SCOTTISH HISTORY SOCIETY

FOURTH SERIES

VOLUME 8

Papers on
Sutherland Estate Management
Volume I

PAPERS ON
SUTHERLAND
ESTATE MANAGEMENT
1802-1816

edited by R. J. Adam, M.A.

Volume I

★

★

EDINBURGH
printed for the Scottish History Society *by*
T. AND A. CONSTABLE LTD
1972

SBN 9500260 3 4 (set of two volumes)
SBN 9500260 4 2 (this volume)

Printed in Great Britain

PREFACE

The Society's invitation to edit these volumes came when I was already engaged on a detailed study of the history of the Sutherland Estate in the eighteenth and nineteenth centuries. That being so, it was necessary to decide on the precise division of material between this work and the book which I hope to publish on the wider aspects of the history of the estate. The decision taken by my fellow-editor, the late Mr A. V. Cole (Senior Lecturer in Economics in the University of Leicester, and one-time Lecturer in Political Economy in the University of St Andrews), and myself was to publish evidence which would illustrate the general working of the estate management, and to concentrate in the introduction, where space was necessarily limited, upon the economic aspects of estate policy. It was our intention, on account of our different disciplinary approaches, that I should assume responsibility for selection and textual preparation, while Mr Cole should analyse the material from an economic standpoint and write a major part of the introduction. I was fortunate to have Mr Cole's help and guidance in the early stages of selection, and to come to know something of his thinking on the broad issues presented by the evidence. But he was unable, to my deep regret, to complete his share of the introduction before his death, and the work is the poorer for it. Had he lived, the introduction would have taken a rather different form.

At the Society's request I have rewritten and expanded my own share of the introduction. In doing this I have endeavoured to concentrate upon the early history of the policy of improvement, upon financial policy, and upon certain important but relatively little-known aspects of estate management. I have made little or no reference to the well-known and controversial themes associated with the Kildonan and Assynt riots of 1813, the Strathnaver removals of 1814, and the trial of Patrick Sellar, although readers will find in the text material relating to all of these. I intend to discuss these episodes in greater depth in my history of the estate.

I have many debts to acknowledge. The first is to my former colleague. Over a number of years I was fortunate to be able to work with Mr Cole, both in Sutherland and St Andrews. The present volumes cannot adequately show how much I have been indebted to his refreshing and critical approach to the subject. They may stand as a tribute, however imperfect, to his memory.

To the Countess of Sutherland, a member of the Society, I am indebted for many years of personal friendship and for the complete freedom with which she has allowed me access to the Dunrobin Castle archives. The work which this has entailed in the–still in-complete–organisation of the archives has, I hope, brought with it a fuller understanding of the working of the estate.

I am further indebted to the Trustees of the 4th Duke of Suther-land, who have deposited the Trentham Papers in the Staffordshire Record Office, and to the County Archivist, Mr F. B. Stitt, and his staff for their courtesy and patience in helping me during my use of these papers.

With the Society, I owe an enormous debt to the Trustees of the Leverhulme Trust, whose generous grant has enabled this work to be published in two volumes. I can only hope that as a contribution to the history of Scotland it will justify their confidence.

I owe further thanks to the Warden and Fellows of All Souls College, Oxford, who elected me to a Visiting Fellowship in 1967. During the time I enjoyed the hospitality of the College I was able to think deeply on the problems of estate accounting and finance. In this I was much helped by discussions with Professor H. J. Habbakuk, now Principal of Jesus College, Oxford, to whom my thanks are also due.

Mr J. M. L. Scott, factor on the Sutherland Estates, has helped me greatly on my visits to Dunrobin Castle. Mr Ian Scott has made elegant and skilful sense of my draft maps. Mrs A. H. G. McNeill has typed much of the manuscript. Lastly, and importantly, Dr T. I. Rae, Secretary of the Society, has been endlessly patient when confronted with the problems of steering editor and manuscript through the press. I have greatly valued the care with which he has read and commented upon the introduction; his suggestions have removed many errors and inconsistencies.

R. J. ADAM

St Andrews
April, 1972

*A generous contribution from the
Carnegie Trust for the Universities of Scotland
towards the cost of producing this volume
is gratefully acknowledged by the
Council of the Society*

b

CONTENTS

Preface   v

Introduction   xi

Introduction

THE HEAD OF THE SUTHERLAND FAMILY during the period with which this work is concerned was Elizabeth, Countess of Sutherland (1765-1839). Left an orphan when she was little more than a year old, she was brought up under the care of tutors, who conducted the defence of her title in the celebrated Sutherland Peerage Case of 1771. She married, in 1785, George Granville Leveson-Gower, eldest son of Earl Gower, who succeeded his father as Marquis of Stafford in 1803; their eldest son, George Granville, born in 1786, took the courtesy title of Earl Gower after his father's succession.

The Countess was the possessor, under an entail of 1705, of the ancient earldom and estate of Sutherland. She also held other lands which had come into the family's hands since 1705, including the barony of Assynt. By her marriage settlement the Countess resigned these for a fresh infeftment in terms of the entail, but made them over in liferent to her husband. The estate of Skelbo, after a legal process extending over almost a century, passed into the joint hands of the Countess and her husband in 1808. Skelbo, a barony held of the Earls of Sutherland by the family of Sutherland, Lord Duffus, was forfeited after the last Lord Duffus' participation in the Fifteen. As the heritable debts on the estate were considerable, the Sutherland family did not choose to resume possession immediately, but instead proceeded over a long period to buy up the debts and then to bring an action of ranking and valuation. This met with opposition from the wadsetters on the estate, and finally the Court of Session ruled that the Countess must either take the estate with the whole debts upon it, or bring it to a judicial sale. The latter course was followed, and Alexander Mackenzie, the Countess' law agent, bought the estate in 1787 for £21,400. He was acting for the Countess, to whom, with her husband, he gave title to hold of him. After his death in 1805 the estate passed to the Countess; in 1808, when the last debts had been paid off and the last wadsets redeemed, she and her husband took a fresh title. Skelbo, together with the earlier acquisitions and others made after 1808, was finally incorporated into the earldom by a new settlement and entail in 1835, following the death of the Marquis (who had become 1st Duke of Sutherland in 1833).

Even including Skelbo, the Sutherland estate did not cover the whole of the parishes of the ancient earldom–Kildonan, Loth, Clyne, Golspie, Dornoch, Rogart and Lairg. In Clyne, the estate of Carrol or Gordonbush (held by John Gordon of Carrol) straddled Loch Brora; in Golspie, Uppat was held by George Sackville Sutherland, and later by William Munro; Dornoch contained two separate estates (Embo and Skibo, held respectively by Robert Home Gordon and George Dempster of Dunnichen); in Rogart, Dempster also held the small property of Langwell, and Duncan Sutherland of Kinnauld that of Lettie; and in Lairg the family lands stopped at the east bank of the river Shin and Loch Shin, beyond which lay the barony of Gruids (Colonel Innes Monro of Poyntz-field) and William Munro's small property of Achany, Munro also holding some lands around Loch Craggie on the east side of Loch Shin. Outside the ancient earldom, the estate included all of Assynt, but in Creich, only Invershin and Achinduich, the remainder of this parish being divided between six independent proprietors.[1] In the parish of Farr the barony of Strathnaver, now part of the earldom, comprised the greater part of the parish, but Armadale and Strathy were possessed by William Honeyman, Lord Armadale, and Lord Reay held the small property of Ardbeg. In the remaining parishes of Eddrachilles, Durness, Tongue and Reay, the Sutherland family held nothing.

Between 1812 and 1816 the Marchioness and her husband took several opportunities to extend their property. In 1812 they bought Uppat and Carrol and in 1813 Armadale and Strathy; they also

---

[1] These were Sir Charles Ross of Balnagown (Strathoykel), William Baillie (Rose-hall), Robert McLeod of Cadboll (Inveran), Hugh Houston (Creich), Dugald Gilchrist (Ospisdale) and George Dempster (Skibo).

rounded off their property in Farr by acquiring Ardbeg from Lord
Reay. The evidence suggests that they were eager to secure Uppat
and Carrol, and that Armadale was considered a sound financial
investment, but there is no sign of an indiscriminate policy of acqui-
sition. The family did not intervene when Rosehall came on the
market in 1806, or Lettie in 1811. By 1816, on the basis of the valued
rent of the shire, the estates extended only to 63% of the total value.
The emergence of James Loch after 1816 may have brought about a
change in this policy, but there are no positive signs of it before this
date.

THE MANAGERS AND THE WADSETTERS

The essential part of the management of this immense estate was a
factor resident in Sutherland. There were three of these during this
period: David Campbell of Combie (1802-7), Cosmo Falconer
(1807-11), and William Young of Inverugie (1811-16), with whom
was associated Patrick Sellar. It was the responsibility of the factor to
handle the revenues of the estate, and to present annual accounts for
audit; in contemporary terms, this was the 'charge' of which he had
to 'discharge himself'. The account was at the heart of his responsibility; the figures which it contained were the products of his actions,
such as leasing lands, collecting rent and arrears, paying taxes and
public burdens, carrying out works and repairs, giving allowances
and charity, selling victual paid in as rent. Certainly, the factor had
other functions too. He oversaw lesser officials – the housekeeper of
Dunrobin Castle, the grieve of Dunrobin Farm, the ground-officers,
wood-keepers, keepers of the Little Ferry mussel-scalps, and others.
He was the family's commissioner for public business, with a vote
at the meeting of the county freeholders. He might, like Young,
have a deputation of admiralty to enable him to deal with wrecked
cargoes, or a vice-lieutenancy. But behind it all lay the annual
account; for some eighteenth-century factors virtually no record but
the account and its vouchers has survived. The factor's responsibility,
before the coming of James Loch, was thus a personal matter, not the
operation of a system. He wrote most of his letters in his own hand,
and evolved his own business methods. It is not surprising, therefore,
to find none of the three have left behind formal letter-books or

much in the way of office records. Campbell left most, because he was untidy and did not bother to collect his papers when he left office; both Falconer and Young, better business-men, clearly considered their papers to be their own property and took them with them when they went. As for Patrick Sellar, the most meticulous of all, he had his own letter-book, but as a personal and not an estate record, and it too went with its owner. The factor, then, had a dignified position in his own right; he also held a farm rented from the estate.[1] Like a great medieval lord's bailiff, he was a full member of the close-knit community of the shire, mixing on equal terms with tacksmen and independent proprietors.

Factors were of no single type. John Fraser, Campbell's predecessor, was the son of an Inverness vintner who had graduated from the position of confidential clerk. Campbell himself, recommended by James Ferrier, the Duke of Argyll's Receiver-General, was a laird from Nether Lord who had farmed widely in the West Highlands and was noted as a cattle-breeder.[2] Falconer was an Edinburgh lawyer, recommended by the family's own law-agents. Young was a small Morayshire proprietor who had made his own way in the world.[3] He came to Sutherland on a business enterprise, thought it good enough to venture farming in, and graduated to be general adviser and confidant, first to Earl Gower and then to his parents, ending up as factor. It was his success in developing improvement, and his inability to control that success, above all in financial terms, that precipitated the passing of the Sutherland enterprise into the all-powerful and all-regulating hands of James Loch.

In Sutherland, except during the relatively brief periods when the family was in residence, the factor was in undisputed command. Yet he was rarely without some form of outside control. During the early part of the period this was provided by the Edinburgh law-agents, whose domination dated back to the period when they had acted as agents and cashiers for the Countess' tutors. They provided,

[1] All three factors in this period lived at Rhives, close to Golspie village.
[2] See *Argyll Estate Instructions 1771-1805*, ed. E. R. Cregeen (Scottish History Society, 1964), 177.
[3] Young once told the Marchioness that he started in business with a capital of £80. In a codicil to his will, dated 1 Jan. 1842, he stated that his estate amounted to £35,000 on 1 Jan. 1841. His brother Robert was factor on the Altyre and Gordonstoun estates of Sir William Cumming Gordon.

during a period when she was either too young or too immersed in the life of the outside world, an element of continuity in estate policy. The factors were under their instructions, and these instructions could be peremptory.[1] The law-agents of the period came from the family of Mackenzie of Tolly in Easter Ross. Alexander Mackenzie had been cashier and clerk to John Mackenzie of Delvine, one of the Countess' tutors and their law-agent, and had succeeded him on his death. By 1802 he had virtually retired from active business, dying in 1805. The active member of the family was his son Colin, who became principal Clerk of Session in 1804. His personality is very evident in the earlier part of the estate correspondence. However, he fell seriously ill in 1806, and thereafter his place was taken by his younger brother William, who took as his law partner a member of the Fife family of Monypenny of Pitmilly. William retained supervision of the political business, but he never exercised the same general control as his brother had done. The Marchioness took him north with her on her visit of 1808, but, having no great respect for his intelligence,[2] never trusted him to the same extent as Colin.

The control of the law-agents was succeeded by a period when the family exercised more direct authority. The personality of Earl Gower, who spent several summers in Sutherland as Colonel of the Volunteers, had a good deal to do with this. Also, his mother's visits to the county sharply increased in regularity. She was in Sutherland in 1802, 1805 and 1808, and thereafter every year between 1810 and 1816 except 1811. The weight of correspondence addressed to her and her son by Young and Sellar indicates that their control was not nominal. It is unfortunate that both Young and Sellar removed all the letters they received, on giving up office, but the fairly continuous series of letters received from them makes it possible to discover the matters under consideration. It should be remembered, however, that many major decisions were taken during the family visits to Dunrobin, and have left no written records behind them. It is rare to find anything like the written instructions left with Campbell in 1805.[3]

It was the weight of business created by Young's expansive plans

---

[1] See below, ii, pp. 17-18, 27-30.   [2] See below, ii, p. 82.
[3] See below, pp. 1-4.

that led to the appearance of a new controlling agent in James Loch.[1] Yet it is important not to over-estimate Loch's role in Sutherland during this period. From his appointment, at the end of 1812, as the Marquis' financial secretary and man of business, he became inevitably involved with Sutherland, but at first only in a secondary way. Where Lord Stafford's personal involvement operated, there Loch functioned. This tended to mean special spheres of interest–as Lord Lieutenant (where Loch made himself useful as a contact-man during the Kildonan Riots of 1813) and as financier of the Brora undertakings (where Loch acted to convey Lord Stafford's wishes to Young and to Robertson, his successor as manager). His correspondence, as preserved at Stafford, indicates very clearly how slowly his influence on the Sutherland operations developed.[2] His importance is manifest in this correspondence, but his part was not that of manager and controller. To Young he could suggest, complain, appeal, but never–except on the Marquis' special business–instruct. It was not until August 1816 that he assumed general control: when he did, Young resigned.

There remains one figure, and an enigmatic one, to be considered –Patrick Sellar. His position in the management was an ambiguous one, and requires close attention.[3]

When Falconer was dismissed in 1810, he was informed[4] that Young and Sellar were to become joint chamberlains at Whitsunday 1811. The terminology was less than exact, as a reflection either of past Sutherland practice or of what was actually envisaged. The office of chamberlain had not been known in Sutherland since the seventeenth century, and joint responsibility not for almost sixty

---

[1] James Loch (1780-1855), chief agent on the Leveson-Gower family estates in England, 1812-55, and in Scotland, 1816-55 (see D.N.B., xxxiv, 26, and D. Spring, *The English Landed Estate in the Nineteenth Century* (Baltimore, 1963), 88-96).

[2] Loch's Out-letters (Staffordshire Record Office, Trentham Collection, D593/K/1/5) show that he wrote 26 letters on Sutherland business in 1813; 30 in 1814; 38 in 1815; 63 in 1816 before Young's resignation; and 85 in the remainder of 1816 (these figures are approximate only).

[3] Donald Sage, *Memorabilia Domestica* (Wick, 1889), 249, describes Sellar as acting 'in the subordinate capacity of legal agent and accountant on the estate'; Thomas Sellar, *The Sutherland Evictions of 1814* (London, 1883), 11, distinguishes the office of factor, held by his father, as 'rather law-agent than factor'; Patrick Sellar himself (ibid., xxxix) apparently described himself as under-factor, 'having a factory for the collection of the rents'.   [4] See below, ii, p. 123

years. Not only this, but the definition of joint responsibility had not been fully thought through, and the problems connected with it first drew attention to those peculiarities of character in Sellar which were to have so significant an effect on the history of Sutherland.[1]

The first attempt at definition followed at once upon Young's acceptance of appointment in August 1810. On 11 August, from Inverugie, he sent the Marchioness a draft, in Sellar's handwriting, of a minute of agreement dividing responsibility;[2] Young was to deal with improvement and public business, Sellar with rent collection, accounts of expenditure, negotiations with tenants, plantations and game, and conveyancing. Sellar, always a stickler for detail, took care to get Young's agreement that they should have strictly equal and independent powers, intervening in each other's departments only when invited.

There was here an ambiguity which required resolution, and which worried the family's advisers as soon as its implications emerged. Was Young in overall control, or was he not? By the beginning of January 1811 Sellar was chafing at the restrictions caused by Falconer's continued presence. As a result, he prepared a commission for Young and a factory for himself, and sent them to Earl Gower.[3] In this way they reached the Marquis and Marchioness without passing through William Mackenzie's hands, a fact the latter did not forget. They were there examined by George Macpherson Grant, who found various points of detail to criticise,[4] considering that the documents should have been revised by Mackenzie in Edinburgh. More fundamentally, he saw the original agreement in a different light from Sellar.[5] There was, in fact, no

---

[1] For two estimates of Sellar's character, see P. Gaskell, *Morvern Transformed* (Cambridge, 1963), 37-42, and E. Richards, 'The Mind of Patrick Sellar (1780-1851)', *Scottish Studies*, xv (1971), 1-20.

[2] See below, ii, pp. 154-5. This division of function is substantially that in the minute of 1811 printed below, pp. 42-43.

[3] Sellar to Earl Gower, 8 Jan. 1811.

[4] Memorandum by George Macpherson Grant, 22 Jan. 1811. Macpherson Grant of Ballindalloch (1781-1846), M.P. for Sutherlandshire, 1809-12 and 1816-26, gave frequent advice on Sutherland estate management. He recommended Young and Sellar to the Marchioness (see below, ii, p. 93).

[5] 'I thought it had been arranged that Mr Young was to have been Commissioner and Factor with power to nominate with their concurrence a Collector of the Rents which would have relieved the Proprietors from any trouble should Mr Young and the Factor not act cordially together.' (Ibid.)

great need for urgency, as a letter from an unknown writer to Sellar on 22 January made clear. Falconer could not be superseded until Whitsunday, and warnings of removal must be applied for in his name. The factory actually made out to Sellar on 19 February described him as acting only from the crop and year 1811 onwards.[1]

Sellar was apologetic for his precipitate action,[2] but not unduly so. By 11 February he was again pressing for his factory to be sent, so that he could examine the county road funds. His intentions became clearer on 23 February, when he wrote to Earl Gower asking that his powers be kept distinct from Young's. Three days later, in dispute with Young over their farming concerns, he repeated the request; he had by then received his factory, and must have noticed that it contained no specific statement on separate powers. The point could not be resolved, however, until Young's commission was prepared. This had been entrusted, in line with Macpherson Grant's comments, to William Mackenzie.

Whitsunday term came and Falconer went, against a background of mounting irritation between his successors. Sellar, with a factory in his hands, pressed his claim to independence hard, to Young's annoyance. The latter even went to the length of having a draft commission drawn up by an Edinburgh lawyer, James Robertson.[3] This was at first accepted, but Robertson appears to have betrayed professional confidence by reporting the fact of its existence to Sellar. On second thoughts, however, the Marchioness hesitated as to whether or not to revert to Mackenzie's form of commission. Young, no great believer in detailed precision, suggested the matter be allowed to stand over.

The tension between the partners did not arise out of a clear sky, for there had been portents for some time. There had been a minor brush on the morrow of their appointment, over plans by Sellar to introduce woollen manufacturers from Elgin to Sutherland. A further clash followed in December, when Sellar had to abandon a projected census in Strathnaver after Young had visited the country;[4]

---

[1] This factory (see below, pp. 43-45) is corrected in line with Macpherson Grant's memorandum. The blank commission to Young (see below, pp. 39-42) appears to be prior to the memorandum.

[2] See below, ii, p. 155.

[3] Robertson later acted as Sellar's agent during his trial in 1816.

[4] See below, ii, p. 132.

Young apparently objected to Sellar intruding on his general plans for the estate. Similar difficulties arose over a number of minor matters, in which Sellar felt himself wrong-footed by Young's actions.[1] There were personal difficulties, too, connected with their joint agricultural operations. Culmaily had now been worked for one season in partnership, they were offering to take over Morvich when the sitting tenant's lease was renounced, and a third farm, Rhives, which had been occupied by the last three factors in succession, had come into the reckoning. By their farming agreement, Young was obliged to offer Sellar either Culmaily or Morvich in the event of a division. Sellar asked for such a division on 6 February, on the characteristic ground that by this means 'our departments under the family and our whole concerns being distinct, such harmony and joint cooperation would go thro' every part of our business that every Step we moved would have effect'.[2] Young, for his part, was not anxious to combine serious farming with factoring, and his preference was strongly for Rhives, the smallest of the three farms and the most adjacent to Dunrobin.[3] Sellar would have preferred Rhives, but could not press his preference in face of Young's views. As a second best, he wanted Morvich, which required a smaller cattle stock than Culmaily. But there were problems over this. Young did not want to keep Culmaily, and soon became anxious not to tie up Morvich in Sellar's hands, as his plans for Strathfleet involved a different use for it. His intention, therefore, was to get Morvich withdrawn from the joint enterprise (indeed there were problems over ending the sitting tenant's lease) and to persuade Sellar to take Culmaily. Sellar did not want Culmaily, as likely to involve him in extra expense.

In this prolonged discussion the Marchioness and her advisers took Young's side. In June, though Morvich was now available, they decided to offer Sellar a lease of Culmaily, and to meet his financing

---

[1] See below, ii, p. 156. The Golspie kirk episode involved a plan to regulate the pews, which had 'become disjoined from the kirk and have been subject of traffic, insomuch, that persons in Glasgow have drawn some pounds of yearly rent from the people, for leave to attend the service' (Sellar to Marchioness, 14 July 1811).

[2] See below, ii, p. 136.

[3] Young to Marchioness, 6 Mar. 1811: 'All I want, or *ought* to have is a home, work for a couple of horses and keeping for a pair to carry me through the Country for I shall seldom be a day without riding many miles.'

problems.[1] This had been done by 10 July, when Sellar wrote to thank Lady Stafford for the lease. The arrangements made do not appear to have included his request for a three-year postponement of rent, but he was allowed to take over an advance of £1,500 for building and fences made under the original tack of 1809, and his tenancy was extended to thirty years, considerably longer than the normal. It was typical of the man that, even at the moment of accepting Culmaily, he should complain that Young was trying to force two of his nephews into his office as clerks. The discussion over the farms, he told the Marchioness, 'never came to the Smallest degree of irritation or heat'; it is not a statement easy to accept.

The great volume of complaint had come from Sellar. Young, by contrast, had relatively little to say. But the tension was obvious to the Marchioness. Earl Gower, coming north in July 1811, had instructions to try to clarify the general position.[2] Not for the first time, Lady Stafford was approaching exasperation with Sellar to the point of contemplating his resignation. She wrote sharply to him, pointing out that Young was intended to be in general control and that he must give him full information. Sellar, in a long letter on 29 July,[3] protested, rehearsing his interpretation of the management arrangements. The Marchioness repeated her instructions on 5 August; Young, she wrote, was principal manager, and always intended as such. Sellar, however, was persistent, and on 12 August he again objected to being made subordinate to Young. But his protests were overridden. Having previously shown Sellar's letter of 12 August to Earl Gower, the Marchioness wrote on 25 August that she had sent Young full powers. At last Sellar saw the danger signals,[4] and the situation was established. As far as can be seen his duties were not seriously altered as a result, although in June 1812 the woods were transferred to Young.[5] His accounts and Young's were also kept separate. At long last a commission to Young could

[1] See below, ii, p. 151.   [2] See below, ii, p. 153.
[3] See below, ii, pp. 154-7.
[4] Young to Marchioness, 15 Sept. 1811: 'Mr Sellar seems to have taken a hint from Your Ladyship and I have of late found him ready to advise with me on all subjects connected with the Estate.'
[5] Probably as a result of the accounting difficulties Sellar had indicated in June 1811 (see below, ii, p. 156).

be made out; on 8 December William Mackenzie finally sent it to the Marquis and Marchioness for signature.

It cannot be said that the problem of the joint management had been well handled. On the one hand the Marchioness and Earl Gower were from the outset interested in Young, as a natural improver and a man of enthusiasm; Sellar was less significant to them—a useful partner to Young in his farming operations and a man whose legal and accounting training equipped him to support Young's wider-ranging plans. On the other hand, the attempt to carry the farming partnership into the business of estate management was not approached with the necessary care. Once in possession of authority, Sellar's instinct was to defend it against all comers, even Young. His natural touchiness did not assist matters. In this situation the minute of agreement of August 1810 was a dangerous guide, for it gave a formal shape to the relationship which hardly coincided with what the Sutherland family had envisaged. The danger of excluding William Mackenzie from the vital stages of the operation was thus apparent. It resulted in bad blood between him and Sellar, shown in a wrangle of 1811 over the duty of framing leases, and reappeared four years later in Sellar's wild suspicions that Mackenzie was behind his arrest. More immediately it left a problem that had to be dealt with as soon as the new management took over. The Marchioness' intervention in the summer of 1811 was necessary and effective, though it was expecting a good deal of a man of Sellar's temperament that he should remain satisfied with a limited subordinate position. It was ironical, too, that the result of the new opportunities opening around the pair was that Young, the farmer, withdrew from farming on his own account, and that Sellar, the lawyer, became tenant of the heaviest-rented arable farm on the estate. Sellar was not yet a sheep-farmer; indeed his references to Culmaily in his letters largely concern the problem of raising a cattle stock. It was the famine of 1812, as he later wrote, that converted him to sheep farming, with all its consequences for the estate. But it was the Marchioness' decision of 1811 that made him into a farmer, a change from which many consequences were to flow.

★

A peculiarity of the estate of Sutherland was the existence of a number of wadsets, a form of land title fallen into disuse in Scotland in general long before 1800. Its persistence in Sutherland is explained by the peculiar nature of the parliamentary franchise for the county, as fixed by a statute of 1742,[1] which reformed the old and disorganised head court of the shire. By this act, the right to vote was extended beyond freeholders to the proprietors of lands valued at £200 Scots per annum, held from a peer or a body corporate or politic. The immediate result of this was to reduce the size of the county electorate; a further consequence was that it became possible for the Earls of Sutherland, and Lord Reay, to create voting rights by a use of their power to give wadsets. Any examination of the Sutherland wadsets, to be fully complete, requires to take into account the political motives involved in their creation and redemption.[2]

Wadsets, however, had a significant financial side also. A wadset, wrote Erskine, 'is a temporary right by which lands or other heritable subjects are impignorated by the proprietor to his creditor in security of his debt. A wadset differs in nothing, as to its constitution by seisin, from other heritable rights. Its specialities lie only in the right of reversion'.[3] A wadset was thus granted in return for the loan of a capital sum, and gave a full title for a fixed term, at the close of which either party had the right to terminate the transaction and to secure the repayment of the capital. Wadsets could therefore be viewed, from the superior's point of view, as a means of raising money, the interest on which was met by the rents of the lands wadsetted; from the wadsetter's point of view, it was an investment secured on property. Where a superior failed to repay at the end of the stipulated term, the wadsetter could, after forty years, exclude any repayment and hold by prescription. The story of the Skelbo estate, as we have seen,[4] was complicated by the existence of a number of wadsets which had to be redeemed in this way.

Both political and financial considerations were involved in the

[1] 16 George II, c. 11.
[2] I hope elsewhere to study in detail the working of the Act of 1742 as it affected the Sutherland franchise. There was at least one serious attempt, in 1792, to challenge wadset rights in the courts.
[3] *An Institute of the Law of Scotland* (Edinburgh, 1824 ed.), 408.
[4] See above, pp. xi-xii.

creation and redemption of individual wadsets on the Sutherland Estate. The political balance of the county franchise, usually, but not always, securely under the family's control, was a constant factor. Some eighteenth-century wadsets can only be described as fictitious. But finance was at times a more important consideration. The eighteenth-century earls appear to have issued wadsets rather freely, either as a means of raising money or to secure existing creditors. The tutors of the Countess Elizabeth, during her minority, made it their business to reduce these debts, and by 1781 only two wadsets existed which diminished the annual estate rental; ten others were probably fictitious, in that the holders had merely deposited bonds for their wadset sums. After the marriage of the Countess, the policy appears to have become more strict, possibly on account of murmurings against the fictitious wadsets. Wadsets based on bonds now gave way to wadsets bought for capital sums. In 1789 ten wadsets were created, some new, others conversions of existing fictitious ones. This was a deliberate borrowing operation. The capital sums raised were calculated on a twenty years' purchase of the free rent of the lands involved, deducting stipend, schoolmasters' dues, and cess. They thus represented a yield of 5% on the money involved. Over £11,776 was raised in this way, the estate rental being reduced by £543 and 300 bolls victual. Between 1789 and 1802 a further six wadsets were added, and one redeemed, with a net capital borrowing of £7,197. A total wadset debt of about £19,000 was thus created. The security of the estate had been used to raise a significant sum, which went to support the Countess and her husband, particularly during his period as ambassador in Paris. It represented a large part of the total capital debt existing in 1802, for between 1787 and 1802 £12,000 was borrowed in other ways and £7,000 repaid, leaving only £5,000 outstanding.

It is against this background that the wadset transactions of the period 1802-16 have to be seen.[1] By 1816 ten of the sixteen wadsets in existence in 1802 had been redeemed; in addition one further wadset had been created and redeemed for political reasons, and two other new wadsets remained in existence. The political balance of the shire was evidently judged secure enough to allow these resumptions. In all £17,783 was repaid to wadsetters on the termina-

[1] See below, pp. 238-40.

tion of their titles,[1] and at least £8,287[2] received either for new wadsets or for prorogations of existing ones. The continuation of the surviving wadsets, with a capital value in excess of £12,000, was due not to any inability to clear off the debts involved, but to the need to consider the electoral balance.[3] It is clear, therefore, that during this period financial needs did not play a major part in wadset policy. Instead, redemptions were taken as far as political prudence allowed. Other borrowings in the period confirm this; the only substantial extra debt (£2,660) incurred and not repaid was, like the £5,000 outstanding in 1802, due to a member of the Countess' family who died before 1816.[4]

There was, however, a third side to the question. Wadsets affected the rent produced by the estate.[5] They could also affect its management, though they did not necessarily do so. In one case, that of Kintradwell, the Sutherland family retained very little control over the behaviour of the holders of the wadset. It had been granted to Hugh Gordon of Carrol as early as 1743, by what appears to have been an exceptional favour, and one in strict terms forbidden by the entail of 1705; this wadset was prorogued in 1761 until Whitsunday 1818. The only other wadset at all approaching this in length was Captain Donald Matheson's holding of Shiness, which was granted in 1779, eiked in 1789, and redeemed in 1809. Kintradwell was held in succession by three generations of the Carrol family–Hugh Gordon, his son John, and his grandson Joseph. Joseph, an Edinburgh lawyer, was consistently unfriendly to the Sutherland family. There was a dispute over the sale of the Carrol estate to the Marquis in 1812, arising out of his wife's claim for an additional sum as the cost of a lady's gown (which she asserted to be a custom of the country). In 1809, soon after his father's death, Joseph was endeavouring to secure an extension of his wadset. In the next year he

[1] The figure was inflated by the repayment of contributions to the county assessment for the building of parliamentary roads.
[2] Loch's payment for his Kirtomy wadset cannot be precisely discovered.
[3] A note on the Sutherland electoral roll as it stood in 1816 shows a total of nineteen voters; of these five were disqualified, five (including one wadsetter) reckoned as probably unfriendly to the family; and nine (including seven wadsetters) as friendly.
[4] Those concerned were Elizabeth Lady Alva, the Countess' grandmother, and Winifred Hairstens, her sister.
[5] See below, p. 240.

attempted to have it bought out at what William Young considered an excessive price.[1] The Sutherland management clearly could not hope to influence the conduct of this wadset, or to integrate Kintradwell into their plans for reform. Joseph, in fact, leased it to a tacksman at a return well above the price the Sutherland agents were prepared to pay. To a lesser degree Lord Hermand's wadset of Helmsdale presented a similar problem. Hermand was not an opponent of the Sutherland family, but he was temperamental and unco-operative in plans for reorganisation. Young hoped in 1810 to obtain land for a fishing village on this wadset, and the failure of this plan delayed the development of a harbour at Helmsdale. It was not until 1816 that the management was able to secure access for the resettlement of tenants removed from the Strath of Kildonan, and then only by the device of the Marquis becoming Hermand's tenant.

A small number of wadsets, such as Shiness and Captain Robert Gordon's holding of Torroboll, were held by resident wadsetters, who managed them directly.[2] But the great majority of the wadsetters were absentees (one, William Huskisson, was not even a Scot, but merely the Marquis' one-time political secretary) whose rents were collected for them and who saw nothing of their lands. John Fraser acted for most of the wadsetters during his factory, being allowed 5% of the rents for his work. Colin Mackenzie was anxious that Campbell should not continue this practice, and tried to persuade him to appoint a clerk, to whose salary the wadsetters' allowances would contribute. Mackenzie himself employed one of the Sutherland tacksmen, Hugh Houston of Clyneleish, on his own wadset. He was not able, however, to prevent Campbell from securing this perquisite, for on 7 November 1803 he authorised him to collect rents on three new and three existing wadsets 'until some other arrangement is made'.

A consequence of this was that the wadset lands were managed

[1] In the course of these negotiations Young drew up a statement of the services owed by the subtenants of Kintradwell, later printed by Loch in *Improvements on the Stafford Estates* (London, 1820 ed.), Appendix I, as an illustration of the abuses of subtenancies by the tacksman-wadsetter class.
[2] There were complaints about their conduct. A tenant on Gordon's wadset complained in 1805 that he had been deprived of part of his holding and had been refused the traditional method of an inquest to divide the crops.

along the general lines of the main estate. In 1805 a prospective tenant on William Dundas' wadset wrote to Campbell to know to whom he should apply for a lease. The complex negotiations over Young and Sellar's entry to Culmaily[1] were only marginally affected by the existence of Colonel Alexander Sutherland's wadset. Sellar's farm of Rhiloisk, when set up in 1814, included lands in Charles Mackenzie Fraser's Badanloch wadset, and a proportion of the rent was paid to Fraser, as it was at Culmaily to Sutherland. When Crakaig farm was let at an increased rent in 1809, William Mackenzie, the wadsetter, wrote to the Marchioness that he would require in consequence to pay an additional wadset sum.

Wadsets, in short, were a variable element in the management of the Sutherland estate. They were an essential part of the family's political control of the county, and they were a useful method of raising capital without interfering with the general policies followed on the estate. In unfriendly hands, however, they could be a political liability and an administrative embarrassment. What appeared sound sense in one generation could, as in the case of Kintradwell, create difficulties in another. The provision in the entail of 1705 that linked wadsets to nineteen years had been, in retrospect, a sound one.

IMPROVEMENT DURING THE FACTORY OF DAVID CAMPBELL

The starting-point for any description of improvement policies on the Sutherland estate may be put in 1799, the year of the recruitment of the 93rd Sutherland Highlanders.[2] The difficulties involved in that operation played a considerable part in turning the minds of the proprietors and managers towards changes in the arrangement of the estate. In addition, measures were adopted to aid recruitment which themselves produced considerable complications in the future.

The raising of the regiment began in the summer of 1799, but the response, both from members of the disbanded Sutherland Fencible Regiment and from the inhabitants in general, was so discouraging that by July the Countess of Sutherland was seriously worried. She

[1] See below, pp. xli–xlii.
[2] The Countess wrote to John Fraser on 29 Mar. 1799 that General William Wemyss, her first cousin, who had commanded the Sutherland Fencibles, was to raise a regiment of the line 'out of its ashes'. General Sir Ralph Abercromby confirmed the intention on 4 Apr.

hinted, in a letter to John Fraser, the factor, at the need to keep a note of defaulters, whilst avoiding any compulsion as likely to produce a bad regiment.[1]

It was against this background that young Colin Mackenzie made an extensive tour of the estate in September and October, in company with General Wemyss and Fraser. His business was to uncover the reasons for the poor recruiting, and to improve the response.[2] In view of the background of the times it was not surprising that he suspected outside contamination from Glasgow and Ireland, reinforced by a dislike of Wemyss on account of an episode during the Fencibles' service in the latter country. It was more interesting that he considered the tacksmen a hindrance to recruiting and suspicious of enquiries about their farms; the management's doubts about their loyalty were to play a part in the events of the next two decades in Sutherland. Most interesting of all, however, was his analysis of the decline of 'the Highland Spirit', and of the need to give tangible reward for 'the continuance of the feudal System'.

This clearly referred to the chief weapon used to attract recruits to the 93rd, the promise of land in return for service. Around these promises a great deal of legend has gathered. John Mackay of Hereford, in evidence to the Napier Commission, gave it as his opinion that they had never been reduced to writing.[3] In fact, several written obligations have survived.[4] They were so framed as to give possession of lands up to Whitsunday 1807, a year when a large part of the estate was to be out of set; in some cases, where immediate entry could be given, this meant a seven-year lease at existing rents, but in many others entry was to be at Whitsunday 1802, when a break in existing leases made it possible. There was no question of unlimited tenure, or of possession until the end of hostilities. The experience of eighteenth-century wars must have sug-

---

[1] Countess to Fraser, 1 July 1799; see also below, pp. 2-8.

[2] See below, ii, pp. 4-5, 6-10.

[3] *Royal Commission on the Crofters and Cottars in the Highlands and Islands of Scotland, 1884*, Evidence, vol. iii, 2510, q. 39195. Sage (*Memorabilia Domestica*, 135) wrote that the promise was 'that the fathers should have leases of their farms', and that it was 'to a certain extent fulfilled'.

[4] The texts of three are extant, for two of which see below, ii, pp. 25, 50-51. A further eleven can be traced from subsequent proceedings; for two of these see below, ii, pp. 12-14.

gested the period given as adequate to cover any likely duration. The promises Patrick Sellar was shown in Kildonan in 1813,[1] and those submitted from Strathnaver in 1815,[2] were presumably of this standard type. It was only the fact that no immediate action was taken in 1807 to re-set these lands that kept the tenures thus created in existence.

An analysis of fourteen petitions arising from disputed promises produces some interesting results. In three cases it is impossible to discover what action was taken, as the lands concerned lay in wad-sets whose rentals have not survived. In five others the rentals show that the redress sought was given.[3] The six remaining cases, where requests were not formally granted, were not straightforward,[4] and illustrate the problems created by such promises in a situation where the pressure of population on land made it difficult to meet all demands. The point of this was early taken. In 1802 the 93rd were on the point of being disbanded, and had actually discharged fifty or sixty men, when the countermanding of his orders forced General Wemyss to recommence recruiting in Sutherland. Colin Mackenzie, writing to the new factor, David Campbell, in November, author-ised him to give assistance, but not 'to include any promise of farms etc'. A few months later Donald Sutherland's demand for possession of Amat or Dalbreck brought from him a reference to 'our Cursed Recruiting business'. The conclusion must be that the management had found that this method of recruiting created more problems than it solved. Indeed, it was never used again. In 1804 and 1805 nothing more was done than to recommend regiments,[5] and to threaten not to give new leases to tenants who gave recruits to other formations. It was the final withdrawal from the attempt to raise and maintain a regiment from the Sutherland estate alone.

---

[1] See below, ii, p. 176.

[2] See below, pp. 162-3.

[3] For two of the cases see below, ii, pp. 12, 13.

[4] Donald Sutherland's father (see below, ii, p. 25) still held a half-tenancy in Riniscane in 1807, and there is no trace of his son in Amat or Dalbreck. Donald McLeod in Lyne (see below, ii, p. 50) is a special case. A letter from Isaac Jopling to Colin Mackenzie (see below, ii, pp. 22-23) shows that he had been given possession but was subsequently removed by Fraser for failure to pay his rent. This case is interesting as showing pressure being put on a tacksman to accommodate a man to whom a promise of land had been given.

[5] See below, pp. 3, 9.

In October 1799 Mackenzie, back in Edinburgh, received a letter from the Countess. This letter is now lost, but Mackenzie sent an extract from it in confidence to Fraser on 16 October, adding a passage from his reply.[1] The general outline of the plans envisaged in this correspondence is clear. There were to be removals and 'a considerable thinning'. Mackenzie hoped that it would be possible to make 'one or More larger farms Commodious and lying together', and directed Fraser to examine Strathnaver with this in view. He also asked whether a fishing village might be settled on the coast of Assynt, with ninety-nine-year leases of building ground. Some of the recurring themes of the next two decades were thus anticipated: the problem of existing leases, surplus population, fishing, village settlements, and the creation of large farms.

The estate's experience of direct sheep-farming before 1799 had been limited and discouraging;[2] also, no farms had been leased out specifically for sheep. Fraser was no friend to sheep-farmers, as shown in his comments in 1792 on offers for Wester Lairg from Walter Ross of Cromarty and Duncan Munro of Culcairn.[3] Yet elsewhere in the Highlands the tide was running strongly towards the introduction of large-scale sheep-farming. The Countess was as aware of this as anyone else, as is shown by her comments in a letter to Fraser on 1 July 1799, when recruiting was going badly and General Wemyss was seriously considering withdrawing from his attempt.[4]

It would be unreasonable to see more than mortification in this statement; certainly no wholesale programme of removals followed

---

[1] See Sir W. Fraser, *The Sutherland Book* (Edinburgh, 1892), i, 483-4.
[2] From 1787 Killin on Loch Brora had been run as a small sheep-farm. It proved unremunerative and was leased off in 1804 (see below, ii, pp. 30, 33). The first references to Border shepherds in Sutherland relate to Killin, which was surveyed by John Bradwood in 1790 and by Andrew Oliver and Thomas Turnbull from Teviotdale in 1793.
[3] Fraser to Alexander Mackenzie, 2 Oct. 1792: 'Mr Ross is at this time advertising parts of the Cromarty estate for Sheep Farms and Culcairn has already Sett the highlands of his own Estate for Sheep also at an increase of Rent. These Gentlemen would reside only for two or three months yearly in Lairg. Bad neighbourhood would ensue twixt them and the poor people, and Incroachments on Forests would become cause of complaint.'
[4] 'I would have him do it, or at least threaten to do it if they do not come in in a certain time, as they are really unworthy of his attention, and need no longer be considered as a credit to Sutherland, or any advantage *over sheep* or any useful animal.'

from it. But there was a flurry of interest in 1802, coinciding with the change of management and a visit paid to Sutherland by the Countess and her husband. Munro of Culcairn, in association with Colonel John Ross, was already making proposals for a farm in Lairg parish, to take in Lairg, Shiness, Corrynafearn and part of Mudale[1]–an area not very different from the Lairg farm actually created in 1807. Colin Mackenzie considered £900 a reasonable rent for this, but was concerned for the future of twenty-five small tenants who would require to be removed. The rent demand must have been too high, however, for in the next year Culcairn and Ross proposed a smaller farm incorporating Lairg, Strathtirry and Achinduich.[2] Again nothing came of the suggestion, but in early 1803 they were offered a four-year tenancy of Corrynafearn. Mackenzie apparently hoped that a sheep-farm might be built around this, taking in Clebrig and Achness. This was dependent on Robert Gordon giving up his tack of Achness, which he was unlikely to do, having already asked that his sons be given Corrynafearn and Clebrig as a farm for sheep and black cattle.[3] Culcairn and Ross had to be content with Corrynafearn, where they became involved in a dispute about stray beasts with the tenants of Truderscaig,[4] recalling Fraser's worries about 'bad neighbourhood'. Their tenancy, with Gordon's at Achness, came to an end with the creation of the 'Great Sheep Tenement' in 1807. It may be suspected that the idea of this particular farm was first suggested by Culcairn's proposals of 1801.

There was a small stirring in other ways also in 1802. In Dornoch and Golspie a small number of building sites were leased out for ninety-nine years.[5] Meanwhile, new leases in Farr parish were for five years only, as the tenants of Farr, Swordly and Kirtomy complained in a petition of 24 August; the target of 1807 was being kept in view, as parts of Assynt were set with the same limitation. But the chief experiment was the nineteen-year tack given in Assynt to Donald McDonald of Tanera.[6] This was specifically designed to promote fishing among the inhabitants, McDonald being a noted fish-merchant and curer. He was expressly forbidden to raise the

---

[1] See below, ii, pp. 10-12.   [2] See below, ii, pp. 14-15.
[3] See below, ii, pp. 15-17.   [4] See below, ii, pp. 36-40.
[5] See below, pp. 59, 85; also ii, p. 43.   [6] See below, pp. 52-53.

rents of the subtenants on his farms around Stoer Head. His holding was increased by lands on the shores of Loch Inver taken over as subtenancies on tacks running until 1812; these included Culag, which he made his fishing base. His rent of £372 was exactly double that paid under the previous set. The tack was a noteworthy innovation, though it did not turn out to be a particularly successful one. McDonald found it difficult to persuade the inhabitants to turn to white fishing in place of reliance on the erratic herring shoals, and was in addition in frequent trouble with his rent.

In general, the first steps towards Mackenzie's new order were halting. There was one major reason for this – finance. Although the estate had produced a surplus income in most years since 1780, this had been deliberately exported to maintain the Countess and her husband; indeed, debt had been contracted through the systematic creation of wadsets. There was no great fund available in 1802 to finance any costly experiments, and Mackenzie's reaction to the offers for sheep-farms suggested that he was aware of the need to raise extra revenue. Restricted by this, and by the existing leases, it was hardly surprising that he had no extensive plans to propose.

He was not, however, short of ideas. This appeared very clearly in 1805, when the first great step forward was taken. By then the financial position had been transformed by the death, on 8 March 1803, of Francis Egerton, Duke of Bridgwater. By his will and a codicil, both of 28 January 1803, the Duke vested all his canals and trade enterprises, together with certain landed estates, in trustees, who were required to pay over the income arising to Earl Gower during his lifetime.[1] On the Earl's death the income was to pass to his second son, Lord Francis Leveson-Gower, and his heirs male, they being bound to take the name and arms of Egerton, enjoyment of the income ceasing should the holder become Marquis of Stafford. Between 1803 and 1816 the Bridgwater Trustees paid to Earl Gower a total of £903,622. An average of £64,544 thus became available each year to him, the highest annual figure being £82,519 in 1805, the lowest £46,570 in 1816. Although the greater part of this was used for English purposes, in particular to expand and modernise the estates in Staffordshire and Shropshire which the

---

[1] For the Duke's will, and for his Trustees' dealings with the Sutherland family see Trentham Collection (Staffordshire Record Office, D593/C/23/4).

Earl inherited through his father's death on 26 October 1803, it was still possible to provide for development in Sutherland.[1] The Sutherland estate was no longer the main source of income for the new Marquis and his wife; instead, it was about to become a major area of investment.

The Marchioness, with her eldest son, the new Earl Gower, sailed from Leith in July 1805 in the revenue cutter 'Royal George' to inaugurate the new era. At Dunrobin she met Colin Mackenzie and his brother William, as well as Campbell. She found the domestic arrangements, and Campbell's closeness with money, rather disconcerting,[2] and the round of entertaining the local notables time-consuming; the castle required cleaning, instructions given three years previously for the upkeep of the grounds had to be repeated, and Hutton, the former gardener, grown senile, had to be removed from direction of the plantations.[3] But the main business of the visit was more serious, as a series of letters written almost daily by the Marchioness to her husband demonstrates.[4] On the day she left Sutherland, 12 August, the main conclusions of a long series of conferences were summarised in a memorandum handed to Campbell,[5] which set out, amongst a mass of small details, the proposed lines of advance.

The guiding hand in the drafting of this plan was that of Colin Mackenzie. It was based on a combination of several elements: sheep-farms, fishing villages, reduction of the authority of the tacksmen,[6] and resettlement of surplus population on reclaimable muir ground. Little could be done immediately, however, beyond the construction of a proposed pier at Dunrobin.[7] This brought into the picture William Pope, whose brother Robert, wadsetter of Gartymore, had recently returned from overseas. Pope was soon being considered as a possible superintendent of two proposed fishing villages at Culgower and Helmsdale;[8] a third village was also envisaged at Golspie.[9] It was clearly understood that these villages would be necessary to provide accommodation for tenants to be

[1] See below, ii, p. 28.
[2] See below, ii. pp. 40, 41.
[3] See below, p. 1.
[4] For examples see below, ii, pp. 39-46, 48-50.
[5] See below, pp. 1-4.
[6] See below, ii, pp. 40-41.
[7] See below, ii, p. 45.
[8] See below, ii, pp. 51-53.
[9] See below, ii, p. 43.

removed to make way for sheep-farms, and that this would also make it necessary to begin reclamation of muir ground. In these circumstances, first attention was given to the construction of a harbour at Culgower, where the first of the fishing villages was to be instituted, the farm of Culgower being due to come out of lease in 1806. The Marchioness visited it on 7 August,[1] and immediate steps were taken to have a survey made. When she left Sutherland, after arranging for Earl Gower to become Colonel of the Sutherland Volunteers (which would necessitate annual visits to the county), she must have been satisfied that the first steps had been firmly taken.

Something else had been discussed at Dunrobin, which found no place in Campbell's instructions. The Marchioness, after a rather prejudiced start, had come, despite amusement at his idiosyncracies, to consider him an honest factor, with a good understanding of the lesser tenants.[2] All the same, she was already considering replacing him in the not too distant future.[3] A good man with cattle, as emerges from his management of Dunrobin Farm,[4] he was a poor hand at paperwork, shown by his difficulties in drawing up a correct rental.[5] Colin Mackenzie went back to Edinburgh with instructions to look out for a successor. One other thing, too, had struck the Marchioness forcibly. If plans were to go ahead regular visits by herself or her family would be necessary. This, as much as his own wish for some sort of military activity, may have lain behind the plan for Earl Gower to command the Volunteers.

Campbell meanwhile set to work on his instructions. There were difficulties involved in preparing a detailed description of the proposed sheep-farms. He did produce a list of the lands involved,[6] mostly in Lairg parish, but Colin Mackenzie was not satisfied with this and on 10 January 1806 was urging the Marchioness to have a plan made.[7] By July this had to be abandoned in favour of a survey by 'skilful sheep farmers',[8] and on 14 July William Mackenzie

---

[1] See below, ii, p. 48. [2] See below, ii, pp. 44-45. [3] See below, ii, p. 55.
[4] See below, ii, pp. 30-36. [5] See below, ii, pp. 27-28.
[6] These were divided into three 'tenements': the forest of Clebrig, Achoul, Altnaharra, Achness, Corryouran, Rhihalvaig, part of Tubeg of Mudale, Letterbeg, and shielings in north-east of Lairg parish; wadset of Shiness, part of Tumore of Mudale; Lairg, Saval, Dalchork, Midpenny, Corrynafearn, part of the forest of Ben Armine. See below, ii, p. 59. [8] See below, p. 8.

wrote to Glengarry to commission one Gillespie to go at once to
Sutherland to value the farms.[1] Advertisement had already taken
place, for would-be tenants were in the county to inspect the lands.
Gabriel Reid of Armadale, the Northumberland son-in-law of Mrs
Mackay of Bighouse, was at Clebrig on 17 July, when he wrote to
Campbell that he had seen 'a great proportion of summering and
not so much of wintering'. Reid raised the question of annexing
shieling ground in the upper Brora valley as wintering for Ben
Armine. This was taken seriously,[2] although years later Patrick
Sellar was to comment adversely on the provision finally made for
wintering.[3] Reid was acting on behalf of south-country farmers,
whose names he did not specify, though they may be assumed to
have been Adam Atkinson and Anthony Marshall from Northumberland, the later tenants of the Lairg sheep-farm, as he acted as
their cautioner when they entered into their tack. He suggested
cautiously that they were likely to come north and would wish to
make a bargain while in Sutherland. Meanwhile William Mackenzie
was re-advertising the farms, apparently with the beginning of
September as the closing time for offers, and by 14 September
Reid's friends were at Armadale, having inspected all the grounds.
They had already met Mackenzie and Campbell, and now awaited
notice of Campbell being ready to treat with them ('It will be necessary that they are either On or Off for the Farms before they leave
Dunrobbin', wrote Reid). When, if ever, Gillespie's report was
received is not known, for it has not survived, but at some point
in September Atkinson and Marshall made an offer, which was
accepted, for the proposed Clebrig and Ben Armine farms, which
thus became the 'Great Sheep Tenement' entered in the rentals.[4]
Entry was to be at Whitsunday 1807, and the annual rent £1,200,
almost three times the figure reported by Campbell in 1805 as the
previous rent of the lands involved. The first major Sutherland sheep-
farm had been created. A second, Shiness, followed in 1808 by the
reorganisation of Captain Matheson's wadset.

   The operation was, in the end, a hurried one, which left various
loose ends. The lack of a plan made the boundaries complex, but
more serious was the problem of dispossessed tenants. One of Cosmo

[1] See below, ii, p. 61.   [2] See below, p. 9, n. 3.
[3] See below, p. 180.   [4] See below, pp. 115-18, 228.

Falconer's first tasks on succeeding Campbell in 1807 was to plan
for their resettlement;[1] as early as 4 July Colin Mackenzie was complaining that 'the measures at Lairg were *too comprehensive* owing to
misinformation as to the number of people involved in the Arrangement'.[2] Falconer appears to have been active in dealing with the
dispossessed tenants,[3] many of whom, from the northerly parts of
the farm, were settled amongst the inhabitants on the north bank
of Loch Naver.[4] William Young, however, was later dubious about
the effectiveness of the operation.[5] Yet it is possible to exaggerate
the change brought about by the creation of the Lairg farm. Subsets
were given by Atkinson and Marshall to some tenants who would
otherwise have been removed.[6] Sellar's comments on the Lairg farm
are also relevant.[7] It was large, unwieldy and unbalanced for lack of
wintering, which goes far to explain why Atkinson and Marshall
were not always prompt in their rent payments, and why they found
it both possible and necessary to give subsets. The difficulty was
avoided in a third sheep-farm created in 1808, Suisgill in Kildonan,
where the tenant, Thomas Houstoun, also held the coastal farm of
Lothbeg, within easy access across the Crask of Glen Loth.

   There had been, too, a failure to co-ordinate the creation of the
farm with other developments in estate policy. The first muir settlements, in Dornoch parish, were not surveyed until 1807, and do not
appear to have attracted a substantial number of the removed
tenants. Campbell, not the clearest of business heads, and nearing
the end of his factory, must carry at least some of the blame for
faulty execution, as Colin Mackenzie years afterwards hinted. Yet
it is also true that Mackenzie himself, who had thought seriously
over the years on the problems of Highland over-population and
improvement, had underestimated the practical difficulties. It was a
barrier that the management of the estate was never to overcome
fully in this period.

   Meanwhile, the other parts of the plan proceeded slowly. In
September 1805 William Pope agreed to superintend Culgower and

[1] See below, ii, p. 65.   [2] See below, ii, p. 70.   [3] See below, ii, pp. 122-3.
[4] See J. Henderson, *General View of the Agriculture of the County of Sutherland* (London,
1812), 24-25. The Marchioness wrote to her husband on 27 July 1808 that 'all those
dismist from Lairg are already settled'; on 29 July the number moved was 300.
[5] See below, p. 209, and ii, p. 114.   [6] See below, ii, p. 161.
[7] See below, pp. 179-80; also pp. 204-5, and ii, p. 35.

another fishing station at Helmsdale. But even here there were problems. The retiring tenant of Culgower was unwilling to give up her lease in 1806,[1] and Pope's entry had to be postponed for a year. More intractable was the question of the harbour. Thomas Telford, called in to make a survey, submitted a detailed estimate of £1,591 in December 1805, almost eight times the original optimistic guess. It was a foretaste of the way in which costs were always to exceed expectations in the family's Sutherland enterprises. In addition the adequacy of the proposed pier was questioned, and new estimates were called for, which Telford did not produce until a year later. Colin Mackenzie, recuperating in Devon from a serious illness, commented that they were high, almost double the original figure, though he was convinced of the need for a real harbour.[2] Doubts, however, were setting in, made stronger by the unenthusiastic response of the Commissioners for Highland Roads and Bridges to a request for a grant.[3] Telford was asked to produce a plan for a smaller pier, which was not forthcoming until April 1808.[4] Even this was expensive and no immediate action was taken. The whole Culgower plan met further difficulties in the same year. The Pope brothers appear to have run into financial trouble, for Robert Pope signed a trust deed in August 1808 and his brother surrendered his lease of Culgower at Whitsunday 1809. He lived on, in reduced circumstances, on the wadset lands of Gartymore, which Robert's trustees did not surrender until 1815, but his part in the village plans was over. William Young, exploring the estate in September 1809, gave the final blow by an outright rejection of Culgower as a site for a fishing village.[5]

At Golspie, too, little had been accomplished. Two boats' crews paid rent there, under an archaic system, at Martinmas 1802, along with three house tenants. The number of tenants had risen by Martinmas 1807 only to nine, and by the following year to ten, while the boats and their crews had disappeared. The figures do not suggest that Campbell took any very strenuous steps to advance the village,[6] any more than he did muir settlement.

The opportunity presented by the long-awaited set of 1807 was

---

[1] See below, ii, p. 58.   [2] See below, ii, p. 67.   [3] See below, ii, p. 73.
[4] See below, ii, p. 79.   [5] See below, ii, p. 101.
[6] In 1811 only six ninety-nine-year leases existed at Golspie (see below, p. 85).

also difficult to grasp. As early as January 1806 Colin Mackenzie had been advising care in granting long nineteen-year tacks.[1] He was cautious about too speedy an introduction of the village system, although he thought it wise to leave the smaller tenants under a year-to-year title, so that they could be directed into villages and new settlements as the opportunity arose. By 14 July it had been decided that no set, apart from a yearly renewal, would be possible for 1807.[2] The Marchioness wished to give titles to the lesser tenants, but was advised to defer this until the large farms could also be set. The problems of the settlement of those to be dispossessed from the Lairg sheep-farm, and of the shieling ground to be taken from the low country farms, were to some extent responsible for the delay.[3]

A further cause, however, may have been uncertainty over the management of the estate. By November 1805 Colin Mackenzie had already found a possible successor to Campbell in Cosmo Falconer, an Edinburgh lawyer.[4] The Marchioness was reluctant to press Campbell, but Mackenzie was instructed to write to him, which he did on 7 December.[5] Campbell, although he had talked of retirement in the summer of 1805, was less anxious when it came to the point.[6] Later, however, he changed his mind,[7] and Falconer was engaged to succeed him at Whitsunday 1807. This led in its turn to further delays, for Falconer required time to become acquainted with the estate,[8] and did not feel able in the short period between going to Sutherland in May and the autumn to do more than survey the east coast, Strathfleet, and the farms adjoining the Lairg sheep-farm, which in consequence restricted the set for Whitsunday 1808.

Campbell's factory thus ended on an inconclusive note. Ever since he had taken office in 1802 the question of improvement had lain behind the general policy of the estate, yet few major changes had taken place. Only the Assynt fishing experiment and the first sheep-farm had been created, and the latter at least had left serious problems behind it. To some extent Campbell's personality had played its part in all this. A cattle-breeder by instinct, deeply

[1] See below, ii, pp. 57-60. [2] See below, p. 10, and ii, pp. 60-62.
[3] See below, pp. 8-10. [4] See below, ii, p. 55.
[5] See below, ii, p. 57. [6] Colin Mackenzie to Marchioness, 21 Dec. 1805.
[7] See below, ii, p. 122. [8] See below, ii, pp. 65-66.

immersed in the management of Dunrobin Farm and the command of the Volunteers, he had changed little or nothing in the detailed control of the estate. Under him it remained an essentially extractive organisation. In his five years as factor, out of a total revenue of £38,655, £22,403, or almost 60%, had been extracted and used for family purposes; the comparable figure for the period between 1781 and 1800, after in both cases allowing for 'capital account' transactions, had been 64%. The era of large-scale investment, foreshadowed in 1805, had not yet arrived in 1807. In this connection Colin Mackenzie's serious illness, which drove him to Devon early in 1807, and effectively removed him from a direct part in the management of the estate, was a serious blow.[1] Mackenzie was undoubtedly the first to see the problem of modernisation in an overall way. No friend to emigration, he was convinced of the practicability of retaining the bulk of the population in Sutherland, if only by drastic reorganisation.[2] In this he was probably an optimist: William Young was certainly to find the task impossible. But there is little doubt that his illness removed the guiding hand behind the 1805 plans. His brother William, who took over the legal management, was a man of narrower views, who inspired less confidence in his employers.[3] To him, and to Cosmo Falconer, there now fell the task of clearing up the confusion of the Lairg experiment, and of resuming the general plans in changing circumstances.

IMPROVEMENT DURING THE FACTORY OF COSMO FALCONER

Falconer's reluctance to commit himself to more than a restricted set in the autumn of 1807, to take effect at Whitsunday 1808, is borne out by the 1808 rental, which shows that this was confined to the east coast, principally in Kildonan (where the rents of farms out of lease were virtually doubled), Rogart and Dornoch. He also

---

[1] Writing to the Marchioness on 12 Jan. 1816, on the publication of the first version of Loch's *Improvements*, Mackenzie commented: 'What has been so very admirably done in one important point is truly the execution of plans formed on a general System relative to Highland population which my Acquaintance with the people early induced me to think the only one Calculated to unite public and private Interests but which I found myself unable while I had the honour to take an humble part in advising the Management of your princely estates to render intelligible to the immediate Managers.'

[2] See below, ii, pp. 68–71.   [3] See below, ii, p. 82.

took the first step towards regulating the new tenancies on the lines suggested in 1805,[1] by producing a set of printed regulations based on the abolition of subtenancy and the removal of the tacksmen's authority, and by allowing improving tenancies for those ready to take muir possessions. The removal of the tacksmen is illustrated by Blarich in Strathfleet, entered in the 1807 rental as held by Robert Gordon of Rhian, and in 1808 as shared with fifteen other tenants. Nothing had changed here except the formal responsibility for the rent. Old habits died hard, for in 1810 steps had to be taken to stop Gordon oppressing the lesser tenants.[2] Repeated all over the estate, such a process must have done much to create a spirit of disaffection amongst the tacksmen.

The set, assisted by William Mackenzie, passed off without difficulty, but already signs of another and more serious problem were emerging. Mackenzie reported that the harvest, both corn and potato, was in danger of total destruction, and that Falconer was preparing to import meal. It was the first time since the bad harvests of 1782 and 1783 (when over 3,800 bolls of bear were imported) that such operations had been necessary on a large scale.[3] Falconer was in Edinburgh in February 1808 to discuss the position with Mackenzie, shipments having already begun.[4] He left behind him a heavy arrear of rent, to which the cost of the famine victual would fall to be added. The point was being reached when the estate could not provide a net income for the family. Quite apart from the famine, expenditure was beginning to mount; there were major works in progress in Dunrobin, and both taxes and contributions to the county roads had increased and were unlikely to decrease.

In the circumstances the completion of the set was deferred yet again.[5] Mackenzie wrote that he and Falconer considered it best to limit the next stage to parts of Dornoch and Golspie parishes. In Dornoch Captain Mackay of Meikle Torboll was given an increased

---

[1] See below, ii, pp. 40-41, 73-75.

[2] Falconer wrote to Earl Gower on 14 Feb. 1810 that Gordon had 'begun to improve upon the kind indulgence shown by Lady Stafford to him'; apparently Gordon was attempting to lay extra rent upon the lesser tenants, which Falconer considered he ought not to be allowed to do, 'they by the late Change having been put upon the Family Rental'.

[3] For the financial transactions arising, see below, pp. 258-9.

[4] See below, ii, pp. 76-77.

[5] See below, ii, p. 75.

d

holding, while a large increase of rent took place at Coul. In Golspie the large farms of Drummuie and Kirkton were set, the latter to Robert Mackid, the new sheriff-substitute.[1] The first attempts at the creation of large arable farms may be seen here. It should be noted that, despite Falconer's earlier views on the need for short leases,[2] these new ones were mainly for nineteen years.

Progress, therefore, was slow. The Marchioness and Earl Gower came north in July 1808, making a detour by Iona and Staffa; the Marquis followed in August. As a result, family correspondence was much less extensive than in 1805; important decisions were taken when all the family were at Dunrobin, and no written records appear to have been kept. Plans were certainly begun for a new sheep-farm in Strathfleet, but the chief interest of the family was in the castle and its policies,[3] and it is possible to get the impression that the momentum for change was being lost. Certainly, it appears that in September the Marquis and Marchioness were considering a postponement of all further removings until settlement experiments had been made;[4] the Lairg episode had left its mark. Falconer reported that it was proving difficult to persuade tenants due to be removed to accept muir settlements;[5] Achavandra had been set aside for this, but had not been taken up. Falconer had come to Sutherland to carry through the plans devised by Colin Mackenzie, but circumstances, and possibly his own nature (William Young considered him good-natured but indolent and circumlocutory in doing business) were beginning to defeat him.

In the summer of 1809 Earl Gower came north to be with his Volunteer corps. The Marchioness wrote on 27 June to warn him that there was resistance to improvement amongst 'the People of the lowest class'.[6] She also reported that there were signs of opposition amongst the tacksmen. Her third piece of information, however, was the most significant. There had been 'a very advantageous offer in the way of improvement and a new system' for Culmaily,

---

[1] MacKid was recommended by William Mackenzie to succeed Hugh MacCulloch, drowned in the Meikle Ferry disaster of 1809 (see Sage, *Memorabilia Domestica*, 246-7). After his involvement in Sellar's trial he gave up Kirkton in 1816, shortly before his resignation as sheriff-substitute (for him see Sage, op. cit., 246-7, 265-6).
[2] See below, ii, p. 66.   [3] See below, ii, pp. 81-82, 87-89.
[4] See below, ii, p. 96.   [5] See below, ii, pp. 95-96.
[6] See below, ii, pp. 90-91.

which would involve giving Colonel Alexander Sutherland, the wadsetter and occupying tenant, every possible inducement to quit.

This offer came from William Young and Patrick Sellar, who thus made their appearance on the Sutherland scene. Young himself wrote to the Marchioness on 5 July,[1] reporting that they had visited Sutherland to seek Falconer's support for the packet service they, with other Morayshire gentlemen, proposed operating from Burghead.[2] On the visit they had been so impressed by Culmaily and the surrounding lands that they had decided to offer for them as a farm. The Marchioness was impressed in her turn, and even more so when she received a letter from George Macpherson Grant,[3] soon to become M.P. for the county, in which he strongly recommended Young and Sellar as improving tenants.

The connection thus established was reinforced by a further circumstance. On 1 August the Burghead packet, on its first return voyage from Sutherland, carried Earl Gower to Moray.[4] Most probably as a result of this journey Young met the Earl, and so impressed him with his ideas that the Earl began to take a direct interest in improvement himself. By mid-August he was writing to Falconer about vacant farms, recent emigration (which did not, Falconer told him, involve many of those removed at Whitsunday) and the prospects for the establishment of a cottage system.[5] The Earl was anxious to postpone further removings until a settlement experiment had been tried on the pattern of Young's Inverugie farm in Moray. The influence of Young himself must be seen in this; he was in regular correspondence with Earl Gower after the latter's return to England, and may already have been engaged as his adviser.

Young's first concern at this stage was Culmaily, and throughout the remainder of the year he and Sellar were engaged in tedious negotiations with Falconer and Colonel Sutherland. Sutherland occupied only a small part of the lands proposed for the new farm, but these were essential to the proper working of the ground. He was an old man, reluctant to move or to accept new ideas, and it proved difficult to make progress. Already in August Young and

[1] See below, ii, pp. 91–92.
[2] See Sellar's description of the visit in Loch, *Improvements* (1820 ed.), Appendix VII.
[3] See below, ii, p. 93.   [4] See below, ii, p. 94.   [5] See below, ii, pp. 94-97.

Sellar were pressing to get entry, at least sufficient to enable them to bargain with the tenants for enough ground to build farm offices and to prepare for green crops in 1810.[1] They offered to allow Sutherland to remain temporarily in his house, Earl Gower having told them that to deprive him of this 'would break his heart'. But by 19 August they were becoming more anxious; they had been unable to fix marches properly with Sutherland, or to get possession of the mill and waterfall on Culmaily burn, so preventing them from establishing a threshing-mill ('the root of all our future doings'). Drainage was also a concern, for the burn was necessary to allow them to dig a large drainage canal through the low ground to Loch Fleet. Urgently, they offered to indemnify the obstinate Sutherland. Young, as he wrote to Earl Gower, was also anxious that the inhabitants should not leave until further plans were properly worked out.[2] Matters made better progress in September, when the partners returned to Sutherland, though the Colonel still retained the dam and mill, and drainage had to be restricted to the western part of the low ground. No sooner were they back in Moray than Sutherland began to interfere with the workmen building the new farm buildings. It was not until the end of November, with the threat that his wadset might be terminated, that Sutherland capitulated, deciding to retire to his hill farm of Braegrudy in Rogart. On this basis, and after a further warning on 24 January 1810 from Falconer that access was required by Whitsunday, he was allowed to retain the wadset. The story was a portent. Sitting tenants were difficult to budge, the tacksman class was not in love with change, and negotiations were bound to be protracted, with the proprietors absent and in any case reluctant to proceed to extremes. Young was becoming aware of the implications when he recommended Earl Gower on 29 October 1809 to stop Falconer giving further long leases without the Marchioness' approval.

Something of the same pattern can be seen in the story of Earl Gower's own attempts to find a farm on which to develop the

[1] See below, ii, p. 93.
[2] Young to Earl Gower, 19 Aug. 1809: 'There is no fear but the younger people of both sexes will soon learn all sorts of field work under our own and the care of a proper Grieve, while the older must get a little land and cottages.' For the population of Culmaily in 1810, see below, pp. 14-16, and ii, p. 113.

village system and at the same time give an example to the smaller tenants. He had already raised this with Young, for on 22 August the latter suggested Culgower as a possible location. This suggestion was dropped, however, after Young's inspection of the place in September,[1] and Achavandra fixed on instead as 'a place where your Lordships Exertions may be better and more agreeably applied'.[2] As at Culmaily, the problem of sitting tenants arose, even while Young was considering what might be done in the way of laying out a village and placing settlers on the muir ground. He soon abandoned the idea of a village, having discovered the disadvantages of the Little Ferry harbour. But the expectation was that possession would be taken at Whitsunday 1810, and Sellar advertised for a grieve for that term; he received eighty-seven applications. In January 1810 everything appeared to be in readiness to start operations. The tenants, however, refused to make any of their arable lands available for a small crop of turnips for winter feed.[3] Falconer appears to have convinced Young of the impossibility of moving them, for on 21 February he was reconciling himself to a delay of a year.

Already in 1809, then, Young had made his appearance on the Sutherland scene as a would-be tenant and as adviser to Earl Gower. In both capacities he was associated with Patrick Sellar. At Culmaily Sellar was a full partner, while the correspondence with Earl Gower suggests that he acted as Young's assistant in that connection. But it is clear that already Young was concerning himself with Sutherland in a third capacity, as adviser on improvement in general to the Marchioness. It is impossible to discover any formal arrangement,[4] or any records of payment to him, but he certainly felt himself free to write to her on general problems.

Young had already made clear to Earl Gower that he was 'an advocate for the Village System'. He took up the theme to the Marchioness on 20 September, instancing the success of Inverugie.[5]

---

[1] See below, ii, p. 101. [2] Falconer to Earl Gower, 12 Sept. 1809.
[3] See below, ii, pp. 110, 112.
[4] A hint is perhaps given in a letter from Sellar to the Marchioness on 31 Aug. 1809: 'It was a sense of . . . the necessity of Mr Falconer's *feeling himself* thoroughly at the head of affairs which occasioned Mr Y. to make the Suggestion to Lord Gower, and of which your Ladyship is pleased to take notice.'
[5] See below, ii, pp. 98-99.

A further visit in October took his thinking a stage further. This time he brought with him William Hay, architect of the Burghead pier, and William Hughes, engineer,[1] to supplement Benjamin Meredith, land surveyor, already engaged by Falconer. Their experience on this visit led Young to abandon the idea of a village at Achavandra and to concentrate instead on Golspie as the site of a pier and village;[2] a new stress was being laid on the importation of fuel and on roads as a means of speeding competition and the spread of new agricultural ideas. Significantly, he also expressed for the first time a lack of confidence in Falconer's initiative,[3] which the negotiations over Culmaily and the Achavandra difficulties did nothing to reduce.

So matters rested over the winter of 1809-10. The county had made a good recovery from the famine, rents and arrears were coming in well, and Young and Sellar's interest had been thoroughly aroused. The evidence suggests that they had come to Sutherland with no other purpose than to open up trade for the Burghead venture. Once there, they had seen the potential of Culmaily, and had been led into a deeper involvement.[4] Young's Inverugie operations had given them a pattern – harbours, reclamation by settlement, villages, consolidated farms. The relevance of all this to the existing Sutherland plans is obvious. Young did not invent these plans: he was, however, the first person to appear on the scene with the capacity to give them real impetus.

Spring brought new developments. In March, with the Achavandra reorganisation held up, a wider horizon opened up at the adjacent farm of Skelbo. Both Baillie James Boog, the tenant, and Matheson of Shiness, his subtenant, died early in the year.[5] Matheson's son, an Edinburgh lawyer, had no wish to continue his

---

[1] Presumably the 'Gentleman of the Caledonian Canal (now engaged here in draining Spynie Loch) who proffers to give us all his Skill, in planning the Culmaily drainage' (Young and Sellar to Marchioness, 19 Aug. 1809).

[2] See below, ii, pp. 105-7, 109.

[3] See below, ii, p. 106.

[4] Young and Sellar to Marchioness, 19 Aug. 1809: 'The very great honour your Ladyship does us by the approbation with which you condescend to look upon our plans, has caused us turn our thoughts more to this subject than we expected, in a matter wherein our engaging was purely accidental.'

[5] There was a serious epidemic fever in Sutherland in the early months of 1810 (see below, ii, p. 114).

father's tenancy, and wrote to Earl Gower on 21 March offering to surrender it to him. The Earl accepted, and Young made rapid arrangements to incorporate Skelbo in his Achavandra plans. On 30 April he wrote to the Earl that he had told Falconer not to remove any tenants in Achavandra during the present season,[1] but that they should be required to give access for roads and for straightening boundaries. At the same time he proposed to cross shortly to Sutherland with workmen to build a new steading on Skelbo to serve both farms, together with a threshing-mill. Meanwhile, he had begun plans for muir settlements, building a specimen cottage at Inverugie for inspection. The stocking of Skelbo was begun, and in September a long-projected plan was put into effect, when a groom was sent to Suffolk to bring north a stallion and some brood mares.[2] The building of cottages was slowed down by the shortage of labour,[3] but by 28 October twelve lots had been laid off on Achavandra muir, and applicants were coming forward. By 14 November the whole of the two farms had been laid out in regular fields for cropping in 1811. Interestingly, Young was dissatisfied with the east coast labourers, and was trying to engage migrant workers from Strathnaver.[4] It was, to him, a reinforcement of his views on the importance of planned resettlement and available work. However, the broad pattern of what he had proposed to the Earl was carried through: a new arable farm, using modern methods, had been created and a settlement for the displaced tenants (there were twenty settlers on Achavandra muir by 1812). Mrs Boog, who retained a liferent, was bought out, accepting an annuity equal to the former rent of Skelbo (one-third of the new rent paid by Earl Gower for the two farms), and retired to the highland farm of Gruby in Rogart.[5] The

[1] Young to Earl Gower, 30 Apr. 1810: 'It woud be unpleasant indeed to dispossess the poor people untill other holdings are chalked out for them, we had too much of that on Culmaily.'

[2] See below, ii, p. 129, n. 1.

[3] See below, ii, p. 129.

[4] Young to Earl Gower, 22 Nov. 1810: 'I was gratified to get a promise from some Strathnaver Lads this morning that they woud work for us at Skelbo. Positively I found much more sense and reason in these Men than our Coast side people are possessed of, at same time they honestly admitted that it was necessity which drove them from home and that they cannot live without going in search of work since the numbers of people have been so much increased by those sent down among them when Marshall and Atchinson got the Sheep Farm.'

[5] See below, p. 66.

whole was not a major achievement in point of size, but as a portent of what could be achieved by vigorous management and an open purse it was very important indeed.

Young's visits to Sutherland in 1809 and his Skelbo operations left him with no great respect for Falconer's abilities. The latter had certainly made relatively little progress with the plans he had come to Sutherland to further. In part this had been the result of circumstances, but there is a marked contrast between his original views on leases and the number of extended tacks he gave at Whitsunday 1809 and 1810. Not all of these were obviously improving tacks; a lease like that of Kinbrace, Shenachy, Achneakin and Achnahow,[1] given to a man who proved to be very inadequate, suggests that he was taking the line of least resistance. Nor does the progress of the muir settlers in Dornoch parish indicate any great urgency in carrying through resettlement. Falconer himself afterwards maintained that his instructions confined him to gradual change, and that he was on the point of moving forward when he was directed to stop his plans.[2] There may have been confusion and misunderstanding here; whatever the reason, a major crisis of confidence was beginning to develop.

Earl Gower's enthusiasm for improvement was infecting his parents. When he and his mother came north in 1810 their journey took them to Elgin and Inverugie, where they met Young and inspected his estate.[3] When the party sailed to Sutherland by the packet Young accompanied them, and took them over Culmaily, Achavandra and Skelbo before Earl Gower went off with the Volunteers. There was 'serious conversation' about improvement and the need for a proper survey of the estate,[4] as a result of which Meredith was sent to Strathnaver. The Marchioness, it appears, was already toying with some idea of dividing the management between Falconer and Young.[5]

Matters then rested until Lord Stafford came north. Thereafter there is silence until the beginning of August, silence that covers the period when a final decision must have been taken. Young was

[1] See below, pp. 103-4, and ii, pp. 206-7.
[2] See below, ii, pp. 125, 126-7.
[3] See below, ii, p. 115.
[4] See below, ii, p. 118.   [5] See below, ii, p. 120.

summoned to return at the end of July;[1] when he came he brought William Hughes to carry out a survey of the Brora coal. There was also a token set of allotments at Achavandra, but the more serious business concerned the management, and on 6 August, immediately after the Achavandra set, the decisive step was taken. Young accepted an offer of the management, with Sellar to assist him, at a joint salary of £1,000. On 9 August the Marchioness drafted a letter to Falconer, announcing the new arrangements, which were to begin at Whitsunday 1811. This was passed to William Mackenzie, to whom the family's views had already been given, before it was sent. Mackenzie, having consulted his brother Colin, concurred, and wrote the formal letter of dismissal to Falconer, in which stress was laid on the need for a more energetic conduct of general policy.[2]

Falconer's protests were dignified,[3] and set out his difficulties clearly enough. His view of Young was reasonably charitable, though it was prophetic that he should feel much less confident about Sellar. He was unwilling, despite encouragement from the family, to consider returning to Edinburgh. It was an old tradition for retiring factors to remain upon the estate as tenants, and he had ambitions to do the same.

On the day after Falconer wrote to the Marchioness to protest at his dismissal, Young, back in Sutherland from Moray, left Golspie Inn on his first extended tour of the estate.[4] From this time the effective management was in his hands, although Falconer continued in nominal office for another nine months. Of twenty-two leases for entry at Whitsunday 1811, all but one were granted by Young. His relations with Falconer were not always easy, but there were good reasons why they should try to remain on reasonable terms. Formal powers for Young and Sellar were not yet prepared, and it was necessary for Falconer to take the preliminary steps for the Whitsunday set. On his part, Falconer was hoping to secure a lease of Rhives, and had in any case to complete his rent collection for 1810.

[1] Young to Marchioness, 27 July 1810: 'I hope something satisfactory will be done in the Cause of improvement, but I am afraid My Lady that it will not be easy to lay down rules for the guidance of any person whose heart and capacity is not enlisted in the service.'
[2] See below, ii, pp. 121, 122-4.
[3] See below, ii, pp. 124-6, 126-8.
[4] See below, pp. 30-35.

Sellar chafed at the delay,[1] but could do nothing, having to accept that Falconer collect the rents due at Whitsunday 1811, though he suspected that the latter might be attempting to secure extra salary. He himself had been drawing salary since 25 February.

The temper of the relationship changed when it became clear that Falconer was not to receive a farm. He complained that Young had deceived him over Rhives, to which Young replied indignantly. Falconer hung on for a while, considering an offer for Midgarty,[2] but by Whitsunday he had given up. On 10 June he was in Edinburgh to submit his final accounts. There were minor problems to be settled, chiefly concerning meliorations to be paid to him for work done on Rhives during his tenancy, but effectively his connection with Sutherland ended at Whitsunday 1811. Though rumoured to have bought an estate in Lanarkshire, he appears in fact to have gone back into business as a lawyer in Edinburgh, where on one later occasion he acted on behalf of a tenant at loggerheads with the Sutherland managers.

Little can be deduced about Falconer's financial abilities. During his term of office the estate ceased to be a net producer of revenue, his remittances to the family being heavily outweighed by funds sent to him. Where Campbell's management receipts, over five years, had exceeded his ordinary expenditure by 42%, Falconer's, over four years, were a mere 5% higher. This was, however, the result of rising expenditure, increased taxation and changing policies, and too much should not be read into the difference. Certainly Falconer's accounts strike the reader as both more businesslike and more realistic than Campbell's. Mackenzie found them accurate, and significantly Sellar, who took over part of Falconer's accounting functions, had no complaint to make. It was a more general weakness in administration, and a temperamental reluctance to accept the logic of his instructions, that led to his replacement. The contrast with the more dynamic Young cannot have been to his advantage. He may have been correct in his assessment of the current situation, but on the other hand his acceptance of the *status quo* came close

---

[1] He wrote to Earl Gower on 1 Apr. 1811, complaining of 'the confusion and uncertainty in which I find matters at Rhives, the prolix details I must listen to in my progress, and the many interruptions I Experience during Calls on Mr Falconer'.
[2] See below, ii, p. 147.

to a counsel of despair. There were certainly major pitfalls, which he was cautious enough to try to evade. Young, more confident and determined, was to find these pitfalls deeper and less easy to avoid than he imagined.

ASPECTS OF THE FACTORY OF WILLIAM YOUNG

1 *Tenurial arrangements*

One of the main features of Young's factory was a major re-arrangement of the estate tenancies. Involving as it did the removal of many small tenants and the creation of both sheep-farms and muir settlements, this constituted a drastic change, which has often been commented upon. It has never, however, been studied in detail, and has tended to become confused with the later changes of the period 1817-20. An attempt is made here to summarise the principal alterations during Young's factory, as a basis for a fuller examination of the complicated problems to which they gave rise. For simplicity, the summary is by parishes rather than chronologically.

ASSYNT

On Young's arrival the interior of the parish was held under tacks due to expire at Whitsunday 1812; the Point of Stoer constituted McDonald of Tanera's special tack, and the remaining coastal settlements were in the hands of small tenants who had been holding at will since 1808.

Young's main proposal, made after a visit to the parish in July 1811,[1] was to create six large sheep- or cattle-farms. This was done, with some modifications, the rents being raised in two stages from £980 to £1,898 for five years, then to £2,679. These new farms all went to old Assynt tenants, including McDonald of Tanera. Around Lochinver Bay McDonald was allowed to keep Culag, but was given Inver and Ardroe on a yearly basis only; Filin, taken from Kenneth Mackenzie of Ledbeg, was occupied in 1812 by twenty-nine small tenants, including two coopers, a gardener and a

---

[1] See below, pp. 126-35.

merchant; at Whitsunday 1813 three ninety-nine-year feus were taken off it. Young looked upon Filin and Inver as likely sites for a village settlement.[1]

The smaller coastal tenants, whose rents were raised to a much smaller degree than the tacksmen's, were not severely treated. Only one farm, Glenleraig, was taken into the new sheep-farms, while the limestone lands of Knockan and Elphin passed out of single tacks; in 1813 there were twenty-seven tenants in Knockan and twenty-eight in Elphin. In 1813, too, the aged minister surrendered his farm for an annuity, and twenty-nine more small tenants were settled there. The small tenants were given nine-year leases to coincide with the expiry of McDonald's tack, while the larger ones received standard nineteen-year tacks. The principles thus followed differed from those used in Rogart and Lairg. No small arable farms were created – indeed the geography of Assynt made that impossible except at the expense of the coastal small tenants. It was fortunate for Young that a native tacksman class existed prepared to venture into the new sheep-farming, for the balance struck in Assynt was thereby more successful than elsewhere.

LAIRG

In Lairg parish Young was faced by the existence of Atkinson and Marshall's large farm, which cut off the remaining tenants from the greater part of the hill ground. To meet this problem, he proposed to adopt a plan he was also to use in Rogart, by setting up a village at Lairg kirk[2] and creating a number of small arable farms. He also took up the idea of muir settlement,[3] which Falconer had tried in a half-hearted way in Dornoch. Over the period 1812-14 he divided the lands of Milnclaren, Lower Lairg and Kinvonovie into nine arable farms, together with a small settlement at Lower Lairg and a division of the adjacent muir ground, originally designed to house the old and infirm.[4] A second stage, to divide the redeemed wadset of Torroboll in the same way, was not proceeded with.

[1] See below, pp. 127-8, and ii, p. 167. Young's claim to have given out twelve feus is not supported by the rentals; possibly not all were taken up.
[2] See below, ii, p. 142.
[3] See below, ii, pp. 145, 159; but see also ii, p. 165.
[4] See below, ii, p. 143.

The relatively small scale of the Lairg operations makes it possible to draw some tentative statistical conclusions. In 1811, there were in the parish a total of fifty-eight named tenants (in fifty-seven tenancies): in 1814, there were seventy (in sixty-five tenancies). The variation in size of tenancy was much increased, muir settlers paying little or no rent, while one or two of the new farms approached £50. It should be noted that at least forty of the 1811 tenants can be traced in 1814, and that of the eleven tenants holding the new small farms at least eight had been tenants in 1811. Young's plans in Lairg meant, on the one hand, a loss of status – though not of security, for muir settlers were given nineteen-year leases[1] – for a large number of tenants. On the other hand, they went some distance towards creating a new class of medium farmers. In this parish at least, the influence of what Young had seen in Moray and Speyside showed itself.

ROGART

Young had envisaged at first a complete reorganisation of Rogart on the Speyside pattern, and Sellar actually drew up regulations for this purpose.[2] In the end, however, Young discarded this, together with ideas for new sheep-farms, with the exception of Rhian, which he set to Dugald Gilchrist of Ospisdale with entry at Whitsunday 1812.[3] He was able the more easily to do this as the wadset of Muie was now redeemed, and Robert Gordon of Rhian and his subtenants could be accommodated in part of the Muie lands. The greater part of Muie was reorganised for the sitting tenants.

Young's general Rogart operations, though aimed at raising rents and consolidating holdings, did not lead to many changes of tenancy. Such reorganisation as took place was mainly round Rogart kirk, with an increase in the number of tenants on the middle reaches of the Fleet. Young told the schoolmaster of Rogart, Alexander Gunn, that he had precise instructions to accommodate the existing

---

[1] There is some uncertainty as to the actual length; in the 1815 rental the tenants are entered as having fifteen-year leases.
[2] See below, pp. 120-6.
[3] See below, ii, pp. 159-60.

tenants.[1] His plans had to undergo some modifications. A proposed village at Pittentrail never got beyond the drawing-board; both there and at Lairg it was necessary to allow the tenants to build where they wished.[2] But the general picture is of detailed changes on a local basis; Young's remarks on the decision not to clear Muie throw some light on this. Although Strathfleet was surveyed during this period, as were the Strath of Kildonan, Strathbrora and Strathnaver, this was not the prelude to a major reorganisation. Instead, something approaching the Dornoch and Lairg system of small arable farms took shape in the lower parts of the parish. The shock to custom was probably severe: the physical dislocation of the parish community was not.

DORNOCH

In Dornoch, a traditional grain-growing parish, the pattern had been largely set by Falconer's leases of 1809 and 1810. There, in addition to leasing arable farms for nineteen years, Falconer had given a number of improving leases to settlers on the muirs of Dornoch and Evelix from 1807 onwards; rents were nominal for seven years, on condition that two-thirds of the land was improved in that time. There were ten of these settlers in 1807, but no more than thirteen by 1809. Young's operations at Whitsunday 1811 largely completed Falconer's pattern of nineteen-year tacks,[3] opportunity being taken to rationalise some boundaries; there were no general rent increases.

There were, nevertheless, some distinctive features in the Dornoch situation. One was the taking-over of Skelbo by Earl Gower, which led to a sharp increase in the parish rental in 1812. Another was the formation of a sheep-farm in Strathcarnoch for Captain Kenneth

[1] Young to Gunn, 16 Dec. 1811: 'While I have to assure you that Lord and Lady Stafford's express instructions are to bring the Country into a progressive state of improvement which can only be done by a different arrangement of the Farms their wish at same time is to provide for every one of the old tenants in some shape or other, and to let them have a reasonable quantity of improveable ground and if possible a little old land at a very low rent.' Young hoped to give nineteen-year leases, or ninety-nine year feus in Pittentrail village. Sellar wrote to Earl Gower on 17 Apr. 1811 that Young had reverted to his 1809 survey, 'namely to put it into compact Small Turnip and Grass farms of from 30 to 50 acres (each having a proportion of pasture) for the accommodation of industrious husbandmen'.

[2] See below, ii, p. 165.   [3] See below, ii, pp. 140-2.

Mackay of Torboll at Whitsunday 1813. The most striking, however, was the development of muir settlement. This was done partly
to meet immediate local needs, as at Achavandra, where ten existing
tenants gave way in 1812 to Earl Gower's farm and a group of
twenty settlers appeared on muir ground, and at Balvraid, which
Young divided into three farms and a muir settlement. In these two
instances it is possible to see something of what happened. Seven
of the Achavandra tenants reappeared as muir settlers, and ten out
of fifteen at Balvraid, while two others may have gone to the
Achavandra settlement.

In the older settlements on Dornoch and Evelix muirs new settlers
were in evidence from 1812 onwards in numbers too great to be
explained by local needs. There were thirty-two settlers in all on
Achavandra, Dornoch and Evelix muirs in 1812, and forty-one in
the following year; in the same period the Balvraid settlers increased
from twenty-three to twenty-seven. A filling-out of a pattern begun
in 1807 is to be detected. But this should not be exaggerated. The
overall total of settlers only increased from ten in 1807 to sixty-five
in 1815. The settlements were surviving at the end of the period,
but it is impossible to rate them more highly than that, and they
were as yet contributing little in the way of rent, beyond a profusion
of probably stringy and tough hens.[1] Young's operations had produced a temporary upsurge of settlement, some of it in all probability from outside the parish, but it would be unwise to see a
highly developed programme in this.[2] The fact that at the close of
his factory the tenants had still not received written titles indicates
how provisional the process had so far been.

---

[1] In 1815 the settlers paid a total of £22 10s. 2d. (£7 of it paid by one tenant) and 58
hens.
[2] That Young had some principles in mind is shown by a letter he wrote to Loch on
*11 Oct. 1815: 'With respect to the lands loted out for the people, the quantity
depends on the age, circumstances and number of Children which each person has, as
well as the Local situation for you know one good acre on the Coast Side is worth
three in the Straths of Kildonan and Fleet. Some of the Skelbo and Proncy moor
settlers have 20 acres others only 5, they get what they ask 7 years rent free under an
obligation to improve the whole within that period, then at a rent to be fixed by men
mutually chosen, or if they agree now at 2s. 6d. per acre. On the whole no fixed
quantity of Land can be named it varys from one to 20 acres.'
[* This sign indicates that the letter in question is to be found in the Trentham Collection in the Staffordshire Record Office (see below, p. ci).]

At Golspie Young had something positive on which to base his intention 'to find situations in each parish to plant Villages'.[1] Falconer had already begun to develop a fishing village there; fourteen houses are entered on the rental for 1809. Young continued this development, though he had to abandon his plans for a new harbour. As early as November 1810 he was urging the Marchioness to allow him to start work, possibly because of the problems which the clearing of Culmaily had thrown up.[2] His plan was to divide Golspymore farm between a new farm attached to Golspie Inn and the factor's farm of Rhives, enclosing a large new park for pasture behind the site of the shore village. At the same time the number of village tenants increased; by 1812 there twenty of these, including a smith, a mason, a baker and a carpenter. There is a curious anomaly in the 1813 figures, which show no fewer than thirty-six tenants paying house and garden rents and forty-seven leasing pasture in the new park, whilst by 1815 there were only twenty-four houses rented and eight pasture tenants. Whether this represents a temporary pressure as a result of famine or whether the lower figure for later years indicates a drift away from the village is impossible to decide. At any rate, by 1815 Golspie had settled down as a rather more diversified community than Young's other village experiments, with a fair sprinkling of tradesmen. Proximity to Dunrobin and the work available there no doubt played its part in this. Meanwhile on the slopes above the Golspie Burn a settlement of small tenants established itself at Backies, where settlers were found as far back as 1802.

CLYNE

The major change in Clyne parish was the creation in 1813 of the large sheep-farm of Kilcalmkill, extending from Loch Brora to the west bank of the Helmsdale. This farm took in the former small farm of Killin, a large part of the old Carrol lands to the east of the loch, and in addition lands in Kildonan parish. The number of tenants on the ground cleared in Clyne parish was seventeen, increased in the following year when some small holdings on the Blackwater were

---

[1] Young to Marchioness, 22 Nov. 1810.   [2] See below, ii, p. 113.

combined and the small sheep-farm of Polly set up. Some at least of these removed were settled on the banks of the river above Loch Brora, where in 1814 a total of sixteen additional tenants appeared in Ascoilmore, Dalfolly and Balnakyle; others may have gone to Rogart parish.[1]

The development of the village settlement around the new Brora harbour is difficult to trace. When Colin Mackenzie's wadset of Inverbrora was redeemed in 1814 the number of tenants in the Doll and Inverbrora increased from ten to thirty-three, which may indicate the beginnings of the new village. A considerable part of Inverbrora, however, passed in 1815 into the farm attached to the coal-works, and the number of tenants decreased by seven. Although negotiations for the granting of building feus were in progress in 1814 and 1815, only a small number appear to have been taken up by August 1816,[2] and the main building work was done by the estate in providing houses for colliers and pilots.

LOTH

The parish of Loth, with its long coastline, was a standing attraction to Young as a possible area in which to combine fishing and agricultural settlements. There was, however, a major difficulty which he was unable to overcome – the provision of an adequate harbour. His own preference, evident from the moment he rejected the long-deferred plans for Culgower, was for Helmsdale. This was, however, in wadset to the temperamental Lord Hermand, and attempts to persuade his tenants to make land available failed. It was not until the very end of Young's factory, in 1816, that access was finally obtained, both for harbour works and for settlement.

Young was forced meanwhile to concentrate on available lands out of lease. The first to appear was Midgarty, which he divided in 1811 into three parts, a small farm at the western end, an inn with a farm in the centre, and a fishing village at the eastern end. He then proceeded to settle tenants as joint fishers and crofters on this last portion, in addition to building a small range of houses specifically for fishermen. He hoped to find fishers from the south shore

[1] See Sellar, *Sutherland Evictions of 1814*, xxxix.
[2] See below, ii, pp. 248, 299. Loch, in *Improvements* (1815 ed.), 18, states that six houses were building at the end of 1815.

e

of the Moray Firth to settle at the proposed new harbour, which
was to be called Portgower. The rentals give some indication of the
progress made. In 1811 eight of the old sub tenants were in possession of Wester Midgarty, and eleven elsewhere on the farm. By
1813 all had disappeared, and twenty-eight tenants were entered at
Portgower, twenty-three of them with building feus. When Sellar
prepared the rental for 1814, carrying out a full check of Portgower,
he found a total of twenty tenants, having seventeen building feus
and twenty lots of land between them; there were also five fishermen occupying houses only, and seven feus and eight lots of land
were vacant. Clearly the establishment of the new pattern took time.
By 1815 some consolidation had taken place, there being, in addition
to the five fishermen, seventeen tenants with sixteen feus and twenty
lots between them. It may well be that the momentum of the operation was modified by the problems of access to Helmsdale as a
harbour, for the Portgower pier site proved too difficult to develop,
in the end a simple capstan and inclined plane being provided
instead. The reorganisation of the arable land, too, was complex.
Of the nineteen tenants named in the 1811 rental only six can be
positively identified in 1814, though in some other cases identity
of family names suggests that sons had succeeded fathers. On any
count, however, there was a bigger influx of outsiders than had
taken place at Achavandra.

Perhaps the most valuable element in the whole situation was
Alexander Simpson, the tenant of the new inn farm. A Morayshire
man, originally a carpenter, he was persuaded by Young to set up
as a herring trader, and became the principal buyer of herring from
the local fishing boats; he filled 2,000 barrels on the shore at Helmsdale in 1813, and planned to double this in 1814. His activities
emphasised the importance of access to Helmsdale. Young did what
he could by leasing an estate store-house there to Simpson and
another merchant in 1815, but complained that he was hamstrung
by his inability to get access to the shorelands. The pressure became
even greater when Robert Pope's trustees at length renounced his
wadset of Gartymore, which was taken into the estate rental in 1815
with thirty-three tenants on it. By closing the gap between Portgower and Helmsdale it made possible even larger-scale settlement,
and made the harbour problem pressing.

Agreement was finally reached in the autumn of 1815 with Lord Hermand's tenants to renounce their leases of Easter and Wester Helmsdale, so giving access to the lands and harbour for 1816. James Loch warned Young not to act precipitately in the light of the new opportunities.[1] It appears that Young was able, however, to go ahead with allotments for a Whitsunday set, for by *26 May he reported that all available land was set, the demand being such as to make it necessary to reduce some lots for tradesmen to a single acre. Some settlers were already in occupation, for ploughs sent from Dunrobin had worked land east of the Helmsdale, in which settlers had planted potatoes. The pressure for holdings at Helmsdale, it appears, was more considerable than it had been in the case of the earlier settlements.

As Lord Hermand's tenant for Helmsdale, the Marquis was now able to consider the construction of a major harbour and attendant offices, to design which John Rennie was called in. It came in time to get for Sutherland a significant share in the expanding herring trade, if not soon enough to enable Young to see his repeated efforts to secure a workable harbour crowned with success.

KILDONAN

The major reorganisation of Kildonan came in 1813, and sparked off the celebrated Kildonan Riots of that year.[2] The set was made in December 1812, and resulted in the creation of three sheep-farms: Ferronich and adjoining lands, set to some of the existing tenants; Torrish, on the east bank of the Helmsdale between Thomas Houston's farm of Suisgill and Kilphedir, set to Major William Clunes; and Gabriel Reid's farm of Kilcalmkill, taking in all the land on the west bank of the river between the Water of Free and the southern boundary of Kilearnan. As a result of these changes a

[1] Loch to Marquis, *30 Nov. 1815: 'I have also mentioned to him respecting the removal of the people to Helmsdale. My anxiety on this subject is very great. For in the first place I do not think a removal of the whole people there at Whitsunday without their own consent, would be just to them. . . . What I should suggest is that they should for the whole of the year 1816 be left in possession of their present possessions, that they should have their new lots marked out and pointed out to them before the end of January, that they should be told you may remove thither at any time henceforward, but you must complete your removal at Whitsunday 1817.' See also below, ii, pp. 261, 270.
[2] See below, pp. 135-44, and ii, pp. 176-93 passim.

total of eighty-eight tenants disappeared from the rental. However, though Donald Sage gives no indication of the fact in his description of the removals,[1] a large part of the low lands along the east bank of the river, between Kildonan kirk and Balnavaliach, was lotted out for settlement by John Roy under Young's direction.[2] The 1814 rental shows a total of forty-four tenants installed there; an approximate count suggests that at least twenty-three has been previous tenants in the cleared lands. Young had intended to make land available at Armadale for others, and had even offered his own ship to transport their belongings, but so few were prepared to accept that he abandoned the proposal in April 1813.[3]

The tenants were not all removed at once, for Gabriel Reid, writing to the Marchioness on 29 August 1816, reported that he had allowed tenants in Free to remain for a whole year there, and then to stay in Borroboll for another two, only removing them when the new lands acquired at Helmsdale were lotted out. But the whole process was precipitate. The system of a winter set, giving in effect only six months' notice to quit houses and pasture, was one that Loch was later to criticise.[4] When it was added to the difficulties caused by Lord Selkirk's intervention and the hurried sale of cattle by many who hoped to emigrate with him, it is hardly surprising that the Kildonan clearance made an unfavourable impression on many contemporaries who were not, as Loch pointed out to Young, opposed to the general policy. Methods which had worked well enough in the east coast parishes, where partial sets had been carried out over a number of years, proved inadequate in Kildonan. The mistake was to be compounded in Strathnaver in the following year. Yet Young had made his plans, in outline at least. John Roy had surveyed Kildonan, and had laid out the new allotments in the settlement area. They were taken up; the trouble was that they were not, and could not be, on a scale adequate to match that of the removals.

A further rearrangement took place in 1816, when Helmsdale became available for settlement. The tenants on the west bank of the

[1] Sage, *Memorabilia Domestica*, 248-9.
[2] See H. Fairhurst, 'The Surveys for the Sutherland Clearances, 1813-1820', *Scottish Studies*, viii (1964), 1-18.
[3] See below, ii, pp. 184-5, 189, 192.   [4] See below, ii, p. 261.

river between Kilearnan and the parish boundary were then removed
– there were eighteen of them in the 1815 rental – and their lands
were added to Kilcalmkill sheep-farm. There may also have been
some adjustment of the boundaries of the Kildonan settlement,
though the latter remained in existence for several years afterwards.

FARR

Benjamin Meredith had surveyed Farr in 1810,[1] before Young
became factor. His plans envisaged two major sheep-farms, one
between Kirtomy and Skelpick, the other largely on the lines of
the Rhiloisk farm later set to Patrick Sellar. He also recommended
the creation of a number of farms, not for sheep, on the west bank
of the Naver, and a fishing village at the mouth of the river. Young,
however, who also toured Strathnaver in 1810,[2] was already aware
of the need for caution. It was this that made him postpone a census
that Sellar had planned in the valley,[3] and led him to leave the tenants
to hold their farms on a yearly basis until he was able to plan a more
gradual change than Meredith had suggested.

This did not begin until Whitsunday 1814, a year after the Kildonan crisis. Then, on 15 December 1813, Young held a set at
Golspie for the upper part of Strathnaver. It produced only one
change, but a major one. Robert Gordon of Langdale was successful
in his bid for Langdale and Skaill, the existing tenants were continued in Syre, Keankyle, Grubmore and Grubeg, but one sheep-
farm was created at Rhiloisk, for which Sellar bid successfully in
competition with the existing tenants and a Caithness shepherd.[4]
This was an extensive farm, taking in the east bank of the Naver
between Achness and Dunviden burn, and extending across the
parish boundary to include Rimsdale and other lands in Kildonan.
Young's intention was to resettle the tenants concerned in the lower

---

[1] See below, pp. 16-30; and also Fairhurst, op. cit.
[2] See below, pp. 30-35.
[3] See below, ii, p. 132.
[4] See below, p. 144. Young wrote to the Marchioness on 16 Dec. 1813 that 'Mr
Sellar was very well handled by Sandsides Shepherd who made him pay £60 more
than he expected for I allowed the Man to mend his offer a second time'. Sellar later
claimed that he had really intended to bid for Langdale but did not proceed out of
regard for Robert Gordon, the sitting tenant.

strath, a move made easier by the buying-out of Captain William Gordon's tack of Clerkhill.[1]

It is impossible, because of the contemporary wadset arrangements, to give complete figures for the consequences of the erection of the Rhiloisk sheep-farm. Four townships which were taken into Rhiloisk (Ravigill, Riphail, Dalachurish, Truderscaig) contained thirty-six tenants in 1813, but four others (Rhiloisk, Rossal, Rimsdale, Garvault) were entered on wadset rentals which have not survived.[2] There must have been removals, forced or otherwise, from other areas also, for the number of tenants in Grubmore and Grubeg fell from thirty-two in 1813 to fifteen in 1814. Something can be deduced from the rentals of the areas lower down the valley to which the removed tenants were directed. There was a major increase between 1813 and 1815 in the tenancies in the area east of the Naver estuary; fourteen tenants became ninety-eight. It should be remembered, however, that Clerkhill had been a single farm and that some of the newly entered tenants had been in all probability subtenants there. Others, however, came from the Rhiloisk removings, for the 1814 rental shows numerous abatements of half-rents to removed tenants both in this area and further up the strath. This was the case at Achalgary, where the old number of three tenants was doubled, one of the new tenants being recorded as coming from Rimsdale and one from Garvault. Similar settlements appear to have taken place at Rhinovie and Dunviden.

The actual method of settlement clearly left a good deal to be desired. The notice given was the traditional one used in the county, but as in Kildonan proved inadequate when used on so large a scale. By it, the outgoing tenant was allowed to retain possession of the arable land and barns until the separation of the crop, having to surrender the houses and pasture lands at the Whitsunday term. It was Sellar's arbitrary interpretation of this practice that caused his difficulties and eventual trial.[3] On the other hand, it should be noted that Sellar had met the tenants concerned at Suisgill in January 1814

[1] See below, ii, p. 205.

[2] This does not agree with the figure of twenty-seven tenants removed at Whitsunday 1814, given by Young in his evidence at Sellar's trial (Sellar, *Sutherland Evictions of 1814*, xxxviii), but it is possible that some had already gone to the new allotments in the lower strath.

[3] See below, pp. 151, 153-68, and ii, pp. 229, 236-49, 253, 255-9, 279-84.

and arranged to give them about half of the ground for a further year.[1] More serious, if Macpherson Grant's comments of 1816[2] are to be believed, was the failure to make a proper division of lots for the resettled tenants, partly caused by Roy's inability to survey early enough in 1814. Loch too remarked unfavourably on the persistence of runrig methods in place of regular lots.[3] Something of the confusion is reflected in a draft rental for 1815, which makes very heavy weather of tenant's names and numbers. As in so many other instances, Young's detailed execution of his plans was not equal to his intentions. The consequences in Strathnaver were, as is well known, very serious indeed.

2 The Brora coal

On 11 February 1810 Young wrote to Earl Gower[4] that he had been discussing the coal and limestone of Sutherland with William Hughes, who had accompanied him on a visit in the previous October. A new and crucial element thereby entered into the Sutherland equation.

Coal-mining itself was not new in the county. The existence of the Brora coal-field had been known so early as 1598, and in the middle of the eighteenth century John Williams had carried out substantial operations under lease from the Marchioness' father.[5] These workings, on Inverbrora point, between the present main road and the sea, were abandoned in 1777, partly on account of the sulphurous quality of the coal. Various other attempts to trace the coal seam were made in the surrounding area – in Dunrobin summer-house park in 1770, and on the shore at Strathsteven in 1797.

Hughes was an experienced miner, having managed a Flintshire colliery before coming to work on the Caledonian Canal and Spynie Loch. He used his powers of observation, on a visit in July 1810, to deduce that a better and deeper coal measure might be found on the north bank of the Brora, some half-mile above the road bridge.

[1] See below, ii, p. 239. [2] See below, pp. 206-11.
[3] See below, p. 193. [4] See below, ii, p. 113.
[5] Sir Robert Gordon, *A Genealogical History of the Earldom of Sutherland* (1813), 237. John Farey's report (see below, p. lxiii) gives a valuable account of the history of the workings prior to 1812. For Williams, see below, ii, p. 222, n. 1.

This recommendation was accepted in discussions with the Marchioness and Marquis during their stay at Dunrobin during the summer, and on 25 September[1] boring was begun under the direction of John Pritchard, a pit-sinker from Denbighshire, who had been working at Spynie with Hughes. The sinking of the trial bore occupied the following winter and early summer.[2] Already in March 1811 Young was becoming excited about the prospects. Boring tools gave constant trouble, but by 4 June the shaft had reached coal, and on 12 June Hughes reported to Young that three usable seams had been found at over 220 feet depth. He recommended that the bore be continued to 500 feet, and that an 8-foot shaft be sunk to work the seams already reached. He estimated the cost of this at £372 – a somewhat optimistic figure as in all over £3,300 was expended by the end of 1812.

Hughes' report was encouraging enough for the Marquis, now beginning to lay out money in earnest in Sutherland, to send Young full powers to sink the shaft. Lord Stafford, with some experience of coal mines on his Staffordshire estates, was taking a more active interest in this than in most of the Sutherland operations. He had already been consulting R. H. Bradshaw, the superintendent of the Bridgwater Trust, and specimens from Brora were being tested in England. His authorisation was at once acted upon, for by 20 July Hughes and Pritchard had gone to Inverness to make preparations for sinking the new shaft. The Marchioness was encouraged to suggest to Earl Gower on 2 August that a mineralogist should go to Sutherland in the following summer to search for coal and alum. By 17 August she was writing again to report that Bradshaw had tested the coal, and found it good enough to warrant sinking the shaft;[3] her imagination was working hard, and she saw manufactures at Pittentrail in Strathfleet and a canal to Loch Shin. Lord Stafford, his mind on the possibility of iron being found in conjunction with the coal, was quite prepared to envisage spoiling the Brora salmon fishings to allow the coal works to go forward. It was a significant moment of involvement which was to lead to a very large expense and a very uncertain return.

[1] See below, ii, p. 129. Young's accounts give 25 Sept. as the starting date.
[2] For a journal of the sinking, supplied by Young, see Henderson, *Sutherland*, 148-9.
[3] See below, ii, pp. 157-8.

Work on the shaft now went ahead. Young was hopeful of a
grant from the government towards the building of a harbour at
Brora that would be adequate to export coal.[1] There were some
problems in the winter, occasioned by 'the religious scruples of the
Sutherland labourers who objected to work on Sunday', as a result
of which every Monday and Tuesday had to be spent draining
water from the shaft; on 2 April 1812 Young was considering
finding more-willing replacements.[2] By 17 May the coal strata were
within reach, Pritchard expecting to reach them within three weeks,
and when the Marchioness came to Dunrobin in July she was able
to test the coal for herself. During August John Farey senior,
employed by the Marquis to make a survey of the coal-field, was
at Brora finding himself obstructed by Pritchard's unwillingness to
release men without positive orders, but managing nevertheless to
sink trial bores and to reconstruct the sections of the original bore
and the new working shaft.[3]

The pit was not yet within sight of operating, however. There
were roads to be driven, and draining and lifting machinery to be
installed (this was started on 25 August, when cases to house two
water-wheels were begun). The machinery arrived at the beginning
of October, but there were unforeseen difficulties and by April 1813
ventilation problems made it necessary to postpone working for
coal until a second shaft was sunk and proper air circulation obtained. This Young estimated would take two months. Meanwhile
he had been making preparations for hauling the coal to the sea,
and calculating selling prices, an agent being engaged in Elgin.[4]
The expectation clearly was that some sales would be possible during
1813.

By May production had begun, the water-wheels far exceeding
their calculated load of five cwts.; twenty tons were out and on the
river bank by 16 May. When the Marchioness came north in June

[1] Young to Marchioness, 15 Sept. 1811.
[2] See below, ii, p. 164.
[3] For John Farey senior (1766-1826) see D.N.B. xviii, 202. He produced a valuable
account of the history and geology of the coal-field, which Dr Charles Waterston, of
the Royal Scottish Museum, hopes to publish (see below, p. 147, and ii, pp. 214,
217).
[4] See below, ii, p. 193.

the difficulties were to all appearances over.[1] But it had been an expensive operation. To the end of 1813 a total of £10,846 was laid out on the coal mine and its approach roads, with nothing to show in the way of receipts but £83 for one cargo exported and some smaller loads sold locally. The problems of transport and management were beginning to obtrude themselves. A great deal would obviously depend on the quality of the management, and on its ability to develop markets round the Moray Firth. On the first of these points James Loch, making his first visit to Sutherland in the late summer, was pessimistic.[2] There had clearly been some discussion about the best method of running the pit, the Marchioness having some doubts about Young's efficiency.[3]

The first solution that suggested itself was an approach to Hughes to take a lease of the whole operation. Hughes, writing on *27 September to Loch as Lord Stafford's agent, was reluctant; he did not consider the works far enough advanced for any permanent arrangement, as salt, lime and brick works might well be added, which could not be separated from the coal. A new dimension was being added to the Brora operations. Hughes, however, offered to raise the coal and deliver it to the river bank at a rate of 5s. 6d. per ton, providing up to 100 tons a day for two, three or four years; he also offered to contract for completing the underground workings. From his technical point of view the mine was not yet in full working order, which lent point to the Marchioness' complaint about Young's eagerness to rush into selling.

Hughes' offer caused a good deal of discussion. Young at first

---

[1] Marchioness to Lady Douglas, 18 July 1813: 'The coal turns out beyond our expectations and a harbour is making to exploit it, it also promises Lime and Tyles, and salt, and to do all that coal does in other parts of the world, and comes up in pieces of 600 weight, or more if you chuse it, and it looks as if there were more strata below, and desires us to bore on. It is worked by water wheels and therefore does not make smoke and look dirty, and as there is a great deal of building about this, the architect has chosen to make a most magnificent water closet over the stream which attracts the attention of the curious before any other part of the work, and looks like a temple near Athens. . . . The natives who work at it do not understand this temple; they think it is either a place of confinement or a *drole magot*; the Welsh colliers say it is quite necessary.'

[2] See below, ii, p. 201.

[3] Marchioness to Loch, 25 Sept. 1813: 'I quite agree with you about a necessity for some measures to be taken about the Coal. Young has an excellent head for *general* affairs but in his eagerness to despatch them I think he has made a bungle with Hughes.'

thought it fair, but suggested a proper inspection of the workings first. Later, his opinion hardened, and he deferred any action, setting Hughes in the meantime to build a small harbour at Brora and a track for a railway from the pit to the sea; he also recommended delay in sending north a brick and tile maker whose appointment had been decided upon in the summer. Loch, characteristically, looked for expert advice, turning to Henry Stainton, London agent of the Carron Company. Stainton was undecided; he found Loch's letter and Hughes' offer contradictory in detail, and thought Hughes' price at first sight high, but considered that there might be special circumstances. There were other problems too. Hughes was preparing to instal a steam-engine to provide more regular power; of this Young was dubious, and inclined to consider Hughes expensive in his workings. His anxiety was to get further expert advice before the next season, and he prepared to look for this when he went to Edinburgh in January 1814.

Before then a minor disaster occurred. On 14 December Young had to report that the axle of the water-wheel working the pumps had snapped. Hughes' credibility was severely damaged. The Marchioness wrote to Young on 20 December that she considered Hughes had too many undertakings to give Brora proper attention, and that she had instructed Loch to look out for an overseer engineer to manage the whole concern. Young wrote anxiously to Loch on *27 December; he was to be in Edinburgh by 6 January, and hoped that a manager could be found to meet him there; he was shaken by the accident, and by the expense. Brora, in fact, was dangerously near to turning into an open-ended liability, and the search for expert advice had become urgent.

Young crossed to Moray at the beginning of January, leaving Hughes at work on the broken wheel. Hughes, possibly also shaken by the accident, made fresh offers to manage the concern; he was prepared to bring the coal to the pit-head for 5s. a ton, or to attend to all the projected concerns – salt, bricks, tiles in addition to coal – for one-quarter of the profits or losses for five or seven years, if a partner could be found to attend to shipping and sales. It was an idea to which Young was to return later in the year, but meanwhile he went to Edinburgh determined to find someone to inspect and report on Brora. Efforts by Loch to find a manager in Staffordshire

were unsuccessful, but Young himself, through an introduction to
Mr Erskine of Marr, was able to go over the latter's Alloa mine with
the manager, Robert Bald. This was a fortunate meeting, for Bald
was an experienced coal engineer and proved helpful, undertaking
to come to Sutherland in February, and to act as an agent in securing
colliers and salt-workers. Young was back in Sutherland by the
end of the month, despite snowstorms, in high spirits, and convinced
that with Bald's advice he would be able to raise coal at half Hughes'
price.

   Bald eventually arrived at Brora on 21 March, and spent a week
studying the pit and the geology of the surrounding area.[1] His report
was encouraging enough to set Young off on plans for brick and
tile making, and also to start work on the projected salt pans on the
shore near Inverbrora point.[2] Hughes' offer was discarded, though
on Bald's advice Pritchard was offered a contract as underground
manager.[3] Ambitious plans to extend the harbour up to the road
bridge were abandoned, and Hughes' interest in Brora was closed
with the completion of the existing harbour. Hughes, then, had lost
both Brora and the Mound,[4] the major works being undertaken in
Sutherland. Long afterwards Sellar complained that Young's eagerness and confidence had driven him out, but there seem grounds for
believing that Hughes, working as he did in close connection with
Telford, was inclined to price his services highly and to overestimate
his indispensability. His influence induced Pritchard, as the latter
afterwards complained, to reject the offer made to him. It therefore
became necessary to call on Bald to find both a general overseer and
an underground manager. Time was running out, for three ships
were already waiting to load on 16 April. Five days later loading
had begun, and Young was busy with plans for a village settlement
at Inverbrora.[5]

   Bald found his men in early May – James Miller from Govan as
general agent and Robert Ramage from Fife as underground manager. Ramage, with some Alloa colliers, arrived in Sutherland at the
end of May, and was immediately sent back to recruit more. Young
was anxious to raise sixty tons of coal daily, but was as yet unable to

---

[1] For his report, see below, pp. 146-51.   [2] See below, ii, pp. 209-10.
[3] See below, ii, p. 209.   [4] See below, p. lxxvi.
[5] Young to Marchioness, 16 Apr. 1814.

get twelve. He was having trouble with the native miners, who went on strike for better terms than the Alloa colliers had accepted.[1] The strike only lasted a week, but the pressure on Young was considerable, and he was relieved when Miller put in an appearance on 8 June, followed by Ramage and his new colliers. When the Marchioness reached Dunrobin at the beginning of July Young had managed to find only twelve or fourteen colliers, instead of the fifty or sixty the demand for coal would have justified. However, a brickmaker was installed, and the harbour was complete. The Marchioness was able to inspect the workings and the harbour on 4 July, with everything apparently set fair.[2] Already, by 11 June, Young had sold 582 tons of coal; the future appeared settled, even if a further £1,761 had been spent since the beginning of the year.

Yet again, however, problems arose. The Marchioness had come north with the question of costs very much in her mind.[3] She talked at length to the overseers and to the miners, as well as to Young, always coming back to the problem of expenditure and prospects. Already she had ordered the salt works to be stopped. The advice of Miller and his colleagues was that it would be sensible to place the colliery on lease. Possibly Miller was painting the prospects in a gloomy light, but whatever the reason the Marchioness' apprehensions were increased. On her suggestion Young decided to approach Hughes again, giving him the first opportunity of making a fresh offer. It is obvious that the advice of the new colliers had contributed to this change of plan.

Hughes came to Dunrobin on 7 July.[4] Pressed to make an offer, he hesitated until Young impulsively offered to share the enterprise equally with him. This episode is a revealing one. As Young admitted, this was the kind of 'active speculation' he enjoyed; he even suggested that his estate salary might be reduced at the same time. Sellar, consulted privately by the Marchioness, was in favour of a lease. He considered that the Alloa colliers were not working at half the rate Bald had predicted, and that a skilled controlling hand was required. Never slow to comment on Young, he told her

[1] Young to Marchioness, 31 May 1814: 'The fact is that these Lads have been spoiled by being on day in place of piece work, but in a concern of this sort when things are arranged nothing else will do.'
[2] See below, ii, p. 216.   [3] Ibid.   [4] See below, ii, pp. 219-21.

on 8 July that the mine had already cost the Marquis £11,000 (a slight underestimate) and that to build the salt pans would increase the total to £14,000. The sting of his letter was in the tail. Young, Sellar said, could not continue as factor once he took over the coal mine; the estate, he continued, could now be managed at much less salary. The Marchioness took his point.[1] But she felt confused by so many conflicting opinions about the coal, and asked for Stainton, or some other competent judge, to be sent. Young's experiment of direct management appeared to be crumbling.

Two days later came a bombshell which altered the whole situation. An informer's evidence came to light, to show that the miners were in a confederation to work slowly and to give a false impression of the mine.[2] Next day the picture became clearer.[3] Ramage was exposed as the instigator of the trouble and dismissed; he was suspected of being unduly influenced by Fifeshire mine-owners who feared competition. Miller was retained on sufferance. The miners, despite their dislike of the informer, David Allen,[4] were induced to return to Pritchard's method of working, using the whole seam instead of only that part above a vein of 'parrot coal' that ran through it. Over the next few days most of them came in to work on new and cheaper terms, although Ramage hung around for several days after his dismissal.[5] By the time the Marchioness left on 22 July opinions on the coal had risen sharply, despite a suspicion that Miller was still acting in the interests of coalmasters in the south.[6] The miners were working at extending the roads, and preparations were being made for new and deeper borings. The salt works were still postponed, but the Marchioness left with a much clearer picture to give her husband, so that he could decide whether or not to continue direct operations.

---

[1] Marchioness to Marquis, 8 July 1814: 'I suppose he thought, as I think too, that he will be thoroughly competent to this for (perhaps) 500£ per annum.' However, her views changed later (see below, ii, p. 229).

[2] Marchioness to Marquis, 10 July 1814: 'The cause of all this extraordinary confusion about the Coal is found out as there is a Collusion among the Colliers just discovered by a Man who was engaged in it, and who has brought another to own it, and is to bring more this evening to Dunrobin. . . . They had taken an oath not to work above a certain quantity and to say that they could do no more and Rammage desired them if they took an oath not to tell him anything of it.'

[3] See below, ii, pp. 222–4.   [4] See below, ii, p. 225.

[5] See below, ii, p. 227.   [6] See below, ii, p. 229.

In the upshot Young's plan for direct management was reprieved, despite the soaring cost of his working. The Marquis decided not to accept Hughes' and Young's offer, but to take a lease of the coal and other workings himself, together with Inverbrora farm; he was given these rent free, in consideration of his expenditure upon the coal. Meanwhile William Daniel, bailiff on the Marquis' colliery at Lane End, Staffordshire, went to Brora during August, and reported carefully to James Loch on his return.[1] There were problems connected with the coal itself, which had gone on fire, but the report was reassuring enough for Loch to engage John Jermyn, a Staffordshire collier, to act as coal overseer at a salary of £120. Loch, for the first time, applied cold financial reasoning to Brora.[2] His conclusions were not optimistic. The gross profit on the existing pit, under the best calculations, was unlikely to be more than £4,000, as against a capital expenditure of £15,000. This was a far cry from Young's wild dreams. Still Loch recommended continuation, not so much because of any notional profit, but for the sake of the secondary benefits to the estate from lime-burning and 'increased industry, Activity and spirit of improvement'. At the same time he made clear to Young that Jermyn must have full control of the workings.[3] It was Loch's first major intervention in the working of the Sutherland management, and Young was open enough in his acknowledgment.[4] The judgment was none the less clear: Young had rushed things and had failed to match detailed control to the breadth of his hopes.

Jermyn reached Brora on 15 September. The day before Young had finally dismissed Miller, after an altercation in which Miller had complained of Young's habit of listening to workmen's complaints.[5] Jermyn therefore had a more or less free hand, as all but four of the

[1] See below, ii, pp. 230-2.   [3] See below, ii, p. 231.
[2] Loch to Young, *3 Sept. 1814: 'He is to be on the same footing there, as to the details below ground, which Burgess is on here, that is without any controul on my part except as to new or additional works, extraordinary outlays, Mens Wages and the like; all of which of course come under the general controul of his Lordships Affairs.'
[4] Young to Loch, *11 Sept. 1814: 'I am well aware that we have been too rapid in our movements and perhaps it had been better that we had not attempted sales untill all the Levels were drawn, but untill Daniell came no Engineer ever told me so and I was glad to see the Coal coming up.'
[5] Cf. below, p. lxxii, n.2, and ii, pp. 294-5.

Alloa miners left at the same time. He reorganised the working and sent for miners from Staffordshire, whom Loch busied himself in finding. In addition to the coal Jermyn interested himself in clay, which was being found in conjunction with the coal seam. Young, inevitably, was attracted by this and started exploring for fresh clay veins, finding a possible one near Lothbeg; a sample was sent to the Potteries for examination. In the meantime he was pressing on with the construction of the salt pans, now authorised, and agitating for a new brickmaker to be sent from the south. When the four Staffordshire miners sent by Loch reached Burghead on 3 January 1815, at much the same time as the last of the Alloa men ran away, prospects again looked hopeful. A summer had been largely lost, less than 150 tons having been sold since June, but Jermyn had quelled a mutiny and new methods were working well. Yet the emphasis was shifting; the coal's limitations were now better understood, and weight was increasingly being laid upon the salt, brick and lime, particularly the outcrop of the latter recently found near Rhives. Total expenditure was over £14,000, but barring accidents was nearing its end: 1815, it was hoped, would be a better year.

Hardly had the Staffordshire colliers reached Brora, however, than alarming accounts began to come south. Francis Suther, writing to Loch on *31 January, repeated reports that the colliers were complaining of low wages, poor housing, and lack of bread and meat. Young had got wind of this discontent before Loch had time to write to him. He questioned the men closely but could find no positive cause for their complaints, beyond homesickness and a natural wish to see their wives and families. He managed to persuade them to sign a paper certifying that their conditions were adequate and as they had been promised, which he sent to Loch in the hope that it could be published in Staffordshire. However the colliers' wives took fright as a body and refused to go to Sutherland.

By 13 February Young considered that the colliers had settled down.[1] John Bloor, a brickmaker sent from Stafford, had at length arrived. Loch, however, poured cold water on Young's suggestions that Staffordshire potters, even the great Spode himself, be asked to come to Brora to inspect the clay, and he was adamant in rejecting Young's request for more money for the works. Lord Stafford, he

[1] Young to Loch, *13 Feb. 1815.

wrote on 14 February, would send none, on account of his English expenses, and was displeased at the request. This did not stop Young from making further plans. On 17 April, reporting that the coal levels were almost complete in preparation for the coming season, he revealed that Jermyn planned to sink two more pits to work the field.[1] By 25 April he was able to tell Loch that salt would be made during the next week, and that demand was high.[2] In short he was being sanguine again, pressing for a decision on the pottery venture. Even Loch caught some of the excitement. Writing to John Farey on *5 May, he was able to deny reports of a fire in the pit (there had been one in the previous autumn before Jermyn's arrival) and to give a glowing account of the state of the workings, including the two proposed additional pits. Still, Young was dissuaded for the present from starting additional salt pans, and his pottery scheme was rejected.

The main concern of all the family's managers, including Young himself, was now to find an overseer capable of handling all the above-ground coal work, together with Bloor's brick and tile operations and the salt pans. Such a manager, all were agreed, was urgently needed. Young's first idea was to call in John Roy, the land surveyor, but this had to be abandoned when Roy became factor on the Invercauld estate on Deeside. A more positive suggestion came from William Mackenzie, who introduced Young, on a visit to Edinburgh, to William Robertson, a clerk and assistant on the Prestonhall estate, who had long coal experience. Young was impressed, but Robertson wanted a salary beyond his limits, and the matter hung fire for the moment.

When the Marchioness, accompanied by Loch, came north in August 1815 the village of Brora was beginning to take shape,[3] and both she and Loch felt confident enough to allow Young to go forward with new tile kilns and salt pans. Loch was cautiously optimistic.[4] He was endeavouring, without success, to persuade Stainton to come to inspect Brora. On the other hand, he was beginning to distrust Young's methods, an opinion supported by other reasons. This was made worse by his discovery, very soon after leaving Sutherland, that Young was proposing to dismiss Bloor the brick-

---

[1] Young to Marchioness, 17 Apr. 1815.   [2] Young to Loch, *25 Apr. 1815.
[3] See below, ii, pp. 247-8.   [4] See below, ii, pp. 254-5.

f

maker and replace him by a young man from Peterhead. He was alarmed too by what he took to be Young's intention to dismiss Jermyn as slow and extravagant. He had his own explanation, not a flattering one, for Young's actions,[1] and he was insistent that the Marchioness should stop any dismissal of Jermyn. The tone of his comments on Young was hardening,[2] and he wrote sharply to him on *9 September, complaining that in Bloor he had dismissed a second brickmaker (one had served briefly in 1814 before being discharged for drunkenness), that he was altering plans agreed during the summer, and that he was running the risk of making Lord Stafford withdraw entirely from Brora. He also advised caution in sinking any new pit.[3] The letter was long and trenchant. Loch was as yet advising rather than instructing, but the change of tone is evident. Meanwhile he resumed the hunt for a general manager for Brora – something that Young himself, in all fairness, had repeatedly requested. But his confidence in Young was shaken. On *11 September he repeated to the Marchioness his criticisms of Young's proposed expenditure, complaining that no hint of this had been given while the family was in Sutherland. It was a serious breakdown in confidence that was to have repercussions in the following year.

For the moment things were patched over. Loch held the whip-hand as Lord Stafford's financial adviser. Young protested on *19 September that he had been justified in dismissing Bloor on grounds of lack of knowledge and expense, and declared that he had no intention of parting with Jermyn. He was now busy with the new salt pans, and the tone of his letters suggests that he was aware that he was getting out of his depth at Brora. Over 1,500 tons of coal, double the quantity raised in the previous year, had been sold in 1815, but another £6,830 had been spent and the enterprises were nowhere near paying their way.

Altogether it must have been a relief all round when in December

---

[1] Loch to Marchioness, *8 Sept. 1815: 'His reason, I know, though he is unconscious of it himself, is because they are English.'

[2] Loch to Marchioness, *8 Sept. 1815: 'It is provoking to see a man of Young's under-standing and other qualifications so much given to prejudice, and so fickle and giddy in his opinions and predilections. Indeed he often changes in the course of 24 hours arising from a bad habit of listening to the opinion of Workmen as to the conduct of their immediate masters.'

[3] See below, ii, pp. 260-1.

William Mackenzie finally reached agreement with Robertson. The latter came to Brora in early March 1816. Terms were arranged for him by Mackenzie and Young: Robertson was to serve a year's trial at £120 salary, starting immediately. Young's management of the coal effectively closed at once, though a number of items in his accounts were not settled until long afterwards. From March 1816 onwards Robertson was the manager of all the Brora enterprises.

Viewed in retrospect, the story of Brora under Young is a microcosm of his whole Sutherland history. Large plans, eager beginnings, defective controls, soaring expenditure, disappointing returns: the catalogue is formidable. The total expenditure, if the harbour and houses are taken into consideration, came to over £30,900. Yet he was a man of resilience, and not a complete failure. At Brora he had formidable problems and a good deal of ill-luck. Loch, from his knowledge of the Staffordshire coal, was probably from the start more aware of the small expectations that Brora should arouse and of the constant need for financial care. Young, the all-purpose entrepreneur, was at a disadvantage against such a trained accountant; he was at an even greater disadvantage in the nature of the enterprise itself. But the account in Loch's *Improvements* is, in the last resort, a tribute to Young. On one small point, too, Young had the last laugh. In August 1816 Loch found himself forced to dismiss Jermyn for idleness and incapacity.[1]

3 *The Fleet Mound*

The story of the implementation of the Sutherland Road Act of 1805, as it affected the construction of parliamentary roads and the commutation of statute labour, is too large a subject to be considered here. The result of ten years' working of the Act was, by 1816, to give the county one main trunk highway along the east coast and a partially constructed one to the north coast at Tongue;[2] in addition

---

[1] Loch to Burgess, *22 Aug. 1816: 'I found him not only lazy and indolent, but utterly incapable of doing his duty – until lately he hardly ever went below and when he is forced to, he lies idle among the rubbish, he had lost all authority or rather never had any.'

[2] For the history of the 'parliamentary' roads, constructed with the aid of the Commissioners for Highland Roads and Bridges, see A. R. B. Haldane, *New Ways through the Glens* (Edinburgh, 1962).

there was the beginning of a system of properly constructed local roads. In all of this the Sutherland estate was closely concerned: it was an important financial contributor;[1] the intervention of the Marquis and Earl Gower was often necessary in the county's negotiations with the Commissioners for Highland Roads and Bridges; and the estate managers were themselves involved, both in the handling of the public business connected with the road programme and the actual work itself. It is one aspect of this latter involvement, the building of the bridge and mound across the estuary of the river Fleet, that is examined here.

The immemorial line of road between Caithness and the south ran along the east coast of Sutherland, crossing the Fleet at the Little Ferry and the Dornoch Firth at the Meikle Ferry.[2] Along this entire route there was, before the coming of the parliamentary road, one single substantial bridge, at Brora. The creation of the parliamentary road removed two major obstacles by bridging the Helmsdale and the Dornoch Firth (upstream from the Meikle Ferry at Bonar).[3] There remained the short but tricky passage of Loch Fleet at the Little Ferry. Thomas Telford, the Commissioners' consulting engineer, in surveying the line of the road, had envisaged new piers there, a bridge being clearly out of the question; money for this purpose was actually allocated in 1811.

The arrival of William Young had its impact on these plans. As early as 1811 he had begun to have different ideas,[4] and brought forward the concept of a causeway across the estuary. The county was impressed enough to ask for an estimate at the very meeting at which it accepted Telford's figures for the Little Ferry piers. Young's reasoning was noteworthy, for he was as much interested in land reclamation as in ease of transit. This may well have arisen from earlier plans to straighten the course of the lower Fleet at Morvich, just above the spot where it ran into the sea. In August the county received and approved the estimate, and submitted a formal request for a mound and bridge to the Commissioners. Telford was in the county inspecting and approving the Helmsdale bridge and the

---

[1] See below, pp. 248-50.
[2] A map of Helmsdale and Navidale in 1778 shows the 'King's High Road to Caithness' crossing the Ord, and passing by 'Montrose's encampment'.
[3] See Haldane, op. cit., 131-2.   [4] See below, ii, p. 147.

completed sections of the parliamentary road, and had undoubtedly been involved in the survey of the proposed crossing, which had fixed on a line between Craigtoun Rock and Cambusmore.

The Commissioners were in some difficulty, the line of their road being already determined and new access roads being necessary to align it with the Mound. They were also somewhat shaken by the cost of the Mound, estimated by Telford at £8,500. On 19 March 1812 they raised the question of the value of the 200 acres expected to be recovered from the sea, and of 108 acres of meadow ground which would be protected from the tide. Young was indignant at what he considered a diversionary move,[1] and even questioned the likely success of the reclamation[2] – something of a change from his earlier view. But the Commissioners were not deflected, and on 30 April called on Telford for an estimate of the value of the ground to be recovered. The result, as Young foresaw, was the loss of an entire season, and it was not until 8 December that the Marquis again approached the Commissioners, offering to contribute £1,000 to the cost of the Mound in consideration of the land to be gained. The Commissioners took their time before responding, but on 24 February they submitted their proposals. The total cost of the Mound with its approach roads they estimated at £9,866, exclusive of £1,200 that Lord Stafford was now prepared to contribute; from this they insisted on deducting £1,087 as the cost of the existing line of road from Golspie to the Little Ferry, leaving a balance of £8,799, against which they set £1,359 already provided for the Little Ferry piers; they then offered to contribute one-half of the remaining £7,420. The county, grumbling, accepted on 3 April, and the Commissioners thereupon sent the specifications out to tender on 29 April, almost exactly two years after the project had first been suggested.

Problems, however, were only just beginning. Contractors were hesitant to offer for what promised to be a difficult operation. William Hughes, already at work at Brora, was approached but was reluctant to commit himself in open competition. By September

[1] See below, ii, p. 163.
[2] Young to Earl Gower, 2 Apr. 1812: 'From whatever source the Commissioners have got notice that profit is to be derived by such a speculation, I am bound in Justice to say that I see no immediate or certain gain.'

only two offers had been received for the Mound itself, whose gross cost Telford had estimated at £8,435. An Edinburgh contractor offered £10,948, and a Morayshire man, James Forsyth, already employed by Young in the county, the low figure of £7,500. The Marquis did not consider Forsyth sufficiently competent, and as a result Hughes was approached again. He remained unwilling, except at an exorbitant price, and probably refused even to submit a formal tender.

In these circumstances, with the whole future of the project in doubt, Young induced Earl Gower to intervene, and on 29 September an offer to undertake the Mound was submitted to the Commissioners by the Earl, in partnership with Young and Sellar.[1] The result was a violent explosion from Telford, who appeared unexpectedly in Sutherland in mid-October. As Sellar explained it,[2] the cause of his anger was simple. He had expected that Hughes would carry out the work, possibly without advertisement, as had happened in the case of the Bonar Bridge contractors, Cargill and Simpson. Sellar reported the virulence of the attack on Young in some detail, though the latter was more restrained.[3] The episode is revealing of Telford's temper and of Young's readiness to undertake enterprises beyond his range of knowledge. The anger of the professional against the amateur is evident. Young, sanguine as ever, attempted to protect himself by engaging Forsyth, the unsuccessful tenderer, as foreman. In doing so, he was placing a good deal of reliance on a man whose capacity was persistently distrusted by the Marquis and by Loch, and who in the end had to be set aside at the crucial moment.

Young finalised the contract when at Edinburgh in January 1814. The plan was to start by building a bridge, with sluice-gates, close to the Craigtoun Rock, on the northern (but usually called the eastern)

---

[1] As Sellar reported to Loch, *16 Nov. 1813.
[2] Ibid.
[3] Young to Loch, *5 Dec. 1813: 'With regard to Telford I really do not think that he is a mercenary but there are a parcel of fellows about him in this Country who are and by whom I suspect he is too much directed, besides the Man has a load of business on his shoulders beyond bearing which makes him capricious and he is in many instances obliged to see with other peoples eyes and is often misled.' 'All in all,' he wrote to the Marchioness on 8 Dec., 'he has done much for us and most people are at times subject to a little spleen.'

shore of the bay; this was to be completed during the summer of 1814, to give it the winter to harden into position. Work on the main embankment would begin in 1815 from both banks using a horse-railway to carry material. Sellar was satisfied that, with 100 barrowmen and 54 men using 27 waggons, the necessary weight of material could be moved into position during one season.[1] On this basis recruiting went ahead and by 26 March 1814 sixty Rogart and Strathnaver men were at work. In May a cargo of freestone from Moray for the bridge was successfully brought up the narrow channel from the Little Ferry.

But there were difficulties. As at Bonar, the rock foundations predicted by Telford were not found, and there had to be a tentative plan to use wood foundations laid on stiff clay. In the end, however, it was decided to carry out extra work to secure a firm rock base. Telford was called in, and on 5 November Young was able to report to Earl Gower that he had given an assurance that the Commissioners would meet the extra cost. Season 1814 closed with some £2,000 already spent, the greater part on labourers' wages and equipment, no bridge ready, and only a small part of the southern (or western) causeway built.

Young was in an urgent frame of mind in the spring of 1815, and work began as early as February. By 4 April he had ordered a temporary embankment to be built round the site of the bridge so that proper foundations might be dug out without holding up the progress of the main Mound.[2] By 12 May solid rock was at last reached, but already the narrowing of the gap between the two arms of the Mound had so increased the pressure of the tide that it was necessary to wait for the completion of the bridge to allow a passage for the water. The bridge and sluice-gates were not in fact finished until 23 July, by which time the season was far advanced. The Marchioness, coming north in August, found sixty people at work and 150 expected in the following week; the Mound, she wrote to her husband on 11 August, was 'a very great work, the bridge, floodgates and about one third of it finished to within six feet of

[1] Sellar to Young, 10 Jan. 1814.
[2] Young to Earl Gower, 4 Apr. 1815: 'We have made a temporary Mound by which the Stuff is now carried forward and having pumps to raise any water which may filter into the foundation we are enabled to do the Bridge and place the valves with greater certainty than if we had been constantly annoyed by this Tide.'

the height, and at present repelling the tide'. But little further progress was made during the remainder of the summer. On 21 August
the Marchioness wrote that 'as the tides do not now admit of working by night, half the workmen and horses are dismist till next
April and they are to finish the present half to its height and width
during the remainder of this Season, in the mean time this will be
quite settled and fixed'. Yet she had her reservations, for two days
later she wrote a note to Loch, who was with her at Dunrobin,
expressing old doubts about Forsyth's competence, and asking
whether an engineer should not now be called in to advise. Loch
apparently was of the same mind, for Young wrote to him on
*19 September regretting his fears that those on the spot might not
be able to finish the work, and estimating that two months only were
required for completion. From this letter it is clear that Loch was
already considering turning to expert advice, for the name of John
Rennie was mentioned. A meeting Loch had had at Clachnaharry
with Matthew Davidson, one of the Caledonian Canal engineers,
had probably occasioned this, Davidson having been very uncertain
about the best method of closing the Mound. The operation was
now running a year behind schedule, almost £5,800 had been spent,
and the most treacherous part of the work, the closing of the final
gap, where the combined force of tide and river pressed most
strongly, still lay ahead.

The winter of 1815-16 passed without any material damage to
the work so far finished. Sellar was unhappy at the expenses to date,
but Young was already purchasing timber for piles to close the gap.
Loch, meanwhile, was following up his worries of the previous
autumn. He wrote to Earl Gower on *11 February that he was
advised by one Jessop, who had designed a major work at Bristol,
that the method proposed by Young – of gradually narrowing the
gap and then closing it at a single low-tide – was impossible.[1] This
serious opinion alarmed Loch sufficiently for him to advise delay
until he had secured an inspection by a competent engineer, especially as he still considered Forsyth unequal to the task. His cousin,

---

[1] '. . . the only way to accomplish it is to heighten the whole gradually but regularly,
from one end to the other at once permitting the tide to flow over it every tide until
it is so high as to be above high Water Mark'. For William Jessop, see K. Hudson,
The Industrial Archaeology of Southern England (Dawlish, 1965), 71-72.

Charles Adam, who was in Edinburgh, acted for him in consulting
John Playfair and James Jardine.[1] Jardine was approached as early
as 18 February and agreed in principle with Jessop. John Rennie was
then called in on 28 February. Meanwhile Sellar was reviewing the
existing plans, which he set out in a letter to Loch on 6 March.[2]
These plans were directly contrary to Jessop's proposals, which had
not yet reached Sutherland in detail. In adhering to the idea of a
single, decisive closure Sellar had, it is worth noticing, Rennie's
support, though Loch did not reveal the fact to him.[3]

Loch followed his own line. In Earl Gower's interest, Jardine was
engaged to inspect the Mound, and nothing, Loch ordered, was to
be done until he had visited Sutherland.[4] It was not until early April
that Jardine arrived and confirmed his previous views.[5] Neither of
the resident contractors was ready to accept these quietly. Sellar
suggested that Hughes might be induced to take over and Young,
keeping Jardine's report with him, went off to Inverness to consult
the latter. He reported that Hughes was inclined to doubt Jardine's
plan, but was unwilling to take on the contract himself. What,
Young asked Loch on *14 April, was he to do – to follow Jardine,
at heavy expense, or to stick to the original plans? Loch, with
Rennie's contradictory advice now before him, hedged. On *29
April he wrote to Sellar that he had sent Jardine's report to Telford.
The next day he wrote to Young: Telford was sending Hughes and
Davidson to inspect the Mound; Young was to do nothing until
their advice was secured, otherwise it would be impossible to apply
to the Commissioners for further financial help.

Hughes and Davidson reached the Mound on 8 May. Their
opinion was basically on Young's side, if with some modifications,[6]
and Telford wrote to Loch that he considered that the resident
contractors should go ahead with their original plan. Loch, reluctantly, agreed on *24 May. It was, in fact, too late to do anything
else, for Young and Sellar were already in action.

On *20 May Sellar reported to Loch that a foot passage had been

---

[1] See below, ii, pp. 276-8.   [2] See below, ii, pp. 273-5.
[3] On *7 Apr. Rennie's son wrote to Loch that his father recommended that the embankment be extended from the bridge towards the south shore, and that the gap be then
completed with as little delay as possible.
[4] See below, ii, p. 277.   [5] See below, ii, pp. 278-9.
[6] See below, pp. 171-5.

opened at ebb-tide and that the piles to exclude the sea were being erected. Thereafter the momentum of the operation increased. Sellar was agitated because Young and Forsyth were erecting only a single line of piles, instead of the double row he had envisaged; he was, he told Loch on *27 May, insisting that the second row be added; he also reported that the tide had cut into the head of the northern causeway, as he had feared it might. This hole, which Young estimated to be fifty-five feet long and six to nine feet deep,[1] was still dangerous when the second row of piles was begun on 31 May. It meant that the closing operations had to be accompanied by the repair of this considerable breach in the work already done. Nevertheless preparations for the assault went on. Sellar went to Ross-shire to recruit men from the road-making squads there, others were taken off the Tongue road, and ten gangs of local workmen were organised under overseers. In all, Young reckoned in a letter to Earl Gower on *31 May, there would be upwards of 700 men, with over 250 barrows and 50 carts, in addition to 40 waggons on the railway.[2]

The crucial day came on Tuesday, 4 June. Sellar was up at 4 a.m., and wrote a hurried note to the Marchioness before leaving Culmaily; the wind was high, and he felt that it would be neceessary to restrict work to closing the breach in the existing Mound. What happened when he reached the scene of operations is described vividly in a letter he wrote the following morning.[3] As this makes clear, the critical failure came at the site of the hole blown in the embankment on 27 May. Yet at 4 p.m. on the previous day Young had been so confident that he had reported success to Earl Gower.

The whole episode shook the mutual confidence of the partners. Sellar, writing to the Marchioness on *6 June, was relieved to report that the damage had been less serious than he had expected; the

---

[1] Young to Earl Gower, *3 June 1816.

[2] 'As your Lordship agrees to it we are all prepared to battle the Sea with at least 600 men in arms on Tuesday (the kings birth day). The piles are all driven, so is an apron of 2 to 3 feet under the sands, the planking is ready with Carpenters to nail it on. Our men and Overseers will all have their stations marked on Monday to avoid confusion. Walklate is brewing 30 hogsheads of ale and the Baker is getting 40 Bolls of Meal converted into bread, for the people must be fed. We shall have a busy and I hope a successful time of it.'

[3] See below, ii, pp. 288-9. The other letters mentioned in this paragraph are in the Trentham Collection.

hole had deepened, but not widened, and the remaining work done during the day had not been harmed. He took what remedial measures he could and prepared for a fresh attack at the next neap tide, but insisted that there be a proper plan and no further mismanagement. His confidence in Young and Forsyth was made still weaker by an episode the same afternoon, when he discussed the next steps with them. He wrote angrily to Loch on the morning of *7 June, complaining that Young would not stick to any fixed plan, that he had failed to carry out preparations properly on 3 June, and that on the morning of 4 June he had crossed to the southern side without seeing to the mustering and feeding of the men, leaving Forsyth with unworkable instructions. His angry conclusion was that he would refuse to take part in a second attempt, unless Hughes, whom Young had agreed should be sent for, would come and take command.

Hughes, however, was far away at the southern end of the Caledonian Canal, and by 12 June, just as the reports of the failure were reaching the south, Sellar was faced with a fresh crisis. Young had recovered his nerve (on *8 June he had been writing to Loch suggesting his retirement from the estate management) and was desperately anxious to make a further attempt before the Marchioness came to Sutherland at the end of the month. Although Hughes had not appeared, Young insisted on a second attack, using stronger timber and properly laid piles across the hole. He was so set on the attempt that he promised to meet all the costs himself in the event of failure. Sellar was reluctant but agreed. The very next day, but too late, Loch was writing urgently to them both to make no further attempt if Hughes had any doubts or proposed any expensive remedy; Earl Gower, he told Young, must no longer be exposed to the blunders of Forsyth, in whom Young had trusted too much.

This time there was no slip, and on 19 June Sellar was reporting that after a night of work the hole had been closed and the complete length of the Mound raised above water level.[1] Young, his relief evident, wrote almost daily to Earl Gower to announce progress. With 400 men at work heightening and widening the embankment, he was able to receive Loch's letter of *13 June with equanimity.[2]

[1] See below, ii, pp. 293-4.
[2] Young to Earl Gower, *21 June 1816.

Sellar, on the same day, was philosophical.[1] There was still some apprehension for another week, as the tides gradually increased, but no accident occurred, and on Wednesday 26 June, the day of the spring tide, the Marquis and Marchioness crossed the Mound by carriage on their way to Dunrobin.[2]

Work continued until the winter, but the crisis had passed, and on 6 December the Local Committee of Superintendence, together with John Mitchell, Inspector of Highland Roads, issued a report that the mound had been, with certain minor qualifications, satisfactorily completed. The cost had not been light. Against the contract price of £8,435 (to which was added £304 allowed for extra work on the foundations) the total expenditure was £9,749; £619 of this was afterwards recovered in sales of horses and equipment. The loss on the contract was thus £391, increased by supplementary works in 1817 and 1818 to £644. This represented a loss on the contract price of almost 8%, high enough to make the professionals' reluctance to tender understandable. The Marquis met the entire balance, thus adding to his previous financial support of the venture.

It had been a considerable operation. In 1814 £2,122 had been spent, of which £1,145 went on labourers' wages; in 1815 £3,667, £2,211 being on wages; and in 1816 £3,960, £2,563 on wages. As an injection of cash into the Sutherland economy it was second only to the Brora works, and probably more concentrated in its effects. As a project in its own right it has considerable fascination. However much Telford and his Inspector, Mitchell, lurked in the background, the brunt of the planning and day-to-day working was in the hands of amateurs and relatively unqualified workmen. Young, Sellar and Forsyth were in no sense trained engineers. Yet, with only occasional help from Hughes and other professionals,

[1] Sellar to Loch, *21 June 1816: 'Davidson said that his principles would have led him to Conclude a blowing up inevitable. But his experience among our Stuff in the North, satisfied him we had no danger to apprehend. We have been most entirely the Children of Fortune in this affair. . . . We entrusted the Timber work in this last attempt to George Alexander, the Superintendence of the Earth work to George Riach one of Mr Telfords people on the Tongue Road, . . . and kept Forsyth to a Squad of 20 men for which he is better Suited than the Conduct of Such an undertaking.'

[2] Marchioness to Earl Gower, 26 June 1816: 'I write this in Forsyth's cottage having just crost the Mound carriage and all. The finishing having been effected the morning of the 19 it is now beyond the height of the highest Tide and appears already secure, though more strength is to be added.'

they battered their way through the difficulties. In the process Young and Sellar demonstrated their very different personalities. It was, ironically, Sellar, the lawyer, who showed more realism. But, in the last resort it was Young's optimism that plucked success from the edge of disaster. He underestimated the technical problems, he overestimated the financial feasibility: but he involved Earl Gower and his money, and he never lost sight of the objective. In a very real sense, the Mound was Young's biggest success-story.

4 *Financial control*

The most striking feature of Young's management was a sharp rise in estate expenditure.[1] Over the period from January 1812 to the arrival of Francis Suther in 1817 management expenditure totalled £140,488, almost double the £70,867 spent in the nine previous years; the average annual expenditure was £28,097, as against £7,874; in each of the three years 1813 to 1815 expenditure exceeded £30,000. Despite an increase in revenue from an average £9,984 to £22,212 Young spent in five years £29,427 more than the estate produced, whereas in the previous nine years revenue had exceeded expenditure by £18,990. This is reflected in the figures for extraction and injection of funds by the proprietors, a net extraction of £13,250 giving way to a net injection of £96,443. After allowing for capital expenditure on purchases and wadsets, and for some rents, mainly salmon ones, collected outside Sutherland, the figure for money actually advanced for the running of the estate was over £46,000. The totals are not capable of precise balance, but the order of magnitude is not in doubt. Although Young's reorganisation, following on Falconer's increases of rent, produced a management income in 1815 approximately three times what it had been in 1803, expenditure had increased nine times. This, more than the rearrangements of tenancies, was the salient feature of the period. It implied a positive change in attitudes, and it entailed a major decision to finance the estate from outside Sutherland.

What is even more striking in any analysis of this situation is that this vastly increased expenditure was neither fully foreseen nor controlled. The broad aims of improvement had been visualised long

[1] For details of the estate accounts during Young's management see below, pp. 241-57.

before, and Young merely put them into effect with greater determination and ingenuity than his predecessors. Resettlement, village
development, farm reorganisation, the refurbishing of Dunrobin
and its policies were all under way in Falconer's time. On these
Young's methods were certainly expensive,[1] and there were serious
questions about the effectiveness of his accounting, but many of the
main commitments had already been made. The new and crucial
factor, beyond any doubt, was Brora.[2] If all Brora expenditure,
including the harbour, pilot's houses and colliers' houses, is taken
together Loch's estimate of £30,000-£40,000 is correct enough, for
the total cost was over £30,900, against which only £3,556 had
been earned by the undertakings by the close of Young's factory.
Loch's comments on the dangers of Brora were fully justified. Yet
the dilemma with which it confronted him is clear enough. Brora,
he recognised, could be of vital importance in transforming the
estate; in addition, expenditure upon it had crept up insensibly, as
one experiment had followed another, and now the money sunk
in it was too great to be written off. But it raised questions of control
and of practicability which he could not finally avoid.

   The question of control is, in fact, the crucial one for the whole
policy of improvement, which ran into such serious financial problems under Young's guidance. Loch was beginning to be aware of
this as early as 1813, though there is no sign that Young ever fully
comprehended it.[3] Equipped with a competent book-keeping clerk,
William Grant, Young was able to produce formal accounts, but
little more. His optimism and carelessness of detail made him a bad
forecaster of expenditure, even when he could be brought to
attempt it. The press of his multifarious enterprises compounded
the difficulty, and produced the state of affairs of which Loch complained in 1816 to William Mackenzie.[4] The evidence suggests that
the traditional method of accountability, through the annual account,

---

[1] See below, ii, p. 290. Loch wrote to Earl Gower in similar terms on *17 June 1816:
'Your Lordship must permit me to state that . . . I have been of opinion that unless a
different direction was hereafter given to the great expenditure at Dunrobin the estate
and your Lordship will lose a great part of the benefit which ought to arise from such
an outlay.'
[2] See below, ii, pp. 294-7.
[3] See below, ii, p. 267.
[4] See below, ii, pp. 303-4.

was proving inadequate in the face of the problems of an investing and improving policy. The division between Sellar, the revenue producing manager, who collected rents and fought with arrears, and Young, the spending manager, continually calling on his partner for money, accentuated the difficulty. It was increased further by a failure to use the family's annual visit to Dunrobin for full discussion of and decisions on projected expenditure; too often decisions were taken from a distance and in a haphazard way. Loch, when his time came, had a simple and rigid system to meet this problem. The wonder is not that he was driven to it, despite William Mackenzie's doubts, but that it had been so long in coming.

The story of Young's financial operations is, in one light, a story of optimism gradually overcome by realities. In another, it is an illustration of the truism that large plans cannot be executed without detailed control. In yet another, it shows how the improver had to give way to the auditor. For with Loch scientific management finally took up the problems which had overcome Young. We shall see later how the change came about.

Meanwhile it is instructive to see how far control was attempted, and how the need for it gradually became evident. Given the basic lines of policy which Young inherited and to which he adhered – with the single great exception of Brora – such control was bound to be financial. The Marchioness, with or without her husband, came north most summers, toured at least the nearer part of the estate, looked with interest but not perhaps much understanding at such figures as were laid before her, and gave her instructions in general terms, largely on what she had herself seen on her tours. When she was accompanied by Loch, as in 1813 and 1815, the financial probing was more persistent. But with Young producing his accounts at increasingly irregular intervals any long view was hard to establish. Large works were in progress, expert opinions were being taken, hopeful estimates were being made, but the financial picture received was essentially a retrospective one, capable of changing abruptly. Young's incurable optimism, and his reluctance to raise money matters until his needs were urgent, extended the problem. On the other hand the position gave Loch, in his capacity as general auditor of the Marquis' money affairs, the opportunity, which he eventually took, of insisting on some fuller method of control. But this did not come quickly, for it was not until the end of 1815 that he moved from the position of an observer and exhorter to that of a controller pressing for compliance – and even then it took a major confrontation in August 1816 to achieve the change.

No serious problem arose in the first year of Young's factory. Indeed, when he closed his first account in January 1812 he offered to give a draft on Earl Gower's Skelbo account to pay up an unexpended balance of £885. He was never again to be in that position for at the end of his next account, on 20 February 1813, he had overspent £7,744 in spite of receiving £2,000 on 6 February from the Marquis. Yet there was little urgency about the situation, with the year's rents still coming in, though he received £1,800 in April to meet current outlays. Ominously, however, he told Earl Gower on 18 May that he would borrow from the bank to meet current needs until the family came north; this may not have happened, for he was sent £5,000 on 26 June.

Loch accompanied the Marchioness to Sutherland in the summer of 1813, and audited Young's accounts up to the beginning of September. He was as yet feeling his way and his remarks were cautious,[1] though he hoped that the Sutherland revenue would in future meet all costs except the coal. This was subject, as he pointed out, to Young preparing proper estimates of expenditure for the year ahead, which he suggested should be done. This was the first of many attempts to persuade Young to apply method to his accounting. There was clearly a considerable deficit building up, for Young's accounts showed an over-expenditure of £10,046, quite apart from the famine victual transactions. For the moment the position was met, Young receiving over the next month £11,500 to put his affairs on a proper footing. £20,300 had thus been injected during 1813.

The situation deteriorated further in 1814. As activity on the Brora and Dunrobin works rose towards a peak, Young's finances came under repeated strain. Already in September 1813 he had advanced £5,258 to contractors to keep the works going, and this sum had risen to £8,973 by the following June. In addition to the coal expenditure, the expenses of Brora harbour, over £2,300, now fell to be met. As early as 3 March Young was borrowing from the

[1] See below, ii, pp. 200-1.

British Linen Company in thousands, despite the fact that rent receipts were at their highest in the early months of the year. The bank, not unnaturally, was looking for security, as Young reported to Loch. His overdraft was £5,800, he told the Marchioness on 2 April, and Sellar would have no funds to pay over before Whitsunday.

Reluctantly, the Marquis made available a cash credit of £5,000 at the bank, which Loch instructed Young was not to be exhausted and was to be replenished from the rents. The assumption was still that the estate could meet all its own costs over the year. But the credit was not enough, for on 6 June Benjamin Ross, the bank's Tain agent, reported to Young that he was in debit to the extent of £8,404; he was honouring Young's drafts, but asked for his personal bill for £5,000 to cover the excess beyond the cash credit. When the Marchioness and Earl Gower came north in July the costs of the coal had risen as high as £14,000, and Young's accounts to June showed him £9,053 overdrawn (he did not enter the cash credit of £5,000 in this account).

Estimating ahead roughly, Young considered that he might require a further £2,000 in the year. Earl Gower, on his return south, discussed the situation with Loch, who wrote to Lord Stafford on 11 August that it would be difficult to send Young more than £5,000 immediately (it was paid on 24 August), and that he was anxious that Young should go over to a proper system of monthly accounts. Already he was growing suspicious as to what would happen to the cash credit, which he feared Young had simply used to meet his current needs. If this were the case, he told the Marquis on 29 September,[1] after another £4,000 had been sent, then Young had still £7,000 of debt to clear. In short, Young had received £14,000, and was still £2,000 in debt—a situation that would decline sharply if he was unable to restore the £5,000 credit from the coming rents. It was not surprising that the Marchioness wrote to Loch on 1 October that she had asked Young for a proper prospectus, and had warned him not to lay out any money except as arranged. Two consecutive seasons had thus made it necessary to find £34,300 for Sutherland over and above the income it had produced. The full cost of Young's works was becoming apparent. Loch did not audit

[1] See below, ii, pp. 232-5.

g

the 1814 account, which went to William Mackenzie in the old manner. Had he done so, the crisis of the end of 1815 might have been anticipated.

With these experiences behind him, Lord Stafford reacted sharply when in February 1815 Young again approached him for money. He was displeased, Loch wrote in reply on *14 February, and would send no more; the £9,000 provided in the previous autumn had been intended to cover all deficiencies, except an estimated expenditure of £2,000 on the Brora salt pans. Loch asked Young for a general state of his accounts since the last balance in June 1814. Young, taken rather aback, wrote on 24 February that he would not trouble the Marquis for money, Sellar having promised him £900. Sellar did rather better than this, paying over £2,348 on 28 February, which brought his total payments to Young since August to £6,340. It is clear, however, that Young was unable to use this to replenish his cash credit. His expenditure was consuming every penny of the estate revenue left after Sellar had met the necessary public burdens and other fixed payments. The weight of continuing outlay on Brora was overshadowing all other considerations.

Young struggled on through the summer, apparently raising no financial difficulties during the visit by the Marchioness and Loch in August. Loch, to judge from a later letter, received a summary of the year's accounts and an optimistic financial estimate. The Marchioness suspected that Young was hurrying too much at Brora in the hope of profits to support his accounts, but as these were not fully prepared when she left the county Loch could not form a true idea of the position. It is possible that Young was deliberately delaying their presentation until Loch had returned south; it is equally likely, however, that his over-worked clerk, Grant, had simply been unable to prepare them in time.

Nevertheless, it is significant that no sooner was Loch back in the south than the old trouble began again. Young apparently wrote to him proposing the construction of much larger brick ovens and sheds at Brora than had been agreed during the summer. It was to be regretted, Loch wrote briskly in reply on 9 September, that these proposals had not been made during the Marchioness' stay in Sutherland, for there was a real danger that the Marquis might become tired out by the constant demands for money. There was, he continued, an urgent need for a steady, systematic plan, as he had previously suggested in September 1814. The Marchioness, writing to Loch on *16 September, agreed with him; it was important, she added, that Young should be kept in order by getting good under-managers for Brora and Dunrobin Farm. This last had already been agreed in principle during her stay in Sutherland.

Worse, however, was to follow. On *18 October Young wrote an excited letter to Loch from Edinburgh. Hearing that Loch had not yet left Blairadam, his uncle's house near Kinross, he had come post-haste from Sutherland in the hope of seeing him, only to find that he had left for England on 15 October. Now he wrote with an air of despair. The bank was demanding the repayment of all bor-rowed money, and nothing could be expected from Sellar under Martinmas. £7,000 was then expected, Young claimed; in the event Sellar actually paid him £2,391 between 25 October and the end of the year, in addition to accepting a three months' bill for £2,500. Having pledged himself to Lady Stafford not to call on the Marquis for more money, Young saw himself threatened with bankruptcy. Ingeniously, he asked for payment for cattle which had been sent to Staffordshire from Dunrobin. Cattle had gone south every year since 1808, but had been entered simply as expenditure in the factor's accounts without money passing. Loch, examining Young's accounts during his summer stay at Dunrobin, had raised the question of payment for the 1815 drove, amounting to £453. Young, seizing on this, was now looking for payment for all such cattle since his factory began in 1811, amounting to some £3,500.

The reaction to this was prompt. Loch, after conferring with the Marquis and Marchioness, emphasised that they were determined to understand what obligations they were accepting and to regulate their expenditure as they saw fit.[1] Pointedly, he asked for details: what sum was required, and for what purpose? When at Dunrobin, he wrote, he had been told that there was an over-expenditure of £7,299 on Young's accounts, from which the old cash credit of

[1] Loch to Young, *26 Oct. 1815: 'After what I have said I am sure I need not intreat of you to apply your mind seriously to the moderation of the outlay and to its proper and methodical arrangement. I cannot easily express to you how earnest and serious both Lord and Lady Stafford are in their desire to have this done which perhaps you will understand fully when I mention to you that his Lordship says it is impossible for him to make any remittance now after having remitted £9,000 last year.'

£5,000 presumably fell to be deducted; if Sellar were able to provide £7,000, then almost all the remaining debt could be paid off
and the cash credit restored, though certainly running expenses
must continue to be incurred. He asked therefore yet again for a
statement of the present position and the probable outlays for 1816.[1]
Surveying the report given him at Dunrobin, he concluded that
only the new salt pans and the Brora farm could be serious new
charges; these would, in any case, shortly be removed from Young's
accounts when the new bailiff agreed upon in the summer arrived.
But it was essential that he be given a correct statement of the present
and future position. There was no desire to halt the improvements,
only to regulate the expenditure, but it was important not to be
too optimistic about returns, especially from the salt. Further, there
could be no new advance. Writing a few days later,[2] he added that
Lord Stafford was prepared to pay for the cattle sent to Trentham
as soon as he received a statement of the amount.

Young replied on 1 November, temporising on the main question, and promising to send his accounts as soon as completed. He
was happy to know that a Brora bailiff was to be appointed, but
rejected any suggestion that any works worth more than £100 were
being carried on that had not been previously approved. The effect
of this letter upon Loch was probably disastrous: he had asked for
information and had received only generalisations. Young himself
was perhaps nearing the end of this tether. On 15 November he
wrote to Lady Stafford,[3] reviewing the state of the works, and suggesting that he might be released at Whitsunday. In her reply of
23 November[4] the Marchioness rejected this idea out of hand, while
insisting that future expenditure be kept in measure.

Young, therefore, had to manage with what money he could raise
from Sellar, even anticipating the rents on 5 November by drawing
on the latter for £2,500, paid through a different bank. The affair
of the cattle still rankled, for on *23 November he complained to

---

[1] 'In making out this last do not understate any thing but give it fully, for the object
is to adjust the Expenditure within bounds and it is not wished to carry on improvements at an expence and at a rate such as the general arrangements will not bear.'
(Ibid.)
[2] Loch to Young, *30 Oct. 1815.
[3] See below, ii, pp. 298-9.
[4] See below, ii, p. 299.

Loch that he had given him reason in the summer to expect payment, which had led him to break faith with the British Linen
Company. Loch was frigid in reply;[1] the demand for the cattle
had been excessive, and though Lord Stafford had been prepared to
meet it at once he (Loch) had held up payment until the settlement
of the accounts. However, the next day he authorised Young to
draw £3,400 as the price of the cattle. Other matters were being
drawn into the correspondence. Loch had complained that Young's
methods gave insufficient warning to tenants to be removed. On
8 December Young defended himself against this charge, but repeated in more general terms his suggestion about resigning.[2] Loch,
however, was not letting him go easily. He wrote again on 18
December, to give Young a long lecture on various topics under
discussion, including Brora, and pressing yet again for an estimate of
outlays for 1816.[3] Young's reply was contained in a letter to the
Marchioness on 31 December, listing a miscellany of works proposed, amounting in all to £1,955 and including £1,080 for Brora.

William Grant finally completed Young's accounts early in
January 1816, drawing them up to 23 December 1815. After all
moneys had been received, and after the much-discussed £5,000
had been taken into credit, Young had over-expended £2,511. All
the money he had received since his October outburst, even including the cattle money, had therefore left his position substantially
as it had been. Indeed, since the closure of the last account on 11
June 1814 the balance of over-expenditure had decreased by only
£1,054. Despite all attempts at closer accounting, and despite all
warnings about the curtailment of expenditure, Young's position
was substantially as it had been eighteen months previously, even
though the Marquis had provided £17,400 to supplement the
£18,500 he had supplied in 1813. Only the debated £5,000 made
the situation appear an improved one.

Grant took the completed accounts south to London, where
Loch audited them in February. His report was careful and detailed,
underlining some of the difficulties he had found in examining
them.[4] There were several points of criticism. The division of expenditure under heads was imperfect; the preparation of the accounts

---

[1] See below, ii, pp. 262-3.   [2] See below, ii, pp. 264-7.
[3] See below, ii, pp. 267-72.   [4] See below, pp. 168-71.

would be much improved by the use of a proper cash book; and the supporting vouchers left a good deal to be desired. Any attempt to analyse these accounts underlines the truth of Loch's comments. Young's habit of making advances to tradesmen, and then reconstructing the accounts later, makes it almost impossible to allocate expenditure accurately. At the time it clearly put a strain on Grant's memory and the tradesmen's honesty. Vouchers which are often as not merely long current accounts with tradesmen make it difficult to pass any judgment on the efficiency with which expenditure was controlled, though they hardly suggest any proper system. In short the accounts, if formally accurate, as Loch acknowledged, were no real guide either to the subjects of expenditure or to the state of the works at the closing date. The general head of advances to contractors, though falling in the period from £8,973 to £3,524, was in itself large enough to complicate any attempt to gain a clear view of the situation. Even on the formal level of accounting practice, Loch's criticisms were justified; Young's accounts were an imperfect record of how he had expended the money that had passed through his hands.

When this is coupled with Young's failure to produce proper estimates, Loch's central argument, so often repeated in his letters, becomes clearer. The Sutherland improvements had proceeded on the basis of broad decisions of principle, unsupported by proper costing, and sustained only by the readiness of the Marquis to meet the deficiencies when they became too urgent. The attempt to prevent this by providing a cash reserve had failed, the money simply being swallowed up into the general funds. Certainly Young had his problems. Tradesmen required cash during the months of summer activity, the very season when rent payments were low; money received from Sellar later could do little more than bring the accounting rather more up-to-date, or satisfy contractors who had been kept waiting at an earlier stage.

Yet the real problem lay deeper. Slowly from 1808, then with a rush after 1812, expenditure was becoming the product of deliberate decisions in the direction of improvement. Income, to a lesser extent, was affected in the same way, but more slowly and less flexibly, for all the increases Falconer and Young had arranged. Expenditure was virtually immediate, and was not related to any precise way to expectations of revenue; to that extent the constant hopes of a balanced Sutherland budget were illusory. Improvement decisions, too, were open-ended. The scale of expenditure upon works, even excluding the Brora complex, is proof enough of this. In 1811, with the heavy expenditure on Dunrobin Castle in Falconer's time being paid off, £5,005 was spent. 1812, with only £1,347 spent, was a relatively lean year, but thereafter the figures rose steadily: 1813 – £5,888; 1814 – £6,728; 1815 – £7,204. This expenditure included some housing, inns and harbour works, but the larger part of it went on the Dunrobin policies and on farms. Loch had his doubts about the validity of some of the works actually carried out, especially the improvement of farms, which again underlines his point about the necessity of estimates. But the main outline is clear enough. Young spent money on projects of which the family approved, without a proper system of financial control being instituted. The scale was formidable. If the Brora costs are added it became more formidable still. No possible rent increases could hope to keep step with expenditure of this magnitude, and so, without at first realising the implications, the Marquis drifted into the position of a source of current account revenue. Given the money he and his wife had drawn from the estate in earlier years, there was a certain poetic justice in this, but there was a great difference between a relatively small annual extraction of money and the massive subventions now called for. Young's management had drastically changed the pattern of the estate's finances.

Expenditure on the scale now involved was only to be controlled through submission of regular accounts and proper estimates. Young's accounts only partially met the first of these conditions. He never realised the importance of the latter – or rather, as he confessed on 8 December,[1] his approach to improvement precluded him from seeing its relevance. To him agricultural improvement on the grand scale was the aim, and finance a secondary consideration. On his home ground he had behaved in much the same way at Inverugie. Far from making the Sutherland estate profitable, he plunged it into an enormous commitment which came to its peak just as the period of rising rents drew to its close. Nothing is further from the truth than to see his factory as a period of rigid all-embracing planning, as

[1] See below, ii, p. 267.

Loch's *Improvements* have tended to make later readers imagine. Instead, with a few general aims in view, he stumbled from one expedient to another, sustained by optimism, a native determination and Lord Stafford's open purse. This was the very antithesis of real planning. Loch's audit of Young's 1814-15 accounts, coming on top of the financial arguments of the preceding autumn, must have finally convinced him that this state of affairs could no longer continue, against a background of falling family revenues (the Bridgwater Trustees' payments to the Marquis declined from £73,206 in 1813 to £46,570 in 1816). Whatever the public face he put on estate policy in his first version of the *Improvements*, he had already weighed Young's management and found it wanting. When the next season of crisis came in 1816 he had resolved to pass from exhortation to action.

5 The end of Young's factory

The first steps towards curtailing William Young's freedom of action had been taken at the end of 1815 with the appointment of Robertson as Brora bailiff and Alexander Stewart as manager of Dunrobin Farm. If Loch had not already reached a decision as to future action after auditing Young's accounts in February 1816, a long letter from Stewart on *24 March must have influenced his thinking. Stewart was uncomplimentary about the state of the farm – the men lazy and badly supervised, the land poor, full of couchgrass and in need of draining, the stock short of straw and turnips, and Young's general management 'the most expensive and extravagant I ever saw'.

Sellar's trial and the Mound crisis diverted attention in the following months, but by May Loch's views had noticeably hardened. When Sellar wrote to him on 7 May[1] on the general question of improvement and the opposition to it, he took the opportunity to raise a whole range of matters concerned with the management. Reading Sellar a lesson on his behaviour,[2] he rejected the suggestion that the difficulties were purely a result of personal hostility to him;

[1] See below, ii, pp. 281-4.
[2] Loch to Sellar, *15 May 1816: 'Let your orders be given directly and distinctly in firm but in moderate language, without Taunt or Joke. And whenever you can, let them be in writing which will avoid every danger of mistake which is particularly desireable where two languages are in use.'

there were problems which Young and he had been unable to overcome, partly due to Falconer's long leases, and many arrangements
would require to be re-examined; the need now was for a steady
system to be laid down for the future. That said, Loch went on to
raise particular questions. Was it possible to remove the whole population of the Strath of Kildonan to the sea-coast? What should be
done with the unarranged parts of Strathbrora (Lairg and Strathfleet should be, he thought, left as at present)? All the information,
he stressed, was needed so that Lord and Lady Stafford could have a
full view of the outline before coming north, 'for there the attention
is so much attracted to the details of particular matters'. The letter
was designed to be shown to Young, and both their opinions were
asked for. This was the first clear sign that Loch was considering a
complete overhaul of the Sutherland management.

Sellar's reply was a lengthy note sent in three instalments at the
end of the month,[1] of which Loch wrote to Macpherson Grant on
*8 June that it contained 'much *very* extraneous matter and his
remarks upon many things shew that satirical turn which does him
so much harm'. Certainly, in addition to some detailed recom-
mendations for future extensive removals, the greater part of the
note was taken up with a denunciation of whisky smuggling, to
which Sellar attributed most of the ills of Sutherland. For any study
of Sellar's psychology this document is of prime importance. There
is no sign, however, that Loch attached much importance to it,
particularly after Sellar sent an appendix on *8 June listing a total
of 1056 families to be removed under his plans. This was too much
for Macpherson Grant,[2] to whom Loch sent the report, and for
Loch himself.

Young's more guarded reply was to point out that no further
removals in Kildonan were possible on account of the shortage of
reception areas.[3] He asked Loch to come north before the Marquis

---

[1] See below, pp. 175-87.   [2] See below, p. 183, n. 2.

[3] Young to Loch, *26 May 1816: 'All the Coast Side Lands suitable for loting out
are now *brimful* and I can think of nothing before the year 18 when Kintradwell will be
open unless a bargain coud be made with Leith of Kilgower which woud accomodate a great many from the interior. There is no other way to dispose of the present
Inhabitants of Badenloch etc. unless the Marquis and Lady Stafford depart from their
present wise system not to turn out a single inhabitant against whom crimes have not
been proved untill a situation on the coast side is pointed out.'

and Marchioness, and to bring Macpherson Grant and William Mackenzie with him; as a result of enquiries, Loch could then 'make up a memorial for consideration'.

Loch replied on *31 May. Young's suggestion fitted with his own ideas, and Macpherson Grant had already agreed to come to Sutherland in August to assist in drawing up a plan for future removals from the hills, even though it might be as much as six years before action could be taken. He agreed on the difficulty of finding coastal land for settlers, suggesting the muir ground between Brora and Clynemilton as a possible solution. On the same day he was writing another letter to Macpherson Grant which showed how far his thinking had moved.[1] It was not merely removal and resettlement that concerned him but the whole question of the conduct of the management. Grant, in his reply, was in general agreement;[2] there had been over-rapid expenditure and Young had been too lavish with the farms taken in hand – this despite Grant's own warnings to him. The picture thus emerging must have been reinforced by Young's confession on *8 June that he was still in debt to the bank. In fact his next account, closed on 29 June, showed that he had reduced his over-expenditure from £2,511 to £698 (the old cash credit of £5,000 still being exhausted), though he had received no money from the Marquis over the period of account; but advances to contractors had increased from £1,237 to £2,315. Loch told him on *11 June to apply to Lord Stafford for money as soon as the letter reached Dunrobin. With a major reorganisation on its way, Loch was clearly not prepared to raise a fresh controversy over the details of Young's accounts.

The full extent of Loch's thinking was revealed in a careful letter he sent on *17 June to Earl Gower, who was to accompany his parents to Sutherland. It was necessary, he maintained, that expenditure on the estate should be 'devoted to these objects which could not be effected except through the assistance which Lord Stafford is pleased and enabled to effect and which could not be so easily undertaken by your Lordship if in possession of the Stafford and Sutherland Estates' – a delicate allusion to the Bridgwater revenue. It was 'the great sinews of improvement', above all roads and bridges, that should command expenditure, not the extravagant land operations

[1] See below, ii, pp. 284-8, 294-7.   [2] See below, ii, pp. 290-3.

practised at Dunrobin and Skelbo and now in contemplation at Morvich and Uppat. The farm improvements had been too rapid, and 'carried farther than even the most active of the old tenants can undertake, understand or keep pace with'; it was essential that 'the original and native population is carried on with them', as Macpherson Grant concurred in thinking. There was, in short, an urgent need for a new direction in expenditure, or the Earl would stand to lose much of the benefit. Loch urged Earl Gower to prevent Young rushing his parents into fresh expenditure before he himself reached Dunrobin. Significantly, he apologised for what he clearly saw as an intrusion 'in a matter not directly under my immediate controul', but justified it as being in both the Earl's[1] and his parents' interests. He wrote more shortly but in much the same terms to the Marchioness on the following day.[2]

Persuaded by the immensity of Sellar's proposals, and by Young's and Macpherson Grant's caution, Loch was thus no longer anxious to rush into large-scale removals. Instead he was concentrating upon the financial performance of the management and on the subjects of expenditure. His former experience of Young's financial optimism, and the worries fanned by Stewart's letter of *24 March, reinforced his natural instincts of orderliness and accountability. Quite clearly he placed great store on Macpherson Grant's advice. Much would depend on the experience of the summer tour which the two were to make of the estate.

The Marquis and Marchioness reached Dunrobin on 26 June by way of the newly completed Mound. Loch, detained by the birth of his fourth son, did not leave London until 16 July, and was still at Blairadam on 1 August. Passing through Edinburgh, he received interesting information from William Mackenzie, to whom Young had written[3] raising the possibility of resignation on the grounds that most of what he had come to Sutherland to accomplish was now finished. The information was confidential, but it must have strengthened Loch's determination to press for a reorganisation. Also, Young must have raised the subject with the Marchioness, for

---

[1] 'Your Lordship's future income in consequence depends most materially indeed upon the establishment and the steady prosecution of a fixed determinate and well considered plan for the future improvements of this princely property.'
[2] Loch to Marchioness, *18 June 1816.   [3] See below, ii, pp. 297-8.

on 16 August Mackenzie wrote to her expressing the hope that he would not retire precipitately.[1] It is possible that Young was already scenting the problems likely to descend on him when Loch and Macpherson Grant reached Sutherland.

The two were in the county not later than 13 August, when they toured Rogart parish. Thereafter Loch appears to have remained at Dunrobin, auditing Young's and Sellar's accounts, while Grant went on an extended tour of Strathnaver.[2] The critical decisions had already been taken before 19 August, and so were independent of the discoveries Grant made about the disorganised nature of Young's earlier resettlement operations on the north coast.[3] Loch, in fact, was engaged on 18 and 19 August in drawing up a series of memoranda,[4] which contained the essential parts of a new arrangement.

These memoranda went to the heart of the problems as he saw them. There was urgent need for a proper organisation of the newly settled areas in Assynt and Strathnaver, through resident sub-factors.[5] Provisions were required for the conduct of Dunrobin Farm, Morvich and the Brora works. But central to the whole scheme was financial control. The entire revenue of the estate, Loch directed, was to be paid into the Marquis' account at Tain, from which Young was not to be allowed to draw. Should he require money he could only receive it on a month's notice and on submission of a monthly cash account. This was crucial. Henceforward expenditure in Sutherland was to come under central control.

The memoranda were sent to Young on 23 August at Lord and Lady Stafford's direction. The next day Young resigned;[6] his resignation was accepted on 25 August.[7] Loch left Dunrobin on 26 August without waiting for Macpherson Grant's detailed report; he

[1] 'I hope along with Your Ladyship that he will not act so wrongly as to retire before his plans are settled and in active Operation. I feel persuaded he will not, he may dislike the curtailing of expence but when this is past he will go on.'
[2] For his report see below, pp. 203-11.
[3] But see Loch's comments below, pp. 191-2.
[4] See below, pp. 191-202.
[5] The men intended for these posts were already chosen, and Loch wrote to them immediately. Lieutenant George Gunn, Royal Marines, claimant to the chieftainship of Clan Gunn, appointed sub-factor of Assynt, had been introduced to the Marchioness by Rev. Alex. Sage, minister of Kildonan (Marchioness to Marquis, 21 Aug. 1815). Captain John Mackay (for whom see Sage, *Memorabilia Domestica*, 227-8) was already resident in Strathnaver, to which he was appointed.
[6] See below, ii, pp. 298-9.   [7] See below, ii, p. 300.

felt, in the words he had written to the Marchioness on the previous day, that 'if I were to remain longer here now I should only be getting entangled in the details of *execution* which I am not competent to attend to'. He had received all that he wanted. A great believer in system and accountability as the solution to problems of management,[1] he was now satisfied that he had provided for this.

There were various loose ends. Young was to retire at Martinmas 1816, but no new factor could be expected before Whitsunday 1817. For the interim, if with misgivings, Loch agreed to a suggestion by Macpherson Grant that Sellar should fill the gap.[2] He was already urgently in search of a replacement, and approached Francis Suther, the family's Northumberland factor at Trentham, on 30 August;[3] Suther accepted, and his entry was arranged for Whitsunday 1817. Loch was anxious, as he wrote to the Marchioness on 28 August from Ballindalloch, that nothing should be done in the way of new plans, particularly for removings, for a further year, so that the new factor could be properly installed.[4]

On his way south Loch wrote a number of letters which reflect his sense of relief at the way things had turned out. From Forfar, on 1 September, he assured both the Marquis and Marchioness, in separate letters, that 'the late changes in place of being a matter of regret, is one which can be attended with nothing but advantage to the character of the family and the prosperity of the estate'. On the same day he wrote to R. H. Bradshaw in less guarded terms.[5] He had obtained what he wanted, and looked forward to better

---

[1] See his remarks to William Mackenzie, below, ii, pp. 302-4.

[2] See below, ii, p. 304. Mackenzie had been even more outspoken in a letter to Loch on *19 Oct. 1816: 'Wherever taste temper or feeling is required or even ordinary discretion he is deficient beyond what I ever met with in any Man, So that I dont know one in the whole Circle of my acquaintance so ill calculated as him to fill the Office of a factor and in such a County as Sutherland.'

[3] See below, ii, pp. 300-1.

[4] The Marchioness agreed (Marchioness to Loch, *31 Aug. 1816).

[5] 'I hinted to you at Worsley that I was not much satisfied with the proceedings at Dunrobin, when I got there I was still less so. I had hitherto gone to that place more as a visitor than anything else, but as I had audited the accounts, I was determined no longer to make myself responsible for the results, without having authority to controul and arrange the outlay, which produced them. This I obtained from Lord and Lady Stafford, and I proceeded accordingly and drew up a set of rules and regulations for each department, they received Lord and Lady Staffords approbation and were given to the gentlemen concerned and it led to Mr Youngs resignation.'

relations with the small tenants, better financial control, and a more realistic policy for expenditure. It was on these three points that he had faulted Young's management and it was on them that he intended to make a fresh start. The broad outline of the policy of improvement remained as it had been formulated by Colin Mac-kenzie over a decade before, but the execution was to be brought back into line after Young's extravagance and over-concentration on the east coast farms. Essentially Loch was passing judgment on Young as a manager.

Young's own interest in the estate rapidly evaporated after his resignation.[1] Although he remained nominally in office until Mar-tinmas his letters decreased sharply in number after August, and there are no signs that he attempted to initiate policy. The problems of the famine which threatened in the autumn of 1816 were left for Sellar and William Mackenzie to face. Only his accounts engaged Young's attention. On 26 August he was no longer permitted to operate the Tain bank account, and on the following day he was given £8,500, out of which the long-standing £5,000 cash credit was finally liquidated. From the balance, another £2,000 received on 30 September, and money advanced by Sellar, he brought his various works to a final close. His accounts were balanced on 24 July 1817, at which date he was, at last, under-expended to the extent of £2,200. This was settled by taking into account his over-expenditure of £561 on the Mound and a further £3,535 owed him by Earl Gower on the Skelbo farm account. The final balance in his favour was cleared for payment by Loch on 30 August 1817, by which time he had left Rhives and returned to Inverugie. Sellar had by the same time relinquished office and become a full-time farmer at Culmaily; his accounts, which contained a disputed item of £621 for his expenses in connection with his imprisonment and trial, were not finally settled until September 1824.

THE PAPERS

The documents here printed are mainly drawn from the Dun-robin Castle archives. The principal source used is a collection of

---

[1] 'His mind is off his employment here', the Marchioness wrote to Loch on *14 Sept. 1816.

letters and papers relating to the period 1810-16, originally arranged
by the 2nd Duke of Sutherland. This has been supplemented in
volume 1 by some miscellaneous documents from the period preceding 1810; for the appendices to this volume use has been made
of three series of papers – Factor's Accounts, Law Agent's Accounts
and Estate Rentals. In volume 2 additional material has been drawn
from a series of letters between various members of the Sutherland
family. In addition letters are printed from the Sutherland Collection
at Trentham, now deposited in the Staffordshire Record Office;
these are taken from the Chief Agent's Correspondence (Stafford
D593/K/1/3 – In-letters, and D593/K/1/5 – Out-letters) and are distinguished in the text by the use of an asterisk. Series D593/K/1/5
contains copies of some letters written by James Loch, the originals
of which are preserved at Dunrobin; in these cases the original text
has been used and asterisks have not been added.

The original spelling and punctuation have been retained, with
the addition of a small amount of punctuation necessary to clarify
the sense. No attempt has been made to standardise proper and place
names. In volume 2 the conventional openings and closings of the
letters have been omitted, together with a small number of passages
not relevant to Sutherland (the subject-matter of these omissions is
indicated). A map to indicate the more important places and boundaries referred to in the text has been provided in the end pocket.

NOTE ON THE MAP

The information presented in the map accompanying this volume has been compiled from: surveys by Benjamin Meredith and John Roy (see below, p. 251); Patrick Sellar's sketch map of the Sutherland Estate, 1815 (see below, ii, pp. 266, 271-2); Gregory Burnett and William Scott's map of Sutherland, 1831-2 (as revised by Hector Morrison, 1853); and descriptions of marches in contemporary leases.

The shading on the map represents land over 500 feet.

The separate estates are shown as they existed in 1802, with the exception that Lettie (Rogart parish) is shown as part of the Achany estate, to which it was added in 1811. The sheep-farms are shown as existing in 1816; farms in Assynt, which were mixed sheep- and cattle-farms, are not shown separately.

The road pattern is taken from Sellar's sketch map, which gives no indication of the condition of individual roads. Some of these, such as that from Kinbrace to Bighouse, were no more than tracks in 1815. The representation of a road on the map is not therefore evidence for the existence of a fully made road.

The place-names shown are a selection from the large number capable of identification; but, although identified, many cannot be located with the precision required by a modern map-maker. Accordingly the principle has been adopted in all cases of indicating the place-name approximately without a definite point of reference. This has resulted in some anomalies in those cases where precise locations *are* known: Backies (Golspie parish) is on the east bank of Golspie burn; Brora village (Clyne parish) is on the south bank of Brora river to the east of the road; Ledmore (Assynt parish) is to the west of the road. For a more comprehensive picture reference should be made to Morrison's edition of Burnett and Scott's map. In some cases spelling has been altered to conform to Ordnance Survey usage.

1802—1807

PAPERS RELATING TO THE FACTORY OF
DAVID CAMPBELL

Memorandums given to Colonel Campbell by Lady Stafford: 12
August 1805

1. HUTTON TO BE REMOVED immediately from the Management
of the Plantations, and to have no situation whatever on the Estate,
merely to have his Annuity paid him. The Cause of his removal to
be explained to him.
2. The Plantation of the Ladies Walk[1] to be placed under the Care
and Superintendence of Fleming the Gardner who is to be instructed
as to thinning and replanting the Same according to such directions
as may be given from time to time. The fence at the bottom of the
Ladies Walk to be immediately renewed and the fences around the
Ladies Walk to be put in Complete repair and so secure as to prevent
Cattle getting in. These repairs must at all events be made before the
ensuing Winter. A sunk fence is also to be made immediately from
the eastern Corner of the Garden Wall so as to join the fence below
the Ladies Walk according to the line of direction presently staked
out and to be planted in Spring according to the directions given
him by Lady Stafford.
3. Mr William Mackenzie will make enquiry at Edinburgh for a
proper person to take charge of and superintend the plantations on
the Estate other than those before mentioned.
4. Colonel Campbell will take particular Care to preserve the Game
on the Estate and in case of any Poacher or person shooting without

---

[1] Immediately to east of Dunrobin Castle, and still known by same name.

A

licence (especially Captain McCulloch)[1] immediately to give information thereof to Mr William Mackenzie.

5. Colonel Campbell will get an accurate description of the proposed Sheep farms in two views: 1. The Names of the places and
possessors included in each:[2] 2. The lines of boundary of each on the
four points North, South, East and West.

6. Colonel Campbell will attend to the bulwarks at Invershin and
Lothbeg, to get the latter finished without delay for fear of a Speat,
to Correspond with Mr Charles Ross[3] as to the other and to ascertain
his paying half of the Expence and propose to him to get an Estimate
for Consideration before Contracting.

7. Colonel Campbell will advert that the harbour at Culgour and
the fisher towns must be kept in View and will form subjects of
frequent Correspondence with Edinburgh until set fairly agoing.

8. Colonel Campbell will examine and report on the damage done
by the Rivers at Evelicks and Blairich and other parts of Strathfleet.

9. The Ice house[4] is to be regularly stocked with Ice.

10. A Game licence to be given Dr Ross and also one to Sandy Noe.[5]

11. Colonel Campbell is directed as to Annuities to advert:

    1. To pay the allowance of £4 per Annum to Chirsty Mackay,
not to herself but to Mrs Keith of Golspie for her use.

    2. The £4 per annum is to be paid Mrs Grant whether she reside
at Golspie or not.

    3. Give Alexander McPhaill in Loth half a boll yearly.

    4. Give Sandy Watson of the Parish of Golspie a boll yearly.

    5. Give Janet McLeod of the Parish of Golspie half a boll yearly.

    6. Give Old Janet at Golspie half a boll yearly.

---

[1] Tenant of Cyderhall (par. Dornoch), son of the Sheriff-Substitute of Sutherland,
and a notorious poacher.

[2] Campbell produced a list of the lands affected, under the three heads of Shiness,
Clebrig and Benarmine; the two latter were joined to form the 'Great Sheep Tenement' set to Messrs Atkinson and Marshall (for boundaries of which see below,
pp. 115-16).

[3] This may be an error for General Sir Charles Ross of Balnagowan (d. 1814), but
it may be noted that Charles Ross of Invercassley, second son of Lord Ankerville,
inherited Invercarron, the property adjacent to Invershin on the Ross-shire side of the
Kyle of Sutherland, under General Ross's will. Charles Ross became Sheriff-Depute
of Sutherland in 1816.

[4] Still existing in woods to west of Dunrobin Castle.

[5] Tenant in Drummuie (par. Golspie) and hunter to Sutherland family.

7. Give Mrs Mackay Teacher in Strathbrora two bolls yearly.

8. Colonel Campbell will give 10s. yearly to John McLeod (son of George McLeod) who has lost an Arm to forward his education.

12. Colonel Campbell will attend to the School Master of Rogart's application for ground say half an acre for a garden in terms of the late Act of Parliament.[1]

13. Colonel Campbell will have James Mackay's[2] boundaries accurately defined in Sleatle.

14. Adam Bannerman's possession is to be given to Bookless[3] rent free and Bannerman to receive £10 a Year till something can be done for him. NB. Enquiry to be made about Sandy Urquhart's Situation which may perhaps be got on his resignation for Bannerman.

15. Colonel Campbell is on no Account to permit Swine to go loose thro' the County unless ringed nor horses or Swine to be tethered upon or within reach of a road or any nuisance to be left on the roads.

16. Colonel Campbell will let Mrs Campbell the housekeeper go away as soon as Convenient paying her wages up to the term of Martinmas and £10 to defray her travelling expences to Edinburgh, attending that she deliver over every thing Committed to her charge per Inventory to Miss McIntyre. Let Mrs Campbell be paid board Wages up to the period of her removal.

17. Colonel Campbell is directed to inform the Kildonan Tenants who furnished Recruits to Captain Cameron of the 79th in preference to the 78th recommended by Lady Stafford[4] that they are not to expect to be continued in their possessions, and this Notice to be given at the ensuing Martinmas.

18. The changes in the Council of Dornoch are to be these:

   1. Brigadier-General J. R. Mackenzie of Suddie, in place of General Fraser.[5]

[1] 43 George III, c. 54 (1803), relating to parish schoolmasters' salaries and to provision of schoolhouses. A school croft first appears in the 1812 rental.

[2] Tenant of Lothbeg (par. Loth).

[3] Manager of Dunrobin Farm, 1787-1802, and later tenant in Drummuie.

[4] The Marchioness had apparently recommended two regiments (see below, p. 9), but the name of the second has not survived. Recruiting parties from both the Seaforth (78th) and Cameron (79th) Highlanders were active in Sutherland in 1805.

[5] John Randall Mackenzie of Suddie was killed serving as Major-General at Talavera in 1809. Major-General Alexander Mackenzie Fraser, elected M.P. for Ross-shire in 1806, died in 1809 after serving in the Walcheren campaign.

2. Thomas Houstoun Esqr at Helmsdale in place of Captain W. McCulloch.

3. Andrew Campbell at Dunrobin, in place of Captain Munro, Kirkton.

19. Let the ground near the Castle above the Garden which is already giving way be gradually Smoothed down and brought to a gradual decline, but before anything is done let some proper Mason examine and report what is best to be done. Let the Porter's lodge go on as already ordered.

20. Colonel Campbell will pay any of the Farm Servants who may have a Claim for Wages which have not been paid by Mr Bookless at the time he was Overseer.

Report by Thomas Telford concerning the proposed harbour of Port Gower: Shrewsbury, 7 December 1805

There is at present no place of Shelter for Shipping on the East Coast of Sutherland, neither Helmsdale nor Brora are safe, or convenient, and the entrances into the two Ferries, consisting of shallow water and shifting Sands, can never answer for regular Navigation.

A small Harbour capable of affording protection for coasting Vessels, and Fishing Boats, appears absolutely necessary for the improvement of this extensive County. The promoting a Fishery along the Coast (where Fish abounds) and facilitating the importation of Coals, are alone important considerations, but the introduction of useful labour suitable for the several adjacent districts, cannot be accomplished untill there is a safe Harbour and Roads of communication opened from the shore into the interior of the Country.

The small Bay, in which it is proposed that a Harbour shall be constructed, is situated a little way to the S.W. of the Promontory, called the Ord of Caithness, and where the Murray Firth is about 15 Leagues in breadth.

The general Line of the adjacent Coast is nearly straight, the beach is composed of Sand, excepting the projecting parts which, are Rock, partly Sand stone and partly of a Calcarious Nature, there is also some appearance of Coal shale; the Country to the N.W. is mountainous.

The Bay is about a quarter of a Mile in depth, and nearly the same in breadth, its direction is nearly N.W. and S.E. The bottom is a clean hard Sand; the only reach of Sea into the Bay being from the S.E., the Pier must of course be so placed as to afford protection against that quarter, this may be done by constructing on the N. shore of the Bay, a little within the N.E. point, as shown on the General Map of the Shore.

From high to low water marks, of an ordinary Spring tide, the distance at this place, is about 100 Yards with a gentle declivity, Rock appears at low water mark, from thence outward, the ground which is a smooth hard Sand, deepens very gradually, as may be observed by the Soundings marked upon the general Map; the Soundings within the Bay are marked in feet; those without it in fathoms, they were taken at the high Water of an ordinary spring Tide, which flows to the S.W. and rises about 14 feet.

The general direction of the Pier, is laid down to point within the head Land of Tarbet Ness, by which means, no great reach of Sea can come within the Line of it, the reach of Sea in this direction is also broken by the Ridge, which at half tide, appears on the South side of the Bay. But that the Vessels lying at or near the Pier may be effectually protected, I have formed the Pier with a returned Head of about 25 Yards in length, which will Cover three Tier of Vessels, about Nine Coasting Vessels will by this means have full protection, or in their place a great number of fishing Boats.

By the Plan of the Pier, which is made to a large Scale, on a seperate Sheet, it will be seen that I have proposed the head of the Pier to be placed upon the Line of low Water mark, at an ordinary Spring Tide, which may be done without making use of a Cofferdam, or being at the Expense of Pumping Water. The general Form is in a small degree Convex, on the outward Side, and Concave towards the Harbour, the breadth on the top is 25 feet clear of the Parapet, which will afford Space for landing goods, and turning a Cart. I propose that the outward and Cross walls be built, in a Workmanlike manner, with good Rubble work, laid in regular Courses, properly connected and bound together, but without Mortar, untill the work is carried to within three feet of the level of the top of the Pier, all above this line to be laid in good Lime Mortar. The spaces between the outward and Cross Walls to be filled with stone Rubble and Rubbish as the Work advances; the top of the Pier to be paved with stones on Edge, not less than eighteen Inches in depth, and set in Lime Mortar. Eight mooring Posts and one Cap Stan to be fixed upon the Pier, and two stairs to be formed agreeably to the Plan.

With regard to materials, there is a considerable number of loose stones lying on the adjacent beach; about 200 Yards to the N.E., Rock appears between high and low Water, and about a Mile and a half along the shore, to the S.W., there is a quarry of Freestone.

Under all the beforementioned circumstances, I have estimated the Expense at £1,591 4s. od.

This would form a safe and Comodious Harbour; by contracting the dimensions the Expense might be lessened, but the saving would by no means compensate for the advantages which would be lost.

The General Map comprehends the adjacent Farm Grounds; which were included in the Survey, in order to afford an opportunity of determining the situation for a Village, but that does not appear to fall within my province.

Remarks by Colonel Campbell as to some Regulations that will be necessary to be adopted in Setting the Estate of Sutherland: 1806

1st. That the number of small horses now kept by the tennants be reduced as much as possible and that in place of every tennant having a plough of his own that each two shall join about a plough and only have each one stout horse. Where it is possible Cart Roads to be made to the respective peat mosses by the Tennants the proprietor giving them an Allowance in Meall or money while employed at said work. Every farm to be summed as to the number of black Cattle, horses and Sheep to be kept and each tennant to keep the proportion he is entitled to by his Rent. Winter herding to be addopted and no person to allow his Cattle to trespass on his Neighbours Grass and the abominable Custom that now prevails of allowing Cattle to go at large over the Country how soon the Cropts are cut must be put a Stop to under the Severest penalties. And no person who possesses houses without Land must be permitted to keep Cows Sheep and horses grasing on their Neighbours without any payment for same: in some Instances they have more Cattle than the Tennant who pays the Rent. To enforce this the Ground Officer of each parish must exert himself to size Cattle of the above description and give Information to the factor of the Owners. Im sorry to say that little trust can be put in the present Ground Officers unless they alter their manner which if they dont, they must be dismissed and steady and determined Men got who will do their duty correctly. And untill the Country is brought into a proper and regular police additional Salaries to be given such people and they to go round the parish and see that the tennants adhere to the Regulations laid down.

It must be expressly understood that when a tennant gets a certain Extent of Land to possess that he is not to Subset any part thereof or give up his possession to any other, if he is inclined to quit his Lands he must apply to the proprietor who is to have the Chusing of the incoming tennant, nor is he to allow any person to build houses and take up a Residence on the lands he rents without a toleration from the proprietor.

As the destruction of the woods on the Estate of Sutherland is become a very Serious Consideration to the proprietor, It is absolutely necessary that some effectuall Measure be taken to put a Stop to it by informing the whole tennants both great and small that it is the proprietors determined Resolution to prosecute every person with the Utmost Rigour and where discoveries are made that such guilty persons (whether the damage is done by themselves, Children or Servants) shall not be continued in their possessions. It is further proposed of which Intimation is now given to the whole tennants that where any destruction appears to be done to Woods that the proprietor shall cause the tennants depone that they have not be guilty nor know of any person that has been guilty of destroying Woods. The Law makes the tennant possessing the Land lyable to the proprietor for any damage done his woods so that every tennant ought to exert himself to make discoveries and report them. If this was done and those found guilty turned out of their possessions the practise of Wood cutting would soon be Stopt. It is also necessary that it shall be publickly known by the Inhabitants at large that the unfortunate habit that prevails among them of being guilty of petty thefts vizt. of taking Corn, Grass, Straw, and wearing Apparell and not considering pilfering of that nature a Crime, nor do the parents correct their Children or Servants when guilty, and as they must be sensible that being encouraged or not punished for smaller Crimes leads them on to commit greater and often ends in their destruction. It is therefore recommended to all heads of families to Attend to this Intimation As the Noble proprietors of the Estate of Sutherland are determined to disposses the persons who permit such practises to be followed and dont inform of those that they know to be guilty. The unfortunate prevailing Idea among the people that they will not discover the person they know to be guilty of Malpractices is ruinous to the peace and happiness of a Country, and causes the honest man to suffer by the Conduct of those inclined to irregular behaviour. It therefore ought to be the pride of the good and well disposed to give every possible Information.

Memorandum relative to the Sutherland Set: July 1806[1]

Sheep Farms[2]

1st. The great Sheep Farms are to be let for nineteen years commencing from Whitsunday 1807. In the view of their management a plan and Survey was wished, but obstacles and difficulties have occurred, and it is apprehended from enquiries made about the expence that that would be very considerable. It is therefore now proposed to rest upon the inspection of Skilful Sheep Farmers both to report upon the best distribution and lines of boundary and to give a Suggestion as to the rents. The suggestion as to this last will be kept confidential. On consideration of the Report an offer will be made to Captain Matheson of the Farm intended for him at a certain Rent. If he declines it will be disposed of like the rest, that is offers will be received from all and Sundry and the Farms will be let to the best account to Substantial people. A distinct Specification of the boundaries will be required for insertion in the Leases, expressing the boundary line on each of the four points as by the course of such a Stream, the ridge of such a hill, and so on.

Tenants to be removed on account of Sheep Farms[2]

Let a Statement be made up immediately of the persons whose removal will be necessary in order to open the range in view, mentioning their names and the rent they pay. It should include Subtenants as well as Tenants. Colonel Campbell will Suggest how far it

---

[1] Sent by William Mackenzie to David Campbell on 14 July 1806.
[2] In margin in original.

is practicable and also how far expedient to give these persons an offer of some accommodation elsewhere. There were Some persons whom it was intended at the general Set to remove altogether. They are Tenants in Kildonan who thought proper in the course of the recruiting to show a preference of other Regiments to the two which the Marquis and Marchioness recommended.[1] It may be made understood that the fault lay in giving the preference. It is not intended ever again to recruit on the principle of giving compensation in land but it will always be expected that those who are inclined to enlist shall go into such Regiments as are recommended by the Family of Sutherland. The possessions of those persons will form a fund of limited compensation to the people dispossessed by means of the Sheep farms.

Shealings on the skirts of the forests annexed to Low Country Farms[2]

There are various shealings belonging to low Country Farms which will form part of the Sheep Range. These must be ascertained,[3] and a proper arrangement made with those in whose possession they presently are. Those persons may be required to make offers for the Low Country Farms alone, and Colonel Campbell will be enabled to judge of these. If they are deemed reasonable bargains can be made accordingly. If otherwise they must be warned to remove, and offers received from others for these low Country Farms. But in the one mode or the other the Shealings must be got out of their hands So as to be open to the Sheep farmers at Whitsunday 1807.

Messrs Forbes's farms[2]

2nd. The farms possessed by Messrs Forbes along with the Salmon fishings will be let to their Successors on a 19 years lease to correspond with their tack of the fishings. The names of the Farms, their present rents, and the rent which they ought to bear on such a Lease will be

---

[1] See above, p. 3.   [2] In margin in original.

[3] A list survives in Campbell's handwriting of 'the Sheilings proposed to be annexed to Benarmine'. This contains the names of 22 shielings attached to tenancies in Farr, Golspie, Lairg and Rogart parishes, together with three others in Rogart which 'some people think' may be required for additional wintering, and concludes: 'Both Achinlucharichs, Dalfosaig possessed by Major Sutherland and Craigachindarroch and Achtomliny if thrown together will be sufficient to grass above 300 Cattle and will Accommodate the tenants of the Parishes of Golspy and Dornoch in Summer Grass for their Cattle in lieu of their former Grasings which is thrown into the Sheep Tenements.'

immediately communicated by Colonel Campbell So as the matter may be adjusted without delay. The current leases had better be sent to Edinburgh. One of the farms is in Lord Hermands wadset[1] but a Statement of it may be made up on Similar principles which shall be laid before him.

Culgower[2]

3rd. The Farms of Culgower will be cleared for Mr Pope by a proper warning and Removing. This lease is nearly adjusted.

As to all the remainder of the Estate it is decided to postpone the Set till another year.

---

[1] Probably part of Easter Helmsdale (par. Loth). George Fergusson, Lord Hermand (d. 1827) was granted a wadset of Wester and Easter Helmsdale and Marrel on 20 May 1793; this wadset was redeemed in 1828.

[2] In margin in original.

1807—1811

Observations by Cosmo Falconer on the present state of the County
of Sutherland: Rhives, 15 January 1808

I HAVE BEEN AT PAINS to ascertain agreeable to Lady Staffords
suggestion to you[1] the real state of the people of this Country with
regard to provisions, particularly the parishes with which her Ladyship is more immediately connected, and can report in general that
with the assistance of a little meal imported for each of these parishes,
a few excepted, the people will be got brought to meet a new Crop,
the expedient having been timeously adopted of converting the surplus Stocks of Cattle to the means of subsistance even to the lowest
ranks of the people. The potatoe Crop having generally failed and in
some of the Highland Districts I may say totally, leaves a difficulty to
Estimate the real effects of this deficiency of a necessary so generally
relied on in this Country, and the severity of mildness of the season
are circumstances which must also have their effect in any estimate
to be made of the Condition of the people, who will support their
Cattle to the last on the little Corn they may have rather than allow
them to die. The season has with the exception of a few weeks been
stormy here beyond example and continues at this moment to
threaten by its severity the Cattle, I may say, of every description
of the people. But a sudden change with a good spring would make
up for the dread which has hitherto attended the passing season
tho' it appears to me almost certain that the loss of Cattle will be
great.

[1] Presumably William Mackenzie.

To come more to particulars I understand that the parishes of Assint Tongue Edrachilles and Durness upon the north west coast have been in use to depend upon Caithness and Ireland for supplies of meal, less or more, in almost every Season and tho' they have a large share of the present Calamity, it is a pleasant thing to understand that they can have their supplies from both these places, particularly Caithness which is certified to Me by a person so respectable as the Sheriff Depute of that County to be capable of exporting at least 20,000 bolls. The greatest difficulty that occurs to me with regard to some of these parishes at least, is the entire want of Money thro' the Failure of the Fishings, the Crops and the sale of black Cattle which will deter Merchants from bringing into the Country what they at once see cannot at present be paid for by the people, and in such a situation nothing but the stepping forward of spirited Individuals amongst them for the sake of humanity, and perhaps too for their own future advantage in Cases where their undertakings depend upon the people, can save some of these parishes from real distress.

The people of the parish of Farr tho' not so well off as usual either for grain or potatoes cannot be Classed amongst the greatest sufferers and may have their small wants supplied as on former and ordinary occasions from Caithness.

The Heights of the parishes of Kildonan and Clyne are sufferers in a very great degree but in the Strath of Kildonan the Crops of grain and potatoes are tolerably good and are well got, but the people there at all times require the Crop for their own purposes.[1] I reckon however that the surplus crop of the parish of Loth will go far to supply the people of Kildonan, as will that of Clyne the people of the upper part of the parish if distillation can be effectually suppressed, which I am certain is the case to the merest triffle both in the highland district of Clyne and in the parish of Rogart, the two places most given to this illicit Traffic.

The parishes of Golspie and Rogart may be reckoned the parishes which have suffered most severely. Dunrobin and the accompanying Farm of Rhives unfortunately had been allowed to dwindle to almost

---

[1] In the 18th century Kildonan rents were paid in money only (see Henderson, *Sutherland*, 177).

nothing in point of agriculture. If the servants and Horses are maintained and the ensuing Crop laid down these farms can boast of little or nothing over. The rest of the farms in the parish cannot put in ¼ of their Victual Rents and Maintain the Families upon them so that a considerable supply of Meal and of seed grain must be imported for the Inhabitants of this parish which are pretty numerous as well as of the parish of Rogart which at best is not a Victual parish.

The parishes of Creech and Lairg have also suffered a good deal but the Inhabitants are not throng in them and will not require a great supply. Dornoch again will supply itself fully having such a Crop as can enable the tenants to pay in their Victual rents in most Instances and some of the Farmers will have something besides to spare.

From this view I have great reason to believe that 900 to 1,000 bolls of oatmeal and perhaps 400 bolls of seed Oats with a few bolls of pease if they can be got[1] and a little seed potatoes (which will be of great consideration as a Change at any rate) will be a supply if cautiously dealt out, which will bring the people of the different parishes not connected with the West Coast to the first of a new Crop with the help of the summer milkness and the command of a little mutton, tho' were they readily to get it they would consume twice or thrice that quantity of meal. But as public roads and other Improvements will be going on in the Country this summer these will not fare the worse that the Inhabitants should experience a certain degree of hardship to lead them to seek after more active scenes than they have hitherto been accustomed to care for at home.

These observations are what occur to me as an answer to Lady Staffords Enquiry in regard to the state of this Country which it will be observed may be affected by Circumstances arising from a good or a bad spring.

---

[1] Between January and July 1808, 2000 bolls oatmeal, 252½ bolls oats, 85 bolls bear, 50 bolls potatoes and 30 bolls pease were bought at Berwick, Leith, Newburgh and Aberdeen and shipped to Sutherland (see below, pp. 258-9, and ii, p. 76).

Census of the Inhabitants on Culmaily: 1810

Names	Places of Abode	Age
1 John Murray	East end of Loch	36
2 Widow Campbell	Coulnacraig	60
3 William Murray Dyker	Loanafrishillock	40
4 Robert MacGregor	Corgrain	33
5 Anne McKay	Corgrain	28
6 Lilly McKay	Corgrain	20
7 Margaret McKay	Corgrain	30
8 A. Murray Soldier 5 Garrison Battalion Ireland	Corgrain	45
9 John Murray Weaver	Loanmore	80
10 John Grant Farmer	Loanmore	30
11 Donald Sutherland labourer	Loanmore	23
Wester Culmaily		
12 Adam Baillie farmer	Culmaily	40
13 John McKay farmer	Culmaily	60
14 William Gunn	Culmaily	45
15 Hugh Innes	Culmaily	50
16 Alexander McDonald Merchant	Culmaily	18
17 Widow Gordon	Culmaily	36
18 James McKay Miller	Mill house at East end of Bridge	26
19 Widow Campbell	Near Colonels Stables	60
20 John Baillie Servant to Colonel Sutherland	Culmaily	30
Rhiorn		
21 James Grant farmer	Rhiorn	30
22 Widow Grant mother of 21	Rhiorn	60
23 Alexander Gordon Farmer	Rhiorn	35
24 Alexander Campbell	Sergeant Gordons Croft	30
Sallichtown		
25 George McPherson farmer	Sallichtown	23
26 Widow Gunn	Sallichtown	36
27 Donald Baillie	Sallichtown	40
28 Alexander McPherson	Sallichtown	40
29 William Ross	Sallichtown	50
30 Widow McPherson	Sallichtown	36
31 James McPherson	Sallichtown	60
32 Donald Gunn Wright	Sallichtown	30
33 Hugh Gunn	Sallichtown	50
34 A. McLeod labourer	Sallichtown	35
35 Anne Gunn	Sallichtown	60
36 Margaret Murray	Sallichtown	30
37 John Ross	Sallichtown	60
38 James Sutherland Dyker	Sallichtown	50
39 John Sutherland Dyker	Sallichtown	50

Families	Total
Five Children – Eldest 10 Years of Age – 2 boys – 3 Girls	7
One daughter married to A. McDonald in Ross militia	2
Married – 3 Children boys – Oldest 13	5
Three Children boys – Oldest five Years	5
None	1
None	1
Soldiers Wife – One Child a boy – 5 Years Old	2
Two boys – 1 Girl – Oldest boy 14 – Girl 10	5
A Son 35 Weaver and labourer – A daughter 26	4
Married to a second wife 6 Children – 1 boy and 5 Girls	8
Lives with 2 Sisters under 30 and a brothers daughter 10 Years	4
Ten Children eldest 16 – 7 boys and 3 Girls	12
Five Children – 3 Boys and 2 Girls – Oldest 26	7
Twice married Five Children – Oldest 15	7
Twice married – 7 Children – Oldest deranged 12	9
Unmarried – Mother – Brother and Sister live with him	4
Four Children – Eldest A boy 7 Years	6
Two Children – A boy and a Girl – Boy 3 Years Old	4
Two Children – A boy and a Girl – boy 16 – Girl 15 – Sister lives with her 50	4
Married – No Children	2
Married – No Children	2
Three Children – Eldest 20 – works at the Canal[1] – daughter 16 – Grandson 1 Year Old	5
Four Children – Boys – Eldest 10 Years	6
Unmarried – Mother – Brother – and Sister	4
Married – 5 Children – 3 boys and 2 Girls – Eldest 12 Years	7
Five Children – 2 boys and 3 Girls – Oldest 10 Years	6
Four Children – 2 boys and 2 Girls – Oldest 18 Years	6
Five Children – 4 daughters and 1 Son – Oldest 12 Years	7
Three Children – 2 Daughers and 1 Son – Oldest 18 Years	5
Eight Children – 2 boys and 6 Girls – Oldest 15 Years	9
One Boy 18 Years	3
Two Children – Daughters – Oldest 3 Years	4
Five Children – 2 Boys – 3 Girls – Oldest 12 Years	7
One Girl 1 Year Old	3
Four Children – 2 Boys and 2 Girls – Oldest 16 Years	5
One Child – A Daughter 6 Years Old	2
Three Children – 1 Boy and 2 Girls – Oldest 18 Years	5
Four Children – 3 Boys and 1 Daughter – Oldest 16 Years	6
Two Children – Young	4

[*Table continued overleaf*

[1] Drainage canal on Culmaily (see Henderson, *Sutherland*, 151).

Names	Places of Abode	Age
Balloan		
40 Hector McKenzie Weaver	Balloan	60
41 Robert Ross	Balloan	65
42 John McLeod labourer	Balloan	35
43 George Gordon	Balloan	35
44 Widow Grant	Balloan	60
45 John Grant	Balloan	65
46 John Innes	Balloan	30
47 Martin Innes	Balloan	65
48 Anne Grant	Balloan	40
49 Robert Grant	Balloan	40
50 Donald Grant	Balloan	30
51 Ebenezer Grant	Balloan	26
52 Widow Grant	Balloan	61

Report on the present state of possessions in Strathnaver, the property of the most noble the Marquis and Marchioness of Stafford: with the probable means of its further improvement. Surveyed by Benjamin Meredith: 1810[1]

General description

Strathnaver is situated on the north coast of the county of Sutherland, the climate adjoining the *sea*, is as salubrious, as the southern coast side, and the crops of grain equally good and early; to a person, who after travelling 20 or 30 miles over rugged mountainous heaths and mosses, with little variety to relieve the eye, the first approach to Strathnaver has a very pleasing and agreeable effect; *the river, natural woods*, and *arable lands*, forming a delightful contrast with the late black moors and morasses. The principal produce of this remote and extensive property, are, *black cattle, small highland garrons, sheep* and *goats*, that roam at large over the adjacent hills; which are upon the whole calculated to support the numbers collectively kept on it, and which are by no means inconsiderable. To the rearing of cattle their chief attention is directed, and from this source the principal money circulation arises, the small portion in aration being only a secondary consideration, and in general insufficient for the home consumption of its numerous population; the most industrious of whom migrate to the south for employment, during the spring and

[1] For the plans accompanying this report see H. Fairhurst, 'The Surveys for the Sutherland Clearances', *Scottish Studies*, 8 (1964), 1-18.

Families   *Total*

Three Children – 1 Son and 2 Daughters – Oldest 20 Years	5
None	1
Three Children – 2 Boys and 1 Daughter – Oldest 6	5
Four Children – 2 Boys and 2 Girls – Oldest 7 Years	6
None	1
Three Children – 2 Daughters and 1 Son – Oldest 25 Years	5
Three Children – 1 Boy and 2 Girls – Oldest 5 Years	5
Four Children – 2 Boys and 2 Girls – Oldest 12 Years	6
Three Girls – her Sister Aged 35, lame – Oldest daughter 10	5
Seven Children – 3 Boys and 4 Girls – Oldest 15 Years	9
Two Children – 1 Boy and 1 Girl – Oldest 3 Years	4
One Child – A Boy 1 Year Old	3
Two Children – 1 Son 14 Years Old – 1 Daughter 16	3
	253

summer seasons, and return with the savings of their labour to pass the winter at home with their families, who conduct and manage their little possessions during the husbands absence; the more idle class remain at home during the whole year, in poverty, idleness and wickedness; their chief employment (if it deserves the appellation) being angling, or shooting, neither are the agricultural affairs of the latter a bit better conducted than are those of the former, but generally worse; where idleness contracted in early life becomes habitual, it is not easily eradicated.

The soil of Strathnaver generally is light and sandy, well adapted for the turnip husbandry, a system much to be recommended where cattle are the principal produce and staple commodity of the country.

The possessions for the sake of arrangement may be divided into three heads, vizt. first, the coast side which will include, Kirktomy, Suardly, Farr, Clerkhill, Bettyhill, Dalharn, Acha, and continuing along the east side of the river *take in*, or include, Achkoilnaburgie, Achlochy and Rhinovy. The second division will comprise all the possessions, west side of the river, as far up as Syre, including Naver, Borgiebeg, Achnaburin, Aphill, Dalhoraskil and Dalvigas in Colonel Clunes wadset,[1] and continuing the same side of the river

[1] Gordon Clunes was granted a wadset of Borgiebeg, Invernaver, Leckvern, Achnabourin, Dalvighouse, Dalchorrisdale, Accobul and Rossal on 20 March 1784; this wadset was redeemed from William Clunes on 7 August 1815.

B

include, Achyalagree, Carnochy, Skeal, Langdale and Syre. The third and last division will continue along the east side of the river, coming down from opposite Langdale, and taking in, all the other possessions on that side, namely, Rheloisk, Girfe, and Enishvloundie, Rhifele, Ravigill, Dunviedan, Achyellan, and Skilpick.

Agreeable to this arrangement I shall endeavour first to shew the nature and properties of the different possessions in their present state, and secondly point out the most eligible plans of improvement, calculated to enhance the value of the property, and meliorate the conditions of the most useful class of its population, drawn with every attention due a subject of such importance, from minute observation, and the best local information that could be obtained and collected; having thus far premised the object of the survey, I proceed to examine and report the nature of the different possessions seperately.

Kirktomy

Is in the possession of small tenants, a poor, light, sandy soil, but manured in such a way as generally to secure a good return, its exposure to the north sea, from which it has no shelter is sometimes attended with a blight or mildew on the crop; but this is not a general case, and when it occurs, the damage sustained is only partially confined to the land contiguous to the Sea. A north east, and north west wind has generally this pernicious effect, if such should set *in*, with violence, while the corn is filling in the ear, or at any time before it has reached maturity. The pasture within dykes, is all natural grass of an excellent quality but very short, and when cut for hay is done with a small hand hook resembling a sickle, the returns in general tho valuable are very light.

The surrounding hills are rocky and rugged, but afford pasturage to great numbers of cattle and sheep; from which source the tenants, in common with the whole tenantry in the Strath, depend more for support, and probably realise more than they do on their arable lands.

There are very good stone in the neighbourhood if quarries were properly opened, of a very hard and durable nature, and may be wrought to any purpose required, as well, and as easily as freestone.

Suardly

In the occupation of small tenants, is a well sheltered situation, the soil in general a mixture of sand and moss, very productive; the low lands are wet, but might easily be rendered perfectly dry at a trifling expence, by a few judicious drains; the arable land is much superior to that of Kirktomy but the pasture and hill grounds are in all respects the same.

Farr

In the hands of small tenants, is a well sheltered situation, the arable land is good and productive, but much neglected, heaps of small stones, or Cairns, and small patches left uncultivated in the midst of their best corn land. Precisely in this state, without the smallest variation, it has remained for time immemorial, from the negligence and want of persevering industry in the possessors, who will do nothing to improve the land or meliorate their own conditions, lest they might by so doing, eventually benefit a successor, at least upon enquiry these were the reasons adduced. Along the bottom and march with Captain Gordon is a ditch that has been cut for the purpose of draining the lands of Farr and Clerkhill, but is now so completely filled with mud and weeds, that its first salutary purpose is entirely frustrated, consequently a good deal of valuable land rendered almost useless or comparatively of little benefit to the slovenly occupiers.

The pasture within dykes is good natural grass, but little hay made; there is likewise the advantage of an extensive range of good hill pasture. The whole coast from Kirktomy to the mouth of the Naver is bold and rocky, with frightful precipices, the disadvantages of which are, that when cattle are on this part they are obliged to herd them, and notwithstanding this precaution some are lost, by being precipitated over the rocks into the sea.

Clerkhill

Or Captain Gordons tack, comprises a part of Farr, the Crask, Renmore, Runachattel, New land, the Erd, Betty hill, Dalharn, Achna, and Achkalnaburgie. The Crask produces good short natural grass, the eastern side and part of its summit may be characterized as good meadow hay, the quality excellent, but the crops light, the small part in aration belonging the Captain is a poor subject and wet with springs oozing out from the adjacent hills; the part occupied by the miller and the glebe, is a light sharp soil and yields good returns of corn and hay.

Renmore and Runachattel are well sheltered situations and good corn land, the latter is much better adapted for perpetual grass in consequence of the unevenness of its surface.

Cramerow may be classed as equal in every respect to Renmore.

Newland, originally a kind of heathy pasture. Captain Gordon on removing some of his tenants from their former situations, placed them here; the soil is a mixture of moss and sand, and some parts of it tolerable productive; but the access to it being so difficult, can never in any point of view be considered an object of cultivation.

The Erd, to the west adjoining the mouth of the Naver river, produces some very good meadow hay; this part might be successfully laid off and feud for building, being the most eligible situation for a village etc. but of this, more hereafter. The other part of the Erd is short green pasture, adapted for sheep or cattle, having a well sheltered hollow, tolerable well defended by rising ground to the north.

Betty hill, a good sharp soil but light. *Campbell*, the tenant, who holds of Captain Gordon, has been very industrious in draining, and improving this small possession; indeed he is the only man I have seen in this part, who deserves the name of an improver. There is some good hill land attached to this possession.

Dalharn, Achna, and Achkilnaburgie, in point of soil, and the hill advantages, are equal in every respect to the last mentioned, but by no means so well laid out and improved.

Achlochy

A run ridge among small tenants, the land is superior to any in Captain Gordons tack, and being a level flat, is easily laboured; the river at some times overflows its banks, and innundates the whole; but this might be easily overcome by a small embankment about 3 feet high, which would effectually do away every inconvenience arising from that quarter; a great part of this land requires draining which might be done at an expense so trifling that half the extra produce gained the first year, would more than cover the expense incurred, yet nothing has been done or attempted.

Naver or Invernaver

A part of Colonel Clunes' wadset, and occupied by the tacksmen of the Naver salmon fishery, is a good sharp soil and very productive, its produce being greater than any other possession of equal extent in Strathnaver; and much more than is at present laboured might be brought into cultivation; which is a desideratum much to be wished, as the crop of this place is much earlier than any other in the neighbourhood which with the other advantages of soil gives it a decided superiority. The face of the hill immediately behind Naver is good short grass, on which several sheep and Cattle are kept, and where they roam at large to the confines of

Borgiebeg another part of Colonel Clunes' wadset. This to its size is a beautiful little place, and in respect to soil and climate equal to Naver; a part of Lord Reay's property intermixes here,[1] between the Borgie water and the Naver, the value of which to the proprietor is very trifling as the Borgie and Naver tenantry at present derive as much benefit from it as does those of Lord Reay; I went over the whole of the hill property adjoining belonging to the Marquis and Marchioness of Stafford, as far up as Langdale, in company with a shepherd (further I have not yet examined) to ascertain how far it might be prudent or profitable to have it stocked with sheep and he condemned the whole of the hill on this side as far up as beforementioned, as unfit to be put under sheep, with any prospect of success to the proprietors or tenant; the whole behind the summit of the hill that faces the course of the river being nothing but moors and [   ][2] of little or no value for sheep.

Were these hills adapted for the sheep husbandry an excambion with Lord Reay would be desireable; but as that is not the case, it becomes a matter of little or no importance. I have endeavoured thus far to elucidate this subject, and set it in its true light in consequence of a hint to that effect from Mr Young.

The remaining part of Colonel Clunes' wadset namely Achnabuin, Aphill, Dalhoraskeil and Dalvigas, come all under one description, viz. a good, sharp and productive soil, with equal benefit of a good hill behind as far up as its summit.

Carnochy

A deep rich sharp soil nearly equal to Naver, a range of good pasture along the side of the river, and along the face of the hill for a a mile and a half in length, makes this a good grazing farm; should a change of system takes place, a great part of this land may be

[1] Ardbeg, which was purchased from Lord Reay in 1814, and entered in the 1815 rental, may have included this land.
[2] MS. blank.

improved, and lotted out for settlers, all the way up the river till they reach the arable land of Skeal; and the land I am presently speaking of could not in my humble opinion be better applied; a total want of good hill in the back ground, entirely precludes sheep, even on a moderate scale; but settlers might in spring and summer derive some small benefit from a hill where sheep could not be kept with any probable chance of success to a person wholly embarking in that line.

Skeal

A good sharp deep soil, but the crop often affected by mildew, occasioned, I apprehend by the humidity of the air, the frequent fogs, and mists rising from the river, and being so surrounded with hills, that wind can have little effect in dispelling it.

A large extent of hill grazing, with natural woods, affording good shelter, makes this a profitable concern to the occupiers notwithstanding the disadvantages the arable lands are sometimes subjected to.

Langdale and Syre

Would be two good little farms if judiciously managed; the soil is of the same nature with that of Skeal, but entirely free of its disadvantages; the pasture within dykes is good strong grass, together with a great range of good hill attached: I did not ascertain by measurement the exact extent of hill belonging or behind the different possessions being restricted from so doing in my instructions; but I am of opinion it would be worth the expense to have the whole of the hills surveyed measured and valued.

Rheloisk

Is a beautiful little place, and good land, the grass among the natural wood is very good, and affords wintering to a number of cattle that are kept in summer on the adjacent hills.

Girfe and Enishvloundi

Are two good little possessions, the arable land according to its extent being very productive. The river has been suffered to encroach and destroy much of the land that originally belonged to the former, for want of proper attention at first; it is now too far gone to have any remedy applied, as the expense would be greater than any advantage now to be gained.

Rhifele

A good sharp and productive soil, with the best and most extensive hill attached of any single farm in Strathnaver.

Ravigill

A run ridge in the hands of small tenants, the arable land the same
with the preceding, beautifully diversified with wood which forms
a good sheltered situation for cattle, the hill behind and immediately
contiguous to this place is much inferior to any of the preceeding;
some parts are likewise much cut for divots; indeed the whole hills
from this place to Skelpick are little better than a black and almost
unproductive heath.

Dunviedan

A good sharp soil, and very productive, were a judicious management of cropping adopted, but under the present system of perpetual
cropping the lands must by consequence be much worn out and
deteriorated.

In my report accompanying the plans the other possessions not
here mentioned are detailed; but the notes from which that report was
taken is by some means mislaid; and cannot at this time for those
reasons be here stated, the original being in Mr Youngs possession.[1]

Having concluded the first branch on the nature and properties of
the different possessions in the present state, I humbly beg leave to
submit to the Noble proprietors consideration, the method of improving this extensive property, in the way nature has evidently
intended it, which are twofold, viz. Grazing or sheep farms, and a
harbour, fishing station, and villages; and first of

Sheep farms

Notwithstanding the great extent of hill and uplands on this property, there is comparatively but a small portion, that can be applied
to the raising of sheep, and that, wholly confined to the east side of
the river Naver. I was at much pains in having this subject investigated, being particularly instructed to that effect by Mr Young, and
went over a great part of the hills, in company with a shepherd sent
here by that gentleman; and afterwards consulted Mr Reid of Armadale and others conversant in the sheep husbandry. Having premised
my means of information, it now becomes my duty to state the result.

One good farm of this description would include all the lands
from Kirktomy to the burn of Skelpick (except what should be
alloted for settlers in the village of Naver to be after mentioned)

[1] This has not survived.

which burn will form its march to the south, and continue that line till it intersect the Armadale property, which will constitute its eastern march, and the river Naver its western one. I made no measurement of these hills, being as before observed restricted from so doing; but from seeing the grounds and observing the stock now kept on it, and receiving the concurrent opinions of those versed in the business, I am warranted to assert, that these grounds would be an object of consequence to a sheep farmer; having plenty of summer, and winter grasses; viz. *Deer hair, moss crops* or ling, etc., etc., with other short herbage of a nutricious quality peculiarly adapted for sheep; add to this the quantity of turnips that may be raised on the arable lands for the animals; where soil and climate are so well calculated to insure success, must enable the farmer to keep a much greater stock than he otherwise could do, besides other advantages arising from locality of situation such as a shipping place, as it were on the farm, for exporting the wool etc., and importing every necessary, requisite for carrying on the concern, without being subject to tedious, long and expensive land carriage; these combined advantages must give these lands a decided superiority, and render them well worth the attention of men in that line, the grounds likewise being perfectly sound.

This farm I should suppose equal to the support of 3† thousand sheep, which taken at an average of 3 shillings a head, allowed as a fair *data* for rent, would make its annual value £450. I state the data for rent as taken from the shepherd, tho' I can discover no reason for its being an established criterion; as the value of property must depend much more on local advantages, or disadvantages connected with its situation than on any other circumstance.

Another Sheep farm, might be up the water from Ravigill, taking in Rhifell and Rhiloisk, and still following the course of the river to Mr Marshalls march at Achness, from thence carried forward, and sweeping round the heights of Kildonan, taking in all the useful lands that way, and from thence again fall down on Ravigill; this farm is supposed equal to the support of 15 hundred or 2 thousand sheep.

---

† The shepherd sent by Mr Young estimated at little more than 2 thousand; but as the raising turnip, and a great extent of hill and arable land, was not taken into that amount, I think myself warranted in stating the number 3 thousand as above. [This footnote is in the original.]

These are the only grounds adapted for sheep farms, as high up as Syre. What the lands are capable of between Syre and Clibrick, I cannot at present say; not having as yet surveyed that part. Humbly presuming that what has been said on the grazing system will be deemed sufficient, will dismiss the subject, and proceed to report the second part of improvements viz.

Harbour, Villages and Fishing station

Among the first and most prominent features of improvement, may be considered a fishing station at the mouth of the Naver; the only objection that can at present be urged against it, is the want of a proper harbour, where boats, and small vessels might at all times come *in*, and remain in safety; the short extent of sea coast, on Lord and Lady Staffords property in this part, and that generally so bold and precipitous, entirely restricts a liberty of choice for such an undertaking, to the entrance into the water of Naver. Stones are in abundance on the spot, and should these be found insufficient for every purpose required, an excellent kind may be obtained, and brought round by water from Kirktomy; I made no correct calculation on the expense of a harbour here, not liking to trust entirely to my own judgment as to its situation etc., without the assistance of some experienced nautical man, whose cooperation would be of great consequences; and the subject appears to me a matter of such importance to the future improvement, and ultimate prosperity of the country, that persons properly qualified should be sent there to examine the place, point out the most eligible situation, and report the expense, with the advantages to be derived from it, if carried into effect. I had no opportunity of taking soundings, as no boat could be procured on the day I had set apart for that purpose, but from the information received, the water is of sufficient depth, to admit vessels of any ordinary burthen, with a little assistance at low water.

I am locally informed (and I believe the information correct) that between Strathy-head, and Whiting head is the best fishing station in the north; *Cod*, ling, haddocks and Skeat, are in abundance, and much larger than those taken in the Moray firth; herrings likewise are here very plentiful; it is not uncommon to see 20 or 30 Smacks[1]

[1] Sellar wrote to the Marchioness on 14 April 1813 that he had counted eleven smacks fishing off Strathy Head and had been informed 'that they belonged to the Thames and had wells in their holds by means of which they carried the fish alive to London'.

from different parts of Scotland and England, fishing off here and not a single boat on the Marquis and Marchioness's property, to share in the advantages which providence has so liberally thrown in the way.

The men who inhabit the coast side are well adapted for this employment were they properly furnished with good boats for the purpose, *lines* etc. I do not mean they are equally skilful in the business with their southern brethren, but from their proximity to the sea, and frequent intercourse with it, their habits and manner of life, are best calculated and suited to that employment.

In support of the beneficial consequences arising from fisheries, I need only adduce as an instance those of Wick and Staxico in Caithness; the produce of which for the last year I am informed, amounted to the enormous sum of 40 thousand pounds Sterling! How great must have been the loss to the country and to the Empire, had any different system been pursued here, than that which nature evidently intended.

The land on the Erd, marked 'meadow grass' on plan No. 2, would be a good situation for building a village, the advantages of which would in my humble opinion be very great. In the first place were a good merchant established here he might have his goods direct from any part of England or Scotland conveyed by water, of course could afford to sell or retail the articles wanted as cheap as in Thurso, at present the emporium of this part of the country, and the general resort either for sale or purchase not only of Strathnaver, but all Lord Reay's country to the west; it is surely an object worthy attention to keep as much as possible the *circulating medium* in a country where so many are interested, and would be ultimately benefitted by such a measure.

Again the great number of vessels that navigate this sea, from England, the west coast of Scotland and Ireland, the Baltic trade, north sea fisheries etc., would doubtless in the event of a harbour and market being established, call here to take in fresh provisions, and I know no place better calculated to supply them than this would be, when in its present state such immense droves are sold off for the south.

Encouragement to a few artizans and mechanics to settle here, would likewise be attended with a beneficial effect, and by a proper division of labour, render it cheaper, and more perfectly executed; probably a woolen manufactory on a small scale for the coarser cloths, blankets, plaidings etc., would be attended with some advantages; it would at least afford employment to a part of the community who have nothing to do at present.

To go a little further into the *minutiae* the number of houses to be built for the fishers would be pretty considerable, as the men employed in the salmon fishery should be removed from their present farming possessions, and set down in the village with their brethren in the white fishery; a farmer-fisher, is a kind of heterogenious jumble, that ought to be seperated, their whole attention should be directed and kept in its proper sphere of action, the same holds good with weavers, taylors, manufacturers etc., or the proper division of labour cannot be accomplished, if they are not obliged to depend on, and follow out the different occupations allotted to them for support; a small portion of ground for a garden is the utmost that should be allowed, and I am not altogether clear whether even that appendage should be generally granted, as in the light in which I view the subject, 2 or 3 moderate sized farms will have to be organized; the disposeable produce from these and others in the neighbourhood, will of course be brought into the market; the villagers by their industry, and following steadily their occupations, will be enabled to purchase, at a cheaper rate, than they could with any small pieces of land in their own possession raise it; the farmer by course finds a ready sale for his disposeable produce; by which means he is enabled to pay a higher rent for the land he occupies.

By these or such like measures, all the useful class of the population that may eventually be thrown out of their possessions by the grazing farm, will be provided for, and be much bettered to what they are at present; their labour by being directed into proper channels will ultimately benefit themselves and the property; as *money*, by the means suggested will be brought into the country, trade must increase and flourish, a greater demand for labour and industry must follow; the property in proportion to the industry of its inhabitants rise in value, and finally all concerned benefitted.

In addition to the town or village of Naver, and to preserve as much as is consistent with true policy the population of the country, more of the inhabitants higher up the Strath, will have to be

provided for; to effect this, between the farms of Carnoghy and Skeal
as before noticed from 100 to 150 acres might be brought into arable
land, which at present pays little or nothing to the noble Family, and
allottments of 3 or 4 acres or any other number that may be thought
better given to each settler with the benefit of the hill behind, for
grass to a cow and a few sheep; and between Syre and Achness another colony of the same description may be placed if found necessary, or upon consideration thought adviseable; the ground will
have to be trenched and small comfortable houses erected, a proper
method of cropping and rotation chalked out, and the tenants become conditionally bound by their leases to follow the course as
pointed out to them; a dyke should be built along the summit of the
hill, to preserve the pasture immediately behind the arable land from
being promiscuously over run or overstocked in summer, when their
few sheep and young stock if they have any, may find support on
the hills beyond, and be brought within the dyke, and immediately
under their owners eye in winter. It is not to be supposed that these
small possessions are intended to support them without directing
their industry to some useful employment, without which they can
be of no real benefit either to themselves or the estate; on the
contrary, all who cannot be usefully employed here, must seek
employment in the neighbouring counties, and in winter when
little labour can be done they have a comfortable home and family
to return to, the savings of their labour imported from other
counties increases the money circulation here, and will assist in
supporting the commercial interests of the place; thus they become
useful members of society, and the strength and support of the
country.

The next object in view is to organize a few moderate sized farms,
and here unfortunately for want of proper extent of arable land,
they must be smaller than what they properly ought to be; however
as I see no way of surmounting this difficulty, proportionally small
they must remain.

Two Farms of this description will be Inver-Naver (after the present fishers are removed) and Carnochy. To the farm of Naver
should be attached, all the other little possessions included in Colonel
Clunes' wadset; and to Carnochy, Achyalague, with the hill grazing
to the march with the new settlers. These two farms by reason of their

proximity to the fishing village and the harbour, would find a ready sale for every article of their produce, in supplying the villagers even those articles at present considered of trifling consequence, such as milk, vegetables etc., would under these regulations be brought to their true value.

Another of these farms would be Skelpick, and to it attached, Achnayellan, and Dunviedan with the benefit of all those hills not included in the sheep farms; the value of which is not very great, but they would be of advantage to the farm of Skelpick; a few sheep, goats and black cattle might be kept on them, and to a tolerable good account if not overstocked.

The last and by far the most extensive would include Skeal, Langdale and Syre, the first of these to be kept principally for meadow hay etc., and the two latter under a regular rotation of crop; as there is a good and extensive hill ground attached to these farms, the occupier will be enabled to rear and support a great number of black cattle, either for exportation or home consumption, which- ever of the two it may be most his interest to accept; as in the event of this plan being carried into effect he would have his election.

In the burn of Langdale there is a good bed of clay, which would be of great advantage to these light lands if applied, but at present paring the surface off 2 acres of the adjoining best hill lands to im- prove half an acre of their arable land is preferred to any other system.

Among other improvements may be noticed a good road to the southern coast side of Sutherland, either to Helmsdale or Brora, whichever according to impending circumstances, may be found best calculated to benefit and connect the two places; the present proposed road to the Bay of Tongue may have many advantages, but few of them will be of any essential service to the further im- provement of Strathnaver.

Having given the outlines of a plan for improving this property; it will be proper in the next place to state the probable rent roll. In making this calculation, I shall consider the arable lands at 20s. an acre; and the hill pasture as equal in value to half the amount of the arable land. This being understood, I shall for brevitys sake, reckon the arable lands only, and call it 30s. an acre.

	Annual value
Sheep farms – Nos. 1 and 2	£750 os. od.
Small tenants or settlers say 200 acres at 30s.	300 os. od.
Farm of Naver – 125 acres at 30s.	187 10s. od.
Farm of Carnochy – 74½ acres at 30s.	111 15s. od.
Farm of Skelpick – 86¾ acres at 30s.	130 10s. od.
Farm of Langdale – 143¾ acres at 30s.	215 10s. od.
	£1,695 5s. od.

Journal by William Young of proceedings to and from Strathnaver: 1810

Left Golspie Inn on Friday morning 24th August. Passed through Dunrobin Mains. Mellick and other Lands east of the Herds House would make a beautiful and advantageous Farm if the Family propose to sett it. An exact plan and measurement shoud be got, the conditions and duration of Lease regulated, the tenant taken strictly bound to preserve planting under a heavy penalty, and to keep and leave the Land the under a rotation of crops to be fixed on. The Farm shoud then be advertised in the Inverness, Aberdeen, Edinburgh, and Kelso Papers desiring Sealed offers to be given in to Lord and Lady Stafford. The water side of Brora both from its local situation, and as the grounds are not adapted for Sheep or tillage Farms of any extent, seems well adapted for settlers. Moss plenty, as well as free stone for building, and a carding Mill might be advantageously placed in this quarter which in all probability woud very soon be followed by a manufacture of course Cloth and Blankets, but nothing decisive can here be fixed on untill the Coal experiment is finished.

Midgarty woud make a Farm well worth the attention of a Man of Capital, but there is much to do in clearing the ground of Stones, and in making covered drains. An exact measurement of this Place shoud also be got, and to induce a Farmer to bring it to the utmost pitch of perfection probably Thirty years Lease woud be necessary, with a progressive rise at each ten. Conditions for leaving the Land dikes and Houses in proper order to be attended to, and no allowance for the two last to be given on this or any other tillage Farm on the Estate but on a plan to be previously approved of.

Helmsdale Salmon Fishing pretty successful at present. Cruives and dikes in excellent order. Fish are boiled and sent to Aberdeen by a small vessell belonging to the Company[1] and reshipped for London by the Smacks,

Bridge Pillars for 2 arches of 70 feet each nearly finished.[2] Timber for one arch getting ready and expected to be finished this Season. Building materials principally Lime Stone with fine beds about one foot thick taken from the Shore of Loth which is said to abound with this valuable article. If Coals are found, it may turn out to great account.

Helmsdale seems extremely well adapted for a Fishing Station, both from its local situation and, as the adjoining Sea is known to contain Cod, Ling, Haddocks, and other White Fish, here the Moray Firth Fishermen frequently come to sett their Lines. Immediate steps shoud be taken to get possession of some ground suitable for a Village and to induce Fishermen from the South side to settle at this place.

From Helmsdale Bridge to Kildonan Kirk 9 miles, a beautiful Strath. Lowest grounds occasionally flooded by the River, people busy at their little Hay Harvest. Crops, Bear, black Oats, and Potato this year midling, but often very uncertain and on an average not equal to half the wants of 1200 to 1500 people living unprofitably by the sale of a few Sheep, Horses, and black Cattle, to subsist which they are often obliged to give part of their dear bought meal in bad Springs, and after all frequently lose numbers.

No marle or Lime Stone ever discovered above Helmsdale, nor does the appearance of the Country warrant a supposition that such is to be found.

Mr Thomas Houston's Sheep Farm betwixt Kildonan Manse and Kinbrace,[3] some low grounds woud be much benefited by a Catch drain, pointed it out to Mr Houston who is desirous to enter on the work when Meredith can find time to plan it out. Perhaps part of Mr Houstons allowance for Houses might be better bestowed for

[1] Messrs Landles and Redpath.
[2] Helmsdale bridge was completed before August 1811 (see Henderson, *Sutherland*, 146).
[3] Suisgill farm, which came out of wadset in 1807, and is entered as set to Houstoun in the rental of that year.

this improvement if he binds himself to leave it in sufficient order at the expiry of his Lease.

Kinbrace and Achinahew sett to Lieutenant Gunn who resides in Thurso, has Sheep Stock on the former, his mother resides on the latter, other pendicles subsett to small tenants. This Farm appears too cold for wintering Sheep to advantage and shoud have had some of the lower strath lands Joined to it. Came to Mr Gordons Dalharn, an industrious man, his possession seemingly very poor Soil. Crops of black Oats and Hay bad in the extreme, and so is his mode of Farming. Rotation 12 years natural grass, dunged, ploughed up for Oats of which he takes three crops running. Still with his superior management of Cattle he contrives to do better than his neighbours, and might be induced to alter his plan of Farming. Lieutenant Gunn shou'd be treated with for a few acres of the Kinbrace land, on the Dalharn side of the burn to be given Gordon, and he ought to have more on the South side.

Here a small Inn and stable shoud be built for the accommodation of travelers going to and coming from Strathnaver.

Left Dalharn on Saturday morning. From that place to Raviegill in Strathnaver entire Hill of Moss. The grounds contain deer hair, moss grass, and heath with inconsiderable spotts of Sour meadow.

In this Hill betwixt Achinhew in Kildonan to the confines of Farr parish Five different settlements on east side the river contain about 28 familys, on west side three settlements with 6 familys, includes Achinmore occupied by Mr Gordon Justice of Peace.[1]

Entered Strathnaver at Ravigill, and proceeded down the East side to Clerkhill, consists of detached Farms, intersected by patches of moor and meadow land to the river side. Crops as in Kildonan, Potato, Bear and black Oats, no attempt to improve; Houses built by alternate layers of Stone and turff, for which, and thatch, the finest ground is dreadfully cutt up.

Clerkhill to the march with Lord Armadale on the East, contains several detached Farms, but well sheltered and provided with good moor pasture. Crossed the Naver at Boiling House, saw 20 grilses and Salmon caught at a haul, cruive and dikes in good order. £150 laid out to force the water (which branches out) into one stream supposed to have an excellent effect. Traveled up the North Bank of

[1] Thomas Gordon, tenant of Achnamoin (par. Kildonan).

the Naver to Achness. Much fine Land especially about Langdale, crops of Potato, Bear and in many places white Oats good. The people complain of increased population in consequence of the Sheep Farming,[1] high Rents and uncertain Harvests. Produce – Horses, sold often when only one year old, Black Cattle (in general a very bad sort), Sheep from which they dispose of woolen yarn to their Caithness neighbours. Population in all about 2000 including wadsetts. Want annually 1800 to 2000 Bolls of imported Meal.

Left the Strath at Achness the east boundary of Mr Marshalls Farm, here a small stage House is wanted, proceeding by Clebrick to Altnaharew Inn occupied by Donald MacKenzie Subtenant of Mr Marshalls on the Road to Tongue House, and here better accomodation woud be desirable. Perhaps Marshall woud agree to build (as he draws a high Rent from MacKenzie) on getting moderate allowance at the expiry of his Lease. Entered the Crask a pass of 10 miles to a small Inn on the Water of Tearey still on Marshalls grounds. Grazings fine. Road desperately bad, had to cross rivers at least fourten times.

Came on Shiness grounds, bounded by the water of Tearey and Loch Shin. Heard of Lime Stone there, but coud not find out the depth of rock and price it cost (2s. 6d. per Boll) astonished us.

Crossed the Tearey at its Junction with the Shin, again on Marshalls grounds to near the Kirk of Larg, east of which a redeemed wadsett[2] full of small tenants well adapted for wintering to sheep. Reached Achinduich, a Farm of Marshalls on which he is raising Turnip (the only ones ever saw since leaving Helmsdale except a few at Shiness). A neat Farm steading finished and Cottage building. Were told by the Grieve that his master intended to root out all the Stones and make the arable but detached Spotts [into] close fields if the new plantation had not encroached so much. From Achinduich to Invershin the grazing and Hill grounds get much worse and seem to be in the hands of small tenants but whither belonging to this Family or Subsetts of Marshalls we coud not learn. Invershin

[1] A reference to the removal of tenants from Atkinson and Marshall's farm (see above, p. xxxv).
[2] Capt. Robert Gordon's wadset of Torroboll, Culmaily, Kinvonovy and Tomich (all par. Lairg), granted on 14 October 1800 and redeemed on 19 May 1810.

C

a flatt of good Turnip land but under bad management, woud be much improved by Lime if put under a regular rotation of crops. Here Mr Dempster of Skibo's property begins.

Found the new Road from Criech to Little Ferry in great forwardness with different Bridges nearly finished.

William Young to Earl Gower (later 2nd Duke of Sutherland)
Dunrobin Castle, September 1810

This and the six preceeding pages contains an account so far as I am capable to Judge of the present situation of those parts of the Sutherland Estate which I have traveled over.

The two arable Farms of Melick and Midgarty cannot fail to find proper tenants, and your Lordship will have to determine what length of Lease shou'd be given on each, and at what period it ought to commence. If it is intended to part with Melick for the ensuing crop, part of the Cattle should be sold by publick Roup about the end of next month, after selecting a sufficient Stock for Dunrobin Mains and Skelbo.

With respect to Kildonan and Strathnaver it is perfectly clear to me and I am Joined in opinion by some good Judges which I have had an opportunity of conversing with, that they are only adapted for the Sheep system, in case a certain and much higher rent is looked for, than it is profitable for the present or any future possessors who may attempt the Corn and Cattle Husbandry to pay.

I do not however feel myself competent to determine in what divisions either Straths ought to be sett, for I had no opportunity of seeing the extent and quality of moor which may be attached to each, neither does my experience in Sheep Farming warrant me to decide on this subject without advice; but the quantity of Land to be lett together shoud not perhaps exceed sufficient maintenance for more than 3 or 4000 Sheep; with this extent the competition will be greater while the numbers of people to be removed at once will be less considerable, and if one or two Farms only are sett annually with sufficient notice to the present occupants to provide themselves the hardship ought to be less felt.

There will after all be many claimants on your Lordships bounty, and to old people a certain quantity of Meal and a little money might be well bestowed, as well as to such as have large familys untill their Children arrive at a certain age, and might be left with a House and Cabbage Garden without Injury to the Sheep Farmer.

Perhaps it may be found that Strathnaver can be sett in four divisions.

1st Clerkhill including Mr Gordons Subtenants and the Lands east ward to Lord Armadales march.

2nd From Clerkhill to Achness or where Mr Marshalls Farm commences.

3rd Naver etc. to Langdale.

4th Langdale to Lord Reays March.

Probably Kildonan might be sett in similar proportions although I fear that part of it will be objected to for wintering. It may be prudent to make the Leases terminate with Mr Marshalls as some advantageous Junction may then be formed as he appears to have too little wintering ground while the Naver has too much for its summer pasture.

I shall be glad to have your Lordships remarks and orders on these matters at convenience.

William Young to Marchioness of Stafford

Dunrobin Castle, 21 October 1810

I had the honor to write your Ladyship before leaving Inverugie, on Wednesday Evening I reached this and found every thing correct at the Castle.

Thursday

Traveled over the Skelbo moors and Embo marches[1] with Mr Berry[2] and the ground officer, but without Captain Mackay, thinking it better to be possessed of every information before meeting the opposite party on matters of this sort; I have heard of, and written for an old plan at Provost Browns[3] which (with the evidence of two

[1] The estate of Embo, formerly the property of the house of Gordon of Embo, was leased by Capt. Kenneth Mackay of Torboll from Robert Hume Gordon, a collateral descendant of the Embo family (Sage, *Memorabilia Domestica*, 147-9).

[2] Thomas Berry, successor to William Hutton as Dunrobin forester.

[3] Provost George Brown of Elgin, a well-known surveyor, must have been an old man in 1810, for he wrote to Falconer in the same year that he had been in business for upwards of 40 years.

men in Dornoch and Tain who accompanied the Surveyor) is likely to throw light on the Subject.

Friday

Went to Blearach plantation with Berry. The old and several of the new planted Oaks are doing well, but owing to the dry Season I could only discover a few of the Firrs which had taken root. They should be replanted, and the arable land in which Oaks are to be put might with advantage be ploughed and harrowed. Berry approves of this and Pringle[1] will send Cattle if your Ladyship agrees to it. The woodkeepers Cattle have yet done no harm and I cautioned him against ever admitting a single beast in future, indeed if the arable ground is ploughed there can be no object for doing so.

Having gone out by Strathfleet and Rovie we returned by the Kirk of Rogart. These Straths seem particularly well adapted for Farms of the Second Class, and if three fourths of this present population could be disposed of as Labourers and Mechanics the remainder might be led on to do well with Farms of 25 to 50 acres arable and a moderate share of Hill.

After having seen the Country I do not think it was proper to give Rovie to Andrew Sutherland who is no more a Farmer than Mackenzie, with this difference that Andrew had already too much, while it will be difficult, (and oblige me to make some sacrifice) to accommodate the other, but I will commune with Andrew and his Son Charles who may yet be induced to give up Rovie which is on the opposite side of the water[2] and quite out of their way.

Saturday

Went to Strathsteven Quarries. The Stone is in my opinion excellent and exceeds that in Morayshire, but although there is a Creek for Boats quite close they are turned to no account and the Quarrier is not up to his business. I wish the adjoining Mill which pays Achany 12 Bolls of yearly rent coud be got for a trifle, it with the Quarries and a small Farm which might be easily laid off wou'd afford constant work for some industrious people and make moderate returns for the money laid out. I have recommended these

---

[1] Alexander Pringle, grieve at Dunrobin Farm.
[2] Andrew Sutherland, merchant, was a tenant in Pittentrail, on the north bank of the Fleet opposite Rovy. Charles Sutherland held Rovykirkton in 1812, and was still in possession in the 1813 rental.

Quarries to Mr Telfords man for the Little Ferry and Iron Bridge Piers.[1]

Found Pritchard had got 39 feet down at the Brora work, still in soft rock. I believe he is using every endeavour and will I hope at last obtain the hidden treasure.

Traveled along the Banks of Loch Brora. Saw some dying Oaks on Mcphersons Sheep Farm[2] which ought to be measured, valued, and offered for sale. Examined Strathbrora which is worthy of more attention than seems ever to have been bestowed on it, and like Rovie is admirably adapted for Small Farms. It is sadly cutt up by the River. I am sure such operations as seem wanted for embanking wou'd return 20 per Cent. Mr Hughes opinion and estimate ought to be got.

Called on Hudson Bay[3] who with his wife and children live in a wretched Timber Hutt open to wind and rain, without a foot of garden ground. Distressed with Rheumatism he cannot long hold out in such a habitation and I coud wish to see him more comfortable. Without saying from whence I came, he pressed me to come in, gave me some detail of his travels and said he liked to see strangers. On remarking that his House must be cold in winter he laughed at my ignorance and said that although I saw the boards open at present the rain wou'd make them quite close and prevent the wind from blowing in. But I had to go by Sibercross and was obliged to leave poor Hudson in the midst of his travels, after telling him at parting what I was, and hoping to see him more comfortable in his native land.

Mr Sutherland has the Sibercross Farm in much better order than that at Brora. His dikes are all good, he has built several Stone embankments along the River, preserves the wood and has a decent House. It might be right to add more to this mans Highland Farm during the Currency of his *present* Lease especially if he agrees to become tenant *at Will* on Brora.

[1] Work on the 'Iron Bridge' at Bonar began in 1811. The Sutherland heritors were at this time pressing for an embankment and bridge at Little Ferry, and sent a memorial to the Commissioners for Highland Roads and Bridges on the subject on 30 August 1811.
[2] Killin (par. Clyne) (see above, p. xxix, n.2).
[3] Precise name unknown. Donald McKay Hudson is entered as a tenant in Ascoilmore in the 1814 and 1815 rentals, but not in previous years.

From Sibercross to Dunrobin Strath the Country is not populous and probably cannot be laid out to much advantage, it faces the north and has not an inviting aspect.

The upper Strath is possessed by Mr MacKay of Ironhill as a Grazing, the lower by Mr Keith and the Innkeeper, under what conditions I have to enquire.

While Sheep ought to be the principle stock in the Highlands, I have now much to my own satisfaction seen that all Strathsfleet and Brora can be advantageously lett for Corn Farms and I shoud hope that many of the present possessors may be trained to a proper mode of Husbandry.

In these districts Turnip, Flax, Barley, Clover and Oats with occasionally a little Wheat will of all others pay best and I cannot too much impress the necessity of having a Flax Mill ready against next Autumn. If during winter this is agreed to I will make it publick before sowing time, and cause some of the Golspie Merchants bring Seed to the Country, having an eye to the quality and price. If Cant does not come forward about the Mills (and our correspondence is at a stand untill the British Linen Company resolve as to the Bank)[1] I can get Mitchell the Mill wright on a moderate Scale and with a loan of 300 £ from a relation.[2]

Sunday

Walked over Lord Staffords intended Willow plantation with Pringle and Berry. It is to be begun to tomorrow morning. Gave Berry a pamphlet on Willows which will enable us to order a variety for this and the Skelbo Ground.

Had a good deal of conversation with our new road Overseer who has been at Lord Reays with a Man of Telfords lining off the Road to Tongue House, the plan differs in some cases from what was given to His Lordship by Wilson and which this Man thinks the best. As I know him to be an intelligent honest Man and an excellent road maker, your Ladyship might Just hint to Lord Reay not to go readily into this new line untill it is a little better investigated, but

[1] A representative of the British Linen Company visited Sutherland in November 1810, but did not recommend that a branch be opened (Young to Marchioness, 22 November 1810). Estate financial business was thereafter conducted through the Company's Tain agent, Benjamin Ross.

[2] Golspie meal and flax mills (the former of which still survives) were built by George Mitchell, millwright, and completed in 1814; the total cost was £840.

without giving Mr Telford any offence. He will listen to reason and we ought all to see that a measure of such importance is not bungled.

The Rooff of the Ice House is in a ruinous condition and so is the dyke round the bleaching ground, they shoud both be repaired and the latter made to sweep round the Ice house.

Meredith has not returned from Strathnaver but I have a young man at work on the Achavandra moors.

I am afraid that Duncan the Innkeeper cannot do well without the shaded Cellars behind his House especially as the Stable and Coach House to which they might have been attached are now to be at such a distance.

Fearing overweight I send this without a cover. A letter Just come in from Mr Cant a Copy of which with my answer,[1] and a Sketch of the Bleaching grounds and small park, will be sent in a day or two.

[1] These have not survived.

1811–1816

PAPERS RELATING TO THE FACTORY OF
WILLIAM YOUNG

Documents relating to appointment of William Young and Patrick Sellar to manage Estate of Sutherland: 1811

A Commission The Marquis & Marchioness of Stafford in favour of Mr Young

KNOW ALL MEN by these presents that I Elizabeth Marchioness of Stafford and Countess of Sutherland with the advice and Approbation of The most Noble George Granville Marquis of Stafford and both of us with mutual Consent and Assent Considering That we find it necessary to appoint a proper person for carrying on the progressive improvement of the different Estates belonging to us in the County of Sutherland; such as the lining out of roads, laying off and valuing farms, setting the same, draining and inclosing of lands, establishing of new Villages and Manufactures, and whatever else may be Considered likely to turn out for the future prosperity of the Estate; and further, for conducting and Executing the whole public business of the County. And having full Confidence in the Abilities and Integrity of William Young Esquire of Inverugie do hereby nominate constitute and Appoint the said William Young to be our Commissioner to the effect after Specified giving, granting and Committing to him full power, warrant, and Commission for us and in our names to investigate into the present Situation of the said Estates, to ascertain what parts thereof are now, or soon to be out of lease and to take and use the measures which may appear most prudent for the improvement and the proper laying out and Setting of all parts thereof as they respectively come into the power of the

proprietors during the Subsistance of this Commission; with power
to him at all times to give the necessary instructions for such removal
of tenants without lease, as may be found necessary in the course of
his duty, to follow out every measure requisite for the lining off and
making roads, and establishing new Villages and manufactures, and
whatever else shall, by and with our advice, be considered conducive
to the future prosperity of the Estate, and to draw from the rents,
to be deposited in the Bank such sums as may be necessary for these
purposes. Further, we hereby authorise the said William Young and
his foresaids to appear as our Commissioner, as often as he finds it
necessary at all meetings of the Freeholders, Courts of Lieutenancy,
Commissioners of Supply, road Trustees, Justices of the Peace, and
others where the Public business of the County of Sutherland is or
may be transacted, and there and upon all other occasions to conduct
and carry through in these Courts the business of our said Estates,
and whatever other business or affairs we may have therein, Hereby
recalling, all powers concerning these matters formerly granted in
favour of Mr Cosmo Falconer at Rhives or any other person and
debarring them from further interfirence in the premisses. We declare
That after this date and untill the recall of these presents the said
William Young Esquire has and shall have the sole power and management thereof, and it is especially provided that the said William
Young shall be Bound and obliged as he, by Acceptation hereof,
Binds and Obliges himself to consult and advise with us before
setting any lands or determining on any measure of importance out
of the common course of business as also, That he shall hold just
compt, reckoning, and payment to us our heirs and successors of his
whole Intromissions in virtue hereof at all times when required,
and shall make payment to us or our order of whatever balance shall
then appear to be owing by him under deduction of Seven hundred
and twenty five pounds Sterling of yearly salary payable to him at
two terms in the year, Whitsunday and Martinmas by equal por-
tions in recompence for the discharge of his duty and without any
extra charge whatever. And further we hereby declare that these
presents shall subsist aye and untill recalled by an express writing
under our hands but that the said William Young shall have three
months written premonition to enable him to wind up the affairs
under his management; during which time his salary shall continue

at the rate per Annum before specified. And we Consent to the Registration hereof in the Books of Council and Session or others competent therein to remain for preservation and Execution and thereto Constitute [   ] [1] Our Procurators.
(To be finished in same Style as the Factory) [2]

B Minute of Agreement between the Most Noble the Marquis and Marchioness of Stafford On the one part and William Young Esquire of Inverugie and Patrick Sellar Writer in Elgin On the other part.

The said Marquis and Marchioness having resolved to part with Mr Cosmo Falconer their present factor, as soon as the nature of his engagements will admitt, and having proposed to Mr Young to take the general management of their Estates, and to consider of the assistance which he should require therein; the said William Young in respect that this management, comprehended not only the duties presently incumbent on Mr Falconer, but the attempting the progressive improvement of the different districts of the country, by the methods most suitable to each, did, therefore, undertake, by and with the Sanction of the family, the direction and conduct of the various *improvements* on the different parts of the Estate, such as lining out of Roads, laying off and Valuing farms, setting the same, draining and inclosing of land, establishing new Villages and Manufactures and whatever else he should consider likely to turn out for the future prosperity of the Estate; and he recommended to the Family the said Patrick Sellar to collect the rents, keep accounts of the expenditure, pay attention to the various rights of the tenants, to their fulfillment of the Conditions in their Tacks, to the enforcing the laws for preserving the plantations and the Game, transactions with Ministers and Schoolmasters, framing Tacks and other writings; And the said Marquis and Marchioness having Approven of this plan, and it being proper to enter into a formal Agreement, to prevent the possibility of any doubt or misunderstanding at a future time. Therefore the said William Young and Patrick Sellar engage and Bind themselves Conjunctly and Severally to conduct and Manage the said Estate upon the plan above mentioned; it being expressly understood however that the special duty of the said

[1] MS. blank.   [2] See below, pp. 43-45.

William Young is, the Conducting of the said improvements, in the discharge of which he may call in the assistance of such people as are versant in the different branches to be carried on and that he shall report their and his opinion to the family and receive their sanction before setting any of the land, or embarking in any undertaking of moment; As also he is to conduct and execute the whole public business of the County; and that the special duty of the said Patrick Sellar is the factorial business before detailed. That once a fortnight at least, or as often as with safety and convenience it can be done, he is to lodge in a Bank the moneys collected by him to bear Interest for Account of the family; That these moneys may be drawn upon by the said William Young for the purposes of the Estate, he accounting to the family for such drafts when required; and that Mr Sellar shall keep regular and distinct Accounts of his Intromissions, receipts and debursements which he shall bring to a balance on the [   ]¹ day of [   ]¹. Yearly; when, or how soon thereafter as is Convenient for the Family or their doers, his last years Accounts are to be inspected, and if found correct, the balance paid and the Accounts discharged. That if the family chuse, he shall enter Agent before the Courts of Dornoch and prosecute such suits for the Family there, as may be necessary and Approven of by them or their doers at Edinburgh. It is further expected that the said William Young and Patrick Sellar will exert themselves to quash all Law suits and quarrels among the tenants, so far as it may be prudent for them to interfere.

c Factory to Patrick Sellar

Know all men By these presents That I Elizabeth Marchioness of Stafford and Countess of Sutherland with the advice and Approbation of the Most Noble George Granville Leveson Gower Marquis of the County of Stafford and both of us with mutual consent and assent Considering That we find it necessary to appoint a proper person for Collecting the rents of our Estates in the County of Sutherland; for keeping Accounts of the expenditure thereof, for paying attention to the various rights of the tenants, to the fulfillment of the Conditions in their Tacks, to enforcing the laws for preserving the plantations and the Game, conducting transactions

¹ ms. blank.

with Ministers and Schoolmasters, and framing tacks and other writings connected with the Estate. And having confidence in the fidelity and ability of Patrick Sellar Writer in Elgin do hereby nominate, constitute and Appoint the said Patrick Sellar to be our Factor and Agent to the effect after specified, giving, granting and committing to him full power, warrant and commission for us and in our names, to collect, and uplift, and if needfull to call, charge and pursue for the rents, maills, farms, profits and duties of our haill lands and Estates in the County of Sutherland, and that for the crop and year of God one thousand eight hundred and eleven and arrears of preceeding years conform to a rental and list of Arrears to be signed by us and delivered to him as relative hereto betwixt and the term of Whitsunday first. And also empowering him to Collect, levy, charge and pursue, for the rents, maills, farms, profits and duties of the said haill lands and Estates for all crops and years to come during the Subsistence of this present Factory, with power to the said Patrick Sellar upon payment of the foresaid rents to grant Discharges therefore which shall be sufficient to the receivers; In general to do every thing for recovering payment of the same as fully and freely in all respects as we could do ourselves if personally present, or which to the office of Factor in the like cases is known to belong; and we further authorise and direct him to make every Investigation concerning the various rights of the tenants and their fulfillment of the Conditions in their Tacks and to take measures if necessary for inforcing the fulfillment of these Conditions and the laws Relative to the preservation of the Plantations and the Game; for all which purposes he is to enter himself Agent before the Sheriff Court of Sutherland and to act as Agent in any suits necessary to be carried on in our names there or before the Justices of the Peace, declaring however as it is hereby specially provided and declared that the said Patrick Sellar shall be bound and obliged as by Acceptation hereof he Binds and Obliges himself his heirs Executors and Successors to hold just compt, reckoning and payment to us for his whole Intromissions in virtue hereof at all times when required and shall make payment to us or our order of whatever balance shall then appear to be owing by him, with the Interests which may arise on the monies Intromitted with as the same shall be ascertained by the Account of a Banker in whose hands the rents are to be periodically lodged as

Collected, once a fortnight if possible or as often as the money can with safety and convenience be conveyed thither, but declaring, that in his said accounts the said Patrick Sellar shall have allowance of Two hundred and Seventy five Pounds Sterling of yearly salary or Factor Fee, and also of the price of Stamps, and Fees paid by him in any suit at our Instance, where the costs cannot be recovered from the other party, which sums are in full recompense to him for the discharge of his duty, and without any extra charge whatever. Further it is declared that these presents shall subsist aye and untill recalled by an express writing under our hands and that the said Patrick Sellar shall have three months premonition to enable him to wind up the affairs under his management during which time his Salary shall continue at the rate per annum before Specified, but it shall be in the power of us or our foresaids, during the said space of three months to debarr him from any act of Management, not connected with the winding up of the Trust. And we Consent to the Registration hereof in the Books of Council and Session or others competent therein to remain for preservation and Execution and thereto Constitute Our Procurators. In witness hereof we have Subscribed these presents written on this and the two preceeding pages of Stamped paper by John Henney, Groom of the chambers to the Marquis of Stafford. At London the nineteenth day of February one thousand eight hundred and Eleven years, before these witnesses The Right Honourable George Granville Leveson Gower, Earl Gower, and John Henney Groom of the chambers to the Marquis of Stafford.

Gower   witness   E. Stafford Sutherland

John Henney   witness   Stafford

Report by Patrick Sellar concerning the State of the Interest of Landlord and Tenant on the Sutherland Estate: March and April 1811

I have the honour to send herewith a correct state of the present position of Landlord and tenant on Lord and Lady Staffords Estates in Sutherland. I have furnished Mr Young with a copy of it, and I hope it may prove of some little use as a book of reference, when, in business or correpondence, enquiry is necessary concerning any particular farm or the possessor of it. I have left, in an additional folio, places opposite each name for such observations as may occur to the family,[1] from time to time, relative to any farm, its tenant, or the business of any particular district. I hope my next may shew every thing in a more perfect condition, than they appear to be at present.

Mr Young I understand, has concerted with Lord and Lady Stafford the sett of the parish of Rogart; which he finds fitted for the occupation of small tenants in allottments of from twenty to forty Arable Acres; each, having a suitable proportion of pasture. It is extremely fortunate, that the valleys of this Country are too wett for the wintering, and the muirs too dry and hard for the summering of sheep; altho' these valleys have always brought corn and cattle to perfection; and the barren ground being *sheltered by the Benevragie range of hills from the sea*, carry, *where tried* pine and Larch to considerable size. There are in the exposed hill above Gordon-bush, trees of old Carroll's[2] planting seemingly as tall as those at Balblair, better than a foot in diameter, and evidently not nearly at their full growth. Besides what the timber may ultimately come to, these trees pay, in a cold latitude, by the shelter they afford, and by the feuel drawn from their weedings.

1st Concerning the farms. I annex a copy of the regulations proposed for this part of the Estate.[3] They have doubtless many defects and require the correction of the Family. When fully matured and fitted, they may be extended on a parchment and signed by the proprietor and by each tenant in the district. A printed copy being given to each tenant, with his lease, he can refer to it at his leisure, and will be thoroughly acquainted with what he has to fulfill.

2nd When Earl Gower comes to the Country he may perhaps order some experiment in planting different places; a thing attended with little expence, and which had it happened forty years ago would have added much to the appearance of the Country, and, possibly, to its wealth and state of Improvement.

---

[1] No such observations are entered.
[2] John Gordon of Carroll was dead by January 1810, when his son Joseph succeeded to his wadset of Kintradwell.
[3] See below, pp. 120-6.

State of Lord and Lady Stafford's property in the County of Sutherland; prepared, with a view to the formation of a correct rentall of
the sums to fall due, Martinmas 1811 and Whitsunday 1812.

EDITOR'S NOTE: The *State* gives information under the following
headings:
>   Farms
>   Tenants
>   Rents
>   Leases – commencement, endurance, expiry
>   Houses, Fences and others – proprietor's interest, tenant's interest
>   Matters requiring attention – immediately, at tenant's removal
>   Remarks.

The entries have been abbreviated on the following principles:
the names of individual small tenants are omitted
where an individual heading is left blank it is omitted (but where
    'not ascertained' is entered, the fact is recorded)
where the details under a heading are identical with those in an
    earlier entry *in the same parish* a reference to that entry is given
where the details under a heading are identical with those under the
    immediate preceding heading the word 'same' is used
in cases where the precise wording of the original is given quotation
    marks are used; the spelling of all proper names is retained from
    the original.

I LANDS IN THE PARISH OF ASSYNT

1 Ardvare, Cromault, Little Assynt, Auldnachie.
Reservations: Kelp shores, power to build a public house.
Tenant: Captain William Scobie, in right of Lieutenant John Scobie
of Sutherland Fencibles.
Rent: Martinmas 1811, tack duty £82; fox money £0 16s. 0d.[1]
Duration: 19 years expiring Whitsunday 1812.
Proprietor's interest: Tenant is bound to preserve houses, etc. as at his
entry; not known if apprisement then made.

---

[1] A County levy on tacksmen, probably based on valued rent. This amounted to
£30 7s. 5¹⁰d. in 1793, but was not apparently levied on tacks granted after 1801 (for
instances see below, pp. 48-55, 95, 109). Payments were made to fox-killers (a small
number of certificates, dating from 1789, survive in the sheriff-court records at
Dornoch).

Tenant's interest: Meliorations of £40, if expended on stone and lime buildings, stone dykes and sunk fences faced with stone, to be left in good condition.

Matters requiring immediate attention: Tenant is bound to preserve natural woods; tenant is bound to plant at least two acres on Ard-vare with firs to be furnished from Dunrobin; houses to be apprised as at tenant's entry.

Matters requiring attention at removal: Houses and fences to be in good repair; natural woods to be preserved; two acres to be planted.

2 Half of salmon fishings in waters of Inver, Culaig and Inverkirkaig.
Tenant: Captain William Scobie, in right of Kenneth McKenzie in Leadbeg.
Rent: Martinmas 1811, tack duty £17 10s. 0d.
Duration: As 1.

3 Auchmore, Rhintraid.
Reservation: Sea ware.
Tenant: Captain William Scobie, in right of deceased Kenneth Scobie in Auchmore, his father.
Rent: Martinmas 1811, tack duty £63; fox money £0 13s. 0d.
Duration: As 1.
Proprietor's interest: Not ascertained.
Tenant's interest: Meliorations of £50.
Matters requiring immediate attention: As 1; two acres to be planted on Auchmore with firs.
Matters requiring attention at removal: As 1.

4 Knockan.
Reservations: Sea ware,[1] power to build a public house.
Tenant: Mr John Robertson late in Keanchilish of Coygash.
Rent: Martinmas 1811, tack duty £30; fox money £0 6s. 8d.
Duration: As 1.
Proprietor's interest: Not ascertained.
Tenant's interest: Meliorations of £15.
Matters requiring immediate attention: As 1, excluding planting.
Matters requiring attention at removal: As 1, excluding planting.

---

[1] A meaningless reservation, the farm being inland.

5 Elphine.
Reservation: Kelp shores.[1]
Tenant: Ensign Alexander McKenzie's heirs.
Rent: Martinmas 1811, tack duty £37; fox money £0 9s. 3d.
Duration: As 1.
Proprietor's interest: Not ascertained.
Tenant's interest: Meliorations of £20.
Matters requiring immediate attention: As 4.
Matters requiring attention at removal: As 4.

6 Leadmore, Badgrinan.
Reservation: As 5.
Tenants: 1. Roderick McKenzie for himself, R. McLeod and J. McLeod; 2. Six named small tenants.
Rent: Martinmas 1811, 1. tack duty £37 12s. 7d.; fox money £0 6s. 3[10]d. 2. tack duty £13 7s. 5d.; fox money £0 3s. 8[10]d.
Duration: As 1.
Proprietor's interest: Not ascertained.
Matters requiring immediate attention: As 4.
Matters requiring attention at removal: As 4.

7 Marble wherever found on Estate of Assynt.
Tenant: Isaac Jopling, marble cutter, late of Newcastle on Tyne, now at Leadbeg.
Rent: Martinmas 1811, tack duty £30.
Duration: 21 years, expiring Whitsunday 1820.
Matters requiring attention at removal: Payment of all claims for surface damage by tenants or others.

8 Rhincreich, half of Unapool.
Tenant: Isaac Jopling.
Rent: Martinmas 1811, tack duty £50; fox money £0 8s. 8½d.
Duration: 18 years, expiring Whitsunday 1820.
Tenant's interest: Meliorations of two years' rents.
Matters requiring immediate attention: Natural woods to be preserved.
Matters requiring attention at removal: As 4.

9 Leadbeg, Fillen, Layne, half of Drumswordland, half of salmon fishings in waters of Inver, Culaig, Inverkirkaig.

---

[1] A meaningless reservation, the farm being inland.

D

Reservations: As 1.
Tenant: Kenneth McKenzie in Leadbeg.
Rent: Martinmas 1811, tack duty £115 1s. 6d.; fox money £1 10s. 0d.
Duration: As 1.
Proprietor's interest: Not ascertained.
Tenant's interest: Meliorations of £50.
Matters requiring immediate attention: Natural woods to be preserved; two acres firs to be planted.
Matters requiring attention at removal: As 1.

10 Stronechrubie, Lower Tubeg, Duchlash, Poulgarvin.
Reservations: As 1.
Tenant: Murdoch McKenzie in Stronechrubie.
Rent: Martinmas 1811, tack duty £82 13s. 4d.; fox money £0 7s. 3d.
Duration: As 1.
Proprietor's interest: Not ascertained.
Tenant's interest: Meliorations of £45.
Matters requiring immediate attention: As 9.
Matters requiring attention at removal: As 1.

Half of Drumswordland.
Tenant: Murdoch McKenzie in Stronechrubie, in right of Kenneth McKenzie in Leadbeg.
Rent: Martinmas 1811, tack duty £7 6s. 6d.; fox money included above.
Duration: As 1.
Proprietor's interest: Not ascertained.
Tenant's interest: Meliorations included in 9.
Matters requiring immediate attention: As 9.
Matters requiring attention at removal: As 1.

11 Inchndamff, Upper Tubeg, house of Inchndamff.
Tenant: George McKenzie.
Rent: Martinmas 1811, tack duty £40; fox money £0 7s. 6d.
Duration: 19 years expiring Whitsunday 1817.
Proprietor's interest: Not ascertained.
Tenant's interest: Meliorations of £40.
Matters requiring immediate attention: As 4.
Matters requiring attention at removal: As 4.

12 Coulin, Torbreeck, half of Camore.
Reservations: As 1.
Tenant: Reverend William McKenzie.
Rent: Martinmas 1811, tack duty £27; fox money £1 7s. 0d.
Duration: From Whitsunday 1766, for life (said to be above 70).
Proprietor's interest : Not ascertained.
Matters requiring immediate attention: Natural woods to be preserved;
thirled to miln of Auldnuagh; houses, fences, etc. to be maintained;
why is fox money out of proportion?
Matters requiring attention at removal: As 4.
Remarks: 'By the Tack the Endurance is mentioned to be the same
as the tenant's Incumbency; but there is a private Minute signed by
the Parson and Mr Fraser[1] conditioning an additional year's lease
provided Mr McKenzie does not augment his Stipend. The stipulation seems unlawful and the Stipend has been augmented. The Fox
money is out of proportion and Mr Falconer knows not how this
happens.'

13 Edracalda.
Reservations: As 4.
Tenant: Mr Alexander McKenzie.
Rent: Martinmas 1811, tack duty £14; fox money £0 2s. 8d.
Duration: As 1.
Proprietor's interest: Not ascertained.
Tenant's interest: Meliorations of £14.
Matters requiring immediate attention: As 4.
Matters requiring attention at removal: As 4.

14 Half of Unapool.
Tenants: 10 named small tenants.
Rent: Martinmas 1811, £50.
Duration: From Whitsunday 1808, at will.
Tenants' interest: Have a right to carry off any bought timber if not
paid for it.
Matters requiring attention at removal: 'What sort are the Houses?'

15 Nedd.
Tenants: 12 named small tenants.

---

[1] John Fraser, factor of Sutherland Estate, 1791-1802.

Rent: Martinmas 1811, £50 8s. 0d.
Duration: As 14.
Tenants' interest: As 14.
Matters requiring attention at removal: As 14.

16 Drumbeg.
Tenants: 15 named small tenants.
Rent: Martinmas 1811, £60.
Duration: As 14.
Tenants' interest: As 14.
Matters requiring attention at removal: As 14.

17 Oldnay.
Reservation: As 3.
Tenant: Mrs Gray, widow of Lieutenant John McKay.
Rent: Martinmas 1811, tack duty £48; fox money £0 9s. 6d.
Duration: From Whitsunday 1793, for 19 years and her lifetime (said to be about 60).
Proprietor's interest: Not ascertained.
Tenant's interest: Meliorations of £30.
Matters requiring immediate attention: As 4.
Matters requiring attention at removal: As 4.

18 Coulkein Drumbaig, ten merks of Durlan sometime possessed by John McLeod and John McKenzie.
Tenant: Heirs of Hugh Clark in Oldnay.
Rent: Martinmas 1811, tack duty £44 10s. 0d.; fox money £0 5s. 3d.
Duration: 10 years, expiring Whitsunday 1812.
Proprietor's interest: Not ascertained.
Tenant's interest: Meliorations of £44 10s. 0d.
Matters requiring immediate attention: Houses to be maintained.
Matters requiring attention at removal: Same.

19 Clashnessie, Achnacarnan Culkein and Achnacarnan excepting Durlan, Clashmore, Balchladich, Store, Clachtoll, Achmelvich.
Tenant: Mr Donald McDonald of Tanera.
Rent: Martinmas 1811, tack duty Clashnessie £58, Achnacarnan Culkein and Achnacarnan excepting Durlan £70 17s. 2d., Clashmore £64, Balchladich £18 15s. 0d., Store £42 5s. 0d., Clachtoll £63, Achmelvich £56; fox money £2 3s. 2^{10}d.

Duration: 19 years expiring Whitsunday 1821, if he lives so long; heirs bound to remove at first Whitsunday after his death.

Proprietor's interest: Seemingly none; to be ascertained.

Tenant's interest: Bound to pay the former tenants their claims of meliorations and to be repaid at end of his lease provided premises be not deteriorated; to get payment for any stone houses or quay or other buildings erected by him not exceeding one year's rent, viz. £372 17s. 2d.

Matters requiring immediate attention: Does Mr Young require access to any part of these farms in his arrangements?; has Mr McDonald's apprisings paid to outgoing tenants been ascertained?; were there any houses, etc. belonging to proprietor at commencement of this tack?

Matters requiring attention at removal: Tenant to furnish apprisings of what he paid for former tenants' meliorations at his entry: see that these have been preserved.

Remarks: Proprietors have right to resume possession of any one or two of these farms on notification of six months before any term of Whitsunday, allowing a proportional abatement of rent; lands are set for the purpose of employing tenants in fishing, and nothing must be charged against them beyond a fair proportion of rent.

20 Inver and Ardroe.

Reservations: Sea ware, right to build store house and public house.

Tenant: Mr Donald MacDonald of Tanera, in right of John McKenzie.

Rent: Martinmas 1811, tack duty £30; fox money £0 3s. 10d.

Duration: As 1.

Proprietor's interest: Not ascertained.

Matters requiring immediate attention: As 4.

Matters requiring attention at removal: As 4.

21 Culaig, including new house etc. built at shore by Murdoch Morrison of Stornoway and bought by Mr McDonald from him.

Reservations: As 20.

Tenant: Mr Donald McDonald of Tanera in right of John McKenzie.

Rent: Martinmas 1811, tack duty Culaig £18, new house £2; fox money Culaig £0 2s. 8d.

Duration: Culaig as 1; new house not ascertained.

Proprietor's interest: Not ascertained.

Tenant's interest: Culaig none; new house not ascertained.

Matters requiring immediate attention: Culaig as 4; enquire into nature of right given Morrison in new house and bought by Mr McDonald.

Matters requiring attention at removal: Culaig as 4; expiscate nature of right in new house.

22 Badidaroch.

Tenants: 7 named small tenants.

Rent: Martinmas 1811, £21.

Duration: As 14.

Proprietor's interest: Not ascertained.

Matters requiring attention at removal: Has heritor any interest in houses?

23 Brackloch.

Tenants: 2 named small tenants.

Rent: Martinmas 1811, £18.

Duration: As 14.

Proprietor's interest: Not ascertained.

Matters requiring attention at removal: As 22.

24 Badynabaan and Knocknach.

Reservations: As 4.

Tenant: George Ross, distiller at Culaig, now residing at Ulapool in Ross.

Rent: Martinmas 1811, tack duty £26; fox money £0 4s. 9d.

Duration: As 1.

Proprietor's interest: Not ascertained.

Tenant's interest: Meliorations of £26.

Matters requiring immediate attention: As 4.

Matters requiring attention at removal: As 4.

25 Inverkirkaig.

Reservations: As 4.

Tenants: Mrs Christian McLeod, widow of late Kenneth McKenzie in Inverkirkaig, and Lieutenant John McKenzie of late Sutherland Fencible Regiment.

Rent: Martinmas 1811, tack duty £20; fox money £0 4s. 2d.

Duration: As 1.

Proprietor's interest: Not ascertained.
Tenant's interest: Meliorations of £20.
Matters requiring immediate attention: As 4.
Matters requiring attention at removal: As 4.

26 Lochbannoch.
Tenants: 5 named small tenants.
Rent: Martinmas 1811, £21.
Duration: As 14.
Proprietor's interest: Not ascertained.
Matters requiring attention at removal: As 22.

27 Glenlerig.
Tenants: 17 named small tenants.
Rent: Martinmas 1811, £89 5s. 0d.
Duration: As 14.
Proprietor's interest: Not ascertained.
Matters requiring attention at removal: As 22.

II LANDS IN THE PARISH OF CREICH

1 Invershin.
Reservations: Market and resting place of Monubuie and dues up-lifted thereat; power to resume possession of 30 acres next adjacent to Portanlick,[1] tenant having a fair deduction of rent therefor.
Tenant: Gilbert McKenzie, Invershin.
Rent: Between Christmas 1811 and Candlemas 1812, 3 bolls bear; Martinmas 1811, tack duty £50; fox money £0 3s. 0d.
Duration: 19 years expiring Whitsunday 1820.
Proprietor's interest: Not ascertained.
Tenant's interest: Meliorations of £50, if expended on houses of stone and lime or stone and clay pinned with lime.
Matters requiring immediate attention: Tenant is bound to preserve wood at Invershin; tenant is bound to uphold houses and fences built or to be built on farm.
Matters requiring attention at removal: Has he preserved woods and houses in terms of his tack?

---

[1] A ferry point across the Kyle of Sutherland, to the west of the present railway bridge (see Henderson, *Sutherland*, 14).

III LANDS IN THE PARISH OF LAIRG

1 Miln of Claren, amounting to 8½ farthings of land.
Tenants: 10 named small tenants.
Rent: Martinmas 1811, £15 7s. 0d.
Duration: From Whitsunday 1808, at will.
Proprietor's interest: Not ascertained.
Matters requiring immediate attention: Ascertain whether any heritor's standard.
Matters requiring attention at removal: Same.

2 Lower Lairg, amounting to 14 farthings of land.
Tenants: 7 named small tenants.
Rent: Martinmas 1811, £22 10s. 0d.
Duration: As 1.
Proprietor's interest: Not ascertained.
Matters requiring immediate attention: As 1.
Matters requiring attention at removal: As 1.

3 Shiness sheep tenement.
Tenant: Duncan Matthieson Esquire.
Rent: Martinmas 1811, £200; Whitsunday 1812, £200.
Duration: 19 years expiring Whitsunday 1827.
Proprietor's interest: Not ascertained.
Tenant's interest: Not ascertained.
Matters requiring immediate attention: Mr Falconer has to settle with Mr Matthieson the terms of his lease, which ought to be given me complete.
Matters requiring attention at removal: Same.

4 Lands lately held in wadset by Robert Gordon; Torrobol (presently possessed by 16 named small tenants), Kinvonovie (presently possessed by 27 named small tenants), Tomich (presently possessed by 3 small tenants).
Tenants: 'Mr Young to say how to be possessed for grass crop 1811 and corn crop 1812, the present tenants having been warned.'
Proprietor's interest: Not ascertained.
Tenant's interest: Not ascertained.

Matters requiring immediate attention: 'I am to procure from Mr Young a correct rental 1811.'

Matters requiring attention at removal: Same.

Remarks: 'Captain Gordon's wadset has it seems been Redeemed but no Rental has been furnished, and Mr Falconer has taken what Rent the people admitted to be due, which he now finds much below truth. Mr Young is to fix a Rent upon it, the difference betwixt which as the Real Rent and what Mr Falconer collected is to be attended to in [   ]¹ of Arrears to be received from Mr McKenzie or Mr Falconer.'

5 Feu Duties. 1. Achany. 2. Water of Shin. 3. Gruids.²

Tenants: 1. William Monro Esquire. 2. Murdoch McKenzie of Ardross. 3. Colonel Munro, Pointzfield.

Duty: 1. £15 5s. 6d. 2. £2 15s. 6⁸d. 3. £31 7s. 11⁶d.

Duration: Said to be perpetual.

Matters requiring immediate attention: See the titles or records and ascertain for what year the payment is and other particulars.

6 Dry multures of Milnchlaren.

Miller is paid for his labour only; Alexander Graham, miller, has mill rent free.

Multures:

William Munro of Achany, £2 13s. 6d.; Duncan Matthieson for Clunas, £5; tenants of Milnchlaren, Lower Lairg, Torrobol, Tomich, Kinvonovie, £8 18s. 6½d.

IV LANDS IN PARISH OF DORNOCH

1 Achinchanter and Castle Yards.

Tenant: Captain William McCulloch in right of his father.

Rent: Crop 1811, payable between Christmas 1811 and Candlemas 1812, 2 bolls victual: Crop 1812, Martinmas 1811, tack duty £14; fox money £0 1s. 10d.

Duration: 19 years expiring Whitsunday 1812.

Proprietor's interest: Ascertained to be £3 12s. 0d.

¹ MS. torn.
² These feu-duties, and a small number of others (see below, pp. 60, 73, 88, 110) were payable from lands held by feudal title from the Sutherland family, as parts of the earldom of Sutherland, barony of Skelbo, or barony of Farr.

Tenant's interest: Meliorations of moss or planted firs to any extent.
Matters requiring immediate attention: Tenant is bound to preserve all trees on the ground; farms are thirled to mill of Cyderhall; tenant is bound to perform a proportionate part of the service necessary to raise and support a proper bulwark on the Evelix in all parts within the thirle of the mill; tenant is bound to support and leave the houses, etc. in good condition and repair.
Matters requiring attention at removal: Trees to be preserved; houses, etc. to be in good repair.
Remarks: Ordered a removing against Captain McCulloch from Achinchanter, Whitsunday and Martinmas 1812, and from Castleyards, both grass and corn, Whitsunday 181[   ]¹; Mr McCulloch contests the point.²

2 Sandcroft.
Tenant: Captain William McCulloch.
Rent: £0 14s. 10d.
Duration: Since Whitsunday 1793, no term stated.
Matters requiring immediate attention: Mr Young to say whether Captain McCulloch is to possess it another year at same rent.
Remarks: Ordered a removing against Captain McCulloch, Whitsunday and Martinmas 1811; Mr McCulloch contests the point;² Mr Young to say how it is to be possessed, grass 1811 and corn 1812.

3 Auchunluie, Achley, Craggy Achlean.
Tenants: Presently possessed by William McIntosh and Andrew McKay; 'Captain Munro has this, but Mr Falconer and he have a difference of 8 bolls rent to ascertain.'³
Rent: 24 bolls victual, £6.
Proprietor's interest: Not ascertained.
Matters requiring immediate attention: 'Have Captain Munro and Mr Falconer ascertained terms of lease?; how do the houses stand?; is there any inventory?; vide old lease.'
Remarks: Tenants warned out; Mr Young to say how it is to be possessed, grass 1811 and crop 1812.

¹ MS. torn.
² McCulloch was still in possession in 1812, having paid a forehand rent at Martinmas 1811; he was no longer tenant in 1813.
³ Capt. John Munro is entered as tenant in the 1812 rental.

4 Auchiroch, Wards, Silver Croft, Garskilly.
Tenant: Reverend Mr Bethune.
Matters requiring immediate attention: No houses or inventory.
Rent: Crop 1812, Martinmas 1811, £28.
Remarks: Tenant warned from Achiroch.

5 Town of Dornoch.
Tenants: 7 named small tenants.
Rent: Crop 1812, Martinmas 1811, £2 13s. 10½d.
Duration: No. 1, 99 years expiring Whitsunday 1902.[1]
Matters requiring immediate attention: Mr Falconer does not know how nos. 2-7 hold; their titles to be examined.
Remarks: 'No. 6 (£0 10s. od.) is the rent of a parcel of hutts which Mr Young has ordered to be removed.'

6 Dean's House Laroch.[2]
Tenant: Angus Fraser.
Rent: Crop 1812, Martinmas 1811, £0 10s. od.
Duration: 99 years expiring Whitsunday 1902.
Matters requiring immediate attention: Void if one dwelling house at least, not under £10 value, not built within 10 years from first date of lease, 31 October 1804, or when said houses not kept in repair; tenant is bound to free proprietor from taxes, cess, stent, etc.

7 East Garden.
Tenants: 4 named small tenants, each with house and garden.
Rent: Crop 1812, Martinmas 1811, £8 14s. 3d.
Duration: Nos. 2 and 4, 99 years expiring Whitsunday 1902; no. 1, 99 years expiring Whitsunday 1904; no. 3, to be ascertained; in all cases gardens at will.
Matters requiring immediate attention: 'Ascertain whether there are any unoccupied lairochs and why they fetch no rent; I understood there are several lairochs unoccupied.'
Remarks: No. 1 warned out from garden; Mr Young to say how to be possessed 1812.

[1] Under an entail of the earldom of 29 March 1706 feus were limited to 99 years. A small number of such feus were given for house-ground in Dornoch and Golspie (see below, p. 85) during Campbell's term of office. Similar terms were offered in the new village at Brora (Young to George Mackay, Inverness, 7 February 1815; see also below, p. 103).
[2] Building site or stance.

8 Croftkaill and house.
Tenant: Philip McKay, wright in Dornoch.
Rent: £0 15s. 3d.
Remarks: Tenant warned out; Mr Young to say how to be possessed.

9 Michaelwells, Torrinroy.
Tenant: George Jaffrey.
Rent: £12 2s. od.
Remarks: As 8.

10 Two bolls pay.
Tenant: 1 named small tenant.
Rent: £1 3s. 8d.
Remarks: As 8.

11 Scottach, 6 bolls pay[1] and house.
Tenant: 1 named small tenant.
Rent: £3.
Remarks: As 8.

12 Feu Duties: 1. Over Skibo. 2. Skibo.
Tenant: W. S. Dempster Esquire.
Duty: 1. Crop 1812, Martinmas 1811, £5 11s. 1¼d. 2. Crop 1811, Christmas 1811 to Candlemas 1812, 1 boll 2 firlots bear; Crop 1812, Martinmas 1811, £5 11s. 1¼d.
Duration: Not ascertained.
Matters requiring immediate attention: 'Endeavour to see titles and ascertain how they stand; uncertain if barley or meal, vide rights.'

13 Pitgrudy.
Tenant: Mr Angus Fraser.
Rent: Crop 1812, Martinmas 1811, £34.
Duration: 19 years expiring Whitsunday 1827.
Tenant's interest: ⅔ of meliorations agreeably to Mr Falconer's Regulations.
Matters requiring immediate attention: Tenant bound to Mr Falconer's printed Regulations.[2]
Remarks: Rises £6 after 6 years' possession.

[1] *Rectius* 6 firlots pay (see below, pp. 222-3).
[2] These have not survived.

14 Croftmeadick, including Bridge Garden possessed by A. Murdoch.
Tenant: John Barclay.
Rent: £13 2s. 2d.
Remarks: As 9.

15 Cyderhall.
Tenants: 1. Captain William McCulloch in right of Lieutenant McKenzie. 2. — Rose, storekeeper.
Rent: 1. Crop 1811, Christmas 1811 to Candlemas 1812, 93 bolls 1 firlot 2 pecks bear; crop 1813, Martinmas 1811, £13 3s. 0d.; fox money £0 8s. 1½d. 2. Crop 1811, Christmas 1811 to Candlemas 1812, 3 bolls bear.
Duration: 1. 19 years expiring Whitsunday 1817. 2. at will.
Proprietor's interest: 1. Not ascertained as to houses and dykes.
Tenants' interest: 1. One year's rent on fences made within 7 years of commencement of lease and on plan approved by Dunrobin overseer.
Matters requiring immediate attention: 1. Tenant bound to preserve woods; tenant bound to maintain dwelling houses, offices, etc. to value at commencement of lease; said value to be ascertained.

16 Miln of Cyderhall, mill croft, multures and sequels, 1 boll pay of land and grass following same.
Tenant: Hugh Leslie, writer in Dornoch.
Rent: Crop 1811, Christmas 1811 to Candlemas 1812, 21 bolls meal; crop 1812, Martinmas 1811, £20 15s. 0d.
Duration: 19 years expiring Whitsunday 1817.
Proprietor's interest: Not ascertained; apparently none.
Tenant's interest: Value of miln, not exceeding £20.
Matters requiring immediate attention: Was any apprising of miln made at entry?
Matters requiring attention at removal: Same.

17 Dalvevie, Teachlybe.
Tenant: Hugh Leslie.
Rent: 22 bolls 2 firlots victual; £14 1s. 11d.
Proprietor's interest: Not ascertained.
Tenant's interest: Value of timber.
Remarks: As 8.

18 Loanmore.

Tenants: 1. Hugh Leslie, 38⅓ acres; 2. Lieutenant McKenzie, Loan-more, 60 acres; 3. Angus Fraser, merchant, Dornoch, 29 acres.

Rent: 1. Crop 1812, Martinmas 1811, £0 19s. 3d. 2. Crop 1812, Martinmas 1811, £1 10s. 0d.; 3. Crop 1812, Martinmas 1811, £0 11s. 0d.

Duration: 1. Not ascertained; 2. 19 years expiring Whitsunday 1817, with 19 years further if improved by Whitsunday 1817, at a fair rent to be then fixed by arbiters; 3. 19 years expiring Whitsunday 1821, with same.

Proprietor's interest: 2, 3. In leases no mention of houses or meliorations.

Tenants' interest: Same.

Matters requiring immediate attention: 'No houses I presume are built; cause Leslie produce his lease.'

Matters requiring attention at removal: Tenants are bound to leave biggings, dykes and fences made or to be built at Loanmore in sufficient repair.

19 Davochfin.

Tenant: William Munro, Dornoch.

Rent: Crop 1812, Martinmas 1811, £17 10s. 0d.; Whitsunday 1812, £17 10s. 0d.

Duration: 19 years expiring Whitsunday 1830.

Tenant's interest: ⅔ of meliorations.

Matters requiring immediate attention: Mr Falconer's printed Regulations.

20 Drumdivan.

Tenants: 8 named small tenants.

Rent: 7 named tenants pay £28 19s. 6d. afterhand rent at Martinmas 1811 for crop 1811.

Remarks: As 8.

21 Ballone.

Tenants: 2 named small tenants.

Rent: £12.

Remarks: As 8.

22 The Park.
Tenant: Robert Clark.
Rent: Crop 1812, Martinmas 1811, £16.
Duration: 19 years expiring Whitsunday 1829.
Tenant's interest: Mr Falconer's printed Regulations.
Matters requiring immediate attention: Same.

23 Little Torbol, Meikle Torbol and mill, Rhiholmy, Achnahuie and miln, Craigablamich, Mains of Little Torbol, Eiden, part of Torfalig.
Tenant: Captain Kenneth McKay.
Duration: Mr Falconer has not finally fixed the lease.
Matters requiring immediate attention: 'Get the lease from Mr Falconer, or have the family's commands, and attend to the heritor's interest in the houses, etc.'
Remarks: 'Why a new lease granted to Captain McKay in the middle of the last without any adequate rise of rent?'

24 Altaduaig.
Tenants: 4 named small tenants.
Rent: Crop 1812, Martinmas 1811, £12 2s. 0d.
Duration: No lease.

25 Achmail[1] and Muir of Achmail.
Tenants: 4 named small tenants.
Rent: Crop 1812, Martinmas 1811, £16 18s. 0d.
Duration: No lease.

26 Turfalaig.
Tenant: 1 named small tenant.
Rent: £3.
Duration: At will.
Remarks: Tenant warned out; Mr Young to say how this is to be possessed; part of it wished by Mr Falconer to be included in Captain Kenneth McKay's lease; requires Mr Young's attention.

27 Cambusavie, Mains of Cambusavie, Blackstones, Croftbain, Rhineceroch, Leadoch, Rhinmunnich, Croftbreak, Croftmore, Londow.

---

[1] *Rectius* Achinal.

Tenant: Mrs M. Sutherland, failing whom Robert Gordon of Rhine.
Rent: Crop 1812, Martinmas 1811, £64; fox money £0 5s. 11½d.
Duration: 19 years expiring Whitsunday 1820.
Proprietor's interest: Appears to be none; to be ascertained.
Tenant's interest: Meliorations of £40 on houses and offices, £24 on stone dykes, enclosures or sunks faced with stone.
Matters requiring immediate attention: Tenant is bound to preserve the woods growing, to assist at loading and unloading vessels at Ferry-oons on business of the family, or to pay a proportion thereof.

28 Cambusmore.
Tenant: Dr Ross.
Rent: Crop 1812, Martinmas 1811, £10 16s. 4d.
Duration: Holds Mr McKenzie's letter for 19 years lease from Whitsunday 1804.
Proprietor's interest: Not ascertained.
Tenant's interest: Not ascertained.
Remarks: 'Mr McKenzie's letter is in the Appendix.'[1]

29 Lednclay.
Tenants: 3 named small tenants.
Rent: Crop 1812, Martinmas 1811, £5 3s. 8d.

30 Muirs of Dornoch and Evelicks.
Tenants: 13 named small tenants.
Rent: Crop 1812, Martinmas 1811, £2 13s. 6d.
Duration: 'Leases said to have been given in a Book to Lord Stafford.'[2]

31 Balvraid.
Tenants: 16 named small tenants.
Rent: 28 bolls victual, £25 2s. 0d.
Remarks: Tenants warned out.

32 Badninish.
Tenants: 5 named small tenants and Lord Gower.
Rent: Crop 1812, Martinmas 1811, small tenants £2 2s. 0d.; Lord Gower, £1.
Remarks: See as to Lord Gower's lease.

[1] See below, p. 118.   [2] This has not survived.

33 Little Garvary.
Tenant: William Taylor, Dornoch.
Rent: Crop 1812, Martinmas 1811, £15.
Duration: From Whitsunday 1811, no lease.

34 Coul, Eachter.
Tenant: Robert Sutherland.
Rent: Crop 1812, Martinmas 1811, £92 19s. 9d.
Duration: 19 years expiring Whitsunday 1828.
Tenant's interest: Mr Falconer's printed Regulations.
Remarks: 'Lady Stafford in her Ladyship's Marginal Remarks speci-
fies of Rent £94 but in drawing the line on the West march the
difference of Ground occasioned the diminution which being 20s.
3d. is laid on the Tenants of Fourpenny.'

35 Fourpenny.
Tenants: 3 named small tenants.
Rent: Crop 1812, Martinmas 1811, £20 10s. 1½d.; Whitsunday
1812, £20 10s. 1½d.
Duration: 7 years expiring Whitsunday 1816; further 7 years if by
end of first 7 years cottages built and inclosures finished.
Matters requiring immediate attention: Have they built cottages and
properly inclosed their ground?; tenants are bound to Mr Falconer's
printed Regulations; Mr Young to point out the inclosures to be
made.
Remarks: After the first 7 years the rent rises to £46 sterling; Mr
Young to point out the inclosures to be made.

36 Part of Knockglass east of Kyle road.
Tenant: — McKay.
Remarks: Mr Young to fix McKay's rent.

37 Skelbo.
Tenant: Mrs Boog.
Rent: Crop 1812, Martinmas 1811, £93 10s. 7³d.; fox money
£0 3s. 7⁹d.
Duration: From Whitsunday 1789, for life (supposed to be above
70).
Proprietor's interest: 'The lease stipulates an apprisement to be made
E

betwixt the date of lease and the tenant's entry but Mr Falconer knows of none that was made.'

Tenant's interest: Meliorations of £104 10s. 7⁸d. on houses, £100 on stone dykes.

Matters requiring immediate attention: To ascertain if any apprisement was made at tenant's entry and to have the value of the houses fixed.

Remarks: 'Mr Young to attend to the distinction between Earl Gower's interest and Mrs Boog's as to meliorations.'[1]

38 Mickle Cubaig.
Tenants: 2 named small tenants.
Rent: £10.
Remarks: As 8.

39 Proncynaird.
Tenant: Mrs McKay.
Rent: Crop 1812, Martinmas 1811, £50.
Duration: 'Mr Falconer is revising the lease it being included in the Torbol one.'
Matters requiring immediate attention: Get the particulars of this lease from Mr Falconer.
Remarks: 'If Captain McKay's lease can be got over it should be done; for what *onerous cause* it was renewed in the middle is not easily found out.'[2]

40 Pendicles of Proncynaird.
Tenants: 4 named small tenants.
Rent: £8 14s. od.
Remarks: As 8.

41 Proncynain.
Tenants: 7 named small tenants.
Rent: 6 bolls victual, £30.
Remarks: As 8.

[1] Mrs Boog, widow of Bailie James Boog (for whom see Sage, *Memorabilia Domestica:* 163), who died in March 1810 (Young to Earl Gower, 14 March 1810). Duncan Matheson of Shiness, sub-tenant on Skelbo, wrote to Earl Gower offering to surrender the property, and Earl Gower appears to have taken possession at Whitsunday 1810. Mrs Boog, who retained possession of the small farm of Gruby (par. Rogart), was paid an annuity of £115 from Martinmas 1813, as a consideration for surrendering Skelbo. In this instance, as possibly in some others, the *State* is not fully up to date.
[2] See above, p. 63.

42 Proncycroy.
Tenants: 4 named small tenants.
Rent: 3 bolls victual, £15.
Remarks: As 8.

43 Evelicks, Milnton of Evelix.
Tenant: Mr William Taylor.
Rent: Crop 1812, Martinmas 1811, £90.
Duration: 19 years expiring Whitsunday 1828.
Proprietor's interest: Not ascertained.
Tenant's interest: Mr Falconer's printed Regulations.
Matters requiring immediate attention: 'His houses must be valued immediately to ascertain what he does under the new lease.'

44 Miln of Evelicks.
Tenant: John Grant.
Rent: 18 bolls meal.
Matters requiring immediate attention: 'How does the value of the mill stand?; Mr Falconer thinks there was an old lease but does not know.'
Remarks: As 8.

45 Dalnamain.
Tenants: 10 named small tenants.
Rent: Crop 1812, Martinmas 1811, £15 15s. 3d.
Duration: Not ascertained.
Matters requiring immediate attention: How do the houses stand?

46 Birichen, consisting of Foa, Fleuchary, Dalchiel, Loanberichen.
Tenants: 4 named small tenants.
Rent: Crop 1812, Martinmas 1811, £3 12s. 3d.

47 Ardochy.
Tenants: 3 named small tenants.
Rent: Crop 1812, Martinmas 1811, £2 10s. 6d.

48–50 Clashalarich, Linagranach, Knockbreack, Leadberichen.
Tenants: 5 named small tenants.
Rent: Crop 1812, Martinmas 1811, £3 14s. 6d.

51 Rhearquhar, pendicle of Osdale, Achosnich, miln of Achosnich, Brea of Dalnamain (excepting George Ross's grazing).
Tenant: Colonel George Sutherland.
Rent: Crop 1812, Martinmas 1811, Rhearchar £42 15s. 3²d., Brea £6 3s. 8⁶d.; fox dues and dry multures £2 12s. 3⁶d.
Duration: From Whitsunday 1789, for life (upwards of 90).
Proprietor's interest: Tenant is bound to uphold houses, etc.
Matters requiring immediate attention: Tenant being bound to uphold houses, etc. value at entry ought as nearly as possible to be ascertained.

52 Kinnauld.
Tenant: Captain Duncan Sutherland.
Rent: Crop 1812, Martinmas 1811, £88.
Duration: 19 years expiring Whitsunday 1828.
Proprietor's interest: Not ascertained.
Tenant's interest: ⅔ meliorations per Mr Falconer's Regulations.
Matters requiring immediate attention: Value of houses at entry to be ascertained.

53 Rhimusaig.
Tenant: Captain Duncan Sutherland.
Rent: Crop 1812, Martinmas 1811, £25.
Duration: 19 years expiring Whitsunday 1828.
Proprietor's interest: Not ascertained.
Tenant's interest: ⅔ meliorations per Mr Falconer's Regulations.
Matters requiring immediate attention: Miln to be inventoried.

54 Part of Kinauld ceded by Captain Sutherland.
Tenants: Messrs Young and Sellar.
Matters requiring immediate attention: Ground to be measured to ascertain rent at 10s. per acre.
Remarks: Part of Kinnauld set to Young and Sellar for 30 years after expiry of Mrs McLeod's lease on Morvich; rent referred to arbiters.[1]

---

[1] See below, p. 90. Young was entered as tenant of this small piece of ground in 1812, but thereafter the entry disappears.

V LANDS IN THE PARISH OF ROGART

1 Eiden.
Tenant: Captain McKay, Torboll.
Rent: Crop 1812, Martinmas 1811, £27 10s. 0d.; Whitsunday 1812, £27 10s. 0d.
Duration: Mr Falconer has not yet settled the terms of the lease.
Proprietor's interest: Houses valued 5 July 1788 at £2.
Matters requiring immediate attention: 'Get from Mr Falconer the lease and attend to the condition of the houses and fences.'
Remarks: Vide Dornoch no. 23.

2 Kintraid.
Tenant: Mrs McKenzie or Clunas.
Rent: 7 bolls 3 firlots victual, £6 2s. 0d.
Duration: From Whitsunday 1801, no lease.
Proprietor's interest: Valued 5 July 1788 at £1 4s. 0d.; 'I see no ascertainment in 1801.'
Matters requiring immediate attention: Tenant is bound to preserve natural woods; tenant is bound to uphold houses, etc. in good condition and of same value as at entry, which value to be ascertained.
Matter requiring attention at removal: In what state are the houses?
Remarks: 'In lease not executed by Colonel Clunas the cautioner and hence null, for 19 years after Whitsunday 1801, I observe an obligation on the tenant to deliver the usual quantity of hens and eggs on demand on the Common Deduction of Rent, and to deliver the usual quantity of Peats and Garden services without any deduction.'

3 Davochbeg.
Tenants: 7 named small tenants.
Rent: £30.
Duration: From Whitsunday 1801, no lease.
Proprietor's interest: Not ascertained.
Tenants' interest: 'Not ascertained whether any Stipulation or if the tenant may carry away the timber agreeably to practice.'
Matters requiring immediate attention: Ascertain tenants' interest in houses.
Remarks: Tenants warned out; Mr Young to say how to be possessed.

4 Rovy Kirkton.

Reservation: Power to resume possession of hill of Strathtolly and pasture ground naturally connected therewith on allowing proportional abatement of rent.

Tenant: Mr Charles Sutherland, son of Andrew Sutherland, merchant, Pittentrail.

Rent: Crop 1812, Martinmas 1811, £22 10s. 0d.; Whitsunday 1812, £22 10s. 0d.

Duration: 19 years expiring Whitsunday 1828.

Proprietor's interest: In dependence in a suit before the Sheriff.

Tenant's interest: Mr Falconer's Regulations.

Matters requiring immediate attention: Mr Falconer's Regulations; value of houses at entry to be ascertained.

Matters requiring attention at removal: Mr Falconer's Regulations.

Remarks: At Martinmas 1815 and Whitsunday 1816, and thereafter, rent is £50.

5 Dalmore.

Tenants: 6 named small tenants.

Rent: Crop 1812, Martinmas 1811, £15.

Proprietor's interest: Not ascertained.

Tenants' interest: As 3.

Matters requiring immediate attention: As 3.

Matters requiring attention at removal: See to the houses.

6 Incheap.

Tenants: 8 named small tenants.

Rent: Crop 1812, Martinmas 1811, £17.

Proprietor's interest: Not ascertained.

Tenant's interest: As 3.

Matters requiring immediate attention: As 3.

7 Achlean of Pitfure.

Tenant: William McKay.

Rent: Crop 1811, 3 hens; crop 1812, Martinmas 1811, £11.

Duration: 7 years expiring Whitsunday 1817.

Proprietor's interest: Last tack expiring 1807 obliges tenant to leave the houses in good condition; not ascertained.

Tenant's interest: As 4.

Matters requiring immediate attention: As 3.
Matters requiring attention at removal: As 5.

8 Inchoraig.
Tenants: 2 named small tenants.
Rent: Crop 1812, Martinmas 1811, £5.
Proprietor's interest: Not ascertained.
Tenants' interest: As 3.
Matters requiring immediate attention: As 3.
Matters requiring attention at removal: As 5.

9 Pitfure.
Tenant: Mr D. McKenzie.
Rent: £45.
Duration: Lease for 19 years expiring Whitsunday 1828 renounced.
Proprietor's interest: Not ascertained.
Tenant's interest: As 3.
Matters requiring immediate attention: As 3.
Matters requiring attention at removal: As 5.
Remarks: 'This man has renounced his lease for Colonel Suther-land's[1] Accommodation. Mr Young to say how it is to be possessed.'

10 Carranlorkan.
Tenant: Mr D. McKenzie.
Tenant's interest: As 3.
Matters requiring immediate attention: As 3.
Matters requiring attention at removal: As 5.
Remarks: As 9.

11 Achtomline.
Tenants: 2 named small tenants.
Rent: Crop 1812, Martinmas 1811, £13.
Proprietor's interest: 'The last lease to Lieutenant George Sutherland and John McKay which expired Whitsunday 1807 provided that the tenants should leave houses in good Condition.'
Tenants' interest: As 3.
Matters requiring immediate attention: As 3.
Matters requiring attention at removal: As 5.

[1] Lieut. Col. Alexander Sutherland, tenant of Braegrudy and wadsetter of Culmaily (see below, pp. 80, 83-4).

12 Rhine.

Tenants: 1. Captain Robert Gordon. 2. 9 named small tenants.

Rent: 1. Crop 1812, Martinmas 1811, £30. 2. Crop 1812, Martinmas 1811, £24.

Duration: 1. Lease expired Whitsunday 1807. 2. No lease.

Proprietor's interest: 1. Rhine house valued 5 July 1788 at £44 19s. 8d.

Tenants' interest: 1. By lease for 19 years dated 11 October 1788 tenant is bound to support houses, and is allowed one year's rent as meliorations. 2. 'These were Gordon's subtenants, and Mr Falconer supposes that they may carry off any bought timber in their houses agreeably to the practice of the Country.'

Matters requiring attention at removal: As 5.

13 Dalmore.

Tenant: Colonel Sutherland of Rhiarcher.

Rent: Crop 1812, Martinmas 1811, £7 10s. 0d.

Duration: 'Mr Falconer says he holds a promise for life – no lease.'

Proprietor's interest: Not ascertained.

Tenant's interest: As 3.

Matters requiring immediate attention: As 3; 'see any letter he may have.'

Matters requiring attention at removal: As 5.

14 Mains of Meikle Rogart, Badachrasky, Balintample.

Tenant: Captain Angus McKay.

Rent: £34.

Proprietor's interest: 'By the lease to Mrs Esther Sutherland which expired Whitsunday 1808 I see £30 were at her entry in the 1794 advanced to her to make the houses sufficient, and she was bound to uphold them to that Amount. The mill too was repaired by the proprietor and she was obliged to leave it in good Condition. McKay entered on this lease and now possesses by Relocation. There is an Apprising of houses on Badachrasky on 28 July 1808, amount £5 10s. 6d.'

Tenant's interest: No meliorations allowed.

Matters requiring attention at removal: Attend to heritor's interest in houses and miln.

15 Part of Balintample.

Tenant: Reverend Alexander Urquhart.

Rent: Crop 1812, Martinmas 1811, £12.
Proprietor's interest: Not ascertained.
Tenant's interest: As 3.
Matters requiring immediate attention: As 3.
Matters requiring attention at removal: As 5.

16 Feu duty: Langwall.
Tenant: Mrs Soper Dempster's heirs.
Duty: Martinmas 1811, £0 15s. 0½d.
Duration: Particulars to be ascertained.
Matters requiring immediate attention: Endeavour to see titles.

17 Balrimore.
Tenants: 4 named small tenants.
Rent: Crop 1812, Martinmas 1811, £11.
Duration: No lease.
Proprietor's interest: By last lease tenants bound to leave houses in good condition.
Tenants' interest: As 14.
Matters requiring attention at removal: As 5.

18 Culdrain.
Tenants: 2 named small tenants.
Rent: Crop 1812, Martinmas 1811, £8 8s. 0d.
Proprietor's interest: As 17.
Tenants' interest: As 14.
Matters requiring attention at removal: As 5.

19 Achnaheih.
Tenant: 1 named small tenant.
Rent: Crop 1812, Martinmas 1811, £1 15s. 0d.
Proprietor's interest: As 17.
Tenant's interest: As 14.
Matters requiring attention at removal: As 5.

20 Achna Garron.
Tenants: 2 named small tenants.
Rent: £10 10s. 0d.
Proprietor's interest: As 17.
Tenants' interest: As 14.

Matters requiring attention at removal: As 5.
Remarks: Tenants warned out.

21 Balchlagin and pendicles.
Tenants: 4 named small tenants.
Rent: Crop 1812, Martinmas 1811, £14.
Proprietor's interest: As 17.
Tenants' interest: As 14.
Matters requiring attention at removal: As 5.

22 Torbreak of Pitfour.
Tenants: 3 named small tenants.
Rent: Crop 1812, Martinmas 1811, £10 14s. od.
Proprietor's interest: By last lease which expired Whitsunday 1807
tenant bound to leave houses, etc. in good condition.
Matters requiring attention at removal: As 5.

23 Milnafua.
Tenant: 1 named small tenant.
Rent: Crop 1812, Martinmas 1811, £1 4s. 5d.
Proprietor's interest: As 22.
Matters requiring attention at removal: As 5.

24 Dalagrunich.
Tenant: 1 named small tenant.
Rent: Crop 1812, Martinmas 1811, £1 15s. od.
Proprietor's interest: As 22.
Matters requiring attention at removal: As 5.

25 Knockinlean.
Tenant: 1 named small tenant.
Rent: Crop 1812, Martinmas 1811, £2.
Proprietor's interest: As 22.
Matters requiring attention at removal: As 5.

26 Dalfeosaig.
Tenants: 3 named small tenants.
Rent: Crop 1812, Martinmas 1811, £24.
Proprietor's interest: As 22.
Matters requiring attention at removal: As 5.

27 Rhianreoch.
Tenants: 2 named small tenants.
Rent: Crop 1812, Martinmas 1811, £9.
Proprietor's interest: As 22.
Matters requiring attention at removal: As 5.

28 Little Rogart and ⅓ of shealing of Craigasnarich.
Tenants: 10 named small tenants.
Rent: Crop 1812, Martinmas 1811, £46 14s. od.
Proprietor's interest: As 22.
Matters requiring attention at removal: As 5.

29 ⅔ of shealing of Craigasnarich.
Tenant: Captain Duncan Sutherland of Kinauld.
Rent: Crop 1812, Martinmas 1811, £10.
Proprietor's interest: As 22.
Matters requiring attention at removal: As 5.

30 Pittentrail.
Tenants: 9 named small tenants.
Rent: £52.
Proprietor's interest: As 22.
Matters requiring attention at removal: As 5.
Remarks: Tenants warned out; Mr Young to say how to be possessed.

31 Achgyle.
Tenants: 2 named small tenants.
Rent: Crop 1812, Martinmas 1811, £3 10s. od.
Proprietor's interest: As 22.
Matters requiring attention at removal: As 5.

32 Rhyline.
Tenant: Captain Duncan Sutherland of Kinauld.
Rent: Crop 1812, Martinmas 1811, £5.
Duration: 18 years expiring Whitsunday 1828.
Proprietor's interest: Not ascertained.
Tenant's interest: As 4.
Matters requiring immediate attention: Ascertain state of houses.
Matters requiring attention at removal: As 5.

33 Rhilochan.
Tenant: George McKay.
Rent: Crop 1812, Martinmas 1811, £12.
Proprietor's interest: Tenant bound to leave houses in sufficient repair.
Tenant's interest: As 4.
Matters requiring attention at removal: As 5.

34 Banscol.
Tenant: 2 named small tenants.
Rent: Crop 1812, Martinmas 1811, £9.
Proprietor's interest: As 22.
Matters requiring attention at removal: As 5.

35 Achvoan.
Tenants: 3 named small tenants.
Rent: Crop 1812, Martinmas 1811, £9 10s. od.
Proprietor's interest: As 22.
Matters requiring attention at removal: As 5.

36 Knockarthur.
Tenants: 2 named small tenants.
Rent: Crop 1812, Martinmas 1811, £10.
Proprietor's interest: As 22.
Matters requiring attention at removal: As 5.

37 Inchomney of Knockarthur.
Tenants: 3 named small tenants.
Rent: Crop 1812, Martinmas 1811, £15 15s. od.
Proprietor's interest: As 17.
Matters requiring attention at removal: As 5.
Remarks: One tenant warned out; Mr Young to say how his lot to
be possessed.

38 Morness, comprising:
   1. Fourpenny land, Badlurgan, Balfruich.
   Tenant: George McLeod's heirs.
   Rent: Crop 1812, Martinmas 1811, £45.
   Duration: 18 years expiring Whitsunday 1828.
   Proprietor's interest: 'John McKay the last tenant without any
   Right of Meliorations bound to leave the premisses in good repair
   – valued at £54 13s. 10d. at Mr McLeod's entry.'

Tenant's interest: As 4.

Matters requiring immediate attention: 'In the minutes of Tack to be prepared the £54 13s. 10d. to be properly Apportioned among the tenants and they made liable therefore.'

2. Torbreak.

Tenants: 2 named small tenants.

Rent: Crop 1812, Martinmas 1811, £20.

Duration: No lease.

Proprietor's interest: As 38.1.

Tenants' interest: Not ascertained.

Matters requiring immediate attention: As 3.81.

3. Forrisaid.

Tenants: 3 named small tenants.

Rent: £17.

Proprietor's interest: As 38.1.

Tenants' interest: Not ascertained.

Matters requiring immediate attention: As 38.1.

4. Brachie.

Tenant: Alexander McKay, Ironhill.

Rent: Crop 1811, 6 hens; crop 1812, Martinmas 1811, £13.

Duration: 'From Whitsunday 1809, Mr Falconer says 7 years. I have his Renunciation, he holds at will.'

Proprietor's interest: As 38.1.

Tenant's interest: Not ascertained.

Matters requiring immediate attention: As 38.1.

Remarks: 'Mr Young to determine how Brachie to be possessed, and if McKay of Ironhill's lease is to be continued.'

5. Bualrurich.

Tenant: 1 named small tenant.

Rent: Crop 1811, 3 hens; ½ face peats; crop 1812, Martinmas 1811, £10 16s. 6d.

Proprietor's interest: Tenant bound to leave premises in good repair.

Tenant's interest: Not ascertained.

6. Upper Croitcroy.

Tenant: 1 named small tenant.

Rent: Crop 1811, 3 hens, ½ face peats; crop 1812, Martinmas 1811, £9 3s. 6d.

Proprietor's interest: As 38.5.

Tenant's interest: Not ascertained.

7. Lower Croitcroy, part of Brandogie.[1]

Tenants: 2 named small tenants.

Rent: Crop 1811, 7 hens; crop 1812, Martinmas 1811, £13 10s. 0d.

Duration: 'From Whitsunday 1809, 7 years Mr Falconer says but they have no written lease. Mr Young to determine.'

Proprietor's interest: Printed Regulations if their leases stand.

Matters requiring immediate attention: 'See their papers if they any have.'

8. Remainder of Brandogie.[1]

Tenants: 2 named small tenants.

Rent: Crop 1811, 6 hens; crop 1812, Martinmas 1811, £7 10s. 0d.

Duration: As 38.7.

Proprietor's interest: As 38.7.

Matters requiring immediate attention: As 38.7.

39 Achanaluacrach.

Tenants: 3 named small tenants.

Rent: Crop 1812, Martinmas 1811, £33.

Proprietor's interest: As 22.

Matters requiring attention at removal: As 5.

Remarks: One tenant warned out; 'Mr Falconer has fixed that he pays £16 and the other two gets an abatement of Rent. Mr Young to see to it.'

40 Bracachy and miln.

Tenants: 3 named small tenants.

Rent: Crop 1812, Martinmas 1811, £13 3s. 0d.

Proprietor's interest: As 22; 'there is a letter of John Sutherland's of Sciberscross saying that the Miln is worth £3 3s. 0d.'

Matters requiring immediate attention: As 3.

Matters requiring attention at removal: As 5.

41 Aultivault.

Tenants: 2 named small tenants.

Rent: Crop 1812, Martinmas 1811, £9 9s. 0d.

Proprietor's interest: As 22.

[1] *Rectius* Rhiandogie.

Matters requiring immediate attention: As 3.
Matters requiring attention at removal: As 5.

42 Dalreoch.
Tenants: 2 named small tenants.
Rent: Crop 1812, Martinmas 1811, £6.
Proprietor's interest: As 22.
Matters requiring immediate attention: As 3.
Matters requiring attention at removal: As 5.

43 Blarich.
Tenants: 1. Mr Robert Gordon. 2. 15 named small tenants.
Rent: 1. Crop 1812, Martinmas 1811, £20 0s. 6d. 2. Crop 1812,
Martinmas 1811, £77 19s. 6d.
Duration: 1. 'Entered Whitsunday 1807. Mr Falconer says he has a
letter giving him a life rent Tack.' 2. No lease.
Proprietor's interest: 1. Ascertained at his entry to be worth
£83 10s. 0d.
Tenants' interest: 1. Meliorations of £30 on offices beyond present
inventory. 2. 'The people were subtenants and supposed to have a
Right to carry off any bought timbers agreeably to practice.'
Matters requiring immediate attention: 1. 'See his letter from Lady
Stafford and get a tack prepared if the tenant entitled to one.'
2. Ascertain state of right in houses.
Matters requiring attention at removal: As 5.

44 Tannachy.
Tenants: 3 named small tenants.
Rent: Crop 1812, Martinmas 1811, £10.
Proprietor's interest: 'By last lease which expired 1807, the tenant viz.
Lieutenant W. Sutherland bound to leave houses in good repair'
Matters requiring attention at removal: As 5.

45 Craggymore.
Tenant: Angus Ross, Golspie.
Rent: Crop 1812, Martinmas 1811, £9.
Proprietor's interest: As 22.
Matters requiring attention at removal: As 5.

46 Craggybeg.
Tenants: 2 named small tenants.

Rent: Crop 1812, Martinmas 1811, £15.
Proprietor's interest: As 22.
Matters requiring attention at removal: As 5.

47 Shanville.
Tenants: 3 named small tenants.
Rent: Crop 1812, Martinmas 1811, £12.
Proprietor's interest: As 22.
Matters requiring attention at removal: As 5.

48 Grudy.
Tenants: 8 named small tenants.
Rent: Crop 1812, Martinmas 1811, £24 10s. 0d.
Proprietor's interest: As 22.
Tenants' interest: 'Not ascertained but supposed to be entitled agreeably to the Practice of the Country to carry off their bought timber.'

49 Brae Grudy.
Tenant: Lieutenant-Colonel Sutherland.
Rent: Crop 1812, Martinmas 1811, £17.
Proprietor's interest: Tenant bound to leave houses in good condition.
Tenant's interest: Allowed one year's rent on houses and biggings if value left to that amount.
Matters requiring immediate attention: Houses on Brae Grudy to be apprised.

50 Easter Kerrow.
Reservation: Power to resume possession of any part necessary in working coals.[1]
Tenant: Captain John Sutherland.
Rent: Crop 1812, Martinmas 1811, rent £7; fox money £0 1s. 6⁷d.
Duration: 21 years expiring Whitsunday 1818.
Proprietor's interest: Not ascertained.
Tenant's interest: ⅔ of any stone dykes or sunks faced with stone built by him.
Matters requiring immediate attention: To ascertain condition of houses.

---

[1] This reservation is clearly intended to apply to Capt. Sutherland's lands at Brora (see below, p. 97).

51 Gruby.
Tenant: Mrs Boog.
Rent: Crop 1812, Martinmas 1811, £11 1s. 1d.
Duration: From Whitsunday 1789, for life.
Proprietor's interest: Not ascertained.
Matters requiring immediate attention: As 50.

52 Wadset of Muie, viz. 1. Laggan of Muie. 2. Claggin of Muie.
Tenants: 1. 12 named small tenants. 2. 3 named small tenants.
Rent: 1. Crop 1812, Martinmas 1811, £35 3s. 0d. 2. Crop 1812,
Martinmas 1811, £9 5s. 0d.
Proprietor's interest: Not ascertained.
Tenants' interest: 'None unless by practice they may remove any
bought timber.'
Matters requiring immediate attention: As 50.
Matters requiring attention at removal: As 5.

53 Achvelie.
Tenants: 8 named small tenants.
Rent: Crop 1812, Martinmas 1811, £25 9s. 0d.
Proprietor's interest: Not ascertained.
Tenants' interest: As 52.
Matters requiring immediate attention: As 50.
Matters requiring attention at removal: As 5.

54 Rossal.
Tenants: 10 named small tenants.
Rent: Crop 1812, Martinmas 1811, £36 18s. 6d.
Proprietor's interest: Not ascertained.
Tenants' interest: As 52.
Matters requiring immediate attention: As 50.
Matters requiring attention at removal: As 5.

55 Mearlig.
Tenant: Captain R. Gordon.
Rent: Crop 1812, Martinmas 1811, £5.
Proprietor's interest: Not ascertained.
Tenant's interest: As 52.
Matters requiring immediate attention: As 50.
Matters requiring attention at removal: As 5.

F

VI LANDS IN PARISH OF GOLSPIE

1 Ferryoons.
Tenants: D. and F. Taylor.
Rent: Crop 1811, Martinmas 1811, £5 5s. 0d.
Tenants' interest: Full meliorations for all houses.
Matters requiring attention at removal: Houses to be attended to.
Remarks: 'These peoples' possession runs from Whitsunday to Whitsunday and their Rent here inserted is from Whitsunday 1811 to Whitsunday 1812.'

2 Craigtown.
Tenant: Mr George McKay.
Rent: 'Owes £26 as bargained Conversion of Victual Rent Crop 1810 also the Market price of 38 Bolls deficient Victual said Crop payable Martinmas 1811 which are Inserted in list of Arrears to be given me.'
Duration: 19 years expiring Whitsunday 1818.
Proprietor's interest: Tenant bound to leave offices and enclosures worth £209 sterling, that sum having been advanced to defray cost.
Tenant's interest: '£80 for building a new house, exclusive of materials of old one, provided information be given so as such materials be comprised before proceeding to build.'
Matters requiring attention at removal: Houses and enclosures to be atttended to.
Remarks: 'Mr Young's Wadset[1] commenced Grass crop 1810 Corn crop 1811.'

3 Ironhill and Baddin.
Tenant: Alexander McKay.
Rent: Crop 1812, Whitsunday 1812, £30 12s. 6d.
Duration: 19 years expiring Whitsunday 1823.
Proprietor's interest: Not ascertained.
Tenant's interest: '£50 Mr Falconer says on dwelling house provided it value at that Amount, ½ of dykes on Ironhill and ⅔ of dykes on Culmaily Angle which however is included in the Culmaily Wadset.'

[1] William Young received a wadset of Craigtoun (par. Golspie) and Rovy Craigton (par. Rogart) on 3 Oct. 1810; it was redeemed from his trustees on 7 Feb. 1843.

Matters requiring immediate attention: 'See whatever lease or writing he has. Ascertain whether the heritor had any Interest in the houses at his entry.'

Matters requiring attention at removal: As 1.

Remarks: 'McKay's lease on Rhives is still unrenounced and his lease on Ironhill unfitted. His general renunciation in P. Sellar's hands shutts the door as to Rhives.'

4 Kirkton and part of Balblair.

Tenant: Robert McKid.

Rent: Crop 1812, Whitsunday 1812, £100.

Duration: 19 years expiring Whitsunday 1828.

Proprietor's interest: Houses and dykes valued at £124 2s. 0d. at entry.

Tenant's interest: Mr Falconer's printed Regulations.

Matters requiring immediate attention: 'There is a Remonstrance by Mr Falconer against Mr McKid's dwelling house as unsuitable to the farm and a Correspondence between Mr Falconer and Mr McKid on the Subject.'

Remarks: 'Nota for Mr Young. I suspect between old and new there will be sunk in this farm on buildings nineteen years' Rent.'

5 Remainder of Balblair.

Tenants: 4 named small tenants.

Rent: £12.

Tenants' interest: Entitled to carry off bought timber by practice of country.

Remarks: Tenants warned out.

6 Part of Culmaily, viz. Sallichtown, Ballone, Rhiorn, including Sergeant Gordon's croft and hill possessions behind Culmaily and Milnton, being in Colonel Sutherland's wadset.[1]

Tenants: Messrs Young and Sellar.

Rent: Crop 1811, 22 bolls 1 firlot 3 pecks bear; Martinmas 1811, £132 15s. 7½d. crop 1812, Whitsunday 1812, £132 15s. 7½d.

Duration: 30 years expiring Whitsunday 1840.

[1] Capt. (later Lieut.Col.) Alexander Sutherland had a wadset of Culmaily and Farlary (par. Golspie) on 21 February 1784, and an eik of reversion on 9 September 1811; the wadset was redeemed in 1823 from his nephew, who had succeeded to it in 1822. For the problems connected with Young and Sellar's entry to Culmaily Farm see above, pp. xli–xlii.

Proprietor's interest: £1,500 advanced on terms in lease.

Tenants' interest: ⅔ of meliorations beyond said £1,500; full value of 8 cottages.

Matters requiring immediate attention: 'To ascertain what part of Colonel Sutherland's houses, etc., are to be valued to the tenants and Get them Apprized. To Get Instructions how the Remainder thereof are to be disposed of. Vide my Letter to Mr Falconer on the subject.'

Matters requiring attention at removal: 'Attend that the houses, etc., on which the £1,500 expended to be in a fair and tenantable Condition. The Rest to be valued and two thirds thereof to be paid for by the Proprietor. Tenant bound to leave the land in the Rotation expressed in the Tack.'

Remarks: 1. 'The Rent is 30 bolls and £370. Deduct rent of Culmaily Wadset payable to Colonel Sutherland 7 bolls 2 firlots 1 peck and £104 8s. 9d. 22 bolls 1 firlot 3 pecks and £265 11s. 3d. Besides interest at 6½ per Cent on £1,500 advanced.' 2. 'Before Whitsunday 1838 to determine Concerning the Sallichtown Plantation.' 3. 'Sergeant Gordon's croft set for the purpose of Accommodating a Tradesman.' 4. 'The victual rent being converted only at 20s. per Boll and payable in kind if Required at Martinmas preceding Intimation to be regularly made – P.S. of course requires none while Factor.'

7 Drummuie and Old Rhives.

Reservation: Sergeant Gordon's croft.

Tenant: Captain R. Sutherland.

Rent: Crop 1811, 15 bolls bear, 15 bolls meal; crop 1812, Whitsunday 1812, £120.

Duration: 19 years expiring Whitsunday 1828.

Tenant's interest: '£800 to be allowed besides £65 2s. 5½d. which he paid outgoing tenants at entry provided he leave houses not under £1,000, proportional payment to be given if houses value under that Sum.'

Matters requiring attention at removal: Houses to be apprised; tenant to leave land agreeably to Mr Falconer's printed Regulations.

Remarks: Links ground not to be ploughed up; printed Regulations to be attended to.

8 Rhives and part of Golspymore.
Tenant: Mr Falconer.
Proprietor's interest: 'Mr Falconer has a letter from Mr McKenzie attested by Lord Stafford showing that he is entitled to repayment of what he has expended on Inclosures conform to Vouchers to be produced by him.'
Matters requiring immediate attention: Houses and enclosures to be handed over on inventory to incoming tenant.
Matters requiring attention at removal: Same.
Remarks: Tenant to remove; Mr Young to say how to be possessed.

9 Golspymore east parks and one upper park.
Tenants: Sundry villagers for cows.
Proprietor's interest: Enclosures belong to Lady Stafford.
Matters requiring attention at removal: Same.
Remarks: Tenants warned out; Mr Young to say how to be possessed.

9A Golspymore lower park.
Tenant: Mr Falconer.
Rent: £15.
Proprietor's interest: Enclosures of Golspymore valued 3 July 1793 at £11.
Remarks: As 8.

10 Golspy gardens.
Tenants: 7 named small tenants.
Rent: £0 13s. 4d.
Remarks: As 8.

11 Golspy houses.
Tenants: 16 named small tenants (2 of whom have left or died).
Rent: Crop 1812, Martinmas 1811, varying amounts, in total £5 6s. 6d.
Duration: Varying: 2 without leases, 5 not ascertained, 1 of 15 years expiring Whitsunday 1824, 6 of 99 years expiring at various dates after Whitsunday 1900, 2 to be determined.
Proprietor's interest: Varying: 1 none, 5 not ascertained, 1 house to be left in good condition, 7 houses Lady Stafford's at expiry, 2 rights to build houses to be left complete at expiry.

Tenants' interest: None or not ascertained, except in one case tenant entitled to ⅔ meliorations.

Matters requiring immediate attention: 'Would any Condition be proper concerning the preservation of the houses?'

Remarks: In two cases (leases granted at Whitsunday 1810) houses to be slated in 2 years otherwise leases null.

12 Golspie lowlands.
Tenants: Sundry.
Remarks: As 9.

13 Golspie Tower.
Tenants: Crop 1811, Captain William Grant, Mr William Rose, William Ferguson, John Ferguson, John Bookless, Reverend Mr Keith, James Duncan: crop 1812, all warned out except James Duncan.

Rent: Crop 1811, 6 warned out tenants, 60 bolls 0 firlots 1 peck bear: crop 1812, James Duncan, Martinmas 1811, £14; Whitsunday 1812, £15.

Proprietor's interest: 6 warned out tenants, not ascertained; James Duncan, 'Inclosures to have been Apprised at his entry, I see in 1788 the inclosures Valued at £22 3s. 6d.'

Tenants' interest: 6 warned out tenants, not ascertained; James Duncan to get ⅔ meliorations on dykes if he possesses 10 years, if less amount to be referred to men,[1] and to get payment by reference for improvements on farm.

Matters requiring immediate attention: James Duncan, enclosures existing at his entry to be apprised.

Remarks: 'Mr Young to say how to be possessed in lieu of the 6 tenants warned out.'

14 Golspie inn and garden.
Tenant: James Duncan.
Rent: Crop 1812, Martinmas 1811, £7 2s. 9½d.; Whitsunday 1812, £7 2s. 9½d. (includes £4 5s. 2d. interest of money expended on furniture).

Proprietor's interest: House is Lady Stafford's; furniture is valued per Inventory at £85 12s. 4d.

---

[1] For valuation of actual work done on dykes.

Tenant's interest: 'To have meliorations for Inclosures – deducting what may be ascertained as value of his Accommodation but if he possess 10 years he only gets $\frac{2}{3}$ of this.'
Matters requiring immediate attention: Dykes at entry to be ascertained.

15 Golspie mill, garden and grass.
Tenant: Angus McKay.
Rent: Crop 1811, $\frac{1}{2}$ multures for mill; crop 1812, Martinmas 1811, garden and grass £1 10s. 0d.
Proprietor's interest: Not ascertained.
Matters requiring immediate attention: 'Fix value of Mill, etc., and ascertain that the tenant is bound for them.'

16 Blarnafidoch.
Tenant: Alexander Sutherland.
Rent: Crop 1812, Martinmas 1811, £3 10s. 0d.
Tenant's interest: May carry off bought timber by practice of country.

17 Glen.
Tenants: Reverend Mr Keith, John Gunn, James Duncan, Adam McKay, piper.
Rent: Crop 1811, 14 bolls 0 firlots 3 pecks bear: crop 1812, Martinmas 1811, £11 15s. 6$\frac{1}{2}$d.
Proprietor's interest: 3 not ascertained; James Duncan, none.
Tenants' interest: James Duncan to have houses paid by apprisement at removal.
Matters requiring immediate attention: 'See what James Duncan paid the former tenant.'

18 Dunrobin.
Tenant: Lord Stafford.
Rent: Crop 1812, Whitsunday 1812, £450.

19 Backies.
Tenants: 2 named small tenants.
Rent: Crop 1812, Martinmas 1811, £7.
Tenants' interest: As 16.

20 New Backies.
Tenants: 17 named small tenants.
Rent: Crop 1812, Martinmas 1811, £5 19s. 0d.
Tenants' interest: As 16.

21 Clashmore.
Tenants: 4 named small tenants.
Rent: Crop 1812, Martinmas 1811, £1 15s. 0d.
Tenants' interest: As 16.

22 Feu Duty: Uppat.
Tenant: William Munro Esq.
Duty: Crop 1812, Martinmas 1811, £3 0s. 8d.
Matters requiring immediate attention: Ascertain state of titles.

23 Strathlundy and Achlundy.
Tenants: 8 named small tenants.
Rent: Crop 1812, Martinmas 1811, £14 7s. 0d.
Tenants' interest: As 16.

24 Inchfoury and Leadreach.
Tenant: Alexander McKay in Ironhill.
Rent: Crop 1812, Martinmas 1811, £8 16s. 0d.
Duration: 'Not ascertained but the door shut by Renunciation in P. Sellar's hands.'
Proprietor's interest: Not ascertained.
Tenant's interest: As 16.

25 Inchlair.
Tenant: Alexander McKay in Ironhill.
Rent: Crop 1812, Martinmas 1811, £5.
Duration: As 24.
Proprietor's interest: Not ascertained.
Tenant's interest: As 16.

26 Badravan.
Tenants: 2 named small tenants.
Rent: Crop 1812, Martinmas 1811, £1 10s. 0d.
Proprietor's interest: Not ascertained.
Tenants' interest: As 16.

27 Croich.
Tenant: 1 named small tenant.
Rent: Crop 1812, Martinmas 1811, £2.
Proprietor's interest: Not ascertained.
Tenant's interest: As 16.

28 Longuish.
Tenants: W. and I. Ferguson.
Rent: £0 6s. 8d.
Remarks: 'Mr Young to say how this place to be possessed and attend that Lady Stafford ordered this man to be removed on Account of his burning Benvragie Plantation last year.'[1]

29 Ledriag.
Tenant: 1 named small tenant.
Rent: Crop 1812, Martinmas 1811, £1 1s. 0d.

30 Easter Aberscross.
Tenant: John Polson.
Rent: Crop 1812, Martinmas 1811, £32 0s. 6d.; Whitsunday 1812, £32 0s. 6d.
Duration: 19 years expiring Whitsunday 1828.
Proprietor's interest: 'By the former lease which expired 1807 conditioned that houses should have been at Commencement thereof valued over to him and that he was to be allowed meliorations above said value to the extent of one year's rent at his Removal.'
Tenant's interest: As 4.
Matters requiring immediate attention: Ascertain state of houses.
Matters requiring attention at removal: See to houses and mode of cropping.
Remarks: Bound to crop agreeably to Regulations.

31 Wester Aberscross.
Tenants: 15 named small tenants.
Rent: Crop 1811, 33 bolls 2 firlots bear: Crop 1812, Martinmas 1811, £28 4s. 6d.
Tenants' interest: Heritor must pay for bought timber if houses left complete.
Remarks: 'Set to Young and Sellar till 30 years after expiry of present tenants' lease in No. 32 – Rent referred to arbiters.' [*This note crossed out, and added:* 'This Lease set aside.'[2]]

---

[1] These tenants were still in possession in the 1815 rental.
[2] See below, p. 90.

32 Morvich.
Tenant: Mrs McLeod.
Rent: Crop 1812, Martinmas 1811, £15; Whitsunday 1812, £15.
Duration: 'In dispute before the Sheriff of Sutherland.'
Tenant's interest: Apparently entitled to no meliorations.
Matters requiring attention at removal: 'Attend at Conclusion of this suit and get state of houses etc., ascertained.'
Remarks: 'Set to Young and Sellar for 30 years from her Removal at £60 Rent the first ten years, £120 the next and £240 the last.'
[*This note crossed out and added:* 'In Lord Stafford's hand. Mrs. M. has accepted an annuity of £50.'[1]]

VII LANDS IN PARISH OF CLYNE

1 Doll, viz.
   1. Easter three lots of Doll of Brora.
Tenant: William Anderson, kenner of fishings.
Rent: Crop 1811, Christmas 1811 to Candlemas 1812, 28 bolls 1 firlot, 1 lippy victual: crop 1812, Whitsunday 1812, £5 4s. 6d.; fox money £0 4s. 0d.
Duration: 19 years expiring Whitsunday 1812.
Proprietor's interest: Apparently none.
Tenant's interest: 'Tenant bound to inclose the whole with stone dykes or sunk fences faced with Stone within first nine years and to leave the same in good condition. And if the same and houses at the end of his lease amount to £80 he is to be allowed £30 and proportionately for a less sum but not beyond £30.'
Matters requiring immediate attention: 'Has Mr Anderson inclosed this farm?: Has he any Apprising of the houses or any other writing to show how they stood at his entry?'
2. Three penny land of Doll.
Tenants: Sergeant-Major John Sutherland, Alexander Graham.
Rent: Crop 1811, Christmas 1811 to Candlemas 1812, 25 bolls 0 firlots 2 pecks 0 lippies victual: crop 1812, Whitsunday 1812, £2 12s. 1d.
Duration: 19 years expiring Whitsunday 1820.
Proprietor's interest: Not ascertained.

[1] See above, p. xix.

Tenants' interest: Bound to build suitable houses and offices, and to enclose with stone dykes or sunk fences faced with stone; to be left in good repair at end of tack, when payment to one year's rent to be allowed.

Remarks: 'Tenants bound further to deliver when Required, 3½ faces of Peats and the usual quantity of Pultry etc. and to assist at loading and unloading Vessels at Brora in the family's business or pay therefore.'

3. Remainder of Doll.

Tenants: 7 named small tenants.

Rent: Crop 1811, Christmas 1811 to Candlemas 1812, 60 bolls 1 firlot 2 pecks 3 lippies victual: crop 1812, Whitsunday 1812, £16 16s. 10½d.

Proprietor's interest: Not ascertained.

Tenants' interest: Not ascertained.

Matters requiring immediate attention: Not ascertained.

Remarks: One tenant warned out; 'Mr Falconer says that she (Mrs Forbes) has a letter of Tack in the hand of Mr Fraser allowing one year's rent of Meliorations. Mr Young to say how to be [   ]¹ Grass 1811 Corn 1812.'

2 Muiemore and Strath Skinsdale.

Tenant: William Munro Esquire of Uppat.

Rent: Crop 1812, Whitsunday 1812, £150.

Duration: 10 years expiring Whitsunday 1818.

Proprietor's interest: Amount not ascertained, but tenant bound to leave houses, etc. in condition and value as at entry.

Matters requiring immediate attention: See houses, etc. valued.

3 Altendow.

Tenants: 2 named small tenants.

Rent: Crop 1812, Whitsunday 1812, £2 3s. 4d.

4 Feu duty: Carrol.

Tenant: Joseph Gordon Esquire.

Duty: Crop 1812, Whitsunday 1812, £4 6s. 1d.

Matters requiring immediate attention: Endeavour to see title.

¹ MS. torn.

5 Ascoilbeg.
Tenants: 5 named small tenants.
Rent: Crop 1812, Whitsunday 1812, £25.
Proprietor's interest: By tack expired in 1807 tenants bound to leave premises in good order.
Matters requiring attention at removal: See houses, etc. are left in good order.

6 Ascoilmore and miln.
Tenants: 4 named small tenants.
Rent: Crop 1812, Whitsunday 1812, £24 15s. od.
Proprietor's interest: As 5.
Matters requiring attention at removal: As 5.

7 Grinan.
Tenant: Reverend Mr William[1] Ross.
Rent: Crop 1811, 28 bolls bear.
Duration: Tenant's incumbency.
Proprietor's interest: 'By lease granted in September 1810 houses and dykes on Grinan ordered to be then Appretiated and like Value left at tenant's Removal – not yet Valued.'
Matters requiring immediate attention: 'Get the houses valued that the Amount to be left by him on the Premisses may be ascertained.'
Remarks: Tenant bound to conform to printed Regulations; former meliorations of £7 on Grinan appear by lease to have been paid him in his first year's rent.
Clyne Kirkton, Tourammore, Crag-roy, Beaugie.
Tenant: Reverend Mr William[1] Ross.
Rent: Crop 1812, Whitsunday 1812, £8 9s. 8d.
Proprietor's interest: 'By the old lease which expired 1807, no mention of any heritor's Inventory.'
Tenant's interest: Old lease allows meliorations of one year's rent.
Matters requiring immediate attention: Same.
Remarks: Same.

8 Rhimiscan.
Tenants: 2 named small tenants.
Rent: Crop 1812, Whitsunday 1812, £14 6s. od.

[1] *Rectius* Walter.

Proprietor's interest: By last lease, expiring Whitsunday 1807, tenants bound to leave houses, etc. in good repair.
Matters requiring immediate attention: As 5.

9 Achness.
Tenants: 2 named small tenants.
Rent: Crop 1812, Whitsunday 1812, £11.
Proprietor's interest: Not ascertained.
Tenants' interest: Not ascertained.
Matters requiring immediate attention: Ascertain state of houses, etc.

10 Crislich.
Tenant: 1 named small tenant.
Rent: Crop 1812, Whitsunday 1812, £9.
Proprietor's interest: Not ascertained.
Tenant's interest: Not ascertained.
Matters requiring immediate attention: As 9.

11 Foich.
Tenant: 1 named small tenant.
Rent: Crop 1812, Whitsunday 1812, £2.
Proprietor's interest: Not ascertained.
Tenant's interest: Not ascertained.
Matters requiring immediate attention: As 9.

12 Cupernahoist.
Tenant: 1 named small tenant.
Rent: Crop 1812, Whitsunday 1812, £7.
Proprietor's interest: Not ascertained.
Tenant's interest: Not ascertained.
Matters requiring immediate attention: As 9.

13 Polly.
Tenant: John Macdonald.
Rent: Crop 1812, Whitsunday 1812, £11.
Proprietor's interest: Not ascertained.
Tenant's interest: Not ascertained.
Matters requiring immediate attention: As 9.

14 Aulmalt.
Tenants: 2 named small tenants.

Rent: Crop 1812, Whitsunday 1812, £15.
Proprietor's interest: Not ascertained.
Tenants' interest: Not ascertained.
Matters requiring immediate attention: As 9.

15 Dalbreak, south side of the water.
Tenants: 2 named small tenants.
Rent: Crop 1812, Whitsunday 1812, £4.
Proprietor's interest: Not ascertained.
Tenants' interest: Not ascertained.
Matters requiring immediate attention: As 9.

Dalbreak, north side of the water.
Tenant: 1 named small tenant.
Rent: Crop 1812, Whitsunday 1812, £3 10s. 0d.
Proprietor's interest: Not ascertained.
Tenant's interest: Not ascertained.

16 Kilfedderbeg and croft.
Tenants: 2 named small tenants.
Rent: Crop 1812, Whitsunday 1812, £11.
Proprietor's interest: Houses, etc. belong to proprietor, tenants being by last lease, expired 1807, bound to leave them in good condition.
Matters requiring immediate attention: As 9.
Matters requiring attention at removal: Houses to be left in good condition.

17 Outfield [of Kilfedderbeg].
Tenant: 1 named small tenant.
Rent: Crop 1812, Whitsunday 1812, £1 10s. 0d.
Proprietor's interest: As 16.
Matters requiring immediate attention: As 9.
Matters requiring attention at removal: As 16.

18 Cluaig and Culrain.
Tenant: 1 named small tenant.
Rent: Crop 1812, Whitsunday 1812, £6 10s. 0d.
Proprietor's interest: Houses, etc. belong to proprietor and must be left complete.
Matters requiring immediate attention: As 9.
Matters requiring attention at removal: As 16.

19 Clyne Milnton and miln.
Tenants: 1. Miss Lucy Gordon; 2. Margaret McLeod, widow; 3. Roderick Cameron.
Rent: Crop 1812, Whitsunday 1812, 1. £11 13s. 8½d.; 2. £18; 3. £32; fox money, 1. £0 1s. 11½d.
Duration: 1. 19 years expiring Whitsunday 1812. 2, 3. No lease.
Proprietor's interest: 1. As 18; tenant bound to leave stone dykes or sunk fences to value of £35; 2, 3. Not ascertained.
Tenants' interest: 1. None; 2, 3. Not ascertained.
Matters requiring immediate attention: 1. As 9: 2, 3. Not ascertained.

20 Knockglass and part of Clynemilton.
Tenant: 1 named small tenant.
Rent: Crop 1812, Whitsunday 1812, £6.
Proprietor's interest: Not ascertained.
Tenant's interest: Not ascertained.
Matters requiring immediate attention: Not ascertained.

21 Clynelish, Craigultan and Badneallan, Ardrochie, Drumie, Achnibrodale,[1] Camlea, Dalchallan, Keilbrora, Islandacra, Fanich, Kilivian, Leadoch, Yarchule.
Reservations: 1. 'Power to Resume possession of any part of the lands necessary in the working of coals on proportional abatement of Rent and allowance for Inclosures or other improvements thereon to be determined by Reference': 2. 'Power to Resume possession of any part of the Muirs between the lands of Aultindown on East, and Church road on West for the Accomodation of salmon fishers without any Allowance.'
Tenant: Hugh Houston Esquire.
Rent: Converted victual crop 1809, Martinmas 1811, £26 14s. 0d.: crop 1811, 44 bolls bear: crop 1812, Whitsunday 1812, £67 4s. 5⁵d.; fox money £0 15s. 0d.
Duration: 27 years expiring Whitsunday 1820.
Proprietor's interest: 1. 'Tenant is liable for value of the houses, buildings, etc. on the premises at his entry and to leave £300 worth more, viz. in dwelling house £150, Stone dykes and sunks faced with stone or hedges, £150, and to keep and leave them in good condition. The Houses, etc. which existed at his entry are ordered

[1] *Rectius* Achrimsdale.

to be valued by four impartial persons and the improvements to be estimated in like manner at his Removal. But I see no Inventory of what was on the premisses at his entry altho' in a memorandum in Combie's hand £7 6s. 6d. is set down as interest of the value of Inclosures then there.' 2. 'Burn of Clynilish to be left straightened in its course thro' the Arable land the proprietor paying half of Expence not Exceeding £10 10s. od.'

Tenant's interest: Meliorations of £100, and half of expense of straightening burn of Clynelish not exceeding £10 10s. od., if not advanced at entry.

Matters requiring immediate attention: 'Tenant is bound to pay a dry multure to the lands of Doll, query – Is this paid?': bound to plant 4 acres of muir with plants from Dunrobin nursery: ascertain state of houses at entry: 'Any advance made at his Entry?'

Matters requiring attention at removal: 'See that the houses and Inclosures, etc. be all complete and of the value expressed in the Tack.'

Remarks: At Whitsunday 1812 additional rent of £15.

22 Glaslochan.
Tenant: Hugh Houston Esquire.
Rent: Crop 1811, 3 bolls 1 firlot bear: Crop 1812, Whitsunday 1812, £1 13s. 10^{6}d.
Proprietor's interest: Not ascertained.
Tenant's interest: Not ascertained.
Matters requiring attention at removal: 'Tenant bound to Render 14 Acres of this farm and Inver Brora (which is a wadset held by Mr Colin McKenzie) arable before his Removal.'

23 House at Brora occupied as a schoolhouse.
Tenant: Hugh Houston Esquire.
Rent: Crop 1812, Whitsunday 1812, £2.
Proprietor's interest: Not ascertained.
Tenant's interest: Not ascertained.

24 Kelp shores between Dornoch and the Ord.
Reservations: 'Red ware to belong to the tenants for manuring their land. The Shore to be put into three Divisions and one Division only cut each year. No ware to be burnt below the farm of Dunrobin when the family in the Country.'

Tenant: Hugh Houston Esquire.
Rent: Crop 1811, Martinmas 1811, £70.
Duration: 7 years expiring Whitsunday 1815.
Remarks: Rent rises to £90 at Whitsunday 1812; 'there appears an error in Mr McKenzie's draft lease. He makes the first year's Rent payable Martinmas 1809 in place of 1808. Had the subject been corn land the first crop would have been 1809 – not so kelp shores – to be investigated.'

25 Brora Easter and Auldririe.
Tenant: Captain John Sutherland.
Rent: Crop 1812, Whitsunday 1812, £50; fox money £0 3s. 2½d.
Duration: 21 years expiring Whitsunday 1818.
Proprietor's interest: 'Would appear from a letter of the tenants in the lease to be £53.'
Tenant's interest: Houses beyond said £53 not exceeding £50; ⅔ of stone dykes, etc. not exceeding £100.
Matters requiring immediate attention: See any inventory made at entry.

Sciberscross and Easter Kerrow.
Reservations: 'As in No. 1st.'[1]
Tenant: Captain John Sutherland.
Rent: Crop 1812, Whitsunday 1812, £40; fox money £0 3s. 6d.
Duration: 21 years expiring Whitsunday 1818.
Tenant's interest: Value of houses to be allowed not exceeding £36.

26 Killian.
Tenant: Marquis of Stafford.
Rent: Crop 1812, Whitsunday 1812, £50.
Remarks: 'Subset to Hugh McPherson Brora for 9 years from Whitsunday 1804 at £100, Meliorations being allowed him to the Extent of £40. The Value of the houses at his entry not ascertained. Perhaps it would make no difference to insert his name and Rent in the Rental in place of Lord Stafford's.'

[1] There appears to be an omission in the immediately preceding entry for Brora Easter and Auldririe. The reservation probably concerned the resumption of land for coalmining (see above, Clyne, no. 21). Capt. Sutherland later complained bitterly of being deprived of land at Brora, in addition to quarrelling bitterly with Hugh Houstoun of Clynelish over their marches. He was suspected of encouraging resistance to removals as a result.

G

27 Kylvrannie.
Tenants: 4 named small tenants.
Rent: Crop 1812, Martinmas 1811, £6 12s. od.

28 Rhiory.
Tenant: 1 named small tenant.
Rent: Crop 1812, Martinmas 1811, £2 10s. od.

29 Badnacardich.
Tenants: 3 named small tenants.
Rent: Crop 1812, Martinmas 1811, £7 10s. od.

30 Rhianbeg.
Tenant: 1 named small tenant.
Rent: Crop 1812, Martinmas 1811, £3.
Proprietor's interest: Not ascertained.
Tenant's interest: Not ascertained.
Matters requiring immediate attention: Ascertain what were houses on
farm at entry.

31 Urachyle.
Tenants: 3 named small tenants.
Rent: Crop 1812, Martinmas 1811, £10 10s. od.

32 Kilfidder and miln.
Tenants: 3 named small tenants.
Rent: Crop 1812, Martinmas 1811, £10 15s. od.

33 Storral.
Tenant: 1 named small tenant.
Rent: Crop 1812, Martinmas 1811, £8.

34 Torry Sulaier.
Tenant: 1 named small tenant.
Rent: Crop 1812, Martinmas 1811, £6.

35 Ellanin.
Tenant: 1 named small tenant.
Rent: Crop 1812, Martinmas 1811, £4 10s. od.

VIII LANDS IN PARISH OF LOTH

1 Lothbeg.
Tenant: Mr Thomas Houston in right of deceased James McKay.
Rent: Crop 1812, Martinmas 1811, £225; fox money £1 5s. 6d.
Duration: 19 years expiring Whitsunday 1816.
Proprietor's interest: 'By the lease in favour of Dougald Gilchrist of date 16th March 1773 the proprietor advanced £260 in houses etc. and the tenant was bound to leave them in good repair. By the present lease the tenant is bound to leave the house biggings and inclosures built on the lands in good condition, and not under same value as they were at his entry. There is no valuation.'
Matters requiring immediate attention: 'Were the houses apprised at his entry and who has the Inventories?'
Matters requiring attention at removal: 'Attend that the houses and Inclosures be left of same value as at tenant's entry; and that all houses built, since beginning of the lease be in good Condition.'

Part of Slatel Forest.
Tenant: Mr Thomas Houston.
Rent: Crop 1812, Martinmas 1811, £10.
Proprietor's interest: Not ascertained.
Tenant's interest: Not ascertained.

2 Whitehill.
Tenant: Mr George Munro.
Rent: Crop 1811, bear deliverable Martinmas 1811, 38 bolls 0 firlots 2 pecks 2 lippies: crop 1812, Martinmas 1811, £17 11s. 0d.; fox money £0 8s. 8d.
Duration: 19 years expiring Whitsunday 1817.
Proprietor's interest: Houses, etc. to have been valued at entry and left of equal value, but no inventory.
Tenant's interest: £50 for stone dykes or sunk fences faced with stone.
Matters requiring immediate attention: As 1.
Matters requiring attention at removal: As 1.

3 Lothmore.
Reservation: Part lying between Whitehill and sea, at an appretiated rent.

Tenant: Reverend George Gordon.

Rent: Crop 1811, bear deliverable Martinmas 1811, 57 bolls: crop 1812, Martinmas 1811, £4 6s. 0d.; fox money £0 10s. 1d.

Duration: From Whitsunday 1801, during incumbency and until next term thereafter.

Proprietor's interest: Tenant bound to uphold built houses or to be built and to leave them in good condition.

Tenant's interest: 'None by law, but by a Correspondence with Mr Falconer in 1807 he was allowed Meliorations on Stone dykes on any line approven to the extent of one year's Rent.'

Matters requiring immediate attention: 'Ascertain how the houses stood at his entry and how they are now. Expiscate the nature of the deduction given by Combie and how the Stipend stands.'

Remarks: 'In Case of his raising a process of Augmentation[1] the lease Immediately falls; and if he violently possess a year longer it must be at double rent. There is a letter of Combie's allowing a Deduction of 10 bolls from Mr Gordon's Rent on Account of his demanding no Augmentation, and this has been allowed by Mr Falconer.'

4 Kilmote.

Tenant: Mrs Elizabeth Forbes or McCulloch, relict of deceased George McCulloch, minister of Loth.

Rent: Crop 1812, Martinmas 1811, £22; fox money £0 7s. 3d.

Duration: 'During Mrs McCulloch's life and for 7 years thereafter provided the Children of the tenant personally possess the same during said last period.'

Proprietor's interest: Tenant bound to leave houses in same condition as found, to value of £71 13s. 10½d. mason work and £61 17s. 4d. wright work.

Matters requiring immediate attention: See houses are left to said value.

5 Culgower and Wester Garty.

Tenant: Miss C. Leith in right of late David Geddes.

Rent: Crop 1812, Martinmas 1811, £100; Whitsunday 1812, £100.

---

[1] In 1791 the presbytery of Dornoch approached John Fraser asking for an early decision on a request for general augmentation of stipend. The Factor's Accounts show that in 1795 stipend payments from the Sutherland Estate increased from £250 to £570. The provision described here appears to be an attempt to prevent further individual applications to the Court of Teinds for augmentations (see also above, p. 51, and below, ii, p. 197).

Duration: 19 years expiring Whitsunday 1828.
Proprietor's interest: Houses said to have been apprised and inventories left with tenant.
Tenant's interest: Mr Falconer's printed Regulations.
Matters requiring immediate attention: 'Get Copy of the Inventories from the tenant and see the parties' Interest in the houses correctly stated.'

6 Midgarty and half davoch of Wester Garty.
Tenants: Captain Baigrie's heirs.
Rent: 46 bolls 0 firlots 3 pecks 2 lippies; £78 3s. 3d.
Duration: Last lease from Whitsunday 1787 expired.
Proprietor's interest: 'There is mention in the Tack of £70 Meliorations allowed the former tenant. The tenant is bound to lay out as follows: Dwelling house and offices (the timber being furnished from Balblair) £150; removing Cairns and draining £60; Inclosures £150. The Apprisements at his entry are: Mason work £49 4s. 8½d.; Wright work £29 4s. 0d.'
Matters requiring attention at removal: See houses are left conform to tack.
Remarks: Tenants warned out; Mr Young to set this farm.

7 Dry multures of Gartymore and miln.
Tenants: Lieutenant McKay, Wester Helmsdale; Landale and Redpath, Easter Helmsdale; Marrel tenants.
Rent: Crop 1811, payable between Christmas 1811 and Candlemas 1812, 2 bolls 2 firlots victual.
Proprietor's interest: Not ascertained as to miln.
Tenants' interest: Same.
Matters requiring immediate attention: Inventory to miln.

IX LANDS IN PARISH OF KILDONAN

1 Costally.
Tenants: 2 named small tenants.
Rent: Crop 1812, Martinmas 1811, £12.
Proprietor's interest: Tenants bound by last lease to leave houses in good condition.
Matters requiring attention at removal: Houses to be left conform to tack.

2 Dalvait and Tuary.
Tenant: Captain Gordon Clunas.
Rent: Crop 1812, Martinmas 1811, £42.
Duration: 7 years expiring Whitsunday 1817.
Proprietor's interest: Not ascertained.
Matters requiring immediate attention: 'Get copy of Minute sent Lord Gower and see every thing properly fitted – if possible insert a Clause forbidding the tenant from breaking up any pasture at his removal.'
Remarks: Lease said to have been sent to Lord Gower by Mr Falconer.

3 Duchyle and Craggy.
Tenant: Captain Gordon Clunas.
Rent: Crop 1812, Martinmas 1811, £12 0s. 10d.
Proprietor's interest: Not ascertained.

4 West Kilernan and miln.
Tenants: 4 named small tenants.
Rent: Crop 1812, Martinmas 1811, £13.
Proprietor's interest: As 1.
Matters requiring attention at removal: As 1.

5 Easter Kilernan.
Tenants: 6 named small tenants.
Rent: Crop 1812, Martinmas 1811, £19 10s. 0d.
Proprietor's interest: Not ascertained.
Tenants' interest: Not ascertained.
Matters requiring immediate attention: See to state of houses.
Matters requiring attention at removal: As 1.

6 Badfleuch.
Tenants: 3 named small tenants.
Rent: Crop 1812, Martinmas 1811, £10 10s. 0d.
Proprietor's interest: Tenants bound to leave houses in good condition.
Matters requiring attention at removal: As 1.

7 Dalcharn.
Tenant: Alexander Gordon.
Rent: Crop 1812, Martinmas 1811, £14.
Proprietor's interest: As 6.
Matters requiring attention at removal: As 1.

8 Balnahown.
Tenants: 4 named small tenants.
Rent: Crop 1812, Martinmas 1811, £14.
Proprietor's interest: As 6.
Matters requiring attention at removal: As 1.

9 Balvoullan.
Tenants: 3 named small tenants.
Rent: Crop 1812, Martinmas 1811, £15 15s. od.
Proprietor's interest: As 6.
Matters requiring attention at removal: As 1.

10 Borable Eachder.
Tenants: 5 named small tenants.
Rent: Crop 1812, Martinmas 1811, £10 10s. od.
Proprietor's interest: As 6.
Matters requiring attention at removal: As 1.

11 Fenofal.
Tenants: 2 named small tenants.
Rent: Crop 1812, Martinmas 1811, £10 10s. od.
Proprietor's interest: As 6.
Matters requiring attention at removal: As 1.

12 Knockfin.
Tenant: Mr George Munro, Whitehill.
Rent: Crop 1812, Martinmas 1811, £31 19s. 5d.
Duration: 19 years expiring Whitsunday 1817.
Proprietor's interest: As 6.
Matters requiring attention at removal: As 1.

13 Kinbrace, Shinachy, Achneakans and Achnahow.
Tenant: Lieutenant William Gunn.
Rent: Crop 1812, Martinmas 1811, £135.
Duration: 19 years expiring Whitsunday 1829.
Proprietor's interest: Not ascertained.
Tenant's interest: Not ascertained.
Matters requiring immediate attention: 'Ascertain the state of the houses and the Interest of parties therein. If possible insert a clause in the

Tack to prevent any of the pasture from being broken up at Tenant's Removal.'

Matters requiring attention at removal: See that Regulations are fulfilled.

Remarks: Ground for the meeting house at Aldnahow reserved without deduction of rent.

14 Altindown.
Tenant: Alexander McKay.
Rent: Crop 1812, Martinmas 1811, £30.
Duration: Renounced.
Proprietor's interest: Not ascertained.
Tenant's interest: Not ascertained.
Matters requiring immediate attention: As 5.

15 Tomich.
Tenants: 2 named small tenants.
Rent: Crop 1812, Martinmas 1811, £15 15s. od.
Proprietor's interest: As 6.
Matters requiring immediate attention: As 5.
Matters requiring attention at removal: As 1.

16 Dallagan.
Tenant: John McDonald in Polly.
Rent: £20.
Proprietor's interest: As 6.
Matters requiring immediate attention: As 5.
Matters requiring attention at removal: As 1.
Remarks: Tenant warned out; Mr Young to say how to be possessed.

17 Calab.
Tenants: 2 named small tenants.
Rent: Crop 1812, Martinmas 1811, £14.
Proprietor's interest: As 6.
Matters requiring immediate attention: Ascertain state of houses and interest of parties therein.
Matters requiring attention at removal: As 13.

18 Terromich.[1]
Tenants: 3 named small tenants.
Rent: Crop 1812, Martinmas 1811, £17.

[1] *Rectius* Ferranich.

Proprietor's interest: As 6.
Matters requiring immediate attention: As 17.
Matters requiring attention at removal: As 13.

19 Branchilly and Reist.
Tenant: Grazing of Dunrobin.
Rent: Crop 1812, Martinmas 1811, £40 5s. 0d.
Proprietor's interest: As 6.
Matters requiring immediate attention: As 17.
Matters requiring attention at removal: As 13.

20 Eachder Free.
Tenants: 6 named small tenants.
Rent: Crop 1812, Martinmas 1811, £15.
Proprietor's interest: Not ascertained.
Tenants' interest: How do the houses stand?
Matters requiring immediate attention: As 17.

21 Cain and Kilfidder.
Tenants: Heirs of Mr Pope, Navidale.
Rent: Crop 1812, Martinmas 1811, £35.
Duration: 38 years expiring Whitsunday 1836.
Proprietor's interest: Tenant bound to leave houses, biggings and fences in good condition.
Matters requiring immediate attention: As 17.
Matters requiring attention at removal: As 13.

22 Torish.
Tenants: 8 named small tenants.
Rent: Crop 1812, Martinmas 1811, £24.
Proprietor's interest: Not ascertained.
Matters requiring immediate attention: As 17.
Matters requiring attention at removal: As 13.

23 Kildonan.
Tenants: Reverend Mr Sage and 8 named small tenants.
Rent: Crop 1812, Martinmas 1811, £43 12s. 0d.
Proprietor's interest: Not ascertained.
Tenants' interest: As 20.
Matters requiring immediate attention: As 17.

24 Dalchalmy.
Tenants: 6 named small tenants.
Rent: Crop 1812, Martinmas 1811, £12 12s. od.
Proprietor's interest: As 6.
Tenants' interest: As 20.
Matters requiring immediate attention: As 17.
Matters requiring attention at removal: As 13.

25 Suisgall.
Tenant: Mr Thomas Houston.
Rent: Crop 1812, Martinmas 1811, £80.
Duration: 19 years expiring Whitsunday 1826.
Proprietor's interest: As 6.
Tenant's interest: Meliorations of £60 for building a shepherd's house; tup park and fank to be built of stone.
Matters requiring immediate attention: 'Nota that a Clause be endeavoured to be got into his lease prohibiting to break up any of the pasture at his Removal.'
Matter requiring attention at removal: 'Attend to comprisement of houses and that none of pasture be broke up.'

26 Kinvaid.
Tenants: 2 named small tenants.
Rent: Crop 1812, Martinmas 1811, £12.
Proprietor's interest: As 25.

27 Balnavalsach.
Tenants: 7 named small tenants.
Rent: Crop 1812, Martinmas 1811, £28.
Proprietor's interest: As 21.
Matters requiring attention at removal: Same.

28 Duible.
Tenants: 6 named small tenants.
Rent: Crop 1812, Martinmas 1811, £10.
Proprietor's interest: Not ascertained.
Matters requiring immediate attention: As 5.

29 Guilable.
Tenants: 3 named small tenants.
Rent: Crop 1812, Martinmas 1811, £12 12s od.

Proprietor's interest: Not ascertained.
Matters requiring immediate attention: As 5.

30 Eldurable.
Tenants: 5 named small tenants.
Rent: Crop 1812, Martinmas 1811, £13.
Proprietor's interest: Not ascertained.
Matters requiring immediate attention: As 5.

31 Grudsary, a pendicle of same.
Tenants: 3 named small tenants.
Rent: Crop 1812, Martinmas 1811, £3 2s. 0d.
Proprietor's interest: Not ascertained.
Matters requiring immediate attention: As 5.

32 Skalbesdale.
Tenants: 6 named small tenants.
Rent: Crops 1812, Martinmas 1811, £16 10s. 0d.
Proprietor's interest: Not ascertained.
Matters requiring immediate attention: As 5.

33 Corrish.
Tenants: 2 named small tenants.
Rent: Crop 1812, Martinmas 1811, £7 10s. 0d.

34 Balintorig.
Tenant: 1 named small tenant.
Rent: Crop 1812, Martinmas 1811, £3.
Proprietor's interest: Not ascertained.
Matters requiring immediate attention: As 5.

35 Achrindle and Prescan.
Tenant: Mr Gordon of Carroll.
Rent: Crop 1812, Martinmas 1811, £6.

Mr Dundas wadset, now redeemed.[1]
36 Ulbster.
Tenants: 7 named small tenants.
Rent: Crop 1812, Martinmas 1811, £14 14s. 0d.

[1] William Dundas (1762-1845), nephew of Henry Dundas, Viscount Melville, was granted a wadset of Ulbster, Loist, Breakachy, Achnamoin, Gearnsary, Grimachory and Arichliny (all par. Kildonan) on 27 March 1797; this wadset was redeemed on 15 May 1810.

Proprietor's interest: By last lease, expired Whitsunday 1807, tenants bound to leave houses, biggings, and fences in good condition.
Matters requiring attention at removal: See that houses are left in tenantable condition.

37 Loist.
Tenants: Captain Baigrie's heirs.
Rent: £10.
Proprietor's interest: Not ascertained.
Matters requiring immediate attention: As 5.
Remarks: Tenants warned out; Mr Young to say how to be possessed.

38 Auchlury.[1]
Tenant: 1 named small tenant.
Rent: Crop 1812, Martinmas 1811, £8.
Proprietor's interest: Not ascertained.
Matters requiring immediate attention: As 5.

39 Outfield of Auchlury.[1]
Tenant: 1 named small tenant.
Rent: Crop 1812, Martinmas 1811, £3.
Proprietor's interest: Not ascertained.
Matters requiring immediate attention: As 5.

40 Breakachy.
Tenants: Thomas and John Gordon.
Rent: Crop 1812, Martinmas 1811, £35.
Proprietor's interest: Houses to be left in good condition.
Matters requiring immediate attention: As 5.

41 Achnamoin.
Tenant: Mr Thomas Gordon.
Rent: Crop 1812, Martinmas 1811, £14 14s. od.
Proprietor's interest: As 40.
Matters requiring attention at removal: As 36.

42 Garnsiry.
Tenants: 2 named small tenants.
Rent: Crop 1812, Martinmas 1811, £15.

[1] *Rectius* Arichliny.

Proprietor's interest: As 40.
Matters requiring attention at removal: As 36.

43 Grimochary.
Tenant: Joseph Gordon Esquire of Carroll.
Rent: Crop 1812, Martinmas 1811, £20.
Proprietor's interest: 'The old Tack is silent.'
Tenant's interest: To be ascertained.
Matters requiring immediate attention: As 5.
Matters requiring attention at removal: As 36.

44 Ascoig.
Tenants: 4 named small tenants.
Rent: Crop 1812, Martinmas 1811, £16 16s. od.
Proprietor's interest: As 6.
Tenants' interest: As 43.
Matters requiring attention at removal: As 36.

X LANDS IN PARISH OF FARR

1 Ardnieskich, Achniskeich, including Bettyhill, Rhinechattle, Docharn, Achana, Achkylnaborgie, Crask, one penny of Farr, Gharve.
Tenant: Captain William Gordon.
Rent: Crop 1812, Martinmas 1811, £62; fox money £1 2s. 5½d.
Duration: 19 years expiring Whitsunday 1812.
Proprietor's interest: Tenant to leave houses, biggings and offices at expiry of lease in condition and repair as found, but no appretiation at entry exists.
Tenant's interest: 'By lease to Charles Gordon and which expired 1793, ½ of all improvements, etc. allowed to the extent of £75, which not to be asked, if tenant Remained 11 years more at old Rent of £33 10s. od. Ascertain what done in 1793.'
Matters requiring immediate attention: Ascertain value of houses at entry, so that any deterioration at removal may be paid for.
Matters requiring attention at removal: See houses are left entire.

2 Miln of Farr and Clachan.
Tenant: Captain William Gordon.
Rent: Crop 1812, Martinmas 1811, £20.

Proprietor's interest: As 1.
Matters requiring attention at removal: As 1.

3 Farr.
Tenants: 12 named small tenants.
Rent: Crop 1812, Martinmas 1811, £54.
Proprietor's interest: Tenants to leave houses, biggings and fences in good condition.
Matters requiring attention at removal: As 1.

4 Feu Duty: Dureness.
Tenant: Lord Reay.
Duty: Crop 1812, Martinmas 1811, £9 0s. 5½d.
Matters requiring immediate attention: 'Endeavour to see the Title.'

5 Swordly.
Tenants: 5 named small tenants.
Rent: Crop 1812, Martinmas 1811, £25.
Proprietor's interest: As 3.

6 Cromeran.
Tenant: 1 named small tenant.
Rent: Crop 1812, Martinmas 1811, £8.
Proprietor's interest: Not ascertained.
Tenant's interest: Not ascertained.
Matters requiring immediate attention: Ascertain state of houses, etc.

7 Ravigill.
Tenants: 11 named small tenants (1 warned out).
Rent: Crop 1812, Martinmas 1811, £31 5s. 1½d.
Proprietor's interest: Tenants to leave houses in good condition.
Remarks: One tenant warned out; Mr Young to say how to be possessed.

8 Rhiphail.
Tenants: 1. Captain Hugh McKay, Tubeg. 2. 8 named small tenants.
Rent: Crop 1812, Martinmas 1811, 1. £12; 2. £18.
Tenants' interest: 'By lease expiring 1807, Meliorations allowed to the extent of one year's Rent on stone and lime biggings or sunk fences faced with Stone for ascertainment of which the premises

were ordered to have been valued at his entry but no Apprisement is extant.'

Matters requiring immediate attention: 'Can the value of the houses at tenants' entry be ascertained?'

9 Rhimoy and Achumore.
Tenants: 1. Mrs Margaret Gordon. 2. 3 named small tenants.
Rent: Crop 1812, Martinmas 1811, 1. £16 18s. 0d.; 2. £4 14s. 6d.
Proprietor's interest: Not ascertained.
Tenants' interest: Not ascertained.
Matters requiring immediate attention: As 6.
Remarks: Mrs Gordon warned out; Mr Young to say how her lot to be possessed.

Achinlochy.
Tenants: 8 named small tenants.
Rent: Crop 1812, Martinmas 1811, £18 7s. 10½d.
Proprietor's interest: Not ascertained.
Tenants' interest: Not ascertained.
Matters requiring immediate attention: As 6.

10 Mudle Tubeg.
Tenant: Captain Hugh McKay.
Rent: Crop 1812, Martinmas 1811, £30.
Proprietor's interest: Tenant bound to leave houses entire.
Matters requiring attention at removal: Houses to be left in good condition.

Grumbeg.
Tenants: 5 named small tenants.
Rent: Crop 1812, Martinmas 1811, £27.
Proprietor's interest: As 10 above.
Matters requiring attention at removal: As 10 above.

11 Dallachavish.
Tenants: 2 named small tenants.
Rent: Crop 1812, Martinmas 1811, £6.
Proprietor's interest: Not ascertained.
Tenants' interest: Not ascertained.
Matters requiring immediate attention: As 6.
Matters requiring attention at removal: As 10.

12 Dimcheory.
Tenants: 3 named small tenants.
Rent: Crop 1812, Martinmas 1811, £10.
Proprietor's interest: As 7.
Matters requiring attention at removal: As 10.

13 Truderskaig, west and east ends.
Tenants: West end, 9 named small tenants: east end, 5 named small tenants.
Rent: Crop 1812, Martinmas 1811, west end, £10 19s. 11½d.; east end, £10 1s. 10½d.
Proprietor's interest: As 7.
Matters requiring immediate attention: As 10.

14 Skelpick and miln.
Tenants: 1. Lieutenant John Gordon. 2. Donald Munro. 3. 10 named small tenants.
Rent: Crop 1812, Martinmas 1811, 1. £16 10s. 0d.; 2. £14 10s. 0d.; 3. £25.
Proprietor's interest: As 7.
Tenants' interest: 'By last lease which expired 1807 tenants allowed Meliorations to the Extent of one year's Rent but state of houses and others at their entry not ascertained.'
Matters requiring immediate attention: If possible ascertain state of houses at entry.
Matters requiring attention at removal: As 10.
Remarks: Lieutenant Gordon warned out; Mr Young to say how to be possessed.

15 Dunveiden.
Tenants: 12 named small tenants.
Rent: Crop 1812, Martinmas 1811, £33.
Proprietor's interest: As 7.
Tenants' interest: As 14.
Matters requiring immediate attention: As 14.
Matters requiring attention at removal: As 10.

16 Grubmore and outfields.
Tenants: 20 named small tenants, 3 unnamed small tenants.
Rent: Crop 1812, Martinmas 1811, £33 4s. 3d.

Proprietor's interest: As 7.

Matters requiring immediate attention: 'Query Ground officer who are the three unnamed tenants of Outfield.'

Matters requiring attention at removal: 'Attend that houses are not destroyed.'

Remarks: 'Mr Falconer Refers to the Ground officer for the unnamed tenants of Grubmore.'

17 Ardraavine of Mudle, with grazings of the braeface of Criggydow.

Tenant: Duncan Matthieson Esquire.

Rent: Crop 1812, Martinmas 1811, £30.

Proprietor's interest: Not ascertained.

Tenant's interest: Not ascertained.

Matters requiring immediate attention: As 6.

The following lands part of the late General McKenzie of Suddey's wadset, now redeemed.[1]

18 Part of Easter and Wester Carnachy.

Tenant: Mrs Diana McKay.

Rent: Crop 1812, Martinmas 1811, £13 13s. 0d.

Proprietor's interest: By old tack tenant to leave houses, fences, etc. in good condition.

Matters requiring attention at removal: As 10.

19 Remainder of Wester Carnachy.

Tenants: 6 named small tenants.

Rent: Crop 1812, Martinmas 1811, £15.

Proprietor's interest: Not ascertained.

20 Remainder of Easter Carnachy.

Tenants: 5 named small tenants.

Rent: Crop 1812, Martinmas 1811, £13 10s. 0d.

Proprietor's interest: Not ascertained.

21 Achalgary.

Tenants: 3 named small tenants.

[1] Gen. Mackenzie (for whom see above, p. 3) was granted a wadset of Carnachy, Achalgary, Skail, Dalcharrel (all par. Farr) and Ascoig (par. Kildonan) on 8 July 1803; his sister, who succeeded to him on 26 April 1810, renounced this wadset on 11 May 1810.

H

Rent: Crop 1812, Martinmas 1811, £9.
Proprietor's interest: Not ascertained.

22 Dalcharrel.
Tenants: 4 named small tenants.
Rent: Crop 1812, Martinmas 1811, £7.
Proprietor's interest: Not ascertained.

23 Skaill.
Tenants: 1. Captain William McKay. 2. 4 named small tenants.
Rent: Crop 1812, Martinmas 1811, 1. £20; 2. £10.
Proprietor's interest: Not ascertained.

24 Outfield of Skaill.
Tenants: 2 named small tenants.
Rent: Crop 1812, Martinmas 1811, £2.
Proprietor's interest: Not ascertained.

The salmon fishings of Naver, Torrisdale, Helmsdale and Brora with the Corff houses and other parts, etc. possessed by Messrs. W. and S. Forbes, Aberdeen,[1] with power to fish anywhere on the sea coast within or without sea march as well as in fresh rivers, excepting in the Ferry of Unes and bays adjacent thereto.
Tenants: James Landles, George Riddell and Philip Redpath of Berwick upon Tweed, merchants: Henry Morton, Esquire, of Berrington, Co. Durham, George Redpath and William Redpath, fishmongers in Billingsgate, cautioners and full debtors with and for them.
Rent: Whitsunday 1811 to Whitsunday 1812, Martinmas 1811 £1,133 10s. 0d.; Whitsunday 1812, £1,133 10s. 0d.
Duration: 19 years, expiring 1 February 1826; with option to tenants to declare lease at an end at expiry of first 9 years, viz. 1816, on giving 12 months' premonition.
Proprietor's interest: 'The Cobles netts and other fishing utensils belong to the proprietor as well as the Corff houses and were delivered over to the Company – Mr Falconer does not know whether there was any Inventory.'

[1] Messrs Forbes' lease expired at Whitsunday 1807.

Matters requiring immediate attention: 'Ascertain whether any Inventory and Apprising of Cobles netts corff houses etc., etc. at entry and get that business fitted.'

Matters requiring attention at removal: Corff houses, etc. to be left in good condition.

Remarks: 'The Family Residing at Dunrobin Castle are entitled to all the Fresh Salmon and kipper necessary for house keeping, not exceeding 100 fish in the year, without any payment or deduction, from the tenant's Rent.'

The Great Sheep Tenement, viz.: 'All and whole the lands and tenement of Bein Clebrig and Beinarmin lying to the north East of the Sheep tenement of Shiness possessed by Captain Donald Matthieson and bounded as follows, viz. By the River Tirry from its Junction with Loch Shin as it runs thro' Midpenny, Lubgorm and Talich, untill it reach a black bank of moss, about a quarter of mile above the Bothy of Bealachriesh and from thence by an Ideal line running in a northerly direction to a cairn on the top of the Crask and from thence forward to the foot of the Rivulet called Aultcroist, and thereafter by the course of that Rivulet and straight forward to Ballacanuaran, where a cairn of stones is erected in a large Rock at the Top of that pass leading to the point of Beinchearel where Cairounaharve begins to take its form and from that point north westerly by a ridge as wind and weather shears towards Toumore and onwards to a hallow or Glack in a Westerly direction to a Water running from Glasloch and by the said Water course till it falls into the large river of Moudale which divides Toumore from Ardraavine and Toubeg of Moudel and by the said river of Moudale (the island thereon belonging to the Possession on the opposite side of the Water from the Sheep tenement) down to Lochnaver and by the River of Naver proceeding from the said Loch down to the mill of Achness. From the Water of Naver where the burn called Mallart empties itself into said river on which burn there is a mill, the said mill and mill croft being within the sheep tenement and alongst said burn of Mallart to Doalone. From thence across a bog by Techvale to the loan of Halmidary and on to Loch Truderscaig by the south-side of the said loch to the mouth of the burn of Cromault and further Eastward half way to Lochnaquin, where a black moss directs

south on the march of Cromault, by the black dyke to Craiglea and
also on Southward to the top of Malour. From thence, as the marches
are known betwixt the forrest ground of Beinarmin and that part of
the Estate of Uppat lately purchased by the Marquis of Stafford from
William Munro of Achany to Craggynadaugh which is wholly
within the sheep tenement and from thence by the course of the
burn till it reach Coirinvtnach which is wholly within said tenement
and from thence in a south west direction dividing Meikle Rogart
shealings from Corifrose, Corifrose being within said tenement, till
it comes thro' Corrieleckach part of which is within said tenement
and from thence to the head of Lochbannach, and alongst the north
side of said loch, and from thence in a Southwesterly direction by
the course of the burn, which runs from said loch, and leaving said
burn still westerly, toward Knockan of Kinnauld, which is wholly
within the Sheep tenement, and extends to the top of Craignaviabeg,
and Craignavimore, on the south side of the water, and as to be seen
from the place of Knockan; here it joins the south side of the Shealing of Clachwall, the south as well as the north side of which being
included in the sheep tenement, directing southwest from the south
side of Clachwall untill the east end of Lochbannoch, parish of Lairg,
the north side of said loch belongs to the Sheep tenement, from the
South end of said Lochbannoch southerly to the top of Knockmel.
From there upon the east side of Aultibreak and Saval which are
both within said Tenement and from Saval Southwestward to
Wester Lairg which is within said Tenement, marching with the
minister's farm into Lochshin. All which lands before described lie
in the Parishes of Lairg, Farr, Kildonan, Clyne and Rogart and
County of Sutherland. As Also all and whole the lands of Letterbeg
in the said Parish of Farr. And also all and whole the lands of Auchin-
duich in the parish of Creech in the County aforesaid as the said
two farms were possessed by the former tenants with free access,
ingress and egress to and from the said lands and every part thereof.'
Reservations: 1. 'Full power and liberty to the said Marquis and
Marchioness and their foresaid to make Roads thro' the said grounds
and to inclose and plant such part thereof as may be deemed necessary for raising wood, allowance being always made to the tenants
and their foresaids, at Counting for their Rent of a fair proportion of
the same corresponding to the Grounds so to be occupied according

as such proportion shall be ascertained by two impartial persons to be mutually chosen.'

2. 'To the Missionary Minister[1] for the time the Accomodation which he presently possesses the rent payable by him to the said Tacksmen in respect of the same to be ascertained by the Factor on the Estate of Sutherland for the time being.'

3. 'Right to such tenants on the Estate of Sutherland as may be authorised to that effect by the Factor for the time the Right of cutting, winning and away carrying peats from such mosses within the bounds aforesaid as may be pointed out by the Factor and that without any exaction of payment for or in respect of such liberty provided that the peats be cut properly and so as to allow the water to run off, and that no spade peats or turff be allowed to be cutt. The places to be pointed out by the Factor and the Tacksmen.'

Tenants: Adam Atkinson of Torbottle near Whittingham, Co. Northumberland, and Anthony Marshall, Alnham, Co. Northumberland: Gabriel Reid, tacksman of Armadale, cautioner.

Rent: Martinmas 1811, £590; Whitsunday 1812, £590.

Duration: 19 years, expiring Whitsunday 1828; 'the tenants entered Whitsunday 1807 but the lease commences only at Whitsunday 1809. Tennants have power to renounce at Whitsunday 1815 on 12 months notarial premonition to the proprietors.'

Proprietor's interest: '£1,200 the first year's Rent allowed the tenant to erect certain houses, stone fences, sheep fanks and wood Bridges and to make improvements by draining and otherwise on the lands sett for which proper Vouchers were to be produced by Whitsunday 1811, Shewing the above sum to be laid out thus – draining £200, Balance on houses etc. £1,000. All to be supported and left in good condition and Repair.'

Matters requiring immediate attention: 1. At Whitsunday 1811 vouchers required of expenditure of £1,200 on meliorations. 2. 'Could the Messrs McKenzies obtain an Obligation from the tenants that they shall break up no part of the sheep walk at their Removal?' 3. 'I see no mention of houses found on the premises at their entry. How do they stand or are they worth Enquiring after?'

Matters requiring attention at removal: 1. Drains, houses, fanks, fences, etc. to be in good condition. 2. No obligation in lease that no part of

[1] At Achness.

sheep walks be broken up at removal; guard against this as much as possible.

Remarks: 1. At Martinmas 1815 and Whitsunday 1816 rent rises to £1500. 2. Rent is divided between Lord and Lady Stafford, and Charles McKenzie Fraser, wadsetter, thus: reversioners, years 1-6 £1180; years 7-19, £1470: wadsetter, years 1-6, £20; years 7-19, £30.

Copy Letter William McKenzie Esquire, ws, to Dr Ross, tacksman of Cambusmore as referred to in No. 29 of the Parish of Dornoch.

'Dunrobin Castle, 8th October 1807. Dear Sir, At your request I write you these few lines to say that I consider you in possession of the farm of Cambusmore (as settled by minute of Sett last month) in the same situation as if you had, had a nineteen years lease from Whitsunday 1804; and accordingly when a general Sett takes place on the Sutherland Estate you will produce this letter and then receive a Regular lease of the same for that period at the rent of £10 16s. 4d. and if we can conveniently add the places held by the subtenants at the rent of £5 3s. 8d. they will be included which will make the rent of Cambusmore and its pendicles Sixteen Pounds, the Rent which you pay this year – as it was the understanding of parties when Cambusmore was given to you that it should be on the Condition of your receiving a nineteen years lease, at £16 of Rent, on the faith of which you have built a good house, and made Inclosures and other improvements. I am etc.

(Doctor Ross says that £1 1s. 0d. of deduction of Rent for Lednaclaish was omitted in Stating the Rent.)'

State of the Customs and Services Exacted in name of the Proprietor from the tenants of the Estate of Sutherland.

There appear to have been formerly a great many Services payable by the tenants to the Proprietors of the Sutherland Estate.

They Consisted of labour in the proprietors farm and Garden, carrying his letters, Foddering his horses and Cattle; furnishing Limestone to his kiln, forwarding deer from the Mountains to his table, and supplying the Castle with wedders, Lambs, poultry, Eggs, fish, Tallow, Peats, etc., etc.

At a time when money was little used, these customs, as they were called, formed a Considerable part of the Rent. I see in the Charter Room Books of their Receipt and debursement dated from 1680 to 1720 which for size might suit a small banking concern. During the minority of Lady Stafford, however, the Guardians converted these Services into money and included them in the tenants Rents, By the following proportions – Labour 4d. per day, Tallow 6s. 8d. per Stone, Wedders 2s. 6d. each, Lambs 1s. 3d., Hens 2d., Eggs 1d. per dozen, and peats 1d. per load. The fish Continued to be paid in kind at the Castle, but latterly at Rhives.

There was at same time a Condition made, that it should be in the power of the family residing at the Castle, to take what part of the Services and Customs they chose in kind, on allowance from the Rent, of a Corresponding abatement, by the same rates. In the Various Succeeding Setts of Parishes, and Farms, and by the absence of the Family, they fell into dissuetude; and so far as I can learn from Mr Falconer and the Ground Officers, the following are all that have of late years been collected. I intend to Expiscate this matter further during the ensuing Summer, and I shall take care, in future, that none are collected, but what are furnished to the Family; and that the fish hitherto taken to Rhives, be sent to the housekeeper at the Castle. I understand they Average, from 12 to 18 fish each day the Boats are at Sea.[1]

	Wedders	Hens	Dozens of Eggs	Loads of Peats	Faces of Peats
Parish of Dornoch					
Achmuil		15			
Dalnamain		10			
Lednoclay		1			
Balvraid		42	42		
Achavandrew		36	36		

[*Table continued overleaf*

[1] Until 1802 the rental for Golspie parish contained victual rents payable for a number of Golspie fishing boats, which appear to have been maintained by the estate. In 1785 there were 4 of these boats, but by 1802 only 2; they are frequently shown as vacant in the Factor's Accounts. The right to receive fish may be a relic of this arrangement.

	Wedders	Hens	Dozens of Eggs	Loads of Peats	Faces of Peats
Upper Proncy		4			
Lednabirichen		24			
Proncy Croy		4			
Torfalig		3			
Wester Altaduaig		6			
Easter Altaduaig		3			
Lower Proncy		7			
Dochfin		14			
Drumdivan		48			
Achlean		17			
Cubaig		3	3		
Parish of Rogart					
Rovy Craig		12		110	
Dalmore		12			
Incheap		16		150	
Torbreak and Achlean		12			
Rossal Achvelie and Muiy		24			
Rhine		12			
Little Rogart		20			
Inchoraig				20	
Parish of Golspie					
Doll of Brora		82	34.2		$9\frac{1}{8}$
Inchfoury		10	4.2		$4\frac{1}{2}$
Parish of Clyne					
Askoilbeg	4	25	22.6	200	
Askoilmore	4	20		160	
Rhimisican	1				
Achness	1				
Cupernahoist	1				
Ammat	2				
Polly	1				
Total	14	482	141.10	640	$13\frac{2}{3}$

Regulations proposed for the parish of Rogart as intended to be put into small farms: April 1811

Conditions, upon which, unless otherwise expressed in the Tacks, the lands and Farms in the parish of Rogart and County of Sutherland pertaining to the Most Noble Elizabeth Marchioness of Stafford and Countess of Sutherland, and the Most Noble George Granville Leveson Gower Marquis of the County of Stafford, are to be set.

Article First

The said lands and farms are to be Sett, with and under the following *reservations* by the proprietors.

1st. Of all mines, minerals, clay, stones (unless so far as necessary for the tenants buildings and Inclosures) and Marle, on any part of their property; with power to digg for, winn, work and carry off the same, and to erect the necessary buildings to that end, on paying the tenant Surface damages to be ascertained by two men to be mutually chosen by the parties, or in case of their differing in opinion by any oversman to be named by them; whose decision shall be final.

2nd. Of power to settle, or streighten, or by the Exchange of ground or otherwise, to render more commodious, marches with other proprietors, or between different farms; to divide commonties by compromise, submission or in any other manner; To Soum and Roum them in order to prevent their being overstocked; to shut up or alter roads; to direct new ones; conduct drains or water courses thro' the lands; and inclose, plant, or improve, for their own use, any barren or pasture ground; all, in the manner they consider most for the General advantage of their Estates: provided always, that, whatever damage may be done to any tenant shall be ascertained and paid for in manner above mentioned, and any benefit derived by a tenant thro' such operations shall, (limited to a fair reimbursement of the proprietors expenditure) be ascertained and paid for in like manner.

3rd. The proprietors further reserve power to dissolve all thirlage to mills upon their Estates, and to cause a fair recompense be paid by the Respective tenants absolved from the servitude, to be ascertained in manner before described. As also to make and enforce such rules and regulations concerning their mosses, and ingress thereto, and egress therefrom, as they consider for the general interest of the tenantry.

Article Second

The tenants and occupiers of the said lands and farms shall possess the same, on condition only, that they observe the following rules which are considered indispensibly requisite on the Estate; and as such agreed to by all parties.

1st. The tenants shall not by themselves or their dependents, servants, labourers or others, tirr[1] any ground, cast or carry off feal or divot,

[1] Pare off the turf or sward; feal is turf.

in any place, or take turff or midden earth from pasture or unimproved ground, or be aiding or abetting thereto; nor shall they permitt of these things to be done, on any part of the ground sett to them without their giving immediate notice to the factor; and the tenant so offending, or suffering his land to be damaged, shall pay twenty shillings sterling, for each load casten or removed, with interest thereof from the date when the transgression was committed, and 'till payment.

2nd. Growing timber having been very much destroyed, and in some places, utterly extirpated, by the practice of peeling bark from Trees for the purpose of Tanning leather, no person in this parish must import hides into the Country, or attempt to tan any skins or leather there; and any tenant contravening this Condition, shall, for each hide or skin, or part of a hide or skin proven to have been in his possession, and for each contravention pay £5 sterling to the proprietor. Further, each and every tenant shall be responsible for all growing timber, plants, or trees, on the grounds possessed by him or them, and shall pay with his or their rent the full value of any damage done to the same during his possession.

3rd. The said tenants and possessors are to refrain from killing Game (without the Proprietors written permission), and Blackfish,[1] and Smolts of Salmon; and from making or using any Engines for the destruction of Game or fish; from burning muirs at unlawful times; and peeling, cutting, injuring, or carrying off any Growing timber plants or trees on the Estate; and it is hereby expressly declared, that, upon the Contravention of any of these particulars, by a tenant, or on such by any of the family, servants, dependants, or Cottars of a tenant without his turning off or removing such offender how soon the matter comes to his knowledge and intimating the fact to the factor on the Estate, the first term of Whitsunday following Such Contravention shall, in either of these cases, be a break in his tack, optional to the proprietors; and it shall be in their power to follow out a process of Removing against him 'as having no Tack or other written right entitling him to possess the lands after the said term'; and that, in the same manner, as if the full term of years first specified in his lease had expired, or such lease never had existed.

4th. The tenants are bound to the accustomed services to Kirk

[1] Spawned salmon.

Manse and Schoolhouse, and to mill dams and weirs; but, excepting
the rents specified in their respective Leases and what may be incumbent on them by the public law of the land, they shall be free of all
other burdens, servitudes, and Exactions whatever.

Article Third

With Regard to the tenants management of the lands hereby sett,
it is Conditioned.

1st. That the lease shall be destined to him, and his heirs, or Assignee
mortis causa; but expressly debarring and secluding all other assign-
ees, and Subtenants legal or Conventional, the necessary number of
Cottars as Servants or labourers whose possession shall not exceed
one Cows grass, and two or at most three Arable Acres, excepted;
As Also, debarring and Secluding the division of any farm, among
heirs portioners, or otherwise, any manner of way.

2nd. The tenant to have such Reasonable and proper Encouragement, for building houses and enclosures suitable to the farm and
upon a plan to be approven of by the Proprietors or their Factor;
and to be bound to such Conditions with regard to the houses and
fences, as shall be expressed in the Contract of Tack to be entered
into with Reference to these Conditions.

3rd. At the tenants entry to his farm he will find traced on it the
lines by which it is intended to be inclosed; by which lines, unless
altered by the Proprietors or their Factors, with the tenants consent,
he shall inclose the lands, and he shall labour and manage the arable
fields thereof, in manner following Viz. Before the second Whitsunday after his entry he shall have one division completely inclosed
with double stone dykes in manner to be pointed out to him, and,
such inclosure, he shall during the Summer immediately ensuing,
fallow or put into green crop, whereby the ground may, effectually,
be cleaned. The next year, he shall with his white crop sow down
artificial grass, by the following proportions [   ]¹ bushels per-
ennial rye grass, [   ]¹ libs. red or white clover, and [   ]¹ rib-
grass per acre. He shall allow no bestial to pasture thereon, betwixt
the first day of November and first day of May ensuing; no swine
to pasture on it during the two following years, nor shall he break
it up untill three crops and years after it was first sown down; at
which period, the tenant may take two white crops in succession;

¹ MS. blank.

the third year, that is the seventh crop and year after the ground was first inclosed and dressed, he shall again fallow and clean it, and he shall proceed by the same six course shift of husbandry, (excepting that on any superior land in good order he may, with the factors written permission, follow alternate green and white crops if he incline) during the whole currency of his lease. Before the third term of Whitsunday after his entry he shall have a second division of his farm so inclosed; which inclosure he shall proceed to clean and crop in manner above mentioned. Before the fourth term of Whitsunday he shall bring a third division into the same train of management, which he shall in like manner continue, and so on with every part of his farm untill the expiry of his Tack. If the tenant neglect to labour the said lands and every part thereof agreeably to these conditions, during the whole years of the lease, he shall pay, yearly along with the Stipulated rent £5 Sterling, for each acre, and proportionally for a less quantity mislaboured.

4th. Each tenant engages and obliges him or herself, to put no bestial on any ground common to Lord and Lady Staffords tenants, besides what are *bona fide* the tenants own property; and in every instance of their doing to the Contrary they engage to pay per head, one shilling Sterling for every day or part of a day in which each beast, was so allowed to pasture.

5th. No tenants shall at any time, or on any pretext remove or allow to be removed, any dung or manure from his farm; nor shall he dispose by sale, barter or otherwise of any straw the growth of these lands. His hay and potatoes too, he shall consume on his farm, excepting any surplus quantity which he may dispose of to any of Lord and Lady Staffords tenants to be consumed on their farms otherwise he shall pay 20s. for each load of manure, and £5 for each load of hay or potatoes so removed from the premisses.

6th. As an Encouragement to tenants to bring new land into Culture and to plant and protect trees on their respective farms, the said Proprietors bind themselves and their heirs and Successors to pay to each tenant, at the next term after his or her removal the sum of five pounds sterling for every such acre, which (with the written approbation of the proprietors or their factors) the said tenant shall have brought into Culture and have managed and left agreeably to the Rotation before set down: As Also, to pay the said tenant the full expence of inclosing any trees or planting done with the written approbation foresaid, and a reasonable sum for the care and protection thereof, such sum to be ascertained by mutual referees in manner formerly described. Provided such trees be left in a thriving, and the inclosure in a fencible condition.

7th. No tenant shall keep goats, or suffer his own cattle horses sheep or swine to roam at large and trespass on his neighbour; or any other persons bestial to trespass on his grounds, at any time of the year; and if he faill to poind all bestial tresspassing on his grounds, as often as they are seen or found thereon, and to cause the owner of them pay the damage done as well as the usual penalty, and divide said penalty equally among the persons acting as servants on his farm, he shall pay to the proprietors or their factor $\frac{1}{2}$ a merk for every trespass of every beast on his ground, of which sums one half to be paid to the informer, and the other to the Ground officer.

Article fourth

Regarding the expiry of the tenants Tacks.

1st. It is conditioned that in the Autumn preceeding the tenants last crop he shall properly plow the inclosure which had that year been in white crop the second year after grass; which park or inclosure he shall effectually harrow in spring before the term of Whitsunday of his Removal; and, at the said term of Whitsunday he shall give the incoming tenant access thereto along with [   ]¹ loads of good dung for each acre of which it consists, as well as to the whole houses offices pasture and grass natural and artificial; the said tenant being as a full recompense entitled to a proportional abatement of Rent for the arable land so given up; and to payment for the grass seeds he had sown with his penult crop, and for the labour he had bestowed on the park above mentioned as the same may be ascertained by Apprisement in manner before Specified.

2nd. He shall, without any payment, permit the incoming tenant to sow, grass seeds, with any part of his last crop, and in respect of the straw he received at his entry, and of the incoming tenants leading home in harvest, and threshing said last crop, he shall leave the whole straw chaff and harpings² thereof to his successor; such

¹ MS. blank.
² Dust sifted from the milled grain (see below, p. 149, for a similar use of the term in relation to coal).

successor being bound to deliver the outgoing tenant his grain clean and in a marketable condition.

And Lastly

That the premisses may be fulfilled with the greater precision.

1st. The tenant is along with each years rent, to bring to the Factor a Certificate under the hand of the ground officer, attesting whether any, and what growing trees or plants on the tenants farm have been, within the then last twelve months peeled, cutt, injured, or carried off; whether any and what feal, divot turff, or midden earth has been cut or carried away on his farm; and what crop the tenant has had in each part of said farm, the said officer, in case he give a false certificate, not only, forfeiting all wages due or to become due to him, and any lease held by him, but being bound to pay the sums conditioned to be exigible from the tenants; which tenants, however shall not be freed from said claims, untill the actual payment of the amount thereof.

2nd. With his last rent and his claim for meliorations the tenant shall further bring to the factor, a certificate from the succeeding tenant or from the referrees named between the parties, that the whole conditions with regard to his removal and the way and manner thereof, have been fulfilled by him. And Finally, There shall no tacit relocation take place at the expiry of the Tacks; and if the tenant faill to give peaceable possession to his successor, in the way and manner before set down, altho no warning or legal process shall be then used against him; it is pactioned and understood between the parties, that he shall pay of Rent for the year succeeding the expiry of his lease, at the rate of twenty Pounds Sterling per Acre, and proportionally for a less quantity, and which rent, he shall pay, during each succeeding year of his possession.

In witness of the haill premisses these presents written on this and the [   ]¹ preceeding pages by [   ]¹ are Subscribed by the said Marchioness and Marquis and by the Respective tenants as follows Viz. [   ]¹.

Report by William Young on Assynt: Rhives, 13 August 1811

During a stay of two weeks in Assynt I embraced every means in

¹ MS. blank.

my power to ascertain the quality of the land, the uses to which it can be most advantageously applied, the value of the Kelp Shores, Salmon and other Fishings, Marble and Lime Stone Quarries, and the result is as follows, so far as I am capable to Judge by myself, or the Gentlemen who accompanied me, Mr Reid of Armadale as a Judge of Sheep grounds, Mr Alexander Simpson as a Kelp maker.

The Parish of Assynt is entirely a pastoral Country, and much of it affords the finest grass I ever saw, but it must not be concealed that several of the hills are very barren and the interior is interspersed with irreclaimable, (but useful) peat bog so far as it affords Fewel to the inhabitants, and for lime buring.

I have no hesitation to say that to turn the greater part of this Parish to the best account it should be under Cheviot Sheep, reserving accommodation for Kelp makers, Fishermen, Lime burners, and other Labourers and after the most minute inspection I am sorry to be obliged to differ with Mr Robert Brown[1] in supposing that Black Cattle have, or ever will be so profitable a stock, but aware as I am that Lord and Lady Stafford will in this and other districts rather sacrifice their interest than that the people should be entirely dispossessed I have in arranging the grounds for a new set keeped them in view.

Kelp Shores

These have been estimated by Mr Brown as equal to an annual produce of 56½ Tons, I have reason to suppose that in this remark he is within bounds, and if I am correct in supposing that the Proprietor shoud derive a benefit of £4 per Ton the return from Kelp woud be £226.

NB Mr Innes of Lochalsh sets his shores at 6 and £7 per Ton but admits that the tenant is a loser, besides, Kelp has of late years been an unusual high price at market.

Marble

This I can form no estimation of. I am afraid it will not turn out an advantageous concern for the present tenant, the report is that he has expended Two or Three thousand pounds on it, and I find that although he has been 12 years in the Country, 90 Tons of block marble have only been shipped, and perhaps 40 Tons more are ready to be put on board. How far a more active man woud make

[1] See above, p. 35.

these quarries an object I cannot pretend to say, but it is not probable that Mr Jopling will, he is old and resides in New Castle; the quarrying and transportation is left to his wife who cannot be competent to carry on such a concern.

Lime Stone

The Lands of Auchamore, Edrachalda and others situated in the center of, and to the confines of the parish on the South, abound with Lime Stone more easily quarried than any I ever saw, and by means of Loch Assynt may be transported to Little Assynt where Fewel on the banks of the lake is in great plenty. There the Stone shou'd be burned and forwarded by Carts to Lochinver about 7 miles distant, if it is considered adviseable to build a Village at that place.

Fishing Stations

Assynt affords the following Sea Lochs safe for Vessels and Boats, Loch Inver and Loch Rou on the West, Clashnessy, Ouldny, Culkein, Ned and Unapool to the east of the head land called Roustore. Of these Lochinver is the most valuable, it combines safety and extent of Bay with beauty, and here the waters of Inver and Culin empty themselves into the Sea, while that of Kirkaig is in the vicinity. A better prooff of the superior advantages attending this Loch cannot be afforded than by seeing that Mr Murdoch Morrison the greatest and most Judicious Fisher in his day had Herring Houses built here, and which are now occupied and enlarged by Mr Donald Macdonald who, (if one may Judge from the correct manner in which all his operations in Ship building and Cooperage, Garden and small Farm are carried on) must see this a desirable situation. I do not hesitate to say that the little ground which is to be found between the waters of Inver and Culin should be fewed out as well as the bank north of the Inver water, and a Village formed to which in the event of some of the principle tenants being dispossessed they could resort to, as well as others who may be inclined to adventure in Fishing or Kelp making. Here also a small Woolen Work might be advantageously placed on the Water of Culin and mechanics settled, in short Lochinver shou'd be the *Metropolis* of Assynt and if an Exchequer grant could be obtained to convert it into a Burgh of Barony the prosperity of the place, and good order of the Country wou'd be better preserved.

At present the people who Fish for Mr Macdonald are settled on the Lands of Roustore, but it is said and I believe with Justice that the situation is inconvenient, affording no tolerable Harbour and no Kelp. My own opinion is (but I give it with diffidence) that Fishermen, and others in the lower part of the Country who may be dispossessed woud be more advantageously placed where Harbours can be found than on an open bold Shore with scarcely a creek to make for, or the means of getting near their homes from the usual Fishing Stations but by land; under this impression I woud in arranging the Farms reserve what of these lands are presently out of Lease for more settlers and as Lochinver affords very little ground around it, a new Lease perhaps shou'd not be given on Mr Macdonalds Inver Farm nor on any lands between this and Clasnessy (Little Assynt to the water of Douie inclusive) untill the fate of Lochinver is known; because in time (and the period may not be distant) all may be wanted for small Farms to the Inhabitants of Lochinver, and being situated between the Lochs South and North of Roustore are well adapted for their accomodation. It has been urged and with much Justice that land is the bane of Fishermen, but in a Country so remote and on a Coast which the Herring do not regularly resort to and where Cod and Ling may not perhaps allways be sold to good account, the meanest person shoud have his Potato ground and Cows grass, the more wealthy settler his small Farm.

Salmon Fishings

The Inver, Culin and Kirkaig waters shou'd certainly afford a considerable quantity of Salmon, but I may be permited to say that the present tenants[1] do not Fish with that attention which they ought, nor do they turn the Salmon to the best account, but different causes may put both partly out of their power. It is likewise said that if the course of Kirkaig water was changed so as to admit Salmon getting up to Span in the interior Lochs, in place of being obstructed in their course by a precipice[2] in the river, that the numbers woud be greatly increased, but I did not estimate the expence of the operation, although when the Fishings are advertised if offerers build much on this it may be considered of.

[1] Captain William Scobie of Ardvare and Captain Kenneth McKenzie of Ledbeg.
[2] The falls of Kirkaig.

I

Interior situation for Settlers

Although it is desirable to place as many as possible of the people round the Shores, numbers will be found whose habits of Life preclude the possibility of making them Fishers or Kelpers, but unprofitable as such a race are the best must be done, and they may be at last useful as road makers and labourers at home and in the low Country in place of, as at present wasting their time in Sloth and idleness.

The Farms of Elphin and Knockan with grazings of Altnachy and Cromalt (detached from the other lands of Assynt by Loch Urgil and the water issuing out of it, and otherwise bounded by Cromarty and Sir Charles Ross' lands) seem the best adapted for inland settlers; Elphin and Knockan although they stand high are excellent soil on Lime Stone, and in tolerable Seasons must afford every convenience to a poor Man, viz. a little Grain and Straw, Potato, Milk and Fewel.

Such Farms as may now be set with entry at Whitsunday next shou'd perhaps be classed as follows.

No. 1

Inchdamph, Stronchrubie, Lyne, upper and lower Tubeg, subject to the *Laird of Leckmellins*[1] *5 years Lease* on Inchdamph and Upper Tubeg, and reserving the House of Inchdamph and grounds between the Rock and burn for an Inn, with permission to hold fairs on the adjoining Land.

Boundings of No. 1

Parsons Farm and Inchdamph House etc. on the North, Sir Charles Ross on the East, Burn of Lyne on the South east, Burn of Rhigruagach up to the hollow North of Canisp Mountain and the water of Fealid which runs into the River Inver a little below and opposite to Little Assynt on the South West, with Loch Assynt on the North West.

Yearly value £525 being equal to the keep of 3,500 Sheep at 3s. each.

No. 2

Ledmore and Rhiancrivach the latter subject to Mr Joplings Lease of eight years.

Boundings of No. 2

Lyne on the North West, Sir Charles Ross on the north and east,

---

[1] George McKenzie, laird of Leckmeln (par. Lochbroom, Ross-shire).

Lochurgil on the South east and the Water from it untill its conjunction with Ledbeg burn on the South West.

Yearly value £300 being equal to the keep of 2,000 sheep at 3s. each.

NB Ledmore may be set exclusive of Rheancrivach during the currency of Mr Joplings Lease although this is not considered so advisable.

No. 3

Ledbeg including the Hill of Canisp, Drimswordland, Dochluish, Polygarvir and Fewlin.

Boundings of No. 3

Water of Inver up to Polygarvir on the North West, Polygarvir burn up to its source at the Hill of Canisp on the North East, from thence to the hollow on the North of Canisp leading into Lochangruigich and on to Lochaw, and forward to a hollow and in a straight to the burn of Lyne continuing this water to Cameloch which are the present boundings of Ledbeg on the east. For the South and West boundings take the water of Culaig from its source by Dremnagrenshich and Cameloch to Lochinfad.

Yearly Value £600 being equal to the keep of 4,000 Sheep at 3s. each.

No. 4

Inverkirkaig, Badenaman, Knocknaneach, Hill of Solvine (Sugar Loaf) and Bracklach of Ledbeg.

Boundings of No. 4

Cameloch on the east, the burn from it to the water of Kirkaig through the Lochs untill they join the Coigach March, down said March to the Sea, on the east, South and West, the Burn of Badenman which seperates this lot from Strahan on the North West untill its source at Loch Fadenamurigil from thence in a line to be marked out by the Surveyor to Loch Assarie which seperates this Lot from Culaig.

Yearly value £300 being equal to the keep of 2,000 Sheep at 3s. each.

NB The Surveyor to consider whither this Lot shoud come so near Culaig in case of too much interference with the Lochinver grounds and how much the value of Kirkaig wou'd be diminshed by a different arrangement if such is judged proper.

No. 5

Achamore, Edrachalda, Tumore and Poltecarakin to the Southside of Glenlerig water.

Boundings of No. 5

Water of Glenlerig from the Balloch on the North West, from thence keep the ridge of the Hill by Spidanconich to Soulac and in a line to the Unapool Marches with Achamore, untill they join Mr Joplings road, and to include the Hill grounds now possessed by the tenants of Unapool (at will) and the Hill grounds of Edrachalda as they bound with Lord Reay and the Parsons Farm on the East, Loch Assynt on the South and water of Dowie on the West.

Yearly Value £450 being equal to the keep of 3,000 Sheep at 3s. each.

NB Reserve the old House of Edrachalda[1] and grounds east of the burn as unconnected with this Lot and more suited to join the Parsons Farm, and if Lord and Lady Stafford desire it the old Castle of Assynt[2] with the Island may be reserved although the Island adds to the value of this Lot.

No. 6

Ardvar, Rhiantrad and part of Glenlerig.

Boundings of No. 6

Water of Glenlerig from the Balloch on the South and West, Sea on the North, present Marches of Unapool on the East, Ridge of hill from Soulag by Spidancoinach to Bellachernish East and North East to West and South West.

Yearly Value £450 equal to the keep of 3,000 Sheep at 3s. each.

NB If Nos. 5 and 6 were joined and a peninsula on the eastside of Rhiantrad occupied by the Unapool people added it is supposed that 1,000 more Sheep coud be kept on both, which at 3s. each woud yield further £150.

Abstract.

No. 1	£525
No. 2	300
No. 3	600
No. 4	300
No. 5	450
No. 6	450
If Nos. 5 and 6 are joined a further rent to be added of	150
	£2,775

[1] For Edrachalda house see *John Home's Survey of Assynt*, ed. R. J. Adam (Scottish History Society, 1960), xii.
[2] Ardvreck Castle.

Besides the foregoing Farms, the following now out of Lease are to be attended to but which in the present instance it may only be prudent to set to tenants at will or to arrange for new Settlers as Lord and Lady Stafford are pleased to direct.

Culaig possessed by	Mr Macdonald
Inver and Ardroe	ditto
Little Assynt	Captain James Scobie
Ned	small tenants
Drimbeg	ditto
West side of Glenlerig	ditto
Culkein[1]	Mrs Clark
half of Unapool	small tenants
Elphin and Knockan	ditto
Cromalt and Altnachy	James and William Scobie

Kelp Shores and Salmon Fishings to be attended to and advertised.

I have according to the best of my abilities aided by the Gentlemen mentioned, given an idea of the annual value of that part of Assynt which may now be set. I am the more confident that the Rents mentioned are within bounds having had a previous opinion much to the same effect from two of the principle people in the Country, still some of the land may be too high valued, part of it too low, but if Lord and Lady Stafford desire it the whole may be advertised. The public will judge for themselves.

Improvements necessary in Assynt and without which the comfort of the people, consequently the Yearly Value of the Land and Fishings will be diminished.

Roads

From Lubcroy in Ross-shire to Lochinver in Assynt there is not the appearance of a Road but that made by Mr Jopling from Rhiancrivach to Edrachalda where it takes off to Unapool,[2] and it is in vain to expect that anything useful will ever be effected by the Statute Labour in a Country so extensive.

The Noble Proprietors shoud use every effort to obtain Government and private aid to bring forward a road to the confines of the Country and on to Lochinver from whence to the North side Fishing Stations.

---

[1] Culkein Drumbeg.   [2] See below, ii, p. 48.

Supposed distance	Miles	
Bonar Bridge to Rosehall	18	
Deduct already made by Lord Ashburton	3	
	—	15
Rosehall to Knockan	3	
From thence to Assynt	12	
	—	15
		—
		30

In which Lady Stafford, Lord Ashburton, Sir Charles Ross, Cadbol, Poyntzfield, Skibo, and Ardross[1] are interested.

From confines of Assynt to Lochinver maybe	28
Lochinver to North side Fishing Stations	10
	—
	38

In which Lady Stafford is solely interested.

I will not enlarge on the *ways and means* for these undertakings untill Mr Telford comes to the Country and his opinion taken with regard to what the Commissioners may be inclined to do.

If Fewing is resolved on at Lochinver, the length and conditions of Lease are to be determined on: 99 years is the usual duration. The price of ground ought perhaps to vary according to the Local situation.

Captain Mackenzie Ledbeg has already built a House at Lochinver which stands well for a line of Street. It is said to have cost him £600. The meliorations allowed by his Lease are only £40 and at this money it is perhaps in Lady Staffords power to take the House. It will be proper to determine whether this shoud be done or a Few given on the ground under the same conditions with other settlers.[2]

Inns

There is not an Inn in this Country nor a room where public business can be transacted. In arranging the Farms I have pointed out the propriety of reserving Inchndamph House and some ground which is a Stage from Lochinver and in the neighbourhood of the

[1] For the lands held by these proprietors, see above, p. xii. Murdoch McKenzie of Ardross was the proprietor of the salmon fishings on the Shin.
[2] In the rental for 1813 Captain Mackenzie is shown as holding this house at £5 annual rent; his widow paid £2 10s. in 1814, 1815 and 1816, holding at will.

Church, and as in this quarter Markets for the sale of Cattle and Sheep shoud be held.

Another Inn will also be wanted at Lochinver on a small scale, but so constructed as to admit of additions, and if the Village is approved of a road to Little Assynt will be absolutely necessary, that the Settlers may have the command of Lime by the Loch and this road.

We heard of much schism among the people, and a few Sectaries have appeared at Roustore – I believe Haldanites[1] – dipping was tried in one instance but not much relished in this climate. If this present pastor Mackenzie lives much longer the flock will go astray, and a good assistant seems much wanted,[2] for in a remote Country the conduct of the people must depend entirely on the example and precept of the Clergyman.

Woods

In the foregoing report it escaped me to say anything on this subject, and I am sorry to have to remark that although Assynt appears at one time to have been very full of timber it is now almost entirely destroyed. Still it is certainly an object to pay attention to what remains and one or two active men if such coud possibly be found in the Country ought to get the charge of it, depredators should be brought before the Justices and severely fined. At present I am told few of the Gentlemen care to act, and that the police of the Country is sadly neglected, Mr Sellar might be interested to put these matters on a better footing, and no time should be lost.

Proceedings on the Kildonan Riots: 1813

Minute for the Procurator fiscal

In cause at his instance against sundry persons in the parish of Kildonan accused of Rioting. The Procurator fiscal craved that diligence might be renewed for citing witnesses to the thirtieth current, and warrant to officers of Court granted for Citing Robert Gordon in Reisk son of Alexander Gordon in Dalcharn, George Macleod in Kildonan, Alexander Gun there, Donald Gun there, Robert

---

[1] James Haldane visited Sutherland in 1799 and 1805 (A. Haldane, *Memoirs of Robert Haldane of Airthrey and James Alexander Haldane* (Edinburgh, 1852), 184-5, 348-9).
[2] Rev. John Kennedy was subsequently appointed assistant in Assynt (for his part in the Assynt disturbances of 1813 see below, ii, p. 197).

Gun his son, John Sutherland there, Alexander Gun there, John Bannerman alias McDavy, and Donald Sutherland in Ulbster, William Sutherland now in Balnavaliach formerly servant to Mr Sage in Kildonan, George Polson in Grudseray, Jean Melville wife of Donald Murray Dram seller in Suisgill, George Macdonald in Dalvait, John Sutherland in Keanakyle, Innes Macleod or Mackay in Auldnabrekach, George Mackay Catechist in Lirrabul, William Sutherland in Balnavaliach and Donald Polson in Torrish to compear before his Lordship for examination at Golspy Inn on the said thirtieth day of January current. (signed) Hugh Leslie.

Kirktown, 27th January 1813

The Sheriff substitute having considered the original Petition at the instance of the Procurator fiscal with the foregoing Minute and precognition taken, hereby grants warrant to Officers of Court with a proper concurrence to pass Search for seize and apprehend the several persons mentioned in the foregoing Minute [the names above follow], and on their being so apprehended to bring them, or such of them as shall be so apprehended, or either of them before me for examination, and further renews the warrant for citing such witnesses as the petitioner may think proper to adduce to appear before me at Golspy Inn upon the [   ]¹ day of [   ]¹ in order to be precognosced upon the facts stated in the petition, each witness under the penalty of one hundred merks Scots. (signed) Robert Mackid.

At Golspy Inn the Tenth day of February Eighteen hundred and thirteen

In presence of Robert Mackid Esquire Sheriff Substitute of Sutherland, The Procurator fiscal represented that on the Thirtieth ultimo the Sheriff had granted warrant for apprehending Robert Gordon in Reisk son of Alexander Gordon in Dalcharn and others of the Rioters in the Parish of Kildonan. That Donald Bannerman one of the Officers of Court was employed to proceed with the warrant to the said Parish and put it into execution. That he has now returned without having effected the purpose for which he was sent and the fiscal craves that he may be ordered to appear before the Court and answer for his conduct. (signed) Hugh Leslie.

¹ MS. blank.

Eodem die

The Sheriff having considered the foregoing Minute ordains the said Donald Bannerman to appear before him for examination. (signed) Robert Mackid.

When compeared the said Donald Bannerman and being solemnly sworn and interrogated Depones That upon Sunday Evening last the Deponent left the parish of Golspy for the purpose of executing a Warrant which was delivered to him by the Sheriff Substitute in order to apprehend the Persons therein named and That early on Monday morning he arrived at Helmsdale accompanied by John Mathison Sheriff Officer at Kintraidwell from whence they proceeded also accompanied by Robert Gray another Sheriff Officer in the neighbourhood of Helmsdale to the parish of Kildonan and reached Suisgal that night where he and his party remained for the night in the House of Donald Murray dram seller there; Depones that being informed by Lady Stafford's Ground Officer that Robert Gordon in Reisk one of the persons mentioned in the warrant was from home the Deponent and his party did not go there but proceeded to Leribol in order to summon John Turnbull shepherd to Mr Houstoun as an evidence which the deponent did. Depones that he and his party proceeded down the south side of the Water of Kildonan until they arrived at the Bridge of Kildonan where they crossed to the north side of the Water. That he left a copy of citation with George McDonald in Delvait to appear here this day. Depones that he did not show the warrant to any person whose name is mentioned in it neither did he intimate to any of them that he had a warrant in his possession for their apprehension, having merely delivered them copies of Citation to appear here this day in order to be examined. Depones that his reasons for so doing was that he and his party were apprehensive of their Lives from the state of Mind in which the people he had then occasion to see, were in, and from the general state of the public Mind there, they having assembled in Crowds around him and his party, and if he had proceeded to attempt to put the warrant in execution against any one of them he is certain that he and his party would have been maltreated if not murdered, as threats of a very alarming and disagreeable nature were made use of upon this occasion, and altho' the Deponent only cited fifteen people to appear here this day, yet there are now upwards of One hundred Men at the Inn-door from the Parish of Kildonan. That while the Deponent was in the execution of his Office he fell in with George Mackay Catechist in Kildonan and one of the people mentioned in the said warrant, who told the Deponent, with Tears in his Eyes, that he was glad to see him as he wished him to communicate a Message to Lady Stafford's Manager and the Sheriff which was that if any man who came down to Golspy upon Wednesday were apprehended as was the case a few days ago at Helmsdale, that there would be such news of it as never happened in Sutherland before, as there would be three hundred Men assembled on that occasion. All of which is Truth as he shall answer to God. (signed) Donald Bannerman, Robert Mackid.

Thereafter and in respect it is now ascertained that the people whose names are mentioned in the warrant which the said Donald Bannerman had received to execute are among the people now assembled at the door of the Inn, The Sheriff ordered the said Donald Bannerman accompanied by a party and Witnesses to proceed to apprehend all or one or either of them, and bring them or either of them before him for examination. And in the meantime would wait until their return. (signed) Robert Mackid.

The Procurator fiscal in respect of the riotous proceedings which have now found their way into the Sheriff's presence, and of the deforcement of the Law before his Eyes, humbly begs leave to decline further procedure in the business until advice of the Crown Lawyers may be had, and for that purpose requests that his Lordship may be pleased to transmit the whole examination to them. (signed) Hugh Leslie.

At Golspy Inn the Tenth day of February Eighteen hundred and Thirteen

The Sheriff Substitute having attended here this day for the purpose of proceeding in the examination of evidences in terms of adjournment, Finds it impossible for him to proceed with safety to himself and the other members of Court, in respect the house is now surrounded by a lawless Mob assembled for the avowed purpose of preventing Judicial investigation, and who have exultingly in his presence, deforced the Officers of the law, by preventing certain Individuals from being brought forward for examination,

The Sheriff is under the necessity of adjourning to Dunrobin Castle there to examine such evidences as the Procurator Fiscal may be able to adduce for examination both as to the original Riot and the present deforcement. (signed) Robert Mackid.

At Dunrobin Castle the Tenth day of February eighteen hundred and thirteen years

Compeared Jean Melville Spouse of Donald Murray Dram Seller at Suisgill who being solemnly sworn and examined Depones That she knew that Messrs Reid and Hall[1] were in the house of John Turnbull at Suisgill on the night of Tuesday the fifth day of January last, That early of the following morning and she thinks before Sunrise two Men viz. Robert Gun son of Donald Gun in Kildonan and Alexander Matheson in Auldbreakach came in to the Deponent's house for the purpose of smoking a little Tobacco, that immediately on lighting their pipes they went out, That the Deponent soon afterwards went out and saw the said two men Standing by the side of the peatstack, That having enquired at the said men who soon thereafter returned to the house what they were about, she was answered, that she very well knew that before at her own expence, meaning thereby as the Deponent understood that she had been one of those that were removed for a Sheep far-mer.[2] Depones, That soon after this the Deponent's husband went out of the house with the view of going to a little distance to his morning devotion, when he soon thereafter returned and told the Deponent that he was apprehensive of mischief, as he saw a number of people assembling and assembled at the back of a rising ground near their house, and requested of the Deponent to go and alarm those who were in Turnbull's house, as she would be less suspected of giving information than her husband. That the Deponent was much agitated at what she herself saw and heard from her husband, and in consequence went to Turnbull's house, and acquainted Turnbull's wife with what she herself had seen and heard from her husband, which the wife immediately communicated to the Shep-herds and the Deponent returned to her own house. Depones That

---

[1] Presumably Gabriel Reid of Armadale, the tenant of the new Kilcalmkill sheep-farm; his companion has not been identified.

[2] This removal presumably took place when Thomas Houston took possession of Suisgill (formerly wadset land, and first entered in rental in 1807, though the actual removal may have been slightly earlier).

soon after the Deponent's return to her own house and as soon as
the Shepherds had mounted their horses and rode off, the Deponent
saw a Crowd of people run down the hill past the Deponent's
house, part running in front and part behind it, taking the route
which the Shepherds had taken. That the Deponent knew two of
the Men who thus run after the Shepherds, viz. William McLeod
in Eldrable, and a William or John Polson son of John Polson in
Torrish. All which is Truth as she shall answer to God, and depones
she cannot write. (signed) Robert Mackid.
At Dunrobin Castle eodem die

Thereafter compeared the said Donald Bannerman who being
again solemnly sworn and examined, Depones That in consequence
of instructions from the Sheriff he did, accompanied by Patrick
Sellar Esquire at Culmaily, Mr Hugh Leslie Procurator fiscal,
William Taylor Sheriff Clerk of Sutherland, John Davidson Wright
in Golspy, George Mackay wright there and James Duncan Innkeeper at Golspy, call over the names of the different people mentioned in the warrant, and they having all answered to their names
except Robert Gordon in Reisk and Robert Gun in Kildonan, and
Alexander Gun there, and appeared in front of the Crowd assembled,
the Deponent intimated to them that he then held in his hand a
Warrant for apprehending the whole of them and bringing them
before the Sheriff for examination. Depones that the moment this
was intimated the people present surrounded them and rescued
them violently from the Deponent in presence of the Gentlemen
and others present, That the two which the Deponent first apprehended were John Sutherland in Kildonan and Donald Polson in
Torrish, and when the Deponent attempted to seize the said John
Sutherland he was prevented by Robert Bruce in Loyst, and as the
whole people mentioned above as being contained in the warrant
were encircled and carried off by the Crowd, it was impossible
for the Deponent to put his warrant in execution as they declared
to a man that none of their number should go to any place for
examination or otherwise unless the whole were present. Depones
that the Sheriff being also present he heard him order the people
quietly and peaceably to disperse and go to their respective homes,
all except those whose names were contained in the warrant, as he
wished them to be brought before him for examination, but they

all positively refused, That he also heard the Sheriff direct the Clerk to order them to disperse in the King's name under the pains and penalties of the Law, and this the Deponent heard the Clerk explain to them in the Gaelic language, but neither of the intimations had the desired effect, all which is Truth as he shall answer to God. (signed) Donald Bannerman, Robert Mackid.

William Taylor Sheriff Clerk of Sutherland being solemnly sworn and examined Depones That he was this day present at the Inn of Golspy when the Sheriff gave orders to Donald Bannerman the preceding witness to execute the Duty mentioned in his deposition. That the Sheriff and the other persons condescended on by Bannerman accompanied him to the outside of the Inn where the Crowd was assembled, and depones and concurs with the preceding witness regarding his being resisted in the execution of his duty, with this exception that the Deponent did not perceive that any person was actually apprehended by the Sheriff officer, altho' two Men, John Sutherland in Kildonan and Donald Polson in Torrish were condescended on from among the rest for being secured, and whom the Crowd by assembling around prevented from being apprehended. Depones that at that time the attention of the Deponent was more particularly employed in noticing and looking after a Man who stepping from the Crowd towards him brandished a Stick at him, as if with intent to strike the Deponent. That the Deponent does not know the name of the Man who thus brandished his Stick, nor did he since see him, altho' he a few minutes afterwards walked through the Crowd in order to recognise that Man and find out his name. Depones that from the attitude and determined language of the persons assembled as aforesaid, it was impossible for the Sheriff Officer to execute his warrant. All which is Truth as he shall answer to God. (signed) William Taylor, Robert Mackid.

The Sheriff adjourns the further Examination of witnesses until nine O'Clock Tomorrow morning, then to take place at Golspy Inn. (signed) Robert Mackid.

Golspy Inn 11th February 1823

Mr James Duncan Inn Keeper of the Inn of Golspy being solemnly sworn and examined Depones that about Twelve O Clock yesterday a vast Crowd of people from the parish of Kildonan assembled at the Deponent's door, each of them armed with a Bludgeon.

That soon thereafter the Sheriff, the Clerk and Procurator fiscal of Court made their appearance, and after some preliminary steps had been taken, the Sheriff delivered a warrant to Donald Bannerman Sheriff Officer with a List of names contained therein with instructions to put the same in execution against the said people, at least in so far as to bring them before him for examination. That after calling over the names which was done in the presence of some witnesses, and the people whose names were called having come in front of the Crowd the said Donald Bannerman was prevented from putting his warrant in execution by the Crowd surrounding the said Men and declaring that none of their number should be laid hold of for any purpose whatever. That among the number who thus surrounded the Men whose names were contained in the warrant the Deponent observed a man of the name of Bruce who was extremely active in preventing the said warrant being put in execution. That he knew a number of their faces but does not know their names. Depones that he was informed by Samuel Matheson Tenant in Kenavaid that if any of their number were laid hold of, the circumstances would be heard of for many years to come. That from the temper of mind in which the men appeared to be the Deponent did not think it safe for the Officer to put his warrant in execution even if he had a party of One hundred men. Depones that he saw the said Bruce put his left hand round one of the people whom the officer apprehended, and pulled him into the Crowd, while with his right he brandished his Stick above the Officer's head. That the said Bruce was aided and assisted by his neighbours armed with Sticks as beforementioned who surrounded the prisoners and carried them into the Crowd. Depones and concurs with the preceding Deponents as to the Sheriff's having ordered the Crowd quietly to disperse under the pains and penalties of the Law, that the proceedings of the day might not be prevented; all which is Truth as he shall answer to God. (signed) James Duncan, Robert Mackid.

Notes by Marchioness of Stafford of conversations with Lord Selkirk: 18 March and 13 April, 1813

March 18th

Lord Selkirk desired General Wemyss to bring him to Cleveland

House to have some conversation relative to the Kildonan People. He said a plan was in agitation to raise a Corps for service in Canada, that it was to consist of married men, and that those who enlisted were to obtain land and settlements for their Families there. He proposed to enlist men from Kildonan provided their Families could still be accommodated there till the war was over. I explained to him the offers made to the People if they chose to remain in Sutherland, which he said he considered as very fair and handsome, but doubted if they would take to habits of Industry at home; and therefore wished to know if such a proposal would be encouraged. I told him it was impracticable as leaving the Families without the men to assist in settling them would only increase the difficulty.

April 13

Lord Selkirk called at Richmond in consequence he said of seeing an advertisement in the Inverness Paper of the 1st of April for Shipmasters willing to convey Emigrants to America from Sutherland. I told him I was surprized at that, having heard from Mr Young that the people again appeared quiet and willing to settle in the manner proposed, and that Mr Young had confirmed the Opinion I exprest that the scheme he proposed was impracticable and also that the men would not leave their Families behind. He exprest a wish (from an idea which he said had at that moment occurred to him on reading a Letter I showed him from Mr Young to Mr Sheriff[1]) to become Lord Stafford's Tenant for some hundred acres of land on Strathy could suitable land be procured, on which he would arrange these people and assist in promoting a settlement there. I told him if he would write any proposal of what occurred to him he might send it to Mr Young. He took down Mr Young's direction, but said he preferred previously corresponding with the proprietor and did not like to make any proposal unless I gave him encouragement to think it would be accepted. I said I could give no encouragement of that sort, till Lord Stafford had seen the proposal and had time to take the full opinion upon it of Mr Young and persons in the country who he might wish to consult with regard to its being practicable or not. We then calculated how many days this would require. I also said that the conduct of the People

[1] David Sheriff of Kinmylies, Inverness, to whom Young wrote a description of his Sutherland plans on 22 February 1813 (see below, ii, p. 191).

after the Offers already made them with regard to settlement in Sutherland was not encouraging, and that we could not interfere in any scheme for sending them to America or make any other proposal for a settlement at home different from what had been already held out to them, and that if our Agents were to make any proposal to them with a view to sending them to America they would suspect they had not fair play and that it would defeat its own purpose.

He said he should go home and set about arranging his ideas and putting them on paper in the form of a Project[1] and send them to me.

Lands on the Estate of Sutherland set at Golspy Inn 15 December 1813.

Farms	Offerers names	Sums offered	Yearly rent accepted
Strathymains etc.	Present tenants	£157	
	John Campbell Skibo	£160	
	George Innes Isauld[2]	£168	
Set to George Innes for 7 years at £168 and for 12 years more at			£180
Rossal and Dalharrold Lots in Strathnaver	Present tenants	£250	
	John Paterson Sandside[3] first 7 years	£350	
	John Paterson Sandside next 12 years	£400	
	Patrick Sellar	£360	
	Patrick Sellar	£410	
Set to Patrick Sellar first 2 years at £200, 3 years at £300 and 14 years at			£438 11s. 6d.
Langdale and Skale	John Paterson Sandside	£175	
	Robert Gordon Langdale	£230	£230
Syre and Kankyle	Present tenants, Left at will	£120	£130
Grubmore and Grubbeg	Present tenants, At will	£100	£105

[1] Nothing corresponding to this paper can be traced, but Lord Selkirk wrote to the Marquis on 22 April 1813, advising that no obstacle should be placed in the way of emigration, and offering to give security for any land given to emigrants' families in Strathy or Armadale.

[2] Par. Reay, Caithness.   [3] Par. Reay, Caithness.

Tubeg and Dymachcarry	Thomas MacKay present tenant	£70	
	Donald Mathieson Dalmore	£80	
	Captain Kenneth MacKay Torbol	£80	£80
Ardravine in Strathnaver	Mr John MacKay Shiness[1]		£40
Pollyour etc. Strathbrora	John Macdonald	£70	
	John Cleugh	£75	£75
	John Sutherland Clyne	£68	
Crislich etc. Strathbrora	Donald Matheson	£56	
	Sergeant Melville present tenant	£52	£60
Achnaluachrach	John Murray	£60	
	Douglass and Murray	£60	
	Ironhill and J. Duncan Golspy	£80	£80
Dalmore in Strathfleet	Angus MacKay Rogart	£42	
	Alexander Gunn Schoolmaster	£30	
	Alexander Campbell Lairg a drunken fellow who could not be trusted	£50	
	Sergeant Robert Macdonald present tenant	£42	£42 10s.
Kintraad and Davochbeg	Present tenants	£60	
	Sheriff MacKid	£80	
	Captain J. MacKay Cambusavie	£85	£85
Achurach and Michaelwells	Alexander Matheson Dornoch	£42	
	William Munro General Merchant	£42	£44

Lands set		£1,590 1s. 6d.
Remainder of Strathnaver may be worth		£753
		£2,343 1s. 6d.

Present rent of the above lands	£1,194 5s.	
Additional rent to be obtained	£1,148 16s. 6d.	£2,343 1s. 6d.

except £74 13s. 6d. amount of Colonel Clunes wadset Lands[2] to be redeemed at Whitsunday per notice given and accepted of

Present rent of Strathnaver including all the Wadsets	£930 2s. 8d.
Increase by the new set	£846 8s. 10d.
Rent now obtained	£1,776 11s. 6d.

[1] Mackay appears to have been in partnership with Duncan Matheson in Shiness sheep farm; Ardravine is entered as part of this farm in the 1815 rental.
[2] See above, p. 17.

K

Report by Robert Bald,[1] Mineral Surveyor, Alloa, relative to the
Field of Minerals which skirts the East Coast of Sutherland Shire
from Golspie to the ord of Caithness, and in particular regarding
the Coal lately fitted at Brora: Rhives, 26 March 1814

At the request of William Young Esquire I have surveyed the
above mentioned district, and from what I observed have to offer
the following remarks.

The Coal Field at Brora has long been remarked by Mineralogists
as singular in its situation being insulated and far disjoined from
what is termed the Great Coal Field of Scotland which stretches
like a Zone or Belt from the Mouths of the Rivers Tay and Forth
to the west Coast in the district of Ayr Shire. Coal has been wrought
west of Brora water upon the Margin of the Sea, and a Salt manufactory there established many years ago, but the quality of the
Coal being so uncommonly sulphurous, and the Field much intersected with slips and troubles, the Colliery was abandoned, and there
only now remain the vestiges of the Pits and Salt pans. I am informed
that the Pyrites were so interwoven with the Coal and so abundant
that when the Coals were laid in a heap and exposed to the air, a
decomposition ensued, heat was generated and actual Combustion
was the consequence. Such a quality of Coal prevented it being
carried to Sea, and it was only fitted for burning in large quantities
such as in the manufacture of Salt and burning of Lime Stone. The
discovery of a good Coal in this remote district of Country so far
North from the Coal districts, was of great importance, as nothing
more directly tends to the immediate improvement of a Country
as abundance of Fuel particularly Coal, and 'tis found from observation that generally in proportion as Coal is in abundance, in like
proportion will be the Population of that District, the Number of
Manufactories and Scale of the general Trade.

The Noble Owners of this very extensive district of Country,
with a Praise worthy Zeal, and with the most Benevolent views have
for some time past paid particular attention to the general improve-

---

[1] Robert Bald (1776-1861), manager of Mr Erskine of Mar's coal-mines at Alloa,
and author of *A General View of the Coal Trade of Scotland* (Edinburgh, 1812); for
him see *Proceedings of the Royal Society of Edinburgh*, v, 29, and *Quarterly Journal of the
Geological Society of London*, xix (1863), xxx. I am indebted to Dr Charles Waterston
for these references.

ment of this district, and amongst the many Improvements, no Pains or Expences have been spared in exploring the district near Brora for Coal, these Trials have been crown'd with a success beyond what the most sanguine could have expected, a Coal has been found regularly stratified, and a Compleat winning has been made of it at the depth of above 80 yards from the surface.

★   ★   ★1

Having thus given a sketch of the general appearance of this mineral field, we now have to consider it in an economical point of view. The Coal has been judiciously fitted under the direction of Mr William Hughes from Wales; it is won at the depth of about 80 yards; a powerfull water wheel Keeps the mine dry, and a small water wheel with reverse Buckets draws the Coal to the Bank; the Pumps are in two lifts with 9½ Inch Barrels, and the Engine manages the whole growth in 3 Hours out of the 24 Hours. Besides the Engine Pit a crop or Relief pit is also sunk from which the Coals are drawn up. The shist in sinking the Pits being uncommonly soft, and full of smooth Backs it was found necessary to case or build the sides of the Pits with ashler stone from top to bottom, which is executed in a workman like manner. The point of Position, with regard to the Engine Pit is well chosen, being intermediate betwixt a shallow and temporary fitting, and a deep and expensive one, the whole is well conceived, and the Machinery executed in a substantial form, the only part I think slight is the Iron Beam which I apprehend ought to be strengthened, in order to run no unwarrantable risques. The Aqueduct is also well executed, and a Supply of Water can be commanded to drive the most powerfull machinery.

I descended the Pit, and found the Coal regular and uniform in its bed, and so far as opened up of the most promising appearance, indeed nothing can be more so. It is of the Cubical Kind, with a small Band of Splint and Pitch Coals; it is singular in its internal structure, and very full of Glazed twisted backs; it burns with a cheerfull Flame, is free of Sulphur, and leaves a residuum of fine

---

1 At this point Bald gives a lengthy survey of the geology of the East Sutherland coast, which is here omitted. Dr Charles Waterston, of the Royal Scottish Museum, hopes to publish this, together with the similar report made in 1812 by John Farey senior (see above, p. lxiii).

brown and white coloured ashes; from this last circumstance it remains red hot for a long time after the bitumen is burn'd off, the fine ashes preventing the action of the air. In my opinion it is fitted for every purpose of Domestic economy and for Public Works. The Main Levels from the Engine Pit are extended but a little way and the Main Roads are in the same situation. The Shropshire plan of working[1] has been begun, and I think it well suited for this Coal; at present there is a wall of 40 yards working forward, in a very regular manner, the strata has not yet made a break, therefore great caution is required till this take place. I have given the manager every injunction to be prepared for this by Keeping the roads clear and secure, so soon as the Break takes place, the work will go on regularly and according to system. At present there are sinkers employed in putting down the Engine pit in the hope of finding these Coals, it is down 6 yards, and only a thin coal of no value has been found.

An excellent Rail Way is now nearly completed from the Pits to the Harbor at Brora and the Harbor is in a great state of forwardness, there is already Berth room for shipping the output of Coals of the largest Colliery in Scotland. The Coal being Tender and full of joints, there is an opportunity of dropping it at a moderate height into the Vessels from the Quay; this will be found very superior to the proposed shipping stations near the Bridge where from the great height the Coals would be shivered to pieces and lose of value from 5 to 10 per Cent.

The consideration is to give an Idea of the best mode now to be pursued in bringing the work to a regular output of Coal, and therefore would suggest, that as a Coal of 3 feet 6 inches has been found of good quality and highly valuable in this northerly district, every attention and energy ought to be directed to this Coal exclusively; with this view the farther sinking of the Engine pit ought to be suspended and also every investigation for other seams of Coal, untill this Seam is in fair and comfortable working order, no other point of pursuit ought to draw aside the attention of these concerned in the work. I therefore earnestly recommend that the Main Levels and Main roads be set forward with double Shifts till

[1] For the 'long wall' or Shropshire method of mining, see J. U. Nef, *The Rise of the British Coal Industry* (1932), i, 364-5.

each be extended fully 200 yards, this accomplished, they can then be carried on with single shifts only. The Crop or Rise Mine ought in the same manner to be pushed forward and not stopped till the Coal is cut off either by the Earth cover or Dead Crop, or by some natural obstruction, these operations would at once open wall, give scope for an increased output of Coals and fair and practical Data be obtained for calculating the extent of this Field of Coal. Without this mode of procedure the work may be brought to an uncomfortable situation by slips intersecting the strata which are to be found in every colliery. By adopting the Plan suggested if such should occur, time is granted to the manager to get beyond these and have Coal wall ready for the workmen as they come forward with their work. So soon however as the Colliery is brought to a regular and Systematic plan of operations, the strata of the Coal formation of this district ought to be explored in a leisurly way by boring, according to a regular laid down Line of Search.

In working this Coal I would in a particular manner advise that it be sent to market according to the Glasgow mode which is business like, and avoid the awkward system of the Lothian and River Forth Collieries. The former sell their Coals in cumulo as they come from the mine, only separating the Dross by a riddle, the latter divide their Coals when wrought into 4 Kinds viz. Great Coal, Household Coal, Chew Coal and Lime Coal, the Household Coals are on the Glasgow plan. The River Forth Coal masters are at this instant making very great sacrifices to be free of their present system, and I therefore the more strongly recommend the avoiding of it at Brora. The Lime Coal can be seperated below ground with a Harp shovel, what passes this can be sent up for salt making and Lime burning.

While inspecting the Coal below ground I observed a slip in the strata of about 3 feet, and I have to remark, that in the whole of my survey along the coast I was surprised to find no Dikes intersecting the strata and few slips of any magnitude, from this I am led to Hope that the Brora Coal may extend to a considerable distance in its line of Bearing. Upon this extention the value of the Coal field depends.

I examined the Uppat Coal[1] 3 feet 4 Inches thick, it has a good

[1] A seam of coal was found on the shore near Strathsteven in February 1814 by one John Mathieson; see also below, ii, pp. 214–15.

appearance at the dead crop, but I would do nothing here till Brora Coal is in regular and compleat order; tis very probable that several other Seams may be found along the Shore.

There is only one good Collier in the work at present under the manager, the others are Natives of Sutherland who already work well, they are hearty and cheerfull at work. The common prejudice against the occupation of a Collier being thus happily removed, we have reason to hope that ere long there will be no want of Colliers in this district. A few good Colliers must in the mean time be instantly procured from the Coal district of Scotland and these would soon establish the work.

I am aware that the establishing of this Colliery must be attended with difficulties out of the common path, on account of its situation, but these difficulties are in narrow compass. The Colliery in other respects will be wrought at comparatively small expence, as the water machinery placed it nearly on a footing with a Level free Coal, and in many instances I know superior.

Salt Pans

It is proposed to erect Salt Pans at Brora to consume the small Coal, these will be an evident good and profitable concern; it is proper to erect no more than Two at present, till it is seen how all other matters go forward.

Clay

The Clay near the Engine Pit tho' rather coarse and free, will I think make good Brick. A Brick Table can immediately be set agoing and if the Clay is found suitable for Tyle, the requisite Buildings may be ready next Season, 'tis not possible to accomplish this at present. The Flat ground near the pits is very suitable for such a work and the Clay can be melled[1] by aid of a water wheel which will be a great convenience.

Lime Stone

Lime stone abounds along the coast and enters into the composition of the greater part of the Strata. I saw no very fine Bands of it, but such may be found upon minute investigation. A coarse sandy Kid and White mottled Lime stone mixed with chert or Petro Silin is seen above the Mill of Golspie, but it does not appear to be worth pursuing after.

[1] Broken down by use of a maul or mallet.

Immediately adjoining Rheves a very fine Lime stone of a Whitish Grey Colour has been discovered, and is now opening up by Mr Young; the appearances are very good and encouraging and am led to conclude that it stretches along the Mountain foot. A Level is bringing up to take off the water, and tis proper to give this Rock a full and fair Trial. An extent of this stone would be very valuable here connected with the Coal, and the situation adjoining the Shore with a moderate declivity offers every facility for erecting Kilns, forming a waggon way and for receiving Coals from Brora by Sea.

To conclude I consider the whole train of operations in this mineral field connected with the general Improvements now carrying on in this district, as directed with Zeal and Benevolence for ameliorating the condition of Man. The state of the Inhabitants here requires a stimulus to exertion in order to render them more usefull to Society and more comfortable at home. If the Colliery flourishes as I trust it will, there is no doubt of the happiest results, which will in every point of view amply repay the Benevolence here exerted, and which is directed with Zeal and Spirit by These to whom the whole train of Improvements is committed in charge.

Heads of the complaints against Mr Sellar contained in the Petition of the Inhabitants presented to Lady Stafford at Dunrobin: July 1814

That in March his Shepherds burnt all the Heath on his Farm to the very enclosures and left none for their cattle.

That a few days after the removing he pulled down all the Houses, Barns, Kilns and Mills, contrary to use and custom of the Country, which is that the removing Tenant has the Barn, Kiln and Miln 12 months after removing for manufacturing the Crop left on the Ground.

That he allowed them a few days to carry off their wood, but on account of distance (some being 12 miles off) they could not within the time. They were afterwards prevented by his Shepherds.

Instructions to Messrs Young and Sellar: July 1814[1]

Instructions for Mr Young

1. Assynt   In the event of Mr Mcdonalds removal his lands to be sett among the people.

2. Creich   Invershin to be advertised and to be publicly set for the duration of Marshall and Aitkinsons lease on the adjoining lands under the usual conditions.[2]

3. Lairg   Tomich to be divided among the people.

4. Dornoch   Castle and Garden to be advertised either for an Inn or for a private family.[3]

Feus may be given on ground in Dornoch for 99 years on building leases.

5. Rogart   Splockton[4] lately held by Captain Angus McKay to be divided between Mrs Urquhart Rogart and Mrs McKay.

6. Golspie   Uppat to be managed with the view of making it a cattle grazing. The roof of the house ought to be inspected and kept tight.

All Cottages should be sett at $6\frac{1}{2}$ per Cent Interest.

7. Clyne   Doll lands South of the road to be offered to Feuars and if they dont require it Lord Stafford to crop it.

Andersons farm to be left in case necessary for the Coal work.

The other people in Doll in like manner to remain tenants at will.

Widow Melville to be removed and have a Cows grass and cottage only.

Mr Walter Ross[5] to be bargained with as Mr Young best can.

Carroll to be lotted among the present tenants at

---

[1] MS. incomplete.

[2] Gilbert Mackenzie, the former tenant, had gone bankrupt. Atkinson and Marshall took a lease of Invershin in 1814, but were replaced in the following year by Messrs Morton and Culley, sheep-farmers in Ross-shire.

[3] Dornoch Castle was renovated between 1812 and 1814 at a cost of £1,745. It was still unlet at Martinmas 1815.

[4] Splockhill is the correct form.   [5] Minister of Clyne.

          the best rent possible but no lease to be given.

8. Kildonan   To lott among the people the lands from Kilearnan
                to Lord Hermands Wadsett.[1]

9. Kelp Shores To be sett for nine or twelve years thus:

        1st.   East of Strathsteven march to a kelp maker on
               proper regulations and after public Advertise-
               ment.

        2nd. West of Strathsteven march thus:

             1st.   From Strathsteven to Golspie burn to
                  be valued to Dunrobin farm.

             2nd. West of Golspie burn to be put into
                  three lotts and Sett publicly, the ware
                  only to be used as manure, the lots
                  which are to be sett up separately thus:

                  1st. From Golspie burn to the West
                     march of Drummuy.

                  2nd. The East side of the Little-ferry.

                  3rd. The West Side of the Little-ferry.

Instructions to Patrick Sellar

    His duty Consists in the Collection of the rents, attending that the
tenants enter into Tacks and fullfill the Conditions of these Tacks,
preventing turff Cutting, in every situation without leave of the
family, and preventing or punishing all transgression of the Game
laws.

Query:[2]   Where Mr Young desires me defer the recovery of a
rent, am I to do so, or in general to use my best Skill and discretion
in discharging this part of my duty?

Documents relating to proposed submission between Patrick
Sellar and tenants of Strathnaver: February 1815

A William Young to Earl Gower (later 2nd Duke of Sutherland)
                                 Rhives, 16 February 1815

    Refering to my letter of 10th Instant with respect to the Colliers
I have now had the honor to receive Your Lordships of 8th covering

---

[1] Elderable, Guilable and Ulbster (par. Kildonan), shown as set to small tenants in
the 1814 rental.   [2] This paragraph is added in Sellar's handwriting.

Petition from the Strathnaver tenants which it is directed that I am to get Mr Cranstoun[1] to determine in.

I presume the short and proper way is for both parties to submit their respective Claims and complaints agreeable to the inclosed Copy of a paper which I have drawn up and which I will instantly dispatch along with your Lordships letter to the Strath drawn up on stamped paper to be signed by the people. I was really in hopes that all this Jarring had been amicably adjust betwixt Mr Sellar and the tenants and that the Noble Family woud never have heard more of it. I wish there is not some incendiary at the bottom of it, however the truth will come out and it is right it shoud.

B William Young to Strathnaver tenants: Rhives, 16 February 1815

Along with this the tenants will receive a letter from Earl Gower and a Submission to be signed by them referring their disputes with Mr Sellar to The Sheriff Depute of Sutherland, but the tenants will consult some person in whom they have confidence to know if this paper is right and proper that no blame nor odium may be attached to me for directing what I consider right.

c Draft Submission betwixt Mr Patrick Sellar and Tenants in Strathnaver: February 1815

The Parties following viz. Patrick Sellar Esquire tenant of the Rossal and Truderskaig Sheep farms in Culmaily on the one Part and [   ][2] late tenants in said farms on the other Part have submitted and referred and hereby submit and refer all demands Claims disputes questions and differences depending and subsisting between them on any account or transaction whatever to the decision final sentence and decree arbitral to be given forth and pronounced by George Cranstown Esquire Sheriff Depute of the County of Sutherland arbiter mutually chosen by the said Parties with power to the said arbiter to receive the Claims of the Parties, take all manner of probation he may think necessary by writ, witnesses or oath of Party for deciding the matters hereby submitted and to hear the Parties thereon and whatever the said arbiter shall determine in the premises by the decreet arbitral to be pronounced by him betwixt

[1] George Cranstoun (d. 1850), sheriff-depute of Sutherland, later Lord Corehouse (see D.N.B., xiii, 32).
[2] MS. blank.

and the [   ]¹ day of [   ]¹ or on or before any other day to
which he shall prorogate this Submission which he is hereby Empowered to do at pleasure.

Both Parties Bind and oblige themselves and their heirs and
successors to acquiesce in implement and fulfill to each other under
the penalty of One hundred Pounds Sterling to be paid by the
Party failing to the Party observing or willing to observe the same,
over and above performance and the said Parties consent to the
registration hereof in the Books of Council and Session or others
competent that letters of horning on six days Charge and all other
execution may pass on a decree interponed hereto in common
form and for that purpose Constitute [   ]¹ Their procurators
etc. In witness whereof these presents written by William Grant
Clerk to William Young Esquire at Rhives are subscribed as
follows etc.

Patrick Sellar to Lord Advocate Colquhoun
                                           Culmaily, 24 May 1815²
It is with great pain and much reluctance that I venture to trouble
your Lordship, on a subject, which may carry *an appearance* of complaint against the person officiating as Judge Ordinary or Sheriff-
Substitute of this County. I am sensible that the conduct of a Judge
is not, on slight grounds to be suspected. I feel what is due to good
order and to the happy government under which we live; and I
have no inclination to accuse or bring disrepute against any constituted authority. As a person, however aggrieved by the contriv-
ances of this man, in danger of being ruined by his machinations,
more *particularly at present* in the opinion of your *Lordship*, I trust
you will have the goodness to forgive me for the inclosed Note;
which, nothing but the necessity of my case would have made me
intrude upon you and of which I humbly venture to beg your
perusal.

Note
At the sources of the rivers Helmsdale and Naver on Lord and
Lady Staffords Estate in this Country, there lies a very great extent

¹ MS. blank.
² Archibald Colquhoun (d. 1820), Lord Advocate, 1807-16.

of high bog land, subject to mildew, and never intended for the residence of man; altho' being covered with the sheathed cotton grass,[1] deerhair,[2] bents, and other Alpine plants that abound in the highest of the border mountains, it is admirably calculated for Stock. The shores of the Country fronting the West side of the Hoy Island in Orkney, and washed by the Atlantic Ocean, near the mouth of the Pentland Frith, abound at all season with fish of the best quality. The London Smacks which supply Billingsgate ply there, continually; and the herring in their season are numerous beyond all computation. These two points which comprehend the sole material wealth of the district, were however lost to the country, the fishing, by the want of people to ply the sea, and the pasture by their presence in the interior where, while they destroyed the winter food for stock and thereby rendered it impossible to use the Alpine herbage of the mountain, they lived in the same degree of civilization, as their fathers had done 500 years ago, altho' in less purity in so far, as, their chief employment was the importation of grain from Caithness, the illicit distillation of it in their impenetrable fastnesses into whisky and the transportation of it in that shape back to the low country.

Lord and Lady Stafford were pleased *humanely*, to order a new arrangement of this Country. That the interior should be possessed by Cheviot Shepherds and the people brought down to the coast and placed there in lotts under the size of three arable acres, sufficient for the maintenance of an industrious family, but pinched enough to cause them turn their attention to the fishing. I presume to say that the proprietors *humanely* ordered this arrangement, because, it surely was a most benevolent action, to put these barbarous hordes into a position, where they could better Associate together, apply to industry, educate their children, and advance in civilization; and I hope I shall be excused for thinking with the greatest deference, that this good motive may be safely applied to a family who have for the last four years to my knowledge, divided, yearly among the

---

[1] The sheathed cotton grass or sedge (*eriphorum vaginatum*) is valued by shepherds as an early bite for sheep at lambing time.
[2] The deerhair sedge (*tricophorum caespitosum*) is of less importance as a food for sheep than the sheathed cotton grass. I am indebted to Dr R. M. Crawford for the information in this and the preceding note.

tenantry in exchange for work, many thousand pounds *beyond the total rental of the Estate.*

This arrangement however, by such as had an interest in the former state of things, or an ill will to the Noble Family or their doers here, and by some well meaning persons influenced by these, was called a very cruel one. Every measure of intimidation as well as of artifice and intrigue was employed to thwart it; and, when these failed, to calumniate, and to entrap and distress the agents.

In carrying thro' the measure, the arrangement of the grounds, and the provision of lotts for the people was in the duty of Mr Young, the Family's commissioner and Manager here, mine was the more unpleasant one of removing them to their lotts and putting the new tenants into possession; in the execution of which, I had to perform a most difficult task, rendered more so by the circumstance, that of the several farms sett for Cheviot stock, I myself required for the maintenance of my stock, access to one of which I had with my employers approbation become tacksman.

In concert with Mr McKid the Sheriff substitute to whom I allude in my letter, a few of these people have been induced to complain of me to my employers; to publish anonymously in the public prints and to petition the Advocate Depute at the Inverness Circuit against me, in all which measures they have carefully avoided the precise discussion of any charge, but have endeavoured to traduce me and to obtain a remitt to Mr Mackid *the silent mover of the business* privately and in absence of me to lead a precognition against me for your Lordships information.

As Mr Mackid never gave me the least notice of the nature of the investigation to be made by him or of the crimes laid to my charge, I can only gather the nature of these things from the anonymous publication made by the party, wherein it is said, that in removing the tenants to their allottments, I *waited* no form of law but applied 'the torch to their dwellings' and involved the country in one general conflagration, or words to that purpose.

If this heavy charge – so heavy indeed as to inferr the punishment of death – be foully and falsely made against an innocent man, I am sure, My Lord, you will pity this man from the bottom of your heart. If the accused person, far from attempting to quibble, to conceal the facts, and evade the law, begs as a most particular favour that your Lordship will be pleased to permitt him lay before you, *evidence of every step he took*, in the Removal of the tenantry, I trust he may in this respect at least be said to differ from the common cast of criminals who come under your cognisance. I do most humbly and earnestly implore this. Earl Gower indeed who *knows* Mr Mackid expected that Mr Cranstoun might be able to do me this Justice, but as this eminent counsel is not resident in the Country and his time is really too precious to be spent in what I flatter myself he considers to be unfounded accusations, may I not be permitted thro' the medium of the Sheriff Depute or Substitute of Inverness-shire, or Ross-shire or the Sheriff Depute of Caithness who reside in the North whom I should willingly pay for the trouble, to lay before you the documents and the evidence on which I found.

My procedure which I will instruct before either of these Gentlemen, was as follows.

1st. The ground having been sett on the 15th December 1813, and Mr Young having in presence of the people begged me to leave on my lott as many of them as possible in possession for one year; I met the people on the 15th day of January 1814, agreed with one half their number to leave them in the best part of my farm at less than a fair proportion of my permanent rent, and then intimated to the rest, that, as my stock were to *come to the ground at Whitsunday*, I could not at that term avoid, but must have complete possession.

2nd. On the 1st, 2nd and 18th days of March I brought regular summonses of Removal, on which the tenants were charged 'to compear before the Sheriff depute etc. on the 18th March and 4th April to hear and see themselves decerned and ordained by decreet and sentence of the Sheriff depute or his Substitute to flitt and remove themselves, wives, bairns, families, servants, subtenants, cottars, dependents, and whole goods and gear, furth and from the possession of the said lands and others at the terms of removal after-mentioned, viz. from the houses, gardens, grass, and mills, at the term of Whitsunday next 1814 and from the arable lands under crop at the separation of crop 1814 from the ground.'

3rd. These Summonses I called regularly in Court on the days of compearance and obtained decreets of removing in terms of the libels.

4th. In the first of May I extracted the decreets and caused charge the defenders in the usual way to remove within six days.

5th. On the 25th May my Shepherd went and requested leave to put his family into the one end, of *one* of the houses, and access to the ground but he was, in a manner very insulting to me, refused the least accommodation for his family, and was obliged to lodge on a neighbouring farm, possessed by Gentlemen in Northumberland, untill measures could be followed.

6th. I of consequence stated the fact of refusal by petition to the Sheriff, and after expiry of the days of charge obtained letters of Ejection.

7th. With this warrant and the Officers I proceeded to the ground about *the 4th June*, waited *patiently on repeated promises by the people as repeatedly broken* untill the *8th*, and the men having at that time disappeared leaving the Women only at home in the hope of baffling me by this manoeuvre and wearying me out, I at length desired the Officers read their warrants and do their duty. They began to eject from a few houses, at the one end of the farm, and *after ejecting*, pulled down the turff cabins which were my property to prevent the people from re-entering. When the men learnt this appearance of firmness they made their Appearance, Set to work to *obey the Sheriffs decreet*, by removing of themselves, and gave me possession on the 13th June *several weeks after the term*, After the new rents had begun to run, and I had, had a very considerable loss of stock by the want of food.

8th. I affirm that notwithstanding the greater part almost the whole of the timber of the hutts was my property, I gave it all but two houses to the people, nor was one hutt or one Stick of a single hutt on the ground taken possession of by me, *burned by any person in my employ*.

9th. So standing the fact, How came such an accusation at all to be brought forward? I beg to inform your Lordship. When I met the people in January they begged that I would assure them of some permanency in the half of my farm which I had assigned to them. I told them I could make no such promise, and added, that there were stealers of sheep as they knew in the Country; and if I lost any in the hirsel marching with them, I should certainly remove every one of them at the end of the first year. Some of the men took me aside and told me they could not be answerable for cattle or Sheep so long as one Chisholm a tinker was permitted to dwell in part of *their* ground. They said he had come some years ago, nobody knew from where, had taken up his residence along with a woman of the country in a moss in one of the wildest parts of the parish, That his first wife who was still alive had lately found him out and come to his house with a parcel of tinkers, and that I must take care to have him removed. Accordingly when we arrived in Strathnaver I sent notice to the tinker that he must be off. I repeated this to him personally on a second occasion; and, he having disregarded the notice, and refused obedience to the Sheriffs decree which run against the principal tenand under whom he possessed, I caused the Officers along with a party of the people who were to possess the ground go to eject him on the 13 June. They arrived at the place I understand about Eleven o clock, read their warrants, ejected him and pulled the roof off and the timber out of the turff house. This they accomplished by four o clock when I arrived there in my return to this Coast. There was a small outer hutt standing untouched into which the woman had removed with some trash of furniture, and by this time every thing was out of the dwelling house, the turff roof taken off and the birch-boughs or sticks etc. laying on the Ground. I advised the people to take the woman into the Strath and build a hutt for her. I told the tinker to be off with himself otherwise I should have him taken up, and I warned the inhabitants to take care he did not erect a new hutt on the premisses. The people replied that he was a daring fellow who certainly would rebuild the hutt and take new possession as soon as I left the Country. And in order to prevent this I said that whatever part of the sticks they could not then carry to the Strath we should burn. Here I must mention that these sticks consisted in part of Moss fir, but most partly of birchen-boughs, cutt on the Noble familys property. This birch wood is at the removal of a householder the property of the proprietor, but the moss fir being dugg by the occupant is either carried away by the Removing tenant, or valued over from him to the entering tenant. In order to prevent the possibility of any impropriety I therefore paid the tinker in presence of the people the comprisement of this stuff, and thereafter presented to the men what part they could carry with them and the officers burned the balance, leaving the tinkers family in the small hutt above mentioned from which we expected he might soon remove. But on my return hither about 50 miles distant, he presently found new birchen-boughs, set up one of their turff cabins as usual in a few hours and I understand is there to this day.

Lastly. It has been Argued by some why not leave the people in their hutts?

I answer 1st. It was my duty to compell them to go to their allottments where they now live and have begun to prosecute the fishing.

2nd. I will prove that they have such opportunities and are so inclined to the stealing of sheep that with every care to keep them off stock grounds, the farmers pay them nearly as much in mutton as they do to the Proprietor in rent! To have run my flocks *in among their residences* would have been *inevitable ruin.*

3rd. I left a barn standing for every 7 acres under crop.

Here I close, after apologising to your Lordship for this intrusion. If I am a criminal, I give you a complete clue to trace my footsteps and bring me to conviction. If innocent I know that I shall experience your Lordships compassion, that you will do me justice.

Patrick Sellar to Lord Advocate Colquhoun

Culmaily, 29 May 1815

Since I did myself the Honour to address your Lordship on the 24th Current Mr McKid the Sheriff Substitute has returned from Strathnaver, and without allowing me at all to be heard, (notwithstanding I applied to him by letter of which I inclose a copy) he has, I learn, forwarded his precognition to your Lordship or Mr Cranstoun.

As I have frequently experienced his ill-will toward me, and have seen how in examining Gaelic witnesses by an interpreter, mischief may be done, expecially where the witness leans to that side, I have little doubt that the precognition contains a tissue of Misrepresentations against me.

In addition to what I took the liberty to state in my last letter I beg to instruct

L

1st. That Mr Mackid told a Gentleman of my acquaintance long before the present affair happened, that he would let slip no opportunity to do me an injury. His words were 'to wind a pirn about my ears.'

2nd. That in examining certain of the witnesses in this private precognition he silenced them as often as they attempted to detail any fact favourable for me.

I humbly lay claim to your Lordship and Mr Cranstouns protection from this oppression. Mr McKid must know me to be innocent, but he hopes to ruin my character, and to injure my fortune by subjecting me to odium, trouble and expences.

I have sent Mr Cranstoun a copy of this letter as well as of my former communication to your Lordship. So far as they concern Mr McKid I humbly consider them part of the precognition. I mean to say that I proceed with no *animus injuriandi*, when I state these facts concerning Mr McKids conduct, which are forced from me by his oppression.

Patrick Sellar to Robert Mackid

Culmaily, 27 May 1815

I learn by common report, that you have been in Strathnaver expiscating for evidence against me, in some charges, which are said to be made against me of a criminal nature, but of the particulars of which I have no notice.

I consider it proper to advise you of consequence that I am at home, that I expect to be informed what crime it is that you lay to my door; and that I am ready to answer any questions which you may think proper to put to me relative thereto.

You will be so kind I hope as to minute this notice in your procedure.

[no answer made.]

Lady Staffords answer to the petition of the Strathnaver people dated 16 August 1815

Dunrobin Castle, 21 August 1815

The persons signing this petition have been allowed to remain in their former situations a year longer than those from other parts of the Strath who have settled in their new lots and who have been occupied industriously and beneficially to themselves and satisfactorily to Lady Stafford. Instead of taking advantage of the time so allowed them for building their homes and taking possession of their lots, these petitioners have either disposed of them to others or neglected them altogether. Lady Stafford is determined that the legal and proper regulations in the improvement of the country shall be carried into effect by the managers and considers this representation as one not founded on fact and consequently that it is unworthy of Attention.

The object of the letter signed by General Wemyss and John Fraser[1] having been long since amply fulfilled and the articles in it fully complied with such letters are no longer of any avail.

*Note humbly Submitted to Mr Cranstoun by Patrick Sellar Factor for the Marquis and Marchioness of Stafford: 14 September 1815

From what Mr Cranstoun, is so good as express concerning the Ejectment of the Tinker I add no more on this subject, unless to express my regret that Mr Cranstoun does not find himself at liberty to examine the witnesses suggested by me to his Majestys Advocate.[2]

Mr Cranstoun is so good as mention the Accusations[3] which were not made known to me by his Substitute. I beg to say a few words on each.

1st. It is, it seems, informed that I ordered a young man to be

---

[1] See above, pp. xxvii-xxviii.

[2] Sellar wrote to Loch (*13 October 1815) that he had named six witnesses. In a lengthy undated 'Statement of Facts' submitted to the Lord Advocate he listed various names in support of particular parts of his case. The six to whom he referred in his letter to Loch were those present at the ejection of Chisholm the tinker: Kenneth Murray, sheriff officer, Alexander Sutherland, Alexander Mackenzie, James Fraser (the last three called by Sellar 'instrumentary witnesses'), John Burns, farmer at Achvarrisdale in Caithness, and Donald Macleod son of William Macleod in Rossal (called by Sellar 'indifferent spectators'). In his letter to Loch Sellar describes Macleod as 'mason in Rossal', which must identify him as the celebrated author of the Gloomy Memories. It is remarkable to find Sellar proposing Macleod as a witness on his behalf. Of the six, only Sutherland, Fraser and Burns gave evidence at Sellar's trial (T. Sellar, The Sutherland Evictions of 1814 (London, 1883), l-liii).

[3] See Sellar, op. cit., xvii-xxii.

removed from a house in Garvault notwithstanding he lay dangerously ill.[1]

Answered. The first house, that we came to, was I think, John
Munro's in Garvault. There was *no appearance* of their attempting
to flitt, upon enquiry for the cause, of this they said that their son
lay dangerously ill, and they had found it impossible on that Account
to go to their new possession. This was a plausible excuse and we
went into the house. The Officers and my Shepherd went into an
Inner Chamber where the supposed sick man lay, and you will
guess my astonishment when I first heard a laugh, and then saw
getting out of bed, dressed, a healthy rosy young man whom I had
*the day before met foxhunting in Beni-Vanton with Robert Gunn my fox
hunter.* Robert Gunn and John Dryden my Shepherd were in the
hill with me when I was in the lads company. Gunn now lives in
Tongue. Dryden is here and reminds me of the imposture. The
Officer and witnesses will I think recollect it.

2nd. It is said that an Old man of 85 of the name of McKay a tenant
of Rhiloisk was Ejected from his house, lay in the wood of Rhiloisk
several days and was then carried to my house of Rhiloisk in a faint-
ing State and was barbarously turned out of it.[2]

Answered. There was no such Old man a tenant or Subtenant in
Rhiloisk. The tenants of that name (vide rental and minute of Set
in Mr Cranstoun's possession) are James McKay or Cooper,
£1 10s., Robert McKay, £1 10s., William McKay, £1 10s. I know
these men to be Young men having seen them when paying me the
above rents.

I am told that there was a hale Old man seen assisting the above
William McKay in removing the timber from his house and that
this was the only old man upon the premises. So altho' I have no
recollection of the Slightest circumstance with respect to him I shall
suppose him the person.

    1st. Then there is no wood of Rhiloisk. The town consists of a
very few Acres of land interspersed among a few birch bushes
on the Water of Naver, Vast extent of hill ground being behind.
The houses of Langdale lye on the Opposite bank of the
Water, within a *few hundred yards of the house* where the Old

---

[1] For evidence on this episode, see Sellar, op. cit., xix, xlix-l.
[2] For evidence on this episode, see ibid., xxxiv-xxxv.

man, I am told, was so employed with William McKay and his family. This William McKay was not Ejected but removed of his own Accord, as did all the other people of Rhiloisk except James McKay Cooper. The brother of the Old man and several others of his relations, and of William McKay's relations and friends, live in Langdale within a *few hundred yards of the house in question*, so, that how he lay in a wood there is beyond my skill to divine.

2nd. However this may be, the following facts must speak for themselves. We got access to the house of Rhiloisk on the evening of Saturday the 11th June. The moment that John Gordon (a lad of 25, in absence of his father, who kept out of the way) gave me the key I gave it to John Dryden my Shepherd. I was not in the house at all and left that Country on Monday the 14th.[1] John Dryden instantly on receiving the keys set out for Culmaily to bring forward the Sheep and owing to the Inconvenience which the want of Access occasioned, was detained from Rhiloisk for better than 10 days thereafter. So it is not possible that this Old man could have been brought to the house of Rhiloisk and turned out of it by Dryden or me. Nota. This *infirm* Old man took the Occasion of my imprisonment and subsequent absence in Edinburgh to fell a tree with a hatchet with his own hand and Steal it from Langdale. And I have not brought him to punishment lest this too should be considered oppression.

3rd. It is said It seems that I pulled down the houses possessed by Sick people in Rhimsdale.[2]

Answered 1st. I was told of people in Rhimsdale said to be sick on the 8th June. I Consented to their remaining unmolested, the inhabitants promising at same time to make the premises otherwise void by the 11th.

2nd. *I left that part of the Country on Monday the 13th* every house in Rhimsdale being then entire. I was called away in consequence of a letter from the Marchioness of Stafford received per Express from Culmaily.

3rd. The Officers found the people with some hundred head

---

[1] *Rectius* 13 June.
[2] For evidence on this episode, see Sellar, op. cit., xxxiv, l-li.

of Cattle horses and Sheep still possessing the premisses, on the 14th. They Ejected them of consequence on the 14th and 15th and pulled down the byres to prevent Cattle being harboured there; *leaving the houses where the sick people were said to be*; and some of them remain there to this day. The Officer and witnesses best know this. John Dryden heard me say to the parties on the 8th that depending on their removing peaceably before the 11th I consented to the people said to be sick staying there.

4th. It is said that I turned a woman who had miscarried out of a house in Ravigill.[1]

Answered. I saw no such woman or heard of any such miscarriage, nor did I turn any woman out of a house in Ravigill nor did any person do so by my directions.

John Dryden tells me that when the Officers were at the west End of Ravigill the people mentioned that a Woman had fallen and hurt herself at the East end of the town; That they mentioned her name; That he knows she belonged to a house from which the family had removed of themselves and had also removed almost all the timber, or boughs of which it consisted; That he does not remember whether I was at Ravigill when this report reached them, but there was no person asked leave for a woman *in that situation* to remain there.

As for my part I recollect nothing of any such matter. Upon asking Robert Gordon in Langdale he says plenty of people saw the Woman who was said to have fallen working unroofing another house or carrying of timber next day and that nothing seemed to Ail her.

I left three widows in Ravigill who dwell in their houses there to this day. If there was a woman hurt *how did she not happen to be taken into either of their houses*.

5th. As to the Muirburning. I cannot at this short notice condescend on what persons from Rhimsdale, Ravigill, Rhiphaill or Rhiloisk were present when I asked leave to burn part of the heath at Suisgill. The room was full of people. I will prove the following facts.[2]

---

[1] For evidence on this episode see Sellar, op. cit., xxxiv, xlii, xlvii. There is conflicting evidence as to whether Sellar's party actually destroyed any houses at Ravigill (ibid., xxxiv, xxxvii, li).

[2] See ibid., xl–xli.

1st. Not one hundredth part of Rhimsdale heath was burned.

2nd. Not one fiftieth part of Garvault heath.

3rd. None of Ravigill heath.

4th. There was not one 1,000th part of Rhiloisk burned.

5th. What was burned of Rhiphaill was Chiefly shealing ground which the tenants did not possess at that time of the year.

6th. There was none burned but high ground not within (the *nearest* of it) *half a mile of the Tenants houses* and land.

7th. I will prove by a Cloud of incontestible witnesses that in this part, burning could not fail to be of the greatest service to the people. The Young herbage of the ling sprouts in a fortnight after burning and continues with the Deer hair to afford the only good nutriment during Spring and untill the soft grass of the meadow pasturage spring in June.

8th. It is a fact that the tenants cattle, notwithstanding the previous severe winter were so much mended by this advantage as to be in better Condition than their neighbouts.

The Barns. The Warrants Ordain the houses to be removed from at Whitsunday, *the haill premises to be then made void and redd.*

Mr Bell, Essay on Leases, page 484[1] has the following passages. 'Patterson was summoned to Remove at Whitsunday 1803 to which he made no Objection, but as he had right to the crop 1803, he claimed a right of retaining the Barns untill the crop on the ground was threshed out and disposed of in conformity with what he maintained to be the Established usuage of the Country; the possession of all the other houses on the farm he gave up at Whitsunday.

'The tenant presented a Bill of suspension praying to be allowed to retain possession of the Barns untill the crop was threshed out and disposed of. But Lord Polkemmet, Ordinary, being clear that the tenant had no right to retain them after Martinmas, he ordered the Bill to be answered on that point only. And after considering the Pleadings on that point, he refused the bill; that is, he found that the tenant *had no right to the Barns after the Whitsunday*, at which he was bound to deliver

---

[1] Robert Bell, *A Treatise on Leases* (Edinburgh, 1803).

up the houses on the farm, and this Judgement was *affirmed by the Court who refused* a petition against the Judgement of the Lord Ordinary.'

Founding on these I did apprehend that they had no *legal right* to retain the Barns after Whitsunday. And, knowing that they would stay in these Barns in place of going to their allottments and harbour horses and cattle, and *Eat my mutton therein*, I considered myself justified in taking possession of them, and I put no hardship on the people, Seeing that harvesting is not done in Barns here as in the West highlands, but in Ricks in the open Air, the Barns here being only used for threshing, and the straw which was to be turned out of the Barns in threshing being my property. I trust it is not possible that I could in this have acted with any criminal intention.

To Conclude, the tenants gave in a specific complaint to Lady Stafford[1] against me in the latter end of July 1814 nearly Six weeks after the period in question.

The whole head and front of this Accusation is that I burned the heath and pulled down the houses and would not allow the tenants 'possess them 12 months after the term of Removing'. Now is it at all Credible that the tenants who were pushed forward by my Enemies with this Complaint on purpose to ruin me with my Employer would have omitted these more heinous Circumstances now brought against me if such circumstances had really existed? Would they not have put them into the most conspicuous part of the Compaint? Their total silence on these subjects must, it is thought, go far to convince Mr Cranstoun that they were fabricated afterwards for the particular purpose of giving a colour to this distressing procedure.

Report by James Loch attached to William Young's Accounts for the period 11 June 1814 to 23 December 1815: 14 February 1816

I have examined the foregoing accounts, and have compared them with the balances of the former year, and with the vouchers and other documents which have been produced to support the same, and find them to be correct, subject to the following obser-

[1] See above, p. 151.

vations as to the mode of stating them and also as to the manner, in which the vouchers are brought forward.

The accounts are kept very accurately and properly by double entry and nothing can be suggested by way of improvement, unless it be that under the head of 'Permanent Improvements' some accounts are placed which would have been more satisfactorily classed under seperate heads, in order to shew their exact expence, such as 'Dunrobin Stables'.

The mode in which the annual accounts are presented with the vouchers in support of them appears capable of considerable improvement, whereby they would be rendered more distinct and intelligible and also more easily made out. The vouchers also would at the same time be more simple and could at once be referred to the sums to which they relate without the explanation which is now necessary.

For this purpose a Cash Book should be kept of a larger size than that now used in which every Cash transaction, both receipts and payments should be entered, the latter in detail and not by reference to the Journal as at present. The Ledger and Journal must of course continue to be kept with the same regularity as they now are.

The Accounts which are in the foregoing pages presented for examination and Audit are a transcript of the Ledger in its Debtor and Creditor shape, rendering them longer than necessary and more complicated. All that is required to be shewn, by these Annual Accounts is the amount of the money received within the year and the payments made which are to be supported by proper vouchers. They ought therefore to be a transcript of the Cash Book not of the Ledger, arranging however the different receipts and payments under the same distinct heads as they appear in the Ledger, and not in the mere order of time only as in the Cash book. The receipts should be 1. Rents; 2. Proceeds of the Farms, including dairy, Glen etc.; 3. of the Lime; 4. of the Coal; 5. of the Salt works; 6. Remittances from Lord Stafford; 7. any other incidental receipts. The payments should be classed in a similar manner, beginning with these of a permanent nature, and ending with those which are temporary.

There may also be a material improvement in the mode of keeping and producing the vouchers. As they have been now produced it has been impossible to refer them to the different items without the

constant and minute explanation afforded by Mr Grant.[1] This is
occasioned by the want of a distinct voucher or receipt for each
payment. The vouchers produced were not receipts, but generally
Bills of Lading or long Accounts Current, not only relating to
many different heads of expenditure, upon the Sutherland Estate,
for articles got for various purposes and at different times, but mixed
up also with Mr Young's personal Accounts and those of various
other gentlemen.

For the future I must earnestly recommend distinct and seperate
stamped receipts being taken for all such payments, excluding all
transactions but those relating to Lord and Lady Staffords affairs.
I may here remark, that in an expenditure of near £32,000, there
are not ten stamped receipts and I cannot help suggesting the
propriety of taking all receipts on Stamps except payments to
Labourers, both on account of the legal security and to avoid the
imputation, perhaps the penalty of evading the law.

Further the vouchers for the payment of many of the workmen
and tradesmen are not in a perfect form being merely references to
particular items contained in accounts current in which accounts are
also contained other items, for which more regular vouchers are
produced. This last irregularity appears to have arisen in many
instances from the practice of paying money on account, leaving the
adjustment of the bargain and the statement of the transactions to
be made up by Mr Grant, from after recollection and calculation.
A stated regular payment in full to the period of payment with
proper vouchers taken at the time, to the different heads of departments and contractors would correct this defect.

I have ordered a proper Cash Book to be made and if any further
explanation is required I will desire Mr Suther to send it from Trentham where Mr Grant saw the method here recommended. The
accounts had better also be written in a quarto bound book as more
easy of reference than when in this shape.

Much confusion has arisen from the account entitled 'Obligations
bearing interest'. I am of opinion that it will be better to pay off
all these people except the money belonging to the poor etc., for
whom it may be an object that it should be retained by Lord
Stafford.

[1] William Grant, Young's cashier at Rhives.

A small explanation as to the money paid to Mr Young by Mr
Sellar, remains to be made, the difference appears to arise from the
deduction of some allowance which has been made in one Account
and not in the other. Subject to these observations there is a Balance
of Two thousand five hundred and ten pounds twelve shillings and
twopence three farthings ($£2,510$ 12s. 2¾d.) due to Mr Young.

Note concerning the Fleet Mound: 15 May 1816

There are two points concerning the Fleet Mound: in both of
which the resident contractors have satisfied themselves by attentive
and Carefull observation and experiment; and, in the most essential
one, they are backed by the concurrent testimony of Messrs
Davidson and Hughes.[1] The first point is the depth of water. From
the river bank on the Cambusmore side of the Fleet (D)[2] to the
head of the west mound (B), the depths are as follow. At the river
bank at a neap tide 5 feet to 5½. At a stream tide 8½ to 9 feet 3. At
the point (A) 50 yards nearer Cambusmore. At a neap tide 2 feet
to 2½; at a stream tide 5½ to six feet 3 Inches. From (A) to the
Cambusmore shore (B) it is with little variation a complete flat;
and the depths are the same as (A). From low water mark at the
Cambusmore side, to low water mark on the east mound head at
(C) (i.e. the river breadth) measures less than 50 yards. The depths
are as follow. At low water variable from 6 to 9 feet. At high water
of neap tides from 11 to 14 feet. At spring tides from 14 to say
18 feet. These depths are proved by *Actual measurement*. The resident
Contractors cannot help what Mr Jardine reports,[3] or what is said
of the general flowings of the Moray Firth. The above are the
Actual measured depths. And the base of the mound is situated one to
two miles up a river, and several feet higher than low water mark
of the Moray Firth. The second and most essential point Concerns
the blowing up of the mound. The Contractors know that the
stones in the stuff do not tumble to the bottom *of the slope*, and
form a drain there. The *water made slope* is *too flat* for this, and the
stones are *seen* to rest thereon. The Contractors have made a small

---

[1] For Matthew Davidson, see Haldane, *New Ways through the Glens*, 79-80.
[2] This reference, with those that follow it, is to the sketch contained in Sellar's letter
of 6 March 1816 (see below, ii, p. 275); a copy is appended to the note.
[3] For Jardine, see below, ii, p. 276.

experiment and conclude from it that very little leakage will happen, on the water being shutt out; and *Messrs Davidson and Hughes have no fear of the blowing up* of what is done. They have three times shifted the bed of the Ness by Mounds of the same sort of stuff; and, by their observation on these occasions they feel the more confident on this subject. Mr Davidson said it was very natural for Mr Jardine to conclude on *theoretical premisses* as he had done, but his (Mr Davidsons) forty years practice led him to entertain a different opinion.

Next, as to the mode of finishing, concerning which so much difference in opinion has existed. Mr Jardine, as mentioned in his report, proposes an extra expence certain, of from £5,000 to £6,000. Mr Davidson proposes the erection of a stage or gangway across the Frith, thro' which the necessary earth to be dropped, untill the mound raise its level along the whole extent above high water. This is more intelligible than Mr Jardines plan and is perhaps less costly by £1,000. Mr Hughes says, this is a mode *quite certain of success in friths of depth*, and is the measure to be resorted to, if cheaper means fail. But, he considers that in such depth of water and in such other circumstances as we have to contend with, several thousand pounds may be saved by the adoption of our plan,[1] provided we be satisfied that we can *at once throw* in the quantity of stuff necessary to give the timber density and strength sufficient to resist the weight and spring of the water. He says he entertains serious doubts of our being able to put in *at once* this quantity of stuff; and therefore we should attempt it *at twice* by first raising the level of the base by means which he points out to a certain height, and then finishing at once.

On questioning Mr Hughes what he considered a sufficient quantity of earth, he said a quantity of the height of the tide along the whole length and sloping to the width of from 12 to 20 feet.

Now the Contractors have most painfully and attentively considered Mr Hughes plan, and they are satisfied and they think they will satisfy Earl Gower.

> 1st. That the first part of Mr Hughes's plan is a work not (if left unfinished) likely to stand the effects of a winter, and that it would occasion such a waste of time as unavoidably to throw the work into winter; and

[1] See below, ii, p. 275.

2nd. That they can put in *at once* the requisite quantity of stuff.
1st. This first part of Mr Hughes plan is the laying along the whole
length of the distance and on *each* side of the piles a line of boxes,
each capable to contain 10 Tons of stones, filling these with stones
and the interval betwixt the lines with earth. Over which boxes
and earth, the sea to ebb and flow during the operation. Now, this
is an operation of several months labour. The stones could not be
laid in sooner than Lambmas. During all this period the sea falls
four times in the 24 hours over the boxes; and the danger of gulphs
being cut by such fall, and during the fall, and of defeat in the
finishing, *at and after the lambmas tides* is very imminent. In the event
of which defeat, these stones lay exposed in the current during the
whole winter; afford occassion to the sea to make innumerable
gulphs along the whole line of operation, and thus, after all the
trouble and expence of season 1816, the Season 1817 begins with
reparations of indefinite extent and endurance.
2nd. But the contractors are confident they can lay in the necessary
quantity of stuff, and they beg to explain the cause of *their certainty*
on this score.

On Monday the third day of June the East mound should have
reached the point A. The piling and shed piling being completed
from B to A and the bay above being at *low* water filled with water
to the line of A and up towards Morvich by reason of the rise of
level of 3 feet from C to A and the use of a temporary sluice at the
upper side of the bridges. This filling diminishes the influx as
$5\frac{1}{2}$ is to $8\frac{1}{2}$ within a trifle of $\frac{1}{3}$rd. The planking is moored along the
line of piling in separate rafts fixed at certain stated distances. 10
Carpenters with their tools and 300 labourers properly officered
stand ready on the beach.

The tide from A to B this day will not by the common laws of
nature exceed $2\frac{1}{2}$ feet it may be 3.

As soon as the sea has left the line of piling dry, the bridge sluices
being hung in their places, every man repairs to his post, the Carpenters under their master, the labourers under Forsyth etc. By the
return of the tide (i.e. 9 hours) the planking is nailed on to the
height of four feet, the earth to three feet sloping to 12 feet base.
A figure of 12 feet base sloping from 3 feet at the one end to nothing
at the other contains 2 cubical yards of stuff for each running yard,

that is 450 running yards contain 900 cubical yards or 3 yards per man, but, each man one with another will with care put in 5 yards during that time. As soon as the sea impedes progress, the men turn to the upper side and work there, untill they have put in the same quantity of stuff on that side. During the day we calculate that they shall by an exertion put in from 5 *to* 6 *cubical yards of stuff*, being $\frac{1}{3}$ nearly more than is accounted necessary. They then retire to rest. Next morning they return to the charge. The sea should rise about 8 inches higher than the day preceeding. They will with great ease put in better than 1 foot of additional stuff, giving it additional breadth in proportion. And so on, as the sea rises to the stream tide; the highest of which, on Saturday the 8th or Sunday the 9th should be 6 feet 3 inches. To raise the mound this height and 24 feet base requires 7,800 Cubical yards of stuff but in 6 days 300 men at 5 yards daily per man will put in 9000 cubical yards; and with care and vigilance the quantity proposed by Hughes should be exceeded.

The case is estimated at £750. If it succeed it will save £5,000 to £6,000 proposed to be expended by Mr Jardine. But if it fail?

In that case there is a loss of	£750
deduce timber which will be recovered in the bay	150
remains of loss	£600

The question is, shall we hazard the *possible* loss of £600 before determining on the certain loss of £6,000.

Mr Young, Patrick Sellar, and James Forsyth agree unanimously in recommending that we should. But there are two previous points insisted on by Patrick Sellar before he will agree and as Messrs Young and Forsyth differ with him he begs to state his opinion.

1st. The first concerns the slope from A to C. The stuff along that slope being composed of the same *soft materials* with the rest of the bay, Patrick Sellar insists on the possibility, or rather the certainty that the bed of the river will never rise to the height of A unless something be done to *harden this slope*, and enable it to resist the power of the water. If left unfortified it *must wash away* into new gulphs how soon the river is displaced, by the mound B; and he thinks, with all deference, that the said slope should be furthwith coated with stones and gravel, so laid, as to exhibit a smooth surface against the action of the water.

2nd. By the Original plan we proposed two rows of piles, the back row driven to the head to support bracers placed for Upholding the front rank, against the pressure of the sea. But, James Forsyth does now propose to leave out the bracers, and rear rank, depending solely on the front rank for success; and calculating that the weight of earth to be wheeled into the line, will render the aid of the bracers unnecessary. Will the gentlemen recollect that it is on the weight of two Cubical yards of earth that they propose to place their *whole* trust! Without opposing the *probability* that this shall repell the pressure and spring of the sea, Patrick Sellar humbly submitts the *possibility* that it may not. He maintains that unlooked for casualties may happen. That the security against casualty, afforded by these bracers is not to be abandoned by men who presume to adventure against the opinion of an Engineer; and that in such cases we are not to expect salvation by an excess of faith, but of good works.

Note concerning Sutherland by Patrick Sellar: May 1816

Culmaily, 24 May 1816

Whether the subject be received with relation to the people themselves, or to the influence their condition must have on the rest of Society, certainly there is no one thing to be imagined more deeply affecting or afflicting, than the absence of every principle of truth and candour from a population of several hundred thousand Souls, the sad remnant of a people who once covered a great part of Europe, and who so long and so bravely withstood the invading strength of the Roman Empire. Their obstinate adherence to the barbarous jargon of the times when Europe *was possessed by Savages*, their *rejection* of any of the several languages now used in Europe, and which being Sprung or at least improved from those of the greatest nations of antiquity, carry with them the collected wisdom of all ages, and have raised their possessors to the most astonishing pitch of *eminence* and *power* – Their seclusion, I say, from this grand fund of knowledge, places them, with relation to the enlightened nations of Europe in a position not very different from that betwixt the American Colonists and the Aborigines of that Country. The one are the Aborigines of Britain shut out from the general stream of knowledge and cultivation, flowing in upon the Commonwealth of Europe from the remotest fountain of antiquity. The other are the Aborigines of America equally shut out from this stream; Both live in turf cabins in common with the brutes; Both are singular for patience, courage, cunning and address. Both are most virtuous where least in contact with men in a civilized State, and both are fast sinking under the baneful effects of ardent spirits.

The Aborigines of America receive this poison in exchange for the few products of their industry which they give to Europe in barter for it. The Aborigines of Britain owe their misfortune to causes totally different and which I shall endeavour briefly to explain.

Government requiring money to be raised by Taxes, luxuries, being the most fit subject for Taxation, and ardent spirits the most fit of all luxuries, the tax imposed on malt wash, and spirits in the different stages of its manufacture amount to about 450 per cent on the prime cost of the article, that is you may buy a boll of barley at 20s. and to make it into whisky in a legal manner you pay £4 10s. of Taxes, the spirits produced fetching in the legal market from six to nine pound sterling. The profits derived by evading the Tax are plain to every understanding. The refuse pays the labour, twenty shillings the prime cost, and from five to eight hundred per cent remains to the smuggler in case he can escape detection. People in an *accessible* country can't escape, the trade therefore falls into the hands of the highlander who lives in an *inaccessible* country. He practices the trade most successfully by tricks by chicnacry, by lies, and by management he evades or brings over the Gauger. By midnight labour he escapes his observation. But all his arts, and all his management would fail him, except for one little secret, which I shall presently communicate, and which I daresay will account somewhat for the astonishing extent to which the trade is carried. The profit does not go into the pocket of the smuggler, but into those, first of his neighbours who buy from him a spirit of first quality at one half its legal value; second of the Justices of the Peace, who get 30s. to 35s. for their Barley in place of 15s. to 20s., 30s. per acre of rent for their land in place of 20s.; third of the Clergy whose stipends are paid by the highest fiar prices; and lastly of the Excise who receive the fines imposed upon him.

The immense Tax of which the Government is defrauded, and which amounts as already stated to £4 10s. per boll or about £27 for each Scotch acre of barley, goes principally into the pockets of those intrusted with the prevention of evil, and instead of enforcing the laws which by the united wisdom of King Lords and Commons have been enacted for the complete suppression of this nefarious and abominable traffic they bring forward the plea of humanity and upon that pretext they mitigate the penalties to what, without doing up the trade may stop the mouths of the Collector and his Officers. These are hard truths, but they certainly are truths, and there is another truth still more afflicting, which is that the poor smuggler gets the least share of the profit, and pays the dearest for it. His life becomes a continued struggle, how by lies, chicnacry, perjury, cunning, midnight journeys, the midnight watching of his wife and family, debasing artifices, and sneaking to his superiors, he can obtain thro' theft a miserable livelihood. Debauchery and beggary follow the total absence of principle, *essential to his* trade. His children trained up in deceit, exceed their father in turpitude, and the virtue of a Scotch Highlander is exchanged for the vices of the Irish Peasantry. If ever there existed an evil crying for the prompt interference of men in power, it is this rapid demoralization of a brave people, for the basest, the most nefarious and the worst purposes. Lord and Lady Stafford have in their own power its correction on the Estate of Sutherland, at least the diminution of it to a very great degree as well as the turning the sentiments of the people and the infusing into them some portion of that stream of knowledge before alluded to, and which had been so successfully communicated in the Highlands of Banffshire to the fathers of Sir William Grant[1] and Sir W. Garrow.[2]

I shall in my next endeavour with every deference and diffidence to suggest what poor ideas occur to me. First on the means of effecting this, and second on the effects likely to follow, first to the people and next to the proprietor.

[1] For Sir William Grant (1753–1832), Master of the Rolls, 1801–17, see D.N.B., xxii, 405–7. His father was a small farmer at Elchies.
[2] For Sir William Garrow (1760–1840), Baron of Exchequer, 1817–32, see D.N.B., xxi, 28–29. His father does not appear to have any connection with Banffshire.

M

The means of Prevention

27 May 1816

The trade explained in my last prevails to a most alarming extent over the whole north south and middle Highlands of Scotland. My observation of it has been limited to Morayshire and Sutherland. In the one I have seen its effects in the low, in the other in the high Country.

The people in Glenlivet Glenrinnis Strathdown and all that district of Country convert the barley grown in Morayshire into whisky. For eluding observation it is delivered by the Moray Farmer to the smugglers on the Banks of the Spey, the price 40s. to 50s. per boll in place of the general *level* of the fair market, that is as nearly as I can compute it, of the defrauded revenue rather better than   20 per cent

They sell to the low country their excellent spirits
at 8s. instead of 16s. per Gallon   50 per cent

And the *periculum* in that country may, one ad-
venture with another be   20 per cent

I daresay the value caught by the Officers of
Excise may average one half the price of the barley. If the whisky be carried across the Grampians,
which the Smugglers frequently do the 2nd article
diminishes, but then the *periculum* increases, and
upon the whole there barely remains to the poor
Smuggler the ordinary profit of fair trade about   10 per cent
                                                                  _____
                                                                  100 per cent

That, in the face of this fact the trade continues and increases, I can't help. There is an *ex facie* profit which deludes the unfortunate man. He plays like a gamester and loses himself because he don't discover that the odds are hollow against him, and it is plain that the odds are against him from this circumstance, that there is not in Britain a trade the possessors of which are poorer or more beggarly in every respect. Now that Morayshire which profits by the corruption and ruin of the Highlanders conterminous to it, and that Caithness and Orkney which profit in like manner by the ruin of the poor people of Sutherland Should encourage the thing, does not at all surprise me. But that any Proprietor in Sutherland should, I dont say on the score of conscience (I spoke to that in my last) but on the score of profit and good policy, tolerate so damnable a traffic on his Estate is perfectly incomprehensible. The means of prevention are just the System followed by Lord and Lady Stafford on their domains in this latter Country:

1st. The bringing the patient from the inaccessible country where alone this mortal complaint rages, to the accessible coast where with proper care it can't exist.

Here are two points and I will speak briefly to each. The first leads me into a good deal of detail, in which I must refer to the map[1] and I shall take each Parish in its order.

ASSYNT comprising Nos. 1, 2, 3, 4, 5, 6, 7, 8, 9, 10, 11 and 12. In No. 7 Coulin and Camore, No. 11 Knockan and Elphine and No. 12 Altnachy, the people have some apology for Smuggling, they are placed in situations where no access exists to any other species of industry. No. 7 may be brought to No. 1 Inver when Lord and Lady Stafford please. Nos. 11 and 12 got Leases to 1831. Assynt is a West Highland Parish more remote from contact with the low country and whisky smuggling exists less there than on any other part of the Estate.

CREICH so far as Lord and Lady Stafford's property[2] is concerned, was a complete nest of Smugglers. It is now put under sheep.

LAIRG so far as not set to Messrs Atkinson and McKay[3] has (No. 72)[4] been lately arranged and divided among the people who are all of them Smugglers. There are a few cottages built there since that time, but there is no room for industry excepting industry in smuggling and I am convinced that in the 1828 the system here will be completely changed, of this I am convinced by two reasons. The one is that it is a situation where people can't get forward, can't pay rent but by illicit practices. The other that Lairg is part of the Winter ground of 73,[5] and owing to want of that ground thousands

---

[1] A sketch map, still surviving, on which Sellar had indicated and numbered the farms and their boundaries. There was an angry exchange between Young and Loch over its existence (see below, ii, pp. 266, 271).

[2] Achinduich and Invershin.

[3] A reference to the two sheep farms in Lairg parish (Atkinson and Marshall's farm, and Shiness held by Duncan Matheson and John McKay).

[4] The remainder of Lairg parish.

[5] Atkinson and Marshall's farm.

of acres of the summer ground of that farm are left to fade unused. For the farmer wanting winter keep dare not venture the necessary quantity of Stock. While I mention No. 73 I may as well notice another point relative to this unwieldy farm. It is held by Atkinson and Marshall at a trifle of rent, it does not pay them at all as might be expected, because it is a collection of the summer ground of the best farms on the Estate without the natural quantity of wintering. Thus Lairg and part of Rogart are the wintering of that range of mountain up Strathtirrie to Ben Clebrick. Strathbrora is the wintering of that part which includes the sources of Brora River, and the South side of Ben Ormin, and Strath Naver the wintering of the opposite sides of the mountains of Ben Clebrick and Ben Ormin. This is plain to any person who has traveled the ground, and when the arrangement comes to be made, a very great increase may be expected to the produce, and of course if well managed by the Agents of that day, to the Rental of the Estate. We can at present do very little for Lairg except by making a good road through it up Strathfleet, to render it more accessible, more easy of course for the people to betake themselves to any fair species of industry, and less easy to continue Whisky Smuggling.

ROGART is entirely packed and crammed with Whisky Smugglers. Excepting Rhien, there is not one rent in it which is not paid very much from the profits of this illegal traffic. A few of these people may be settled in allottments at Rearquhar, Evelix and the district towards Dornoch which will certainly at present pay more under people than under farms. But I am humbly of opinion, that as many of these people as possible should be put into Brora, and the grounds which lye betwixt Strathstiven on the West, Kintradwell on the North, and Lothbeg on the East. This is a tract of low lying favourable and most improveable land of great extent, a fine river flowing thro' it, a bridge across the River and thoroughfare connecting it along its whole extent a harbour in its centre, the finest fishing ground in Scotland along six miles of coast, and coals salt brick tyles pott clay etc. ready for the hands of the manufacturer. It is not easy to figure anything more favourable. Nothing I am sure exists like it in the North of Scotland, and it must, and will become a place of more bustle and stir than is yet imagined. The people should be *directed with effect to this common centre*. As long as without plan they are kept in separate groupes nothing like the industry of a Town can exist for want of that bond of Society and Junction of effect necessary to the scientific direction of labour and on the other hand, nothing like perfection in farming, like a fair rent of land can exist, while those who should be forwarding the industry of a Town, are doing every thing possible to ruin the industry of the Country.

As I mean to say a few words on this subject in the last part of this Essay, I shall not enlarge at present, farther than merely to suggest the idea that Mr Loch may carry it along with him, in considering the few poor observations which I shall immediately hazard. In the meantime I proceed to mention the use for which nature seems to have intended the Parish of Rogart. And that is most decidedly the wintering of those extensive flocks of Sheep for the maintenance of which in summer the interior of which is entirely applicable. Without such an effectual arrangement justice is not done either to the people who reside where they cant benefit Society, or to the Country which by the presence of people where they should be absent, and by their absence where their industry is required, cant come to its push and vigour.

We are told that Merino sheep can never suit Sutherland for want of winter keep, but it is wonderful how any sheep suit it in its present most imperfect state of arrangement. They suit it or rather it suits them most imperfectly. There will yet occurr an amazing improvement, not merely on the numbers kept on the same extent of ground but on the quality and condition of the sheep and the Rent afforded from them; and those who live here 50 years hence will be at a loss to see how we have at all got forward under so many disadvantages as at present oppress us.

DORNOCH is beyond my skill. The grounds of this Parish are in general low and free from *mill dew*, and consisting not of regular fields but of patches interspersed in an improveable moor of great extent, there is a great population gathering thither and getting forward with the culture of the wastes. I see no harbour or interior country behind it, and I shrewdly suspect that, that will happen to it which has frequently happened in other countries after these men have improven the ground and rendered it fit for the regular operation of husbandry. These allottments will by 1836, be in all probability be put into regular farms and the present possessors drawn into some Town or Village.

What I have ventured to Prophecy as to Dornoch has already taken place as to GOLSPIE except in Wester and Easter Aberscross Strathlundie and Scottery districts, the inhabitants of which inaccessible places all live by smuggling whisky. All that remains to be done is to bring these families into Golspie or Brora, laying Aberscross to Morvich, Strathlundie to Culmaly and Scottary and these grounds along the Brora lake and river to the Dunrobin Glen pasturage. Nature has pointed these things out and they are scarcely to be avoided without compromising the interest of the Noble Family and their people.

CLYNE. What I have said concerning Rogart applies to Clyne. Draw the people to the *Centre point* where Lord Stafford has done so much to forward the industry of a town and set the interior for sheep stock.

The interior of LOTH is entirely under stock. I am of opinion that all that tract betwixt Kilmot and the Ord of Caithness will pay more in the possession of fishermen than in any other manner. I include Culgower, Wester, Mid, and Easter Garty or Gartymore Wester and Easter Helmsdale and Navidale. Besides the tillage land which should be lotted out among them, there is some extent of improvable ground all equally adapted for the occupation of these people.

I would entirely bring down the people of KILDONAN to this district. They pay their rents by Smuggling barley brought over the mountains from Caithness, returning the Whisky to that County and Orkney and by stealing sheep from the neighbouring farm.

I say the same thing concerning what of the Parish of FARR lies above Dunveidan, and Carnachy on the Naver, and on the Strathy water on the Armadale property. I include Langdale farm which is at present entirely subset by Mr Gordon the tacksman to a parcel of people that live almost entirely by illicit distillation.

Altho we heard much of Mr Roys laying off allottments in STRATHNAVER, the truth is there is not one single allottment in the whole district.[1] But the people of the upper districts were

[1] See Macpherson Grant's observations (below, pp. 206-7) and Young's evidence at Sellar's trial (Sellar, *Sutherland Evictions*, xxxviii).

packed in among those below and the whole occupy the old tillage land merely in the old run-rig fashion, as their fathers did in the days of Sir Patrick Gordon.[1] The families to be brought down consist as follows.

Syre Farm and Grubmore farm	54 families
Langdale's Subtenants	43 families
Strathrathy tenants	32 families
total	129 families

and by a judicious allottment of the ground betwixt Bighouse march and Dunvidan room might be got for 10 times that number.

In the Appendix[2] will be found a state of the number of families to be removed from each District. The particular dates at which these removals can take place and the particular spots for each, are matters which may be more easily discussed, in conversation and which require the consideration of plans and maps, careful examination of the ground, and a comparative attention to many and minute details not possible to be conveyed in a paper of the nature of the present.

But nothing is more plain than that by an arrangement to be matured on a prudent considerate and systematic plan, the people may (as they ought) be brought from the inaccessible interior of the country where smuggling is the only possible means of life, where man is shut out from every rational pursuit to the accessible sea coast where all his motions are distinctly seen, where so many different fields for his industry lie open, where his children are educated and bred to honest and useful trades and where the presence of people firmly knit together in the bond of one Society is necessary for any such things as scientific direction of labour wealth and prosperity in a Country. Next, as to the medicines for the mind which I ventured to speak of as necessary to change the sentiment and feeling of the people and to induce them willingly to bend to this new state of things, I beg leave with the greatest deference and

---

[1] Probably an error for Sir Robert Gordon (1580-1656), first baronet of Gordonstoun, the historian of the Sutherland family.

[2] This has not survived, but according to Macpherson Grant (to Loch, *5 July 1816) it included 1,056 names. Macpherson Grant was clearly apprehensive of the scope of Sellar's proposals: 'I confess my Nerves are hardly equal to the contemplation of removing 1056 Families at once even supposing you could acquire the Means for their Accomodation.'

respect to express some surprise that Lord and Lady Stafford who have been so long at pains to enforce industry among their people and so long in the practice of employing their servants in Sutherland from a different Country, should entirely entrust the essential duty of teaching and preaching to their people to men not of the new but of the old school. I venture to say that what we have seen among the people during the last four years could not have happened had the Teachers of Youth, and the Ministers of the several Parishes been men brought from an industrious Country the sons of industrious Parents, and with a passion for industry in them, had they not been completely the reverse of all this bred in a country of sloth and idleness the sons of highland tenants and whisky smugglers, and with a tone imbibed from the earliest infancy of detestation to every introduction to industry or innovation on the ancient language and manners of the Gael. I think if Lord and Lady Stafford were pleased to fill up a few of the first vacancies with persons to be searched for in Aberdeenshire or Kindardineshire districts, where the people are extremely industrious it might have the happiest effect. The sure road to the head is by the heart and while the heart is kept subject to ignorance and prejudice, little genuine co-operation can be expected. The want of the Gaelic language will at first be quibbled on by the Clergy, but without much reason, for during the whole line of coast betwixt the Meikle Ferry and the Ord, there are very few old people who do not understand the English language, and except the Golspie Fishers very few young ones who cannot speak it fluently.

Effects to be expected

31 May 1816

If what I have said in the two proceding parts of this Essay carry with it any appearance of common sense, the sense is not mine. I have merely reported what is observed on the subject by a Gentleman of great worth and erudition, to whom I shall presently introduce you. But before doing I humbly beg your consideration of two very curious facts of the causes of which I would be glad to hear any satisfactory solution. The first fact is that in no country of which I have yet read or heard is there in every one person such an accumulation of offices as in the highlands of Scotland. Every man is a

Quarrier, mason, woodman, carrier, square wright carpenter, cooper, turff cutter, thatcher, wood destroyer, currier, tanner, shoe-maker, saddler, shepherd, wool comber, spinner, farmer, cattle dealer, distiller, poacher, and God knows what, and yet with all this bountiful provision for every man of them, are they not de facto (but as Lord and Lady Stafford well know) de Jure beggars. The second fact is that no where is to be found a peasantry richer, more independent, better lodged, better fed, more virtuous, of higher and nobler spirit, and of more sterling value to society than the people of England, and yet strange to tell, no man there can get hold of more than one trade or calling, and some only part of one. Witness those who live by the one twentieth part of the busi-ness of a Scotch weaver, or the one tenth part of the making of a pin. These are very curious paradoxes, but yet they are founded upon plain matter of fact. Now let us hear what is said by the old Gentle-man to whom I promised to introduce you.

'Among savage nations' says he 'every individual who is able to work is more or less employed in useful labour, and endeavours to provide as well as he can the necessaries and conveniences of life etc., such nations however are so miserably poor, that from mere want they are frequently reduced to the necessity of directly des-troying, and sometimes abandoning their infants their old people and those affected with lingering deseases to perish with hunger, or be devoured by wild beasts. Among civilized and thriving nations, on the contrary though great numbers of people do not labour at all many of them consume the produce of ten times frequently of a hundred times more labour, than the greater part of those who work. Yet the produce of the whole labour of the *Society* is so great, that all are often abundantly supplied, and a workman even of the lowest and poorer order, if he is frugal and industrious may enjoy a greater share of the necessaries and conveniences of life than it is possible for any savage to acquire.'

The causes of this improvement on the productive power of labour he goes on to explain. 'The greater improvement on the productive powers of labour, and the greater part of the skill dex-terity and Judgement with which it is any where directed or applied seem to have been the effect of the division of labour, in the lone houses and very small villages which are scattered about in so desert a country as the Highlands of Scotland, every farmer must be a butcher baker and brewer for his own family. In such situations we can scarce expect to find a smith a carpenter or a mason within twenty miles of another of the same trade. The scattered families that live at a distance of eight or ten miles from the nearest of them, must learn to perform themselves a great number of little pieces of work, for which in more populous countries they would call the assistance of those workmen. A man commonly saunters a little in turning his hand from one sort of employment to another. When he first begins the new work he is seldom very keen and hearty, his mind as they say does not go to it, for some time he rather trifles than applies to good purpose, the habit of sauntering and of indolent careless application, which is naturally or rather necessarily acquired by every country workman who is obliged to change his work and his tools every half hour, and to apply his hand in twenty different ways almost every day of his life renders him almost always slothful lazy and incapable of any vigourous application even on the most pressing occasions.' *Wealth of Nations*, Book I, chapter 1st.

Upon these corroborating and convincing data I maintain with the greatest deference and humility, that the people should not be dissipated and Scattered in lone and helpless hutts, and small villages and hamlets over every part of the Estate. That what is left in Scattered villages should only be considered a temporary delay, rather than a solid establishment. That the attention of the Noble family so far as concerns the forwarding the industry of the people should be concentrated in the Coal district along the Post road betwixt Strathstiven and the Ord. That the Tenantry should be drawn down and settled along this line of coast, in the middle of coal, salt, lime, fisheries, water carriage, waterfalls for machinery, good roads and in a word every convenience suited to such an undertaking. That there is great danger of planting them too thin, but none of their being too thick, because the means of support and living here to people who choose to join together in the bond of an industrious society is beyond anything that can be imagined, because division of labour can't exist without numbers *thickly* settled, because scientific direction of industry can't be while a man is half a farmer, or till he find it necessary to apply to one trade, not to many, and he can't apply to one trade alone until one closely joined society find him with customers for his own surplus labour and workmen in every department necessary to his line of industry.

I have heard a great deal of progressive improvements but I beg Mr Lochs cool consideration of this fact. That while these deliberations are in progress, while the thing hangs thus in suspense, instead of an emulation in industry, there exists a spirit of warfare, betwixt those who should be forming the industry of a town and those who follow the industry of the Country, to the injury of both, and most of all to the Noble Proprietors of the Estate. To sum up all, the effects to be expected from the measures most humbly suggested are. First to the Tenant, in place of smuggling, perjury and canting hypocricy, the independent look of an honest man, in place of sneaking indolence malice and envy, spirited industry. In place of a Jack-pudding mass of confusion, correct division of labour, in place of the poverty beggary of a savage Country, that state of affluence mentioned by Mr Smith 'where a workman of the lowest and poorest order, if he be frugal and industrious, may enjoy a greater share of the necessaries and conveniences of life than it is possible for any savage to acquire'.

With regard to the interest of the Proprietors Rent being the landlord's share of the produce of his country, and the produce of the country being infinitly increased by the usual causes of 'the Wealth of Nations' the landlord is above all others interested in the prosperity of his people. He has a share of every mans prosperity, or adversity, and the amount of his rental depends on that prosperity or adversity, and the degree of utility to which the industry and produce of his country are applied. 'How preferable', says Mr Burke in one of his admirable speeches on American affairs 'How preferable are the overflowings of a prosperous country to all the miserable trash that can be expressed from the dry husks of poverty by the most dexterous management and chicnacry.'

Report by Patrick Sellar and John Lawson concerning the natural woods on the Sutherland Estate: 27 July 1816

Wednesday 17 July. On inspecting the wood of Scale this day we found it pretty free from damage. It consists in a great measure of stunted Birch trees, which, being, every Winter, cropped by the tenants horses and cattle make no progress. We are of opinion it may remain as it is, untill Langdales subtenants be removed from it; and, how soon that is done, and the ground put under sheep stock, as intended by his lease, the stunted stuff should be thinned out, to give room for Young vigorous plants to come forward. This wood is situated on the banks of the Naver. The timber is entirely Crooked consisting of knees for boat building and they should be sold at the Naver mouth at the above period; and the bark exposed at same time in parcels among the fishermen on the Coast, who will come to need such for their netts, sails and lines.

18 July. After inspecting this wood, proceeded thro the grounds possessed by the tenants as allotments, inspecting their houses; made up a list of how much timber was required by each for repairing his Cabin. Found as annexed[1] that 915 trees were required, and appointed the people to receive this timber from the wood of Letterbeg, on the 19th and 20th Current.

19 and 20 July. Letterbeg wood consists entirely of Birch of pretty good size, very much suited for boat building. It adjoins the Reay Estate, the tenants of which are permitted to destroy wood as they please; and it is much damaged. In examining the Strathnaver Lotts particular notice was taken by Mr Lawson and the keeper and Ground Officer, to find bark or new timber, but none was found; and we are convinced, of Consequence, that this damage is not done by these people. In our opinion, this wood cannot be kept, but at an expence exceeding its Value, and therefore, the tenants had better be served from it, taking care to give them always any peeled or damaged timber, before fresh timber be served out; so that they, as well as the proprietor may feel a loss, in the damage, and Consequently an interest to check depredations. Served out the quantity required in the Strathnaver lotts (except, to 4 men concerned in the Strathnaver Combination),[2] warning the tenants, at same time, that, hereafter no timber would be given but to tenants whose houses were thatched with straw or heath. If they be, *but brought to thatch,* one tenth of their present wants will serve them. At present the

---

[1] This appendix lists 126 tenants in lower Strathnaver, with the number of trees required for each house; included in the names are John Munro and John Mackay in Rhinovie (see below, p. 202).

[2] Presumably including John Munro and John Mackay in Rhinovie.

more wood they allow to rot in their Cabins, the more they annually require, and *the more bark they, of consequence acquire with it.*
21 July: Sunday. Went to Armadale.
22 July. At the Strathy mains. There are the ruins of an old mansion house and Garden, a complete wreck. Round the garden are a few stunted damaged trees, long the prey of the tenants and their Cattle and horses. Mr Young desired this to be comprised, as it is to be sold for boat building. They amount as follow

114 trees at 10d.	£4 15s.
49 beech, Elm and poplar at 3s. 6d.	£8 11s. 6d.
Brush wood and thorns supposed	£3 10s.
	£16 16s. 6d.

It is, for Mr Young to take measures for selling it, if the Family see proper.
23 July. Returned up Strathnaver and inspected the woods of Ravigill, Rhiphail and Rheloisk which have already begun to shoot out, since the removal of the tenantry. That part thinnd last Year, by the tenant, shews a new appearance of health. Some depredations having been recently committed on it, Enquiry was made and bark and wood found in the houses of Angus Mackay Drover, Charles Gordon Elder, William Mackay all on Langdales farm.
24 July. This day inspected the houses of Scale, Langdale, Syre, Kenakyle, Grubeg and Grubmore. The quantity required to repair them is 380 trees[1] but none were given out, as it is understood to have been in the Arrangement for Strathnaver determined on by the noble Family in 1813, that the people in this high situation should be brought down to the fishing grounds. Thereafter, examined the woods of Achoul and Clebrig on Loch Naver and found them thriving beyond our most sanguine expectation. The bark clean and fresh, many trees shooting up from 18 to 25 Feet in height, and most of the wood which was there, when the people possessed it, appearing to have decayed or been removed. Some damage has been done to the wood of Achoul. On search, bark was found with George Munro Grubeg, John Mathison, Murdoch Mathison and Hugh

---

[1] An appendix lists 64 tenants in upper Strathnaver with the number of trees required for each house.

Mackay in Grubmore, a skin in Tan with Angus Mackay in Syre; and their names are set down for prosecution and removal.

25 July. Crossed the mountain Clibrig to Tow Garrow wood, which extends several miles along Loch Corr. We traversed the whole wood and minutely examined it. Found no damage done this Year. However, the grounds are extensive, and Gunn the keeper reports a few trees peeled next Rogart. He luckily stopped the depredators in the beginning of their work. They had with them four horses with Creels for carrying off the bark, and proved to be tenants of Mr Munro Achany vizt. Hugh Mackay Saval, John Mackay there, Hugh Ross Balinloch and [   ]¹ son of Adam Tarral in Doula whose names are set down for prosecution.

The woods on Mr Marshalls farm, which have now been eight Years under sheep, bear in general, the most flattering appearance. They give crooked timber of a very tough quality and are of the best sort for boat building. There are not less than 10,000 trees on it, which ought to be furthwith cut down and disposed of, for the good of the wood; and if the family think it proper to *do anything for these woods*, perhaps they will consult with Mr Young, who is entrusted with the disposal of every thing on the Estate, and who can take such measures as may be thought most proper.

After getting out of Towgarrow wood near Halmidary, we proceeded to Bracachy. There was formerly a great deal of wood here, but during Mr Fraser, Colonel Campbell and Mr Falconers management, it was destroyed by the Contiguous tenantry, excepting a small part furthest from them, on Loch Badinloch side. Finding that this had been considerably damaged during the last Year we made enquiries as well at Mr Gordon the tenant as among the Badinloch people, and got evidence against William McBeath and his sons, Donald Gunn and his sons John and Donald Gunn all in Badinloch, whose names are accordingly set down for prosecution and removal.

26 July. There are a good many promising Young plants at Liraboll, formerly a Wadsett held by Popes heirs, who damaged the woods, under his trustees authority. Finding, that a good many Young trees had been damaged there, we made search, and discovered that one Donald Gunn in Mid Badinloch had cutt some hundred of these plants, and we set his name down for prosecution and removal.

¹ MS. blank.

Suisgill was only the other Year committed to Major Clunes and was in 1815 damaged to the extent of 500 trees. A pretty sharp correspondence passed betwixt Mr Sellar and the Major, which was last year laid before Mr Loch. This year it has been better preserved. We discovered no more than 8 trees destroyed. We found that William and Joseph McLeod and Alexander and John Gordon Eldurable had bark in their possession and Mr Sellar accordingly noted them for prosecution and removal.

Memoranda by James Loch on estate management: August 1816

A Memorandum respecting the management of the Estate of Sutherland

Dunrobin Castle, 18 August 1816

The great extent of this property, and the details connected with its management, makes it impossible that the principal Agent should have it in his power to visit its more distant districts as often as the interest of the proprietors and the wants of the people require. It is proposed therefore to Lord and Lady Stafford that a resident person or Agent should be fixed in Assynt and another in Strathnaver. The estate of Assynt should be entrusted to the former. Those parts of the estate which are situated upon the waters falling into the North Sea should be entrusted to the latter.

The Necessity of this arrangement is pointed out by this circumstance alone, that whenever a dispute now happens the parties are obliged to submit to the inconvenience and the very great loss of time of coming over to the coast, with a complaint which must probably be referred back to some third party for settlement, thus leaving a very material branch of the arrangement of the estate and its inhabitants to persons unconnected with its management, by which all plan and system is lost.

The adoption of these two appointments is the more necessary because much discontent exists (and it is well founded) in these districts and especially in Strathnaver in consequence of the people who have been removed to the valley, from their various habitations in the hills, having been thrown into one common lot, without any division having been attempted.[1] The inconvenience and loss of this

[1] See Macpherson Grant's comments (below, pp. 206-7).

mode of holding not having here the only circumstances which can ever attach men to so unprofitable a way of using their land, namely, ancient habits and long possession. This arrangement bears moreover peculiarly hard upon a portion of these settlers who possessed distinct holdings in severalty among the hills. This state of things must have tended to keep alive that feeling of regret and disquietude which their sudden and not well digested removal from the hills in the first instance produced.

The first duty of these two resident persons or Agents will be to divide these settled lands with care among the different settlers now possessing them in common. Their local residence and daily intercourse with the people will enable them to do this in a manner which no occasional surveyor can do. Their authority will readily repress all disputes and by proper management and attention to the feelings and wants of the people their present irritation will gradually subside. They will be able to encourage the industrious and push on the idle. Their attention must also be turned to how far the allotted lands within their districts may be capable of holding more settlers whom future but gradual arrangement may make it adviseable to remove from the mountains, and they will have constantly in view the encouragement of the fisheries.

Their attention must also be particularly directed to the prevention of subsetting and the sub division of their allotments by the people and the establishment of new settlers who have had no ground heretofore – and no alienation of a lot by assignment should be permitted without leave first asked and obtained.

In the collection of the rents of these districts also they may be of essential service. In many instances these are collected with much difficulty and occasionally with some hardship to the people, it not being possible, always to make, at present, the proper distinction between the man who cannot pay owing to temporary difficulties and he who is incorrigibly lax and behind hand in his arrears. Severity and strictness in the collection of Rents can only be effectual when it is executed with judgement and discrimination. The want of this in many cases, arising in a great measure from the great extent of the estate and the impossibility of one person being able to become acquainted with the character and circumstances of every man in his collection, together with the practice of charging interest on the arrears from whatever cause the arrear arises (where it arises from misfortune it only makes the man less capable of discharging what he owes), has produced much complaint, and is not just nor calculated to obtain its proposed end.

There exists another practice which bears most severely upon one class of people that is where land is held in run ridge and although the people pay distinct rents each man is made answerable for his neighbours rent[1] and although he may have paid his own most regularly, he is subjected to the payment of his neighbours, together with the expense of legal process and the interest, upon a debt not his own. This bears peculiarly hard upon those Strathnaver men who until settled on the shore possessed their lands in severalty. This practice ought to be abolished and if a man will not pay his rent let him be ejected.

It is recommended that a similar plan should be adopted on the Sutherland estate as has been adopted with success at Trentham etc. The Audit for each district should be held in the centre of the collecting district. Upon the sea coast and on those parts of the estate not included in Strathnaver and Assynt, the factor can probably of his own knowledge with such information as he receives from the ground officer judge of the nature of the different arrears and act accordingly – against the obdurate instant process ought to be issued – in the case of the less obdurate the ground Officer should be sent with a list to collect the arrears as Mackay does at Lilleshall and in the case of the unfortunate more time still should be allowed. A Strict attention to the audits in as far as practicable should be enforced and the neglect of two even in the case of a deserving man should not be passed over without an admonition or proceeding suited to the case. All over Scotland a man paying his rent at the Audit gets a dram, as in England they get a pint of beer. Mr Sellar thinks this practice would have great good effect here and I am of the same opinion. The expense would be very trifling indeed.

The Collection of the farm rents above a certain Sum should be left to the factor.[2] When the state of the affairs upon the Sutherland estate renders a double management upon the Coast side unnecessary,

---

[1] A common practice in Assynt in the 18th century (see *Home's Survey of Assynt*, xlix).
[2] The main factor at Dunrobin. The rent collection books after 1817 follow this division.

the factor should have two Clerks, one to keep the Accounts, the other the rental – this latter should also have two smaller collecting days on the Coast side previous to the Audit as Henney[1] has – in the same way as all rents above £10 are left in Suthers own collection, and as to Assynt and Strathnaver the factor should send to the resident Agent a collecting sheet of all rents under a sum to be fixed about a month before the district audit; that they should have lesser district rent days to collect these sums and that they should at the principal district audit pay over to the factor, their collection, accounting for the arrears. Their local knowledge will assist as to advising where severity was required or when lenity should be shewn and this want of connection with the district will prevent the factor shewing undue favour to any.

By being upon the spot they will be able to collect many rents which otherwise may be lost, as it is well known that a man often has a small sum which if not instantly demanded by a person on the spot and acquainted with their circumstances would be spent. It is in this way Burgesses[2] and Henneys collections are so perfect, and the Newcastle[3] one improving.

The attention of these local Agents must also be directed to the erection of proper houses by the people – thatching with straw or heather – the preservation of the woods – of the Salmon fishings – And to transmit through the principal agent a monthly report to come to London of every thing within their district, in a form hereafter to be settled.

The Assynt and Strathnaver Agents must remit whenever they receive £100 to the factor, and he must never have more than £300 in his hand. All the collections must be paid into the British Linen Companys office at Tain to his Lordships account and to be drawn from thence only by his Lordship.

The Rental would be much simplified as would all the Accounts, if the remaining Victual rents and payments in kind as far as possible were converted into money rents. The accomodation to the tenants would be equal.

[1] Clerk at Trentham.
[2] Burgess was responsible for the collection of cottage rents paid by colliers at the Lane End (Staffs.) coal-mines.
[3] Newcastle-under-Lyme (Staffs.).

It is proposed to give these resident agents £100 per annum each and £20 a year each for expences. These sums to be deducted from Mr Youngs Salary.

[NOTE] The factor to transmit a Monthly account of his accounts and also a state of the balance of his Lordships account at the Bank. A Copy must be sent to Mr Loch that he may be able to advise with his Lordship on the subject.

B Mr Youngs accounts and expenditure of the Estate
                                                    19 August 1816

Lord Stafford having been again called upon and at a very short interval to pay a very large sum for the expenditure upon the Sutherland estate, is determined not again to be subjected to the payment of money borrowed without his consent or control. He therefore desires that it may be distinctly understood for the future that he will be answerable for no money borrowed without his knowledge and approbation.

For the purpose of securing this object and of putting the expenditure of the Scotch estates upon the same footing as that upon the English, and that the accounts may be similarly kept, his Lordship has directed that Mr Sellar shall pay all the rents etc. directly into the Bank to be subject to his Lordships order only. All payments upon the estate must also be paid into Mr Sellar as rents or produce of the estate, except the Coal etc., which is to pay directly into the bank.

Mr Young before he can receive any money must transmit a monthly account of his Cash account, open and under cover to his Lordship to Mr Loch in order that both the amount may be regulated and the expenditure in the two countries kept from interfering – which can only be done by a compliance with this direction. Mr Young must instruct Mr Grant to consider this direction as positive. A Months notice to be given when money is wanted.

Money must not be advanced upon loan without express leave whether to the public or to individuals and it is creating infinite trouble to say no more of it, to pay accounts for others and take the labour and risk of recovering the amount.

The Packet must be immediately put under Robertson's[1] charge

---

[1] William Robertson, manager of the Brora undertakings.

as it must be employed as much as possible for the use of the coal and salt works, which it can only be, by being put under the orders of the Manager of these works.

Lord and Lady Staffords distinct directions about the Saturdays slap[1] must no longer be neglected or opposed. And the prevention of Subtenants and new settlers upon the Moors must be enforced. This appears so serious to the estate that Mr Loch will not fail to press every deviation from the rule upon Lord and Lady Staffords attention.

Mr Young must in conjunction with Mr Sellar take the proper steps immediately for converting the Victual and kain[2] rents into money rents at the prices of 1815 where the same is practicable. In the case of hens and eggs the payment must be left in the alternative to be taken in kind or not, as the family is here or not.

[NOTE] Mr Sellar has directions not to honour any orders for money paid by tenants as rent, as they are alone to be paid to him.

c Mr Sellar

19 August 1816

Mr Sellar is to make no payments for the future but into his Lordships account at the British Linen Companys office at Tain, public burthens and gratuities excepted.

He is to render a monthly State of his payments into his Lordships account at the Bank and one of his own receipts and payments. When he wants money he must give a months notice. A Copy of these accounts must be sent under Cover to his Lordship open directed to Mr Loch.

Mr Sellar must lose no time in assisting Mr Stewart to inventory the implements upon Dunrobin farm, a duplicate of this account to be placed in the Charter room, and to inventory and value the Stock upon it and to consider the rent of the mains, of Dunrobin Glen and of Uppat with Stewart and Mr Young – and a new one fixed – the rent and overplus to be payable to Mr Sellar like any other farm upon the estate.

Mr Young and Mr Sellar to take the proper steps to convert the Victual and kain rents into money rents at the price of 1815 where

---

[1] See below ii, p. 150.
[2] Small rents paid in kind (for a list see above, pp. 118-20).

it is practicable and leaving sufficient to pay the Victual stipends, the hens and eggs to be left in the alternative to be taken as the family is here or not.

All payments upon the estate must be made to Mr Sellar as rents or produce of the estate except the Coal etc., which is to pay directly into the Bank.

Mr Sellar to retain a balance of Cash in his hands not exceeding £600.

Mr Sellar to appoint Mondays and Thursdays for receiving Rents. In charging interest upon rents in arrear where the amount is small Mr Sellar will use his discretion whether it should be charged or not according to the case. Where the amount is considerable he will refer the consideration of it to London.

D Memorandum respecting the Appointment of Captain Mackay and Mr Gunn as Strathnaver and Assynt Agents

19 August 1816

To the former gentleman is to be committed the management of all the country situated upon the Waters running into the North sea. To the latter the estate of Assynt.

In addition to any Commission which they may receive from Lord and Lady Stafford, they will both be made justices of the peace.

The ground officers of these Districts are to be entirely under their control and when the Woodman Lawson is employed by Lord and Lady Stafford's direction in cutting the woods in their districts he will follow such directions as he receives from them and as are calculated to accomplish their orders. The proceeds will be paid into Mr Sellars hands as rent payable for the woods. The future preservation and encouragement of these woods will form a particular object of their attention and of their instructions to the ground officer within whose district they may be.

The division of all the run ridge land within their districts must form an immediate object of attention. The lots should not be too large and they ought to be distinctly and permanently marked upon the ground. Captain McKay and Mr Gunn will both consider in their laying off these allotments whether the lands given to these settlers may not be capable of holding more people. And in this case they must reserve this surplus land accordingly, permitting the people to occupy it in the mean time in the most convenient way, letting it be distinctly understood that this land is to be resumable at pleasure as soon as it may be wanted for settlers. It must also be very particularly attended to that no one gets a settlement who had not a former occupation in the hills which would both be unjust to the people to be moved and would load the estate with a population which it cannot support. No settler must be allowed to assign or subset his lot without leave asked and obtained and particular care must be taken to prevent them subdividing their lots.

To direct them generally to active and industrious (and in the case of the younger persons) to seafaring habits will be considered an essential object of attention and to endeavour to prevail upon them to build their houses of stone and gradually to substitute straw or heath thatch for turf roofs.

The preservation of the Salmon fishery is also a material object of attention, particularly in Strathnaver, where Captain Mackay will have to enforce strictly a due attention to the law on the part of the lessees both as to the proper observance of the close season and the opening the Saturdays slap, which has been neglected in opposition to Lord and Lady Staffords express directions and wishes in a very improper manner, to the injury of the fishing. The preservation of the Salmon fry must also be attended to.

The collection of all rents below and inclusive of Ten pounds within these two districts is to be committed to Captain Mackay and Mr Gunn and for this purpose Mr Sellar must transmit to them half yearly a collecting sheet, and they will do their utmost in getting in these rents and will remit the proceeds to Mr Sellar as soon as they amount to £100. *They are to make no payments whatever.* Mr Sellar will still receive the farm rents as heretofore.

Captain McKay and Mr Gunn are fully aware of the nature of the people from whom these small rents are to be collected and of the constant attention which this may require, especially when the people have money – and in all practicable cases they will enforce payment, an arrear of rent is as bad for tenant as landlord as it soon becomes a debt which bears him down and it is often the kindest act that can be done a man, to remove him. The determined idler must be used strictly, but occasional or accidental difficulties must be treated more gently. A man ought not to be made liable for more than his own rent, but then the idle must be more strictly dealt with.

Captain McKay and Mr Gunn will make out a quarterly report of all that they think worthy of notice and fit for consideration marked '1' '2' '3' etc., and transmit the same to Mr Young to be forwarded to her Ladyship.

It may be added that Lord and Lady Staffords wishes being the improvement and happiness of the people, are desirous that this should be accomplished upon a fixed and regular plan, that nothing should be done which will require to be undone, and that in inducing them to adopt more industrious habits as little as possible should be done to hurt their feelings, both for their sakes and the success of the measures themselves.

[NOTE] In order to relieve Captain Mackay and Mr Gunn from any difficulty if they should be applied to by any gentleman for leave to shoot, they have to state that Lord and Lady Stafford retain that in their own hands.

E Dunrobin Farm including Uppat and Dunrobin Glen
                                               19 August 1816

The detail of this farm to be carried on by the Bailiff,[1] and the super-intendance of the servants and men while employed within its limits to be under his orders. The buying and selling the cattle, crop, etc., to be entrusted to him.

Mr Stewart is to continue to transmit regularly to Lord Stafford his monthly report, even when his Lordship is in the country.

An Inventory and valuation of all the Stock upon the estate must immediately be taken and also an inventory of all the implements, one copy of the latter to be placed in the Charter room, another to be left with the bailiff.

No Cattle or horses whatsoever must be turned into any park upon the farm without the bailiffs permission and with his knowledge and if the circumstances of the country render such a practice indispensable a particular field must be set aside for the purpose. It is a bad practice however and ought to be discontinued. A list of the Cows grassed upon the farm must be made out and they also must be placed in a particular field.

[1] Alexander Stewart.

The farm at present appears to be rated much too low in point of rent, a new valuation should be made including the Glen and Uppat. To do this and to make the inventorys above mentioned Mr Sellar is a fit and proper person from his acquaintance with the subject and his accuracy in figures. Mr Stewart must recollect that a proper economy in all his transactions is expected, a steady adherence to the directions he receives from Lord and Lady Stafford and a strict attention to the preservation and protection of all the plantations within Dunrobin and Uppat.

A Monthly statement of his Cash transactions debtor and Creditor must be made out and transmitted directed to Mr Loch open under his Lordships cover, that he may be enabled to advise with Lord and Lady Stafford on the propriety and amount of the current expenses of the farm. No demand for money to be made under a months notice and any payments which Mr Stewart has to make, must be to Mr Sellar like any other tenant upon the estate.

Mr Stewart to keep a proper Cash book journal and ledger and to take stamp receipts – except for wages.

F Skelbo and Morvich Farms

19 August 1816

Barclay[1] must understand very distinctly that these two farms have no connection whatever and that their Accounts are to be quite distinct, the proceeds of Skelbo belonging to Lord Gower and to be remitted regularly to his Lordships account at Messrs Drummond through the medium of the British Company's office at Tain.

A monthly report and account of the proceeds of the farm must be transmitted to Mr Loch to be forwarded to Lord Gower, this his Lordship expressly directs. A Valuation and inventory of the Stock must now be taken and also an inventory of the implements belonging to the farm, a duplicate of which to be placed in the Charter room.

Morvich is at present in hand on Lord Staffords account and until his Lordship gives express directions for any extra work there is none to be begun, a Monthly account and also an inventory to be taken as in the former case.

[1] Thomas Barclay, Earl Gower's grieve at Skelbo, now employed also to manage Morvich for the Marquis.

G Brora Coal and Salt works etc.

19 August 1816

Mr Robertson is in every instance to bear in mind that in the management of these works (which are put under his control) strict and accurate economy is necessary and is expected. Being held answerable for the success of the concern, he must take upon himself the entire direction of the men. He is not to turn away any man capriciously, but he is not to employ any one who either from idleness or being too expensive is unfit to be employed. He must get all work done in the cheapest and the best style and whatever can be done by contract must be so executed, he is in short to follow the instructions in this respect he received from Mr Mackenzie.[1]

The Selling price of the Great Coal to be 7s. 6d. the Ton of 20 cwt., the Small Coal to be furnished the works at prime cost or 4s. 6d. the Ton. The Salt to be 8s. the Bushell.

By accurate experiments it appears that there is a loss of 2s. 3d. a ton upon all great coal used in making salt. The sale of the great coal must therefore be the object to be pushed and the Salt pans etc. must only be considered as for using the small coal which is made in working the great coal.

The present pit to be continued for the next season. A stair in the Engine pit at an expense as much under as possible and by no means exceeding £50, and doubling the railways below so as to enable the present pit to put out 50 Ton of coal a day at an expense also as much under £50 as possible, to be constructed. The drift way to the rise to be carried on so, as if possible to ascertain the existence of Mr Fareys great fault.[2] The South West lead also to be carried on 200 yards further than it now is to ascertain the quality and extent of the Coal field in that direction.

Mr Robertson to make out a monthly report of the Salt and Coal works including his Cash transactions in the form approved of to be sent under cover to his Lordship directed to Mr Loch and in order that there may be no difficulties as to money a Months notice

[1] William Robertson was engaged by William Mackenzie as manager of the Brora undertakings in March 1816, at a salary of £120 per annum.
[2] John Farey (for whose report see above, p. lxiii) had predicted that a major fault would be discovered in the coal-seam.

to be given his Lordship and Mr Loch that arrangements may be made regarding it.

All payments made by Mr Robertson to his Lordships account must be into the Bank. He must keep his accounts with a debtor and creditor side of the account and except for workmens wages he must take stamp receipts. The farm must form a seperate branch that it may be seen what it produces.

The Packet is to be put under Mr Robertson's direction. A seperate account must be opened for it and it is expected that he will make the most of her.

These general directions being attended to, it is hoped that these works will be put upon a better footing than they have yet been and experience will point out many improvements which do not at present suggest themselves and from a review of the monthly reports many suggestions will occur to Lord and Lady Stafford which they will communicate from time to time either directly or through Mr Loch as suits their convenience.

An Inventory of all the implements belonging to the works and farm must be made out and a copy deposited in the Charter room and another to be left with Mr Robertson.

It is Lord and Lady Staffords wish that Berry who occupies 4 Colliers houses should find lodgings.

[NOTE] Anderson should be removed and accomodation would be found at once for the Overseer, the Grieve and the farm servants and would save every expense of rent, building etc. for lodging them.

H Memorandum

19 August 1816

No delay should take place in communicating to the following persons in Strathnaver, who were connected with the late occurrences, that they are to be turned off at Whitsunday, which ought to be done without fail.

John Munro Rinovie   John Mackay

1 Memorandum: *for consideration*

BRORA TOWN   24 August 1816

The people meant to have come to day to represent to me that I might lay the same before Lord and Lady Stafford that they had got none of their leases, which Mr Sellar says he cannot make out until he gets the description of the different lots.

Both Mr Sellar and Mr Robertson have stated that the building at Brora is much checked by the high rent put upon the lots about 30s. and if they were made more moderate during the first periods of the lease, the progress of the Village would be more rapid.

Mr Sellar says that the value of the land is about 40s. an acre and recommends a scale as follows: that for the

1st 20 years the rent should be at the rate of per acre	£2
2nd do.	£4
3rd do.	£8
4th do. and the residue of the 99 years lease	£12

This only applicable to building ground.

Besides the settlement of these lots, the whole of the DORNOCH etc. Moors and the ROGART etc. settlers require to be arranged that the bargains made with them may be reduced to writing and where the lots are not marked out they ought to be so, that they may not rest upon recollection alone, otherwise these matters will be productive hereafter of much difficulty and confusion.

Memorandum of observations on an excursion into the Interior of the Sutherland Estate from the 19th to 23rd August 1816 Inclusive: by George Macpherson Grant

In going up Strathfleet the lands from that part of the Farm of Kinnauld which it is proposed to annex to Morvich, to Pitfour, appear well adapted for Settlers, partly in small allotments and partly in farms of a small size. From Pitfour to Mr Gilchrist's Sheep farm of Rhyne both sides of the Water are adapted for Settlers. The South Side is already regularly lotted out and the people appear to have commenced improving, they should be encouraged and directed to drain and grub out the brush wood from such parts of their allottments as are suited for arable land. The Birch wood of

Inchship has at present the aspect of brushwood and there can be no benefit in preserving any part of it that is capable of being advantageously converted into arable land, such of it as does not admit of being made arable should be thinned out by the Tenants leaving the leading tree of each bush and pruning off its lower branches, this the Ground officer said they would do if permitted. There are six wretched corn milns between Kinnauld and Muie where one proper Miln would suffice. The Settlers appear to be doing a great deal in erecting comfortable stone dwellings and they should be encouraged by furnishing them with lime to harl them. When we went through the Parish of Rogart on the 13th I understood that this species of encouragement had been in Active operation but the Ground officer says that although some Individuals may have got lime he never heard of a General order to call for it till that day.[1]

Major Gilchrist has been doing a great deal for the Improvement of his Sheep farm by conducting the Water in a Main Drain through the valley and making numerous catch water drains on the slopes of the hills; his Sheep walk is a very pretty one and the ground is evidently much better suited for that purpose than for Settlers. From the termination of his Farm to the Manse of Lairg the Land has been lotted out to Settlers and it is very agreeable to see the exertions they are making. These people are much pinched from the want of any hill ground for their Cattle, this circumstance and the prospect of assistance to be derived from the example and exhortations of the Clergyman who is a good farmer, renders it desirable that the attention of the Proprietor should be turned to the encouragement of sowing artificial Grasses in this quarter; supplying some of them with Seeds and giving a small premium would probably be attended with the best effects. From the confines of the Parish of Lairg the Commutation money has been admirably expended in making an excellent piece of road and it is highly important that it should be speedily extended down to Strathfleet,[2] thus an easy communication would be opened to the Coast for those interesting Settlers.

At the Manse of Lairg we entered on the overgrown Sheep walk

---

[1] Young's accounts show that in February 1817 88¼ bolls were credited as having been given to people who had built cottages; the dates of issue are not given.

[2] Sellar's map (see above, p. 179) shows this road, but does not indicate its condition.

of Messrs Marshall and Atkinson which we did not quit until we reached the Water of Mallard at the Foot of Lochnaver. They appear to have more ground than they can beneficially occupy and indeed it is understood that they set part of it to the Tenants who are in want of hill ground. On the opposite side of Lochnaver are the Lands of Grubmore and Grubby which are crowded with small Tenants occupying the farms in run ridge. These farms appear to be adapted for Settlers but from the rocky nature of the ground I understand that it woud be very difficult to throw the lands into allottments, it could be advantageously lotted into a few small farms but then the question of providing for the extra population occurs. It might be well to consider whether the most opulent of the Tenants might not be provided with regular allottments out of it and those less able to pay accomodated with a piece of ground and a Cows grass from its pendicles.

The Meeting House of Achness is in Ruins one end of it having fallen in and the Tenants who frequent it are so unsettled and un-certain of their Tenures that they feel no encouragement to repair it.[1] It would probably have a good effect were the proprietors to be at the Expense of repairing it and the Tenants to be bound to keep it in thorough repair. Much less Accomodation than formerly is required, the Timber is good and the expense of repairing it would not be material.

Opposite to Achness and below Grubby is Dalihurish a detached pendicle of Syre which should be let as a single farm. The whole of Strathnaver so far as not occupied by Mr Sellars Sheep farm is possessed by a very large population and it does not appear at all desirable that they should be disturbed or that any extension of the Sheep Farming system should be contemplated so far as regards these lands. The object therefore which should be aimed at is the best arrangement of them under their present population and I am decidedly of opinion that a most material improvement will arise from lotting the possessions. Keanchyle is the first possession and I think the upper end of it might be divided into larger and the lower

---

[1] For the mission and mission church at Achness see Sage, *Memorabilia Domestica*, 262–5. According to Sage, the missionary received £50 from the Royal Bounty, but Sellar's accounts show that the estate paid him £50 in 1816, through the ministers of Farr and Kildonan.

into smaller allotments the lines of division to run from the Water to the hill. Syre is capable of the same arrangement; there is a most improveable flat next the River which would require a drain to lay it dry and the lotts should run from the river to the top of the hill even beyond the present ring fence. Langdale is possessed by Mr Gordon under Lease, a part of it being occupied by himself and the remainder subset. Scale has likewise been let to Mr Gordon under Lease for 19 Years in 1814, and is entirely subset by him. This farm is peculiarly well adapted for allottments but requires a drain at the foot of the bank to make the Meadow land properly dry. Mr Young says that he has no doubt Mr Gordon would be very ready to give up his Lease of it. The Birch wood of Scale appears to have come to maturity, it is of a very crooked quality and should be rouped off in lotts for boat building but the purchasers should be bound to cut the trees close to the ground and not peel the wood until cut; at present they cut it standing and leave large stumps of the tree which probably did not suit their purpose, the consequence is that no fresh shoots will spring from the stumps so peeled. There is a promising appearance of young trees from the seed but they will probably be kept under by the browsing of Cattle and I do not think that they would pay the expense of Inclosure.

Carnachy[1] is possessed by Captain [   ][2] and sundry Tenants. Captain [   ][2] is building a good house and seems desirous to forward improvement. The same mode of arrangement applies to all the farms in this Strath. A drain is required on some of them particularly on Achanlochie. The lotts further up the river should be as large as the accomodation of the present population will admit, those near the mouth of the River as small as possible not to exceed two Acres. The farms of Achnapool and Achanneiskick are possessed by the Salmon Fishers and subset by them, it is stated that this was necessary in order to give them the command of people to assist them at the fishing, how far this is the case may be enquired into as it does not appear to be in general requisite that Fishers should possess such accomodation.

The lands in Strathnaver are stated to be sett in Allotments, no

---

[1] Carnachy is entered in the 1815 rental as held by Mrs Mackay (£37) and by 11 named small tenants (£37).
[2] MS. blank.

vestige, however of allotment Appears. A dispossessed Tenant is
merely told you are to have an allotment in such a Farm and a new
division of every patch of ground of that farm is made by persons
called the Inquest who portion out the different patches according
to the population which the farm is destined to accomodate.

Mr Roy the Land Surveyor was employed by Mr Young to
Make the allotments and we were certainly led to believe that he
had actually done so but that the people had disregarded the boun-
aries pointed out to them and had resorted to their own favorite
system of dividing the ground by the Inquest. Upon a Minute
enquiry however the real state of the case appears to be this. That
Mr Roy in fixing the allottments in the Parish of Lairg and elsewhere put a value on a farm, then divided it into allotments and
proportioned the value of the Farm on each Allotment. As he could
not possibly judge so accurately of the value of every different
field as those locally acquainted with their produce and accustomed
to judge of them it of course happened that some of the lotts were
considered as higher valued than others and this sometimes to a
considerable degree. When the Measure was therefore proposed in
Strathnaver the Tenants were naturally alarmed and requested to
be allowed to divide their lotts by the Inquest and they were told
that if they would pay their Rents as one Individual and give no
trouble to the Proprietor or Factor they might divide their lands
as they pleased. The people do not seem to have any predilection
for their present most unprofitable mode of occupation further than
they think it secures them an equality of Rent And to Accomplish
this a mode has occurred to me which is this that the allotments
should be regularly marked off by the Factor or by a Surveyor
where Acres are to be the rule of divisions, that a rent should be put
on the Farm And that the Inquest (in whom the people have
probably with reason so much confidence) should fix the proportion
of Rent to be paid by each allotment.

In lotting out a farm the Circumstances of its present occupiers
should be considered and lotts might be formed suited to their
Circumstances.

The Lands about the Church of Farr and Clerkhill should be
portioned out in small allotments not exceeding two Acres but
much consideration will be required in arranging these lotts and it

appears highly desirable that they should be laid out and the houses erected in a regular manner as much as possible in the form of a Village. The nature of the ground will not admit of this being done to perfection but I cannot help thinking that the houses might in many instances be placed in the form of a Street instead of every man dropping down his house where he pleases. The house of Clerkhill is going to ruin from the roof being neglected. It is a good house and the Expense of repairing it will not be great, some Accomodation is wanted in that quarter for the Manager of the Estate when he visits it, as at present he must sorn[1] on the Clergyman which is neither pleasant nor respectable. Two rooms of the house of Clerkhill might be fitted up for that purpose and the Miss Gordons might occupy the rest of the house as a school and attend to the keeping of the two rooms aired.

A small country Inn for the accomodation of the Publick is much wanted at Bettyhill. The lands, presently allotted to Bettyhill are at a distance from the ruinous fabrick which bears the name of an Inn and I understand that this has arisen from the Circumstance of lotting out the ground intended for an Innkeeper in a situation to suit the proposed Parliamentary road from Tongue to Thurso.

The Water of Naver and other Waters on the Estate are doing considerable damage to the Lands through which they run. Where there are many Settlers it might be well to have them taken bound to 3 or 4 days service each Yearly for erecting Bulwarks against the encroachment of the River in the Strath where their Lands are situated. This would secure hands on any emergency and a shilling a day might be deducted from their present Rents as a compensation.

The situation of the Tenantry in Strathnaver strongly confirms the necessity of the recent Appointment of a local Factor in that District, its remote and almost inaccessable situation having prevented the superintendance of the General Manager being at all felt in this Quarter. He can have acquired no knowledge of their different situations and Characters. When he did at any time go over a crowd of Applicants oppressed him whose Claims were all left to be settled by the Ground officer or referred to some other more convenient opportunity. This Strath is a most interesting and beautiful portion of the property but its improvement must be

[1] Impose himself for board and lodging.

indefinitely protracted unless a Communication is opened between
it and the opposite Coast of the Estate and likewise to Thurso. The
roads for that purpose might be constructed of a moderate breadth
say ten or twelve feet and an Annual sum appropriated to this purpose and judiciously expended would add more to the permanent
Improvement of the Estate and to the comfort and Amelioration
of its Inhabitants than any other mode that can be devised. The most
important Lines of communication appear to be a continuation
of the road from Lairg to Strathfleet which could be done at no
great Expence: a road by the Crask of Kildonan to Farr, from Farr
to Thurso and ultimately a road to Assynt.

The difficulty of arranging the Lands of Strathnaver in consequence of the great population to be provided for is to be attributed
to the mode resorted to when the great tract of Country given to
Atkinson and Marshall was cleared of its Inhabitants; No Occupation having been then provided for Settlers on the Coast those
people were crowded into possessions in the Strath and on the
opposite side of the Loch, where it would have been more desirable
to have enlarged the Possessions and when Mr Sellars farm was
laid out the evil was of course extended, but it is pleasant to find that
even from the Upper parts of the Strath the want of land has driven
the families of the occupiers to the herring fishing where they make
very handsome wages and generally return in sufficient time to
earn additional Wages in reaping the Harvest. It is however too
evident that the generality of the people are much reduced in
Circumstances and that in the present depressed state of the Cattle
Markets they cannot be expected to make punctual payment of the
Rents now exacted from them and any deficiency in this respect
must be attributed to the times and not laid to the Charge of the
new measures recommended for the amelioration of the Condition
of the people by altering the present mode of tenure. The Lands
occupied by Mr Sellar are certainly better calculated for Sheep than
for Inhabitants and there are very high grounds about Badinloch
which might be more beneficially occupied in the same way did
not a difficulty occur in finding a situation for the present occupants.
(QUERY? would it be advisable to reserve Kintradwell for any such
purpose.)

The Settlers about the Manse of Kildonan have had their allot-

o

ments regularly laid out and the advantage of such an arrangement is very evident in the Improvement they are making. A road to connect them with Strathnaver would have the best effects in communicating the same spirit of Industry to the Inhabitants of that Strath. The Lands laid under Sheep in the lower part of the Strath of Kildonan are well suited for Stock and the Tenants of that part which has this Year been given to Major Clunes must experience the greatest comfort from being permitted to occupy their present possessions until they have got rid of their Cattle and erected habitations on their new allotments which they are busily employed in doing. But no regular plan has been pointed out to them as to the situations on which they should build, but they are permitted to plan their houses at random on their lotts.

The disturbances in Strathnaver appear to have had their origin in neglecting to have the allotments intended for the dispossessed Tenants divided and pointed out to them in proper time. The term of their removal was the 26 of May and it was not till the Middle of June that they were told in what farm they were to be placed Mr Sellar having indulged them at Mr Youngs request until that period. After they were told where they were to be settled Mr Sellar allowed a fortnight to remove their articles of Furniture etc., but *they state* that the sacrament happened during one week of that period and the Tenants of Garvault who had to remove a great distance over the most wretched road complain that Mr Sellars Shepherds after the fortnight was expired would not permit them to remove the wood of their houses through the Grounds and that it lay exposed to the Weather till Lady Stafford on her arrival in the Country gave directions that they should be permitted to take away the wood. This statement was made by John Munro in Rinovie who by no means seems to give a fair state of the Case. He seems to have been the Active Instigator in pressing the other Tenants to proceed by Criminal prosecution. He admits that he was advised by Captain Sutherland[1] in London and by Mackid but evaded admitting that Mr Sutherland Brora[2] gave him any advice. John Mackay admits that he was misled by John Munro Mr Mackid and Mr Sutherland Brora who advised him as he had a good action on Account of the

---

[1] Alexander Sutherland.
[2] Captain John Sutherland of Sciberscross.

Injury sustained by his wife, not to submit the question of Damages but to proceed by criminal Action. On the whole since they chose to prefer the advice they did to that of the Lord Advocate[1] and Mr Young who recommended a Submission I think those two men should be removed from the Estate as an example.

[1] John Campbell, joint Crown Agent, wrote to Rev. David Mackenzie, minister of Farr, on 25 December 1815, stating that in the Lord Advocate's view a submission should be entered into between Sellar and the Strathnaver complainants, and recommending the sheriff-depute of Sutherland or of Caithness as a proper arbiter ('I trouble you with this Communication because we understand that the Complainants would be likely to take your advice on the subject'). Sellar complained (Sellar to Marchioness, 16 March 1816) that Mackenzie sent this letter to the *Military Register*, and that the crown lawyers in consequence decided that a public trial was necessary. It would appear that the complainants refused the suggested submission, as they had earlier when proposed by Young (see above, pp. 153-5). It should be noted that in the same letter Sellar complained that the trial judge was to be Lord Pitmilly, 'brother of the partner of Mr McKenzie's; whose influence, I believe, did at *the first* foster and bring forward this and similar oppressions against me'.

Appendices

🗿🗿

Appendix A

TABLES RELATING TO SUTHERLAND ESTATE
MANAGEMENT

1802-1816

TABLE I

RENTALS OF THE ESTATE OF SUTHERLAND

The two rentals here printed in parallel are those for Victual Rent, Crop 1807, and Money Rent, Martinmas 1808 (by Cosmo Falconer), and for Victual Rent, Crop 1815, and Money Rent, Martinmas 1815 and Whitsunday 1816 (by Patrick Sellar). The earlier of these is the first rental to be arranged completely by parishes: the second is the last to be prepared during William Young's period of office.

To reduce the material to manageable proportions, the following conventions have been followed:

Martinmas 1815 and Whitsunday 1816 rents have been added together.

Tenancies rented below £20 have been summarised; their names, and the number of tenants in each, are given in footnotes to each parish.

A small number of tenancies are dual; these have been counted as single tenancies.

In farms listed separately, individual names of tenants are given where these do not exceed three; in other cases totals only are given.

Rents in kind, not listed in 1808 but amounting in 1815 to 12¾ faces peats, 9 wethers, 339 hens and 820 eggs, have been ignored.

Direct comparisons between the rentals are complicated by the purchase of the estates of Armadale, Carrol and Uppat between 1808 and 1815; by alterations in the number and extent of wadsets; by the conversion of victual rents to money; and by the fact that some tenancies over-ran parish boundaries (e.g. Kilcalmkill sheep-farm). The following summary must therefore be interpreted with caution.

SUMMARY

Parish	1808	1815
Victual		
Clyne	190.1.2.2	143.0.2.0
Creich	6.0.0.0	—
Dornoch	425.1.2.0	143.1.2.0
Golspie	498.0.0.0	85.3.3.0
Loth	143.3.2.0	87.2.2.2
Rogart	79.0.0.0	—
	Total: 1,342.2.2.2 bolls	459.3.2.1 bolls

Money

	£	s.	d.	£	s.	d.
Assynt	1,518	2	11^{10}	3,869	1	6
Clyne	759	16	7^8	1,619	18	$8\frac{1}{2}$
Creich	50	3	0	220	0	0
Dornoch	968	11	2^2	1,762	4	6
Farr	508	14	11^{10}	2,214	9	$11\frac{1}{2}$
Golspie	936	10	3^{11}	2,090	10	$4\frac{1}{2}$
Kildonan	715	1	2^8	1,091	5	5
Lairg	1,703	18	1^4	2,372	2	11^{11}
Loth	427	11	8^9	932	0	$3\frac{1}{2}$
Rogart	835	12	6^{10}	1,950	1	6
Salmon fishings	2,267	0	0	1,650	0	0
Total:	10,691	2	9	19,762	15	2^{11}

PARISH OF ASSYNT: 1808

		Money		
		£	s.	d.
Cromalt, Ardvare, Little Assynt, Auldnachie, half of salmon fishings	Capt. William Scobie	100	6	0
Knockan	John Robertson	30	6	8
Elphine	Ensign Alexander McKenzie's heirs	37	9	3
Leadmore	Roderick McKenzie and 8 named tenants	51	10	0[6]
Riencreach, Marble Quarry, ½ Unapool	Isaac Jopling	70	8	8[6]
Ledbeg, Fillin, Layne, ½ Drumswordland, half of salmon fishings	Capt. Kenneth McKenzie	116	11	6
Stronechrubie, Lower Tubeg, Duchlash, Poulgarvir	Murdoch McKenzie	90	7	1
Inchnindamph, Upper Tubeg	George McKenzie	40	7	6
Torbreak, Culin, ½ Camore	Rev. William McKenzie	28	7	0
Auchmore, Rhintraid	Kenneth Scobie	63	13	0
½ Unapool	10 named tenants	50	0	0
Nedd	13 named tenants	50	8	0
Drumbeg	15 named tenants	60	0	0
Oldany	Mrs McKay	48	9	6
Culkein Drumbeg, Durlan	Lieut. Hugh Clark's heirs	44	15	3
Ruestore etc.[1]	Donald McDonald	375	0	4[10]
Inver	Donald McDonald	30	3	10
Culag	Donald McDonald	20	2	8
Baddidarroch	7 named tenants	21	0	0
Badinabaan, Knockineach	George Ross	26	4	9
Inverkirkaig	Lieut. John McKenzie	20	4	2
Lochbannoch	5 named tenants	21	0	0
Glenlerig	17 named tenants	89	5	0
2 farms below £20 rent[2]		32	2	8
	Total:	1,518	2	11[10]

[1] Clashnessie, Culkein Achnacarnan excepting Durlan, Achnacarnan, Clashmore, Balchladich, Store, Clachtoll, Achmelvich.
[2] Edrachalda (1 named tenant), Brackloch (2).

PARISH OF ASSYNT: 1815

		Money		
		£	s.	d.
Layne, Stronechrubie, Lower Tubeg, Drumbegg Island	Heirs of Murdoch McKenzie in Stronechrubie, Alexander McKenzie in Poulgarvir	302	14	0
Inchndamff, Upper Tubeg	George McKenzie	40	7	6
Ledmore, ½ Rheincrevoch	Roderick McKenzie	150	0	0
Ledbeg, including Canisp, Drumswordland, Duchlash, Poulgarvir, Culkein Island	Heirs of Kenneth McKenzie, Ledbeg	430	9	6[6]
Clashnessie etc.[3]	Donald McDonald	870	10	10[4]
Feullin	John and Hugh McLeod and 4 named tenants	65	11	4[8]
Achumore etc.[4]	William and James Scobie	700	0	0
Little Assynt, Cromault	John Mackenzie, Little Assynt	120	0	0
Aultnachie	Roderick and Donald McLeod	70	0	0
Culkein	sundry tenants	77	10	0
Drumbegg	sundry tenants	80	0	0
Loch Beannoch	sundry tenants	35	0	0
Brackloch	4 named tenants	29	0	0
Baddydarroch	sundry tenants	30	0	0
Bady Grinan	sundry tenants	20	0	0
Elphine	sundry tenants	150	17	6
Knockan	sundry tenants	143	15	6
Marble Quarries	Isaac Jopling, New Castle	40	0	0
Rheincrevich, ½ Unapool	Isaac Jopling	50	8	8[6]
½ Unapool	10 named tenants	50	0	0
Coulin, Camore	30 named tenants	132	19	0
Torbreck	sundry small tenants	40	0	0
Oldany	Mrs Gray, widow of Lieut. MacKay	48	9	6
Nedd	sundry small tenants	50	8	0
Salmon fishings	Landles and Redpath	100	0	0
Kelp shores south of Row Stoir	sundries	35	0	0
2 farms below £20 rent[5]		6	0	0
	Total:	3,869	1	6

[3] Clashnessie, Culkein Achnacarnan excepting Durlan, Achnacarnan, Clashmore, Balchladich, Store, Clachtoll, Achmelvich, storehouse, Inverkirkaig, Badinaman, Knocknaneach, Soulvine, Brackloch of Ledbeg, Coulack and Straan, Inver Island, house at Coulkein, kelp shores north of Row Stoir.

[4] Achumore, Edrachalda, Tumore, part of Poltacarkan, Ardvare, Rheintraid, Glenlerig, part of hill ground of Unapool.

[5] Chalda pendicle (1), Durlan, a pendicle of Culkein (3).

PARISH OF CLYNE: 1808[1]

		Victual	Money		
			£	s.	d.
Strathskinsdale	William Munro of Achany		150	0	0
Doll	10 named tenants	115.0.2.2	24	17	5[3]
Ascoilbeg	5 named tenants		25	0	0
Ascoilmore and miln	4 named tenants		24	15	0
Grinan, Furranmore, Altivulen, Clynekirkton, Badenlois	Rev. Walter Ross	28.0.0.0	10	10	0
Clynemilton and miln	Roderick Cameron, Miss Lucy Gordon, Hugh McLeod		61	15	7[6]
Brora	Capt. John Sutherland		50	3	2[8]
Sciberscross, Easter Kerrow	Capt. John Sutherland		40	3	6
Clynelish etc.[2]	Major Hugh Houstoun	47.1.0.0	98	9	4[11]
Kelp Shores	Major Hugh Houstoun		50	0	0
Killean	Marquis of Stafford		50	0	0
19 farms below £20 rent[3]			174	2	5[4]
	Total:	190.1.2.2	759	16	7[8]

[1] The following wadset existed at Martinmas 1808: no. 12 (see Table III below, p. 239).

[2] Clynelish, Dalhalmy, Ardochy, Dromy, Achoimsdale, Kyle Brora, Islandnacra, Fanich, Kilivian, Gearchyle, Leadoch, Glaslochan.

[3] Altindown (2 named tenants), Craigroy and Renagive (1), Rhimiscan (2), Achness (2), Crislich (1), Foick (1), Coppernusgach (1), Polly (1), Ammott (2), Dalbreck (3), Kilfidderbeg (3), Cluaig and Culrain (1), Knockglass (1), Strathroy, including Kylvrannie, Rhivoy, Badnicardoch, Rhianbeg (9), Urachyle (3), Kilfidder and miln (3), Storral (1), Torry Seilzier (1), Ellanin (1); also feu-duty on Carrol.

PARISH OF CLYNE: 1815[4]

		Victual	Money		
			£	s.	d.
Doll and Inverbrora	26 named tenants	25.0.2.0	40	13	1
Muiymore	James McKay and D. Ross		33	0	0
Knockanachalich	Alexander McKay		30	0	0
Achumore	Widow McPherson		50	0	0
Grinan excluding Altnavoullen	Rev. Walter Ross		20	0	0
Clynekirkton	Rev. Walter Ross	44.0.0.0	9	8	9½
Ascoilbeg	Rev. Walter Ross		25	0	0
Ascoilmore and miln, Ballaidan	9 named tenants		49	5	6
Dalfolly	5 named tenants		31	10	0
Balnakyle	Alexander Sutherland		22	2	0
Crislich, Foick, part of Cupernahoul	Alexander Melville		60	0	0
Clynemilton and miln	Roderick Cameron, Miss Lucy Gordon, Margaret McLeod widow		61	15	7½
Clynelish	Major Houstoun	47.1.0.0	111	9	5
Easter Brora, Auldriry	Capt. John Sutherland		32	3	2½
Sciberscross, Easter Kerrow	Capt. John Sutherland		40	3	6
Strathroy, including Kylvrannie, Rhivoy, Badnacardich, Rhianbeg	12 named tenants		23	2	0
Carrol	6 named tenants	6.0.0.0	25	4	0
Kilblair and mills	6 named tenants	10.3.0.0	34	19	0
Dalvait	William McDonald, Margaret Sutherland Hugh McLeod	4.0.0.0	15	18	0
Scottary	4 named tenants		22	0	0
Achnakyle	Ann Bruce, A. Sutherland McCarlish, A. Sutherland Clyne		21	0	0
Kilcalmkill[5]	Gabriel Reed		531	18	3
Salmon fishings in Loch Brora	Landles and Redpath		45	0	0

[4] The estate of Carrol was purchased from Joseph Gordon in 1812; many of the additional small farms listed in 1815, together with a large part of the sheep farm of Kilcalmkill, were formerly part of this estate.

[5] This figure includes £45 payable at Whitsunday 1816 as half-year's rent of Lirriboll, par. Kildonan, and £28 14s. 10½d, as half-year's rent of Aultivoullan; the rent of Kilcalmkill proper was £452 10s. 3d.

PARISH OF CREICH: 1808

		Victual	Money £ s. d.
Invershin	Gilbert McKenzie	3.0.0.0	50 3 0
Achinduich	7 named tenants	3.0.0.0	
	Total:	6.0.0.0	50 3 0

PARISH OF DORNOCH: 1808

		Victual	Money £ s. d.
Achlean	William McIntosh and Andrew McKay	32.0.0.0	6 0 0
Acheroch, Wards, Silvercroft	Rev. John Bethune		23 0 0
Pitgrudy	Angus Frazer		34 0 0
Cyderhall	Capt. William McCulloch, in right of Lieut. William McKenzie, and Alexander Rose, storekeeper	96.1.2.0	13 11 1[4]
Teachlybe	Hugh Leslie	15.2.0.0	11 0 0
Teachlybe miln	Hugh Leslie	20.0.0.0	13 17 9[4]
Davochfin	Hugh McKay and John Munro	14.0.0.0	3 0 0
Achloie	Charles McKenzie, Robert Sutherland, James Clark	16.0.0.0	4 10 0
Drumdivan	8 named tenants		30 0 0
Little Torboll	Capt. Kenneth McKay and 6 named tenants		28 0 8[6]
Cambusavy	Mrs Sutherland		64 5 11[6]
Balvraid	Baillie James Boog and 15 named tenants	28.0.0.0	25 2 0

		Victual	*Money*		
			£	s.	d.
Kelp Shores from Ord to Strathsteven	Alexander Simpson		75	0	0
21 Farms below £20 rent[6]			209	6	4
	Total:	143.0.2.0	1,619	18	8½

[6] Altindow (2 named tenants), Rhimiscan (2), Achness (1), Amott (2), Dalbreck (2), Kilfidderbeg (3), Cluaig and Culrain (1), Knockglass and part of Clynemilton (1). Urachyle (3), Kilfidder (3), Storral (1), Tory Sulzier (1), Ellanin (1), Corriscaig (6), Kildoir (1), Achucragach (1), Achcork (1), Aldintorig (1), Dalvolian (1), Dalvaddie (1) Badnillich (1). The Marquis of Stafford held the Brora Coal Farm rent-free.

PARISH OF CREICH: 1815

		Victual	*Money*		
			£	s.	d.
Invershin	Morton and Culley, in place of Atkinson and Marshall		220	0	0

PARISH OF DORNOCH: 1815

Achinchanter	William Rose	3.3.0.0	34	19	0
Cyderhall	Capt. William McCulloch	93.1.2 0	13	11	1[6]
Achinluie, Achley, Craggy, Achlean angle	Capt John Munro		50	0	0
Pitgrudy	Angus Frazer		40	0	0
Achlean	Angus Frazer		50	0	0
Acheroch, Michaelwells	William Munro senior		44	0	0
Mill of Cyderhall	Hugh Leslie	21.0.0.0	20	15	0
Dalvevy, Teachlybe	W. and G. McIntosh	3.3.0.0	34	19	0
Davochfin	William Munro junior		35	0	0
Drumdivan	Alexander Gunn and 4 named tenants		60	9	11[6]
Meikle and Little Torboll etc.[2]	Capt. Kenneth McKay		235	0	0
Cambusavie	Mrs Sutherland		64	5	11[6]
Balvraid	Dr Ross and 4 named tenants	8.3.0.0	115	4	3[9]
Coul, Eachder	Robert Sutherland		92	19	9

[2] Meikle and Little Torboll, Esavreck, Airds, Achu of Eiden, mill of Torboll, Achinal, muir of Achinal, Achladuaig, Torfalig, Lednoclay, Dalnamain, Brae, Strathtolly, Garskally, Craigulichy, Aultanrevach, Rossal grazing, Strath Achuvaich.

| | | Victual | Money |
| | | | £ s. d. |

		Victual	*Money*		
			£	s.	d.
Kinauld, ⅔ shealing of Craigachnarich	Lieut. Duncan Sutherland		90	0	0
Coul	4 named tenants	16.2.0.0	14	0	0
Achavandra	8 named tenants	36.0.0.0	24	0	0
Fourpenny	John McDonald, Alexander Mathieson	24.0.0.0	10	0	0
Eachder	4 named tenants	24.0.0.0	12	12	0
Proncy	Mrs McKay and 8 named tenants		46	4	0
Proncynain	7 named tenants	6.0.0.0	39	10	7
Proncycroy	4 named tenants	3.0.0.0	15	0	0
Milltoun of Evelicks and miln	6 named tenants	36.0.0.0	13	0	0
Knockglass	Rev. John Bethune and 3 named tenants	24.0.0.0	12	0	0
Skelbo	James Boog		93	14	2[11]
Evelicks	William Taylor	22.0.0.0	19	0	8[6]
Rearcher, Brea	Col. George Sutherland		51	11	3[2]
Meikle Torboll, Achnahue	Capt. Kenneth McKay		51	8	7[10]
38 tenancies under £20 rent[1]		12.0.0.0	220	2	2[1]
	Total:	425.1.2.0	968	11	2[2]

[1] Achinchanter, Sandcroft (1 named tenant), Castle Garden (1), Achley (1), Garskelly (1), Dornoch town (7), East Garden (4), Croftkeil (1), 2 bolls pay (1), Scottach, 6 firlots pay (1), Croftmeadich (1), Lonmore (3), Dalvevy (1), Ballone (1), the Park (1), Airds of Little Torboll, Wester Rhihalmy and miln (1), Achinal with pendicle and muir (4), Esavreck (1), Torfalig (1), Michaelwells, Torrenroy (1), Cambusmore (1), Lednoclay (3), Evelicks and Dornoch Muir settlers (13), Badninish settlers (6), Rimusaig (1), shealing of Little Garvie (1), Cubaig (1), Altaduaig (4), Dalnamain (10), Gruby (1), Toar (1), Fluchary (1), Dalchiell (1), Ardochy (3), Loanberichen (1), Clashnalarich (1), Lenagranach (1), Knockbreack (1), Leadberichen (2); also feu-duties of Skibo and Overskibo.

PARISH OF FARR: 1808[1]

		£	s.	d.
Fisherlands, Crask, Gharve, part of Farr	Capt. William Gordon	63	2	5[6]
Part of Farr	12 named tenants	54	0	0
Swordly	5 named tenants	25	0	0
Clachan and miln	Janet McKay widow	25	0	0
Ravigill	12 named tenants	31	6	0
Rhiphail	Capt. Hugh McKay, Clebrig, and 8 named tenants	30	0	0

[1] The following wadsets existed at Martinmas 1808: nos. 8, 10, 19, 20 (see Table III below, pp. 238-9).

		Victual	*Money* £	s.	d.
Fourpenny	Alexander Mathieson, William Gunn, Andrew McKay		41	4	3
Skelbo, Achavandra	Earl Gower		300	0	0
Proncynaird	Mrs Mackay		50	0	0
Proncynain	Hugh Leslie	5.2.0.0	52	11	10[6]
Proncycroy	William Ross	2.2.0.0	24	12	8
Evelix	William Taylor		90	0	0
Rhearquhar	Col. Sutherland		57	11	3[6]
Pendicles of Proncycroy	13 named tenants		21	11	10[9]
Kinnauld	Capt. Sutherland		88	0	0
32 tenancies below £20 rent[3]		1.2.0.0	145	8	5
	Total:	143.1.2.0	1,762	4	6

[3] Castle Yards (Marquis of Stafford and 1 named tenant), part of Achlean (1), Wards, Silvercroft (1), Torrinroy (1), Dornoch town (5), Dornoch schoolhouse (3 named heritors), East Garden (5 named tenants), Powder magazine (Collector of Supply), Croftkail (1 named tenant), 2 bolls pay, Scottach, 6 firlots pay (1), Croft-meadien (1), Croft opposite Cyderhall (1), Lonemore (3), Park (1), Cambusmore (1), Knockglass (1), Evelix mill (1), Muirs of Dornoch (38 settlers: 22 paying no rent), Balvraid Muir (27 settlers paying no rent), Badninish (5 named tenants), Fleuchary (1), Dalchiel (1), Loanberichen (1), Ardachu (3), Clashalarich (1), Linagranach (1), Knockbreck (1), Leadberichin (2), Teachlybe (1), kelp shores south side of Little Ferry (2); also feu-duties of Skibo and Overskibo.

PARISH OF FARR: 1815[3]

		£	s.	d.
Braerathy	9 named tenants	100	0	0
Dalangdale	4 named tenants	30	0	0
Bowside	4 named tenants	31	10	0
Daltine	6 named tenants	30	0	0
Swordly	8 named tenants	26	0	0
Farr, Clerkhill pennyland	31 named tenants	90	0	0
Ardbeg, Clerkhill	7 named tenants	25	0	0

[3] The following wadset existed at Martinmas 1815: no. 8 (see Table III below, p. 238). The estate of Armadale was purchased from Lord Armadale in 1813; many of the additional farms listed in 1815 were formerly part of this estate. Ardbeg was purchased from Lord Reay in 1814.

		Victual	Money		
			£	s.	d.
Rhinovy	14 named tenants		40	0	0
Mudle Tubeg	Capt. Hugh McKay, Clebrig		30	0	0
Grubbeg	Lieut. John McKay, William McKay, and 4 named tenants		27	0	0
Grubmore	17 named tenants		29	6	3
Skelpick and miln	Lieut George Gordon and 11 named tenants		56	0	0
Dunveidan	12 named tenants		33	0	0
6 farms below £20 rent[2]			65	0	3[4]
	Total:		508	14	11[10]

[2] Dallacharish and pendicles (3 named tenants), Dimichory (3), Truderskaig (9), east end of Truderskaig (5), outfield of Grubmore (4), Ardraavine of Mudle and Braeface of Craggydow (5); also feu-duty of Durness.

PARISH OF GOLSPIE: 1808[1]

			£	s.	d.
Craigtown	George Mackay, assignee of Mrs McLean	38.0.0.0	62	18	7
Kirktown	Capt. John Munro	34.0.0.0	18	5	8
Ironhill, Badden	Lieut. Alexander Mackay	17.0.0.0	30	0	0
Sallichtown	9 named tenants	54.0.0.0	9	0	0
Ballone	7 named tenants	46.2.0.0	6	0	0
Rhiorn	James Grant, Hugh and Alexander Gordon	21.0.0.0	5	0	0
Old Rhives	4 named tenants		27	5	0[8]
Drumuie	7 named tenants	55.0.0.0	8	14	1

[1] The following wadset existed at Martinmas 1808: no. 3 (see Table III below, p. 238).

		Victual	*Money*		
			£	s.	d.
Rhinachattle, Rhianmore	10 named tenants		31	0	0
Achnieskich	9 named tenants		22	12	6
Invernaver	Landles and Redpath		48	15	0
[ ]ie[4]	12 named tenants		25	0	0
Achinlochy, ⅓ Achmore	9 named tenants		25	0	0
Rhinovie, part Achmore	5 named tenants		25	0	0
Achinellan	9 named tenants		22	0	0
Dunveidan	12 named tenants		33	15	0
Carnachy	Mrs MacKay and 13 named tenants		74	0	0
Mill of Farr	astricted tenants		20	0	0
Invernaver Inn lot	William Gordon		20	0	0
Rhiloisk Sheep Farm	Patrick Sellar		169	5	0
Langdale and others	Robert Gordon		230	0	0
Syre, Kennakyle	20 named tenants		130	0	0
Grubmore, Grubeg	15 named tenants		105	0	0
Mudle Tubeg, Dinachkary	Capt. Kenneth McKay		80	0	0
Mains of Strathy	George Innes, Isauld		168	0	0
Remainder of Strathy and Armadale	Mr Innes, Sandside		350	0	0
Armadale Fishertown	sundry small tenants		65	0	0
Portskerra[5]	Hugh Mcdonald		100	0	0
11 farms below £20 rent[6]			137	12	5½
		Total:	2,214	9	11½

[4] MS. torn.
[5] In par. Reay.
[6] Achrugan (4 named tenants), Crask (7), Cromeran (5), Newland (18), Betyhill (5), Dochain (6), Accoboll (4), Chrat (3), Dalcherisgill (4), Dalvighouse (5), Achalgarry (6); also feu-duty of Durness.

PARISH OF GOLSPIE: 1815[6]

			£	s.	d.
Ironhill, Baddan	Alexander McKay		30	12	6
Kirktown etc.	Robert Mackid		120	0	0
Culmaily	Patrick Sellar	22.1.3.0	352	9	8½
Drummuy	Capt. Robert Suther- land	30.0.0.0	120	0	0
Rhives, Golspiemore	William Young		120	11	7
Golspie houses, shops	22 named tenants		97	18	8
Golspie houses and gardens	James Dallas, saddler, and David Gunn, shoemaker		20	3	0

[6] The following wadsets existed at Martinmas 1815: nos. 3, 7 (see Table III below, p. 238). The estate of Uppat was purchased from William Munro of Achany in 1812.

P

		Victual	*Money* £ s. d.
Golspymore[2]	5 named tenants	30.1.0.0	0 13 4
Golspytower[3]	9 named tenants	82.2.3.0	10 17 9[4]
Low-lands of Golspy[4]	11 named tenants		47 3 6
New Inn and lands	James Duncan		41 8 7
Glen of Dunrobin	4 named tenants	22.0.1.0	11 15 6[6]
Rhives, part of Golspy-more	Cosmo Falconer		40 0 0
Dunrobin, Croftfruich	Marquis of Stafford		450 0 0
Golspymilns	Angus McKay	10.0.0.0	10 16 4
Balblair	John McPherson, Gilbert Mathieson, Donald Bannerman and widow McLeod	24.0.0.0	0 12 0
East Aberscross	John Polson and 5 named tenants		64 1 0
West Aberscross	11 named tenants	36.0.0.0	22 0 0
Morvich	Mrs McLeod	20.0.0.0	3 1 4
18 tenancies below £20 rent[5]		7.3.0.0	66 17 6[5]
	Total:	498.0.0.0	936 10 3[11]

[2] 'The former Money rent of these Cease this year except what may be got for spots of grass set to some people for Cows and they will be met by New arrangements connected with the Village next year.' The money rent shown is paid by 5 non-tenants for gardens and pasture-ground.

[3] The 9 tenants pay victual rent; in addition 4 tenants pay money rent, and 2 non-tenants also pay a small amount of money rent.

[4] Divided into small pasture-grounds, measured in acres.

[5] Ferryoons (2 named tenants), Croftvaliach of Old Rhives (1), Golspy (12: house rents only), Blarnafidoch (1), Backies (2), New Backies (17), Clashmore (5), Lonmore (3), Coirgrean (1), Strathlundy (12), Achlundy (1), Inchlair (1), Ledroach (2), Inchfoury (1), Badravan (1), Croich (1), Longuish (2), Ledriag (1); also feu-duty of Uppat.

PARISH OF KILDONAN: 1808[1]

		£ s. d.
Knockfin	George Munro	31 19 5
Kinbrace, Shunachy	9 named tenants	53 9 0
Badicharlist or Reisk	4 named tenants	20 5 0
Achneaken	5 named tenants	21 0 0
Achnahuach	Lieut. Patrick Matheson	24 0 0
Branchilly, a shealing of Badinarib	Marquis of Stafford	20 0 0
Cain, Kilfedder	Robert Pope	35 0 0

[1] The following wadsets existed at Martinmas 1808: nos. 1, 11, 17, 19 (see Table III below, pp. 238-9).

		Victual	*Money*		
			£	s.	d.
Golspie Mills etc.	John Morrison		51	18	10
Golspie Tower	Rev. William Keith		36	0	0
Inn and farm	James Duncan		108	5	7
Dunrobin Glen etc.	Lord Stafford		80	0	0
Dunrobin	Lord Stafford		450	0	0
Uppat Mains,	Lord Stafford		235	16	0
Strathsteven					
West Aberscross	15 named tenants	33.2.0.0	28	4	0
East Aberscross	John Polson		64	1	0
Morvich	Lord Stafford		80	0	0
14 tenancies below £20 rent[7]			94	9	6
		Total: 85.3.3.0	2,090	10	4½

[7] Ferryoons (2 named tenants), Golspy New Park (8: pasture rents), Blarnafidoch (1), Backies (16), Clashmore (4), Croick (1), Longuish (2), Crooks (1), Strathsteven cottages (4), Strathlundy (7), Achlundy (2), Top of Benevragie (Patrick Sellar), Baduchrasky (7), Dalfudrick of Aberscross (3).

PARISH OF KILDONAN: 1815[3]

		£	s.	d.
Torrish	Major Clunes	182	0	0
Kildonan	39 named tenants	181	12	0
Ferranich, Tomich,	Hugh Sutherland,	80	0	0
Fenofal, Dallagan	Alexander McDonald,			
	Andrew McBeath			
Knockfin	George Munro	31	19	5
Cain, Kilfedder	Robert Pope's heirs	35	0	0
Suisgill	Thomas Houstoun	80	0	0
Bracachy, Achnamoin,	Thomas Gordon and	105	0	0
Gairnsary	others			

[3] The following wadset existed at Martinmas 1815: no. 1 (see Table III below, p. 238).

		Victual	Money		
			£	s.	d.
Torish	8 named tenants		24	0	0
Kildonan	Rev. Alexander Sage		47	1	6
	and 9 named tenants				
Suisgill	Thomas Houstoun		80	0	0
Balnavaliach	7 named tenants		28	0	0
28 farms below £20 rent[2]			330	6	3[8]
		Total:	715	1	2[8]

[2] Costally (2 named tenants), Dalvait, Tuary (1), Wester Kilernan (4), Badfleuch (3), Duchyle, Craggy (1), Borable: Dalcharn (1), Borable: Balnashawn (4), Borable: Balvullin (3), Borable: Eachter (5), Fenofal (2), Tomich (2), Dallagan (2), Calaab (2), Altindown (1), Eachter Free (4), Dalhalmy (6), Kinvade (2), Duible (6), Guilable (3), Eldurable (5), Grudsary, a pendicle of Eldurable (3), Skalbesdale (6), Badintarig (1), Corrish (2), East Kilernan (6), Achrindle, Preschon (1).

PARISH OF LAIRG: 1808[1]

		£	s.	d.
Great Sheep Tenement	Atkinson and Marshall	1,200	0	0
Lower Lairg	Rev. Angus Kennedy	22	10	0
	and 6 named tenants			
Shiness, part of Mid-	Capt. Matheson	400	0	0
penny, Lubgorm				
Feu-duties of Achany,		49	9	0[10]
Water of Shin, and				
Gruids				
1 farm below £20 rent[2]		31	19	0[6]
	Total:	1,703	18	1[4]

[1] The following wadset existed at Martinmas 1808: no. 16 (see Table III below, p. 239); no. 15 (Shiness) was not formally redeemed until 1809, but is included in 1808 rental.

[2] Milnchlaran (10 named tenants); also multures of Milnchlaran.

		Victual	Money		
			£	s.	d.
Reisk	Alexander Murray and Angus McBeath		63	0	0
Grimachkary	Adam Gordon		20	0	0
Achnahow	Lieut. William Gunn		80	0	0
Shunachy	4 named tenants		24	0	0
Kinbrace and miln	William Sutherland, Donald McKay, widow Gunn		26	5	0
Kerrow of Kinbrace	William Gordon, Donald Matthieson, Oliver Fraser		24	15	0
Achintoul	6 named tenants		40	0	0
11 farms below £20 rent[4]			117	14	0
		Total:	1,091	5	5

[4] Kildonan mill (1 named tenant), part of Kilernan (3), Dalcharn (1), Guilable (3), Eldurable (5), Grudsary (3), Ulbster (7), Ellig grazing (Marquis of Stafford), Achneakin (1), Rhinacoinich (2), Torwrae (1).

PARISH OF LAIRG: 1815

		£	s.	d.
Shiness Sheep Farm	Duncan Mattheson and John McKay	431	10	0
Lairg Sheep Farm	Atkinson and Marshall	1,500	0	0
Culmaily	Alexander Gunn and James Gray	25	0	0
Balquhairn, Glack	Angus Gunn and John Sutherland	25	0	0
Wester Badnadielson	Donald Matheson, Kinvonovie	27	0	0
Easter and Middle Badnadielson	John Murray, late in Tomich	46	0	0
Milnclaren	Hugh Ross and Alexander Graham, miller	45	0	0
Lower Lairg	Rev. Angus Kennedy and 9 named tenants	46	4	5[2]
Muir Settlements	25 named tenants	28	16	0
Torroboll	23 named tenants	78	5	0
Tomich	4 named tenants	20	5	0
Feu-duties of Achany, Water of Shin, and Gruids		49	9	0[8]
4 farms below £20 rent[3]		49	13	6[1]
	Total:	2,372	2	11[11]

[3] Culbuie (1 named tenant), Rhianmore (1), Knockdow (1), Rhimarskaig (1); also multures of Milnclaren.

PARISH OF LOTH: 1808[1]

		Victual	Money
			£ s. d.
Lothbeg	Thomas Houstoun, subtenant of James Mackay's heirs		226 5 6
Whitehill	George Munro	38.0.2.2	17 19 7[10]
Lothmore	Rev. George Gordon	57.0.0.0	4 16 1[1]
Kilmote	Mrs McCulloch		22 7 3
Culgower, Wester Garty	William Pope		105 0 0
Mid Garty	Capt. Robert Baigrie	46.0.3.2	41 3 2[10]
1 tenancy below £20 rent[2]		2.2.0.0	10 0 0
	Total:	143.3.2.0	427 11 8[9]

[1] The following wadsets existed at Martinmas 1808: nos. 2, 4, 5, 6, 11, 12 (see Table III below, pp. 238–9).
[2] Part of Sleatle Forest (1 named tenant); also multures of Gartymore miln.

PARISH OF ROGART: 1808[1]

			£ s. d.
Eiden	12 named tenants	16.0.0.0	35 15 6
Kintraid	Mrs McKenzie	7.3.0.0	6 2 0
Davochbeg	6 named tenants	24.0.0.0	30 0 0
Rovykirkton	Donald McKenzie and 7 named tenants		32 10 0
Pitfour	10 named tenants	1.2.0.0	21 12 0
Rhine	Capt. Robert Gordon and 9 named tenants		29 0 0
Badchrasky, Corryfrose,[2] Lubvrick	Capt. Angus McKay		35 0 0
Little Rogart, ⅓ of shealing of Craigachnarich	10 named tenants		42 0 0
Pittentrail	Andrew Sutherland and 7 named tenants	28.1.0.0	52 0 0
Moriness	Lieut. John McKay and 14 named tenants		61 0 3

[1] The following wadset existed at Martinmas 1808: no. 13 (see Table III below, p. 239).
[2] Corryfrose was part of Atkinson and Marshall's Sheep Tenement, and included here in error.

PARISH OF LOTH: 1815[3]

		Victual	Money £ s. d.
Lothbeg	Thomas Houstoun		226 5 6
Glenloth and miln	Thomas Houstoun		25 0 0
Whitehill	George Munro	38.0.2.2	17 19 7½
Lothmore	Rev. George Gordon	47.0.0.0	4 16 1
Culgower	Mrs Leith		196 7 6
Midgarty	Alexander Simpson		110 0 0
Wester Garty	Mr Mackenzie, merchant		65 0 0
Port Gower	18 named tenants		34 9 2
Gartymore	Alexander Simpson		45 0 0
Gartymore	33 named tenants		128 15 6
6 tenancies below £20 rent[4]		2.2.0.0	69 6 11
	Total:	87.2.2.2	923 0 3½

[3] The following wadsets existed at Martinmas 1815: nos. 2, 4, 5, 6 (see Table III below, p. 238).
[4] Slatel Forest (1 named tenant), Duchyle Park (1), Kilmote (1), Fisher-houses at Portgower (5), Helmsdale Inn and fisherlands (1), Salt-cellar and granary at Helmsdale (1).

PARISH OF ROGART: 1815[4]

		£ s. d.
Eiden	Earl Gower and John Campbell	75 0 0
Kintraid, Davochbeg	John Mackay	85 0 0
Dalmore	Robert Sutherland and 2 named tenants	47 10 0
Pittentrail	Andrew Sutherland and 13 named tenants	112 2 8
Rovykirkton	Charles Sutherland	42 0 0
Incheap	10 named tenants	51 15 0
Pitfure	Lt. Col. Sutherland	38 0 0
Achtomliny	William Ross and William McDonald	48 0 0
Blaremore	8 named tenants	22 2 0
Bank	Adam Sutherland, James Matthieson, Alexander McDonald	29 4 6
Little Rogart and Improvement	14 named tenants	53 2 6
Lonemore	Lord Stafford	70 0 0
Achnagarron	A. Grant, senior and junior	30 0 0
Torbreck of Pitfure	5 named tenants	20 0 0

[4] The following wadset existed at Martinmas 1815: no. 7 (see Table III below, p. 238).

		Victual	Money
			£ s. d.
Achunoluachrach	George McKay and James Douglas, Alex. Murray		34 0 0
Blarich and miln	Robert Gordon, John Munro, and 14 named tenants		100 0 0
Grudy	8 named tenants		24 10 0
35 farms below £20 rent[3]		1.2.0.0	332 2 9[10]
	Total:	79.0.0.0	835 12 6[10]

[3] Dalmore (6 named tenants), Rovycraigton (5), Incheap (8), Inchoraig (2), Achlean (2), Ballintample, Skiag and Lonmore (2), Culdrain (2), Dalmore (1), Achtomliny (2), Blarimore (4), Achnaheisk (1), Achincarron (2), Balchlagin (4), Torbreck and Ballifure (3), Mulnafua (1), Dalaguinich (1), Knockintian (1), Dalfosag (4), Rheanreoch (2), Rhiline (1), Achgyle (1), Rhilochan (2), Achvoan (3), Knockarthur (2), Inchomney (3), Shanville (2), Bracachy and miln (4), Aultivault (2), Dalreoch (2), Tannachy (3), Wester Kerrow (1), Craggymore (1), Craggybeg (2), Banscol (1), Braegrudy (1); also feu-duty of Langwell.

SALMON FISHINGS: 1808[1]

		£ s. d.
Salmon fishings of Brora, Helmsdale, Naver, Torrisdale	Landles and Redpath	2,267 0 0

[1] See also par. Assynt.

		Victual	Money
			£ s. d.
Rhimusaig, Rhyline	Capt. D. Sutherland		30 0 0
Inchomney	James Sutherland,		30 0 0
	Duncan Campbell,		
	Adam McKay piper		
Moriness	Donald Mackenzie		25 0 0
Torbreak	Peter Matthieson,		20 0 0
	Adam Baillie		
Croitroy, Rhiandogie	4 named tenants		30 3 6
Achnaluachrach	Alexander Murray and		57 0 0
	son, Rev. George		
	Urquhart and James		
	Douglas		
Braecachy and miln	4 named tenants		27 0 0
Blarich	Mrs Gordon and 7		59 6 4
	named tenants		
Rhine	Major Gilchrist		273 0 0
Tannachy	5 named tenants		20 2 0
Craggymore	William and Angus		20 0 0
	Ross		
Craggybeg	6 named tenants		31 10 0
Shanville	4 named tenants		24 0 0
Grudy	8 named tenants		24 10 0
Muiy	7 named tenants		32 15 0
Milton of Muiy	11 named tenants		45 3 6
Achvreal	6 named tenants		32 7 0
Rossal	12 named tenants		65 19 0
35 farms below £20 rent[5]			378 8 6
	Total:		1,950 1 6

[5] Inchoraig (3 named tenants), Achlean of Pitfure (1), Dalmore Brora (1), Mains of Rogart (1), Culdrain (1), Balnachlaggin (3), Splockhill (1), Mill Croft (1), Milnafua (1), School Croft (1), Kirkton (1), Dalfeosaig (3), Corrish (1), Rhianrevach (2), Craigachnarich (tenants of Little Rogart and Capt. D. Sutherland), Rhilochan (1), Banscol (3), Achvoan (3), Clachbhoun (1), Knockarthur (1), Achcork (2), Torresaid (3), Brachu (3), Bualmach (1), Altivault (2), Dalrevoch (2), Tressady Wood (Lord Stafford), Brae Blarich (1), Achucork (2), Mount Babel (3), Brae Grudy (1), Gruby (1), Wester Kerrow (1), Achorsal (2), Achvelie (4); also feu-duty of Langwell.

SALMON FISHINGS: 1815[2]

		£ s. d.
Salmon fishings of	Landles and Redpath	1,650 0 0
Brora, Helmsdale, Naver,		
Torrisdale		

[2] See also par. Assynt, Clyne.

TABLE II

CHANGES IN RENTAL: 1802-1815

The following table and notes are drawn from a series of annual rentals, which survive for the years 1802, 1807-9, and 1811-15; these have been supplemented by the abstract totals given in the Factor's Accounts. The 1802 rental gives the victual rent for the year's crop, together with the money rent due at Martinmas 1802; those for 1807-9 give the victual rent for the crop of the preceding year, together with the money rent due at Martinmas; from 1811 onwards the victual rent for the crop of the year of account is again given, together with the money rent due at Martinmas and the following Whitsunday. In the table victual rent is shown under the year of the actual crop; thus the victual rent given for 1808 in Table 1 (see above, p. 214) is entered under 1807.

The rentals are organised by parishes, but those for 1802 and 1807 show the Skelbo Estate separately; this has been corrected in the table. The accompanying notes indicate major changes in the rent structure; they do not list all changes. Figures are given to the nearest pound.

It should be noted that the money rent totals shown are not a precise indication of the actual revenue received in the year indicated. Martinmas rents were in practice collected from December onwards, and the rentals therefore effectively relate to the following year; they are in fact so described in statements of alterations in rents drawn up by Sellar to accompany the 1814 and 1815 rentals. Further, account must be taken of changes in arrears, abatements and remissions of rents due, rents of lands kept in hand, and variations in the cash product of the victual rent of the preceding year. For an estimate of actual revenue received, see Table v below, p. 244.

TOTAL RENTS

	Money Rent	Increase	Victual Rent	Increase
1802	£5,499		1,343 bolls	
1803	5,748	£249	1,266	77 decrease
1804	5,868	120	1,320	54
1805	5,859	9 decrease	1,320	
1806	5,858	1 decrease	1,343	23
1807	6,811	953	1,343	
1808	10,691	3,880	1,316	27 decrease
1809	11,367	676	1,316[1]	
1810	11,367[1]		934	382 decrease
1811	11,843	476	794	140 decrease
1812	14,828	2,985	577	217 decrease
1813	17,128	2,300	544	33 decrease
1814	18,974	1,846	487	57 decrease
1815	19,934	960	460	17 decrease

[1] Estimated.

MONEY RENT BY PARISHES

	1802	1807	1808	1809	1811	1812	1813	1814	1815
Assynt	£1,333	£1,410	£1,518	£1,518	£1,528	£3,447	£3,746	£3,811	£3,869
Clyne	354	490	760	760	841	1,059	1,440	1,658	1,620
Creich	66	50	50	50	50	50	50	147	220
Dornoch	742	833	969	1,193	1,067	1,543	1,729	1,756	1,762
Farr	790	445	509	527	617	617	1,330	2,093	2,394
Golspie	397	839	937	1,174	1,321	1,840	2,019	2,121	2,090
Kildonan	260	412	715	711	957	960	957	1,044	1,091
Lairg	214	125	1,704	1,704	1,847	1,717	1,857	2,059	2,369
Loth	352	428	428	445	517	649	711	754	923
Rogart	590	645	836	1,018	1,137	1,303	1,639	1,882	1,945
Salmon fishings	400	1,134	2,267	2,267	1,959	1,650	1,650	1,650	1,650

NOTES

Year	Money Rent	Net Increase
1803	1 wadset redeemed (par. Dornoch, Farr, Golspie)	£106
	Dunrobin Farm (Golspie) rent increased	£333
1804	3 wadsets granted (Farr, Kildonan)	£220 decrease
1807	2 wadsets redeemed (Golspie, Kildonan, Loth)	£221[1]
	Salmon rent increased (½ year)	£734
1808	Strathskinsdale (Clyne) lease bought in	£150
	Lairg and Shiness (Lairg) sheep farms set[2]	£1,600

[1] Approximate; the new rent of Wester Garty (Loth) is not precisely stated.
[2] Lairg sheep farm was actually set in 1807, but the first year's rent was allowed to be retained for meliorations. The rents of the lands which comprised this farm were estimated by Campbell at £439 in 1805.

Year	Money Rent	Net increase
1808	Increases in Dornoch	£133
	Kildonan	£303
	Rogart	£182
	Salmon rent increased (full year)	£1,153
1809	Drummuie (Golspie) and Kirkton (Golspie) set	£202
	Increases in Dornoch	£224
	Rogart	£182
1810	4 wadsets redeemed (Farr, Kildonan, Lairg, Rogart)	£492
1811	1 wadset granted (Golspie, Rogart)	£87 decrease
	Skelbo (Dornoch) rent postponed	£104 decrease
	Culmaily (Golspie) set	£330[1]
	Salmon rent reduced (½ year)	£308 decrease
1812	Uppat Estate (Golspie) purchased	£250
	Carrol Estate (Clyne) purchased	£210
	General set of Assynt	£1,921[2]
	Skelbo (Dornoch) set to Earl Gower	£300
	Balvraid (Dornoch) set	£85
	Rhives (Golspie) set	£83
	Golspie village and adjacent lands increased	£199
	Lairg rents postponed	£126 decrease
	Midgarty (Loth) set	£110
	Rhine (Rogart) sheep farm set	£146
	Salmon rent reduced (full year)	£309 decrease
1813	Armadale Estate (Farr) purchased	£711
	Coulin and Camore (Assynt) increased	£105
	Little Assynt (Assynt) increased	£120
	Kilcalmkill (Clyne, Kildonan) sheep farm set	£64
	Torboll (Dornoch) increased	£128
	Morvich (Golspie) and Dunrobin Glen (Golspie) set to Marquis of Stafford	£137
	Torrish (Kildonan) sheep farm set	£99
	Kildonan settlement set	£93
	Lairg settlement set	£279
	Tomich and Torroboll (Lairg) rent postponed	£56 decrease
	Increases in Rogart	£336
1814	3 wadsets redeemed (Clyne, Farr, Loth)	£658
	1 wadset granted (Farr)	£56 decrease
	Polly (Clyne) sheep farm set	£64
	Invershin (Creich) set	£97

[1] Including £86 interest on capital advanced.
[2] Of which:

farms set to Messrs Scobie, Achmore	£536
farms set to M. Mackenzie, Stronechrubie	£213
farms set to K. Mackenzie, Ledbeg	£313
farms set to D. McDonald, Tanera	£399
Ledmore	£99
Knockan	£95
Elphin	£87

Year	Money Rent	Net increase
1814	Armadale and Strathy Head (Farr) increased	£125
	Rhiloisk (Farr, Kildonan) sheep farm set[1]	£80
	Skail and Langdale (Farr) set[2]	£198
	Golspie mills added	£52
	Tomich and Torroboll (Lairg) set	£98
	Increases in Rogart	£243
1815	2 wadsets redeemed (Farr, Kildonan, Loth)	£399
	Kilcalmkill (Clyne, Kildonan) sheep farm increased	£74
	Brora Coal Farm (Clyne) set rent free to Marquis of Stafford	£78 decrease
	½ year rent remitted in 1814 to removed tenants (Farr) added	£117
	Lairg sheep farm increased	£300

Victual Rent

Victual rents were paid in 1802 from the parishes of Clyne, Creich, Dornoch, Golspie, Loth and Rogart; in 1815 they were confined to Clyne, Dornoch, Golspie and Loth. The greater part (70 per cent) of the rents in 1802 came from Dornoch and Golspie parishes. These were reduced between crop 1809 and crop 1812 from 899 bolls to 241 bolls. Major reductions were:

Dornoch	crops 1810/11	Coul and Eachder	41 bolls
		Evelix and miln	41
	crop 1812	Achavandra	36
Golspie	crops 1810/11	Craigton	38
		Kirkton	58
		Culmaily	100
		Golspie Tower	60

In other parishes the most important reductions were:

crops 1810/11	Pittentrail (Rogart)	29 bolls
crop 1813	West Midgarty (Loth)	47
crop 1814	Doll and Inverbrora (Clyne)	65

[1] Gross rent £230; part in wadset redeemed in this year, and part of new rent payable to a continuing wadset.

Part in wadset redeemed in this year.

TABLE III

WADSETS ON ESTATE OF SUTHERLAND: 1802–1816

Wadsets in existence during whole period

1. Badanloch, Elig, Garvault, Halmidary, Rhimsdale (par. Kildonan):
held in 1802 by William Huskisson, who disponed in that year to Col. Alexander Mackenzie of Inverallochy, who was succeeded in 1810 by Charles Mackenzie Fraser.
2. Crakaig (Loth):
held in 1802 by Alexander Mackenzie, W.S., who disponed in 1804 to his son, William Mackenzie.
3. Culmaily, Farlary (Golspie):
held throughout by Capt. (later Col.) Alexander Sutherland.
4. Helmsdale Easter and Wester, Marrel (Loth):
held throughout by George Fergusson, Lord Hermand.
5. Kintradwell (Loth):
held in 1802 by John Gordon of Carrol, who was succeeded in 1810 by his son, Joseph Gordon.
6. Navidale (Loth):
held in 1802 by Gen. James Grant of Ballindalloch, who was succeeded in 1807 by George Macpherson Grant.

Wadsets granted during period and still in existence in 1816

7. Craigtoun (Golspie), Rovy Craigton (Rogart):
granted in 1810 to William Young.
8. Kirtomy (Farr):
granted in 1803 to David Monypenny of Pitmilly, who disponed in 1805 to Sutherland Mackenzie, who in turn disponed in 1813 to James Loch.

Wadsets in existence in 1802 but redeemed before 1816

9. Balblair (Golspie), Dalchalmy, Kildonan, Suisgill, Torrish (Kildonan):
held in 1802 by Alexander Brodie; redeemed in 1807.

10. Borgiebeg, Accobul, Achnabourin, Dalchorrisdale, Dalvighouse, Invernaver, Leckvern, Rossal (Farr):
held in 1802 by Gordon Clunes, who was succeeded in 1814 by William Clunes; redeemed in 1815.

11. Gartymore (Loth), Achintoul, Leriboll (Kildonan):
held in 1802 by Robert Pope, who disponed to trustees in 1808; redeemed in 1815.

12. Glenloth, mill of Lothbeg (Loth), Balinledan, Balnakyle, Clynekirkton, Dalfolly, Inverbrora (Clyne):
held in 1802 by Colin Mackenzie; redeemed in 1813.

13. Muy, Achvelie, Achvreal, Dalnessie, Marlick, Rossal (Rogart):
held in 1802 by Major John Macdonald, who was succeeded in 1807 by his grandson, John Small Macdonald; redeemed in 1811.

14. Rhives, Achlundy, Drummuie (Golspie), Cambusmore (Dornoch):
held in 1802 by John Fraser; possession was resumed, but Fraser's creditors were not repaid his wadset money until 1816 under a decreet of division of the Court of Session.

15. Shiness (Lairg):
held in 1802 by Capt. Donald Matheson; redeemed in 1809.

16. Torroboll, Culmaily, Kinvonovy, Tomich (Lairg):
held in 1802 by Capt. Robert Gordon; redeemed in 1810.

17. Ulbster, Achnamoin, Arachliny, Breakachy, Gearnsary, Grimachary, Loist (Kildonan):
held in 1802 by William Dundas; redeemed in 1810.

18. Wester Garty (Loth), Balnavaliach, Eldrable, Duible, Guilable (Kildonan):
held in 1802 by Lieut. Lewis Houstoun, who was succeeded in 1806 by Hugh Houstoun of Berbice; redeemed in 1807.

Wadsets granted during period but redeemed before 1816

19. Carnachy, Achalgary, Dalcharrel, Skail (Farr), Ascoig (Kildonan):
granted in 1803 to Gen. John Randall McKenzie of Suddie, who was succeeded in 1810 by his sister, Mrs Henrietta Wharton McKenzie; redeemed in 1810.

20. Langdale, Kenakyle, Rhiloisk, Syre (Farr):
granted in 1803 to James McDonald; redeemed in 1814. (McDonald was granted in 1814 a fresh wadset of Skelpick, Achana, Achnabourin, Borgiebeg, Leckvern (Farr), but the transaction was not completed and the lands involved reappeared in the 1816 rental.)

RENTAL CHANGES RESULTING FROM WADSETS

Year	Wadset No.	Rent Increase	Rent Decrease
1803	14	£106	
1804	8		£38
	19		£79
	20		£103
1807	9	£122	
	18	£100 approx.	
1808	15	£400	
1811	7		£87
	13	£112	
	16	£143	
	17	£120	
	19	£117	
1814	10	£118	
	12	£212	
	20	£328	
	20 new		£56
1815	11	£214	
	20 new	£185	

TABLE IV

ABSTRACT OF SUTHERLAND ESTATE ACCOUNTS: 1803-1817[1]

Year	Receipts			Expenditure		
	Management	Capital	Injected	Management	Capital	Extracted
1803	£7,703	£2,543		£3,596		£5,872
1804	7,427	1,000		3,259	2,011	3,565
1805	7,354	2,660		5,036	2,304	3,899
1806	7,391	40		4,514	1,046	3,599
1807	8,780	2,201	1,291	6,129	2,887	4,394
1808	8,402	1,610	10,611	8,026	9,767	2,264
1809	10,526		1,813	10,758	1,818	2,800
1810	15,148	200	6,799	11,322	6,973	4,100
1811[2]	17,026	1,493	799	18,227	100	4,070
1812	13,120	1,877	25,336	11,729	28,579	2,661
1813	18,770	107	45,302	30,802	27,738	1,375
1814	23,711	252	14,000	30,379	353	1,226
1815	24,879	10	8,539	32,974	3,304	2,327
1816	22,765	40	14,635	14,905	3,505	2,130
1817[3]	7,816	20		19,699		1,650
Total	£200,818	£14,053	£129,125	£211,355	£90,385	£45,932

[1] Excluding famine relief (see Appendix B, p. 258).
[2] Estimated figures.
[3] Including Dunrobin funds handled by Young and Sellar only, and including transfers to and from new management.

NOTES

1. This table, together with Tables v-vii, has been extracted from:

A. *Factor's Accounts:*   David Campbell's accounts for crop and Martinmas rent, 1802-6 (but excluding crop 1806).

Cosmo Falconer's accounts for cash product of crop of previous year and for Martinmas rent, 1807-10.

William Young's opening account to 31 January 1812.

Patrick Sellar's opening account to Martinmas 1811.

Q

William Young's accounts: 31 January
1812–20 February 1813; 22 February
1813–3 September 1813; 3 September
1813–11 June 1814; 11 June 1814–23
December 1815; 23 December 1815–29
June 1816; 29 June 1816–24 July 1817.
Patrick Sellar's accounts for cash product
of crop of previous year and for rents
payable at Martinmas and following
Whitsunday, 1811-16.

B. *Law Agent's Accounts:* Messrs Mackenzie's (subsequently Messrs
Mackenzie and Monypenny's) accounts,
by calendar year, 1803-17.

C. In a small number of instances where the normal channels were
not used, information has been extracted from *correspondence* (an
example of this is the purchase of Uppat in 1812, which was paid by
a direct draft on the Marquis' bank account).

2. Falconer's account for Martinmas 1810 and Young's opening
account to 31 January 1812 do not survive in completed form.
Estimates have been reconstructed from the vouchers. All figures for
1811 are therefore approximate.

3. The year of account has been obtained by taking the Martinmas
rent as relating to the expenditure of the following year. This involves only a slight distortion, as it is clear that rent collection did
not begin until December and was mainly carried out in the following year. It should be noted that the rent collected was based on the
rental of the previous year (as given in Table 11 above). From 1811
onwards Young's accounts are incorporated on the basis of date of
entry (as is always the case with the Law Agent's Accounts). Thus,
the totals for 1814 take together Sellar's Martinmas 1813 account,
items from Young's accounts for 3 September 1813–11 June 1814
and 11 June 1814–23 December 1815, and Mackenzie and Monypenny's account for 1 January 1814–31 December 1814. The only
exception is 1811, which takes together Falconer's Martinmas 1810
account, Young's opening account to 31 January 1812, and Sellar's
opening account to Martinmas 1811.

4. To allow standardisation, Campbell's accounts have been credited
with the cash product of the crop of the previous year.

5. The following items have been ignored in drawing up this and the following tables: money advanced for work on turnpike and commutation roads (see above, p. lxxiii); famine relief (see Appendix B, p. 258).

6. No attempt has been made to establish an annual balance-sheet. The system of charge and discharge accounting, together with a final settlement with the individual factor (see above, p. xiii), involves much carrying forward of credit and debit balances. After 1812 Young's use of advances (see below, p. 250) and his irregular accounting periods produce further complications. It has not proved possible to clarify the situation produced by John Fraser's death in 1802 (see below, ii, p. 27), but the accounts have been carried forward into 1817 to incorporate Young and Sellar's final settlements. The overall excess of expenditure over receipts of £3,676 should be modified by the tentative receipts of £2,666 suggested from the examination of the problem of famine victual in Appendix B below. The resulting discrepancy of £1,010, bearing in mind the incomplete figures for 1811, is not unacceptable. Certainly, the general order of sums involved appears to be substantially accurate.

7. Totals are given to the nearest pound sterling. Scots money, in the smaller denominations, was used as a unit of account in the early years of the period, but had disappeared by the close.

8. The table is grouped under three headings: *Management* (see Tables v and vi), *Capital* (see Table vii), and *Injected–Extracted*. The last represents money provided by the Marquis and Marchioness to the factor or law agent, and money remitted to them by the factor or law agent. Transfers of money between the factor and the law agent have been ignored.

TABLE V

ABSTRACT OF SUTHERLAND ESTATE MANAGEMENT REVENUE: 1803–1817

	1803 £	1804 £	1805 £	1806 £	1807 £	1808 £	1809 £	1810 £	1811[1] £	1812 £	1813 £	1814 £	1815 £	1816 £	1817[2] £
1. Net rental product	5,305	5,794	5,844	5,916	6,541	7,900	10,630	11,415	11,193	11,626	14,912	16,973	18,933	19,883	4,925
2. Value of victual of preceding crop	1,273	1,258	1,456	1,386	1,386	1,477	1,961	2,181	1,879	1,454	1,306	1,260	989	724	478
3. Reduction of arrears[3]	535[6]	60–	32	50	270–	975–	2,608–	24	2,725	1,037–	641	329–	1,240–	[4]	2,573–[5]
4. Dunrobin Farm gross product	499[6]	400[6]			1,123[6]		259[6]	271[6]	511[6]	552[6]	986[6]	3,071	2,441	457	331
5. Other farms in hand gross product											305	657	770	383	38
6. Industrial undertakings gross product											83	976	2,234	263	
7. Interest	91						55	344	248	214	389	366	269	330	185
8. Miscellaneous		35	22	39			229	913	470	311	148	737	483	725	102
9. Management transfers															4,330
Total	7,703	7,427	7,354	7,391	8,780	8,402	10,526	15,148	17,026	13,120	18,770	23,711	24,879	22,765	7,816

[1] Estimated figures.
[2] Including Dunrobin funds handled by Young and Sellar only.
[3] When the arrears total is increased rather than decreased, a minus sign follows the entry.
[4] Not ascertainable.
[5] Including special item of £1,378 outstanding debts on Young's account.
[6] Net profits only.

NOTES TO TABLE V

1. These figures [*net rents*] are based on the rental drawn up in the preceding year (see Table II above). To this have been added: payments towards schoolmasters' salaries (by an Act of 1696 heritors were empowered to recover one-half of their contributions from their tenants), fox-money dues (see above, p. 47), kain rents not taken in kind, small additional rents, and alterations in afterhand rents (payable in arrears, at Whitsunday following). Both Campbell and Falconer take afterhand rents into the charge account of the following year; until 1811, therefore, it is necessary to calculate the difference between afterhand rents charged (from the previous year) and discharged (carried forward into the following year), and to add or subtract this from the total rental. With Sellar this practice ceases, rents being specifically stated to be for Martinmas and the Whitsunday following. Abatements and remissions of rent have been deducted. The figures for 1817 include cattle taken in lieu of rent.

2. Until 1806 the normal procedure in accounting for *victual rents* was to enter rents due, and payments made in kind, in the account for the current year; the balance was then transferred to the succeeding year's account as either undelivered arrears or delivered victual sold out on credit; this balance was valued at the price ruling at the following Martinmas, and any sums unpaid at the close of that accounting year transferred to arrears. Campbell did not account in this way for crop 1806, which was transferred to Falconer. Falconer charged himself, in his annual accounts, with the cash value of the preceding year's victual, and discharged himself by charging expenditure at its cash price also. Sellar followed this practice. It is thus difficult to identify payments made in kind after crop 1805. Previous to that year they varied between 317 and 396 bolls, being mainly for stipend, fees to ground officers and others, and charity. To simplify presentation of the figures, Campbell's victual accounts have been valued out on the basis used by Falconer and Sellar. Table V therefore shows the value placed on the crop at the succeeding Martinmas (when payment of arrears and sales fell due), while Table VI includes payments in kind at their cash value. It should be noticed that the figures appearing under any one year relate to the crop of two calendar years preceding (see note 3, above, p. 242).

A tenant not paying in kind took the risk of having to pay more highly (or alternatively the chance of paying at a lower rate), dependent on the variation in price. The table of ruling prices (below) shows how wide such fluctuations could range. In general single prices were fixed at Martinmas, but some variations occur. For crop 1807 Falconer charged a rate 7s. lower than standard to tenants paying less than £20 rent; for crops 1810-13 Sellar fixed a price for meal in addition to that for grain (5s. to 7s. lower in 1810-12, but 1s. higher in 1813); some victual was also charged at prices different from the ruling one. Rent victual, when delivered, went into the storehouses at Helmsdale, Dunrobin and Cyderhall, from which it was issued against written orders from the factor during the difficult spring and summer months. In some cases, however, tenants owing victual rent gave it out directly to those holding written orders.

Ruling Prices for Crops

1801	20s.	1806	22s.	1811	42s.
1802	20s.	1807	33s.	1812	45s.
1803	23s.	1808	33s.	1813	36s.
1804	21s.	1809	30s.	1814	28s.
1805	21s.	1810	33s.	1815	20s.

3. Under the charge and discharge system, the factor charged himself with *arrears* outstanding at the start of his financial year, and discharged himself of those outstanding at its close, these being carried forward to the following year. The difference between these two totals represents the net alteration to the revenue for the year. Arrears include money rents, victual balances not paid for, long-standing arrears for imported victual (see below, pp. 258-62), and miscellaneous items such as payments owing for timber sales. The figure for 1817 includes £1,378 of debts on Young's account, here taken in for the first time because of the impossibility of calculating them on a yearly basis (these amounted to £672 at 3 September 1813, £272 at 11 June 1814, £2,011 at 31 December 1815, and £1,533 at 29 June 1816).

4. Earl Gower (later 1st Marquis of Stafford) and Campbell worked *Dunrobin Farm* (with Killin sheep-farm) on a joint basis between 1803 and 1807; the figures entered show the Marquis' share of the

profits, as paid over by Campbell. Falconer managed Dunrobin between 1807 and 1811 at £200 annual salary, Killin being sub-let; the figures entered are the net profits. Young managed Dunrobin between 1811 and 1816, when he was succeeded by Alexander Stewart (see above, pp. 199-200). Until 1813 he accounted on a net basis only, but in 1814 and 1815 full revenue and expenditure figures are incorporated in his General Account. The figures for 1816 and 1817 represent the winding-up of Young's management, not the total revenue and expenditure for these years.

5. These *other farms* were Morvich (1813-16), Dunrobin Glen sheep-farm (1814-16), Uppat (1815-16), and parts of Doll-Inverbrora (1815-16), all managed by Young. As part of the 1816 reorganisation, Young was replaced at Morvich by Thomas Barclay, at Dunrobin Glen and Uppat by Alexander Stewart, and at Doll-Inverbrora by William Robertson (the last being worked as an adjunct to the coal-mine). The figures for 1816 and 1817 represent the winding-up of Young's management.

6. *Industrial undertakings:* Brora coal, salt and brick works, and Rhives lime works, managed by Young until Robertson's appointment in 1816; also freights earned by sloop 'Dart'.

7. *Interest* on debts, overdue rents, and (during Sellar's term of office) on money deposited with the British Linen Company's agent in Tain.

8. *Miscellaneous:* Sales of mussels from the Little Ferry scalps, timber etc.; casual rents; and extraordinary receipts, viz.:

    1810   £220 from wadsetters towards repairs to kirks and manses.

          £568 from Government and County for repair of dykes opened by building of the parliamentary road along the East Coast.

    1811   £121 for same.

    1814   £116 repaid by tenants for improvements carried out.

          £288 profit on victual imported in 1812.

    1815   £130 repaid by tenants for improvements carried out.

    1816   £400 for same.

9. *Management transfers:* Receipts from new factor (Francis Suther) and payment by Young of balance outstanding (see above, p. *c*).

TABLE VI

ABSTRACT OF SUTHERLAND ESTATE MANAGEMENT

	1803	1804	1805	1806	1807	1808
Public burdens (1)[2]	£304	£398	£874	£690	£726	£2,299
Religion and education (2)	802	943	1,208	922	831	1,016
Annuities, pensions, charity	151	203	149	159	110	114
Management (3)	836	659	582	706	981	920
Surveying (4)						24
Woods and nurseries		37	33	122	2	249
Game (5)						
Castle and family (6)	859	448	1,126	306	685	756
Dunrobin Farm (7)						
Other farms in hand (8)						
Works (9): Castle and policies (10)	24	30	251	410		20
Works: Dunrobin Farm (11)						
Works: Farm buildings (12)						
Works: Inns, harbours, piers (13)						253
Works: Others (14)	29	83	55	129	302	144
Undertakings: Brora coal						
Undertakings: Brora others						
Undertakings: Rhives lime						
Ships (15)						
Meliorations and premia for leases (16)						13
Cattle bought for Trentham (17)		148		451		270
Political (18)	10	17	372	307	625	1,336
Interest (19)	528	250	325	265	277	248
Special items (20)						225
Miscellaneous	53	43	61	47	99	139
Management transfers (21)					1,491	
Total	£3,596	£3,259	£5,036	£4,514	£6,129	£8,026

[1] Excluding famine relief.
[2] The numbers in brackets refer to the main notes following.

EXPENDITURE: 1803-1817[1]

1809	1810	1811[3]	1812	1813	1814	1815	1816	1817[4]
£3,207	£2,436	£2,020	£2,813	£5,305	£3,262	£4,147	£2,133	£3,030
1,762	1,669	1,638	964	1,124	2,047	1,111	2,027	1,848
430	329	232	293	303	363	294	420	204
814	862	2,148	875	2,014	2,223	2,934	1,951	1,159
		294	28	129	149	155	62	
739	518	620	72	530	756	55	163	194
		69	8	166	214	137	36	93
935	440	878	704	2,457	612	973	1,044	896
442	1,497				2,385	3,356	386	395
		68	9	1,648	1,567	3,285	517	428
568	1,795	3,739	477	1,267	1,483	2,096	101	319
468	500	557	179	1,905	328	765	3	
		159	79	334	853	1,102	187	2,387
21	44	645	38	107	3,026	879		25
223	130	905	574	2,275	3,408	2,977	209	1,070
		1,081	3,303	7,345	4,028	3,673	306	913[5]
					373	3,157	2,524	
				11	397	374	174	134
	300				507	50	78	
18	12	1,592	313	291	758	408	1,672	1,468
376	489	1,013	521	762	909	453		
359	6	14	250	20	11	9	272	12
254	203	160	86	423	314	496	462	46
				2,137	200			621
142	92	165	143	249	206	88	178	324
		230						4,133
£10,758	£11,322	£18,227	£11,729	£30,802	£30,379	£32,974	£14,905	£19,699

[3] Estimated figures.
[4] Including Dunrobin funds handled by Young and Sellar only, and including transfers to and from new management.
[5] Total for all Brora undertakings.

NOTES TO TABLE VI

The totals given under each head represent payments settled during the calendar year: they do not indicate the year in which work was actually done, or to which payments refer. Young's practice of making advances on account to tradesmen (for Loch's views on which see above, p. 100) is a serious complication. Advances feature in Young's accounts in two forms. In places he carried forward a total already accounted for and called it an advance, so producing a cumulative total for the operation concerned. Elsewhere, however, he made large advances to contractors and tradesmen, merely entering a single total to be carried forward to the next account. Thus at 20 February 1813 he had advanced £1,445 to seven contractors; at 3 September 1813 a single total of £3,214 was entered; at 11 June 1814, £3,168; at 23 December 1815, £1,237; and at 29 June 1816, £2,315. The impression given is of a financial system under severe strain. In general advances were used for works and undertakings, while public burdens, stipend, annuities and pensions, salaries and wages were settled inside the relevant year (though Young's own salary for Martinmas 1811–Martinmas 1812 was not paid until February 1813, while he received payment for two years during 1815). The figures, as presented, therefore tend to postdate the execution of various works, and are to that extent artificial.

A second artificial feature arises from the fact that individual operations were kept distinct from each other. Thus, Dunrobin Farm paid rent, though it was in hand during most of the period, but also received payment for supplies to Dunrobin Castle. Similarly coal supplied from Brora to the Castle, Rhives lime works and other accounting units was entered as paid for. Both revenue and expenditure are therefore inflated by 'internally consumed' items. No attempt had been made to remove this, as the gross totals give a realistic indication of the scale of activity.

1. These include taxes and heritor's contributions to the cost of Parliamentary roads, bridges and the Mound. Of the total of £33,744 under this head, road contributions amounted to £13,673 (for the financing of the road programme see A. R. B. Haldane, *New Ways through the Glens* (1962), 44-51).

2. Heritor's obligations for the payment of ministers' stipends (in

some cases mainly in kind) and schoolmasters' salaries, together with the expenses of repairs to kirks, manses and schools.

3. Factors' salaries are included under this head. Campbell received £400 per annum, Falconer £450 (including an allowance for his clerk), Sellar £275 and Young £1,000.

4. The chief surveyors employed were Benjamin Meredith, who was responsible for the survey of Strathnaver, and John James Roy, who surveyed Strathbrora and Kildonan (see H. Fairhurst, 'The Surveys for the Sutherland Clearances', Scottish Studies, 8 (1964), 1-18).

5. No gamekeeper was employed at Dunrobin before 1811, when Walter Nash was sent from Staffordshire.

6. Under this head are included wages and maintenance of house and garden staff, food supplies, equipment, furnishings and running repairs for the Castle, seeds and tools for the garden, freight of goods and miscellaneous expenditure for the family. In years during which members of the family were in residence at Dunrobin (e.g. 1805, 1813, 1816) such expenditure rose considerably, but a permanent staff was in fact maintained.

7. See above, p. 246, n. 4. The expenditure figures for 1809 and 1810 represent the value of Campbell's half share of the farm stock (worth originally £1,186 in 1803). This had been taken over by Falconer on Campbell's retirement, but this arrangement was subsequently changed when Falconer became paid farm manager. Falconer was paid only a part of the cost of the stock in 1809, it being intended that he take over Robert Pope's wadset of Gartymore in exchange for the remainder. When Falconer was dismissed in the following year this arrangement fell through, and he was paid the remainder of the stock price in cash.

8. See above, p. 247, n. 5. Expenditure on these farms began before revenue was received.

9. Young's accounting methods make any precise allocation of expenditure on works very difficult. Although some of this expenditure is entered under separate heads (e.g. Brora Harbour, Golspie Inn, Dornoch Castle), a high proportion appears under the general head of 'Improvements' (a term used in the accounts in the 18th century to cover all works). An attempt has been made to allocate this expenditure, on the basis of a close study of the accounts and a personal knowledge of the geography involved. It has, however,

proved impossible in all cases to distinguish between 'Castle and Policies', 'Dunrobin Farm' and 'Others'. Young's habit of settling accounts with individual tradesmen without fully distinguishing the work involved has added to this difficulty, and has made it necessary to include under 'Others' works which should probably be more precisely classified. Finally, it is far from clear on what basis Young and his accountant Grant distinguished between improvement expenditure and maintenance and miscellaneous items entered elsewhere.

Young himself appears to have been aware of these problems. In 1815 he produced separate abstract accounts for Dunrobin Farm and Rhives Lime which transferred expenditure from these heads to 'Improvement'. It is likely that he was endeavouring to show these operations in a more favourable light, although he debited the Rhives Lime account with interest at $6\frac{1}{2}\%$ on the expenditure shown as transferred. In drawing up this table such exercises have been ignored, and the arrangement of the main accounts has been retained, except in a small number of instances which represent a lack of consistency on Young's part. However, separate work accounts have been grouped as far as possible under the heads used in the table, though this must be recognised as to some extent tentative. Industrial works have been separated under the general heading of 'Undertakings'.

10. Works in the Castle were largely internal, following on building operations in the 1780s, which filled in the south-east side of the Castle courtyard and produced the building to be seen in William Daniell's well-known prints. Amongst other improvements were a piped water supply and a bath-house. Works in the policies included a new gate-house and stable buildings at the junction of the main avenue and the new Parliamentary road, together with the draining of the present Review Park to the north-west of the Castle.

11. These included a complete range of farm buildings, draining, dyking and enclosure, together with a lade from the Golspie Burn. The field pattern of the present farm was created at this time.

12. The main expenditure under this head was on Lothbeg farm (£2,061), Morvich farm (£1,204), Rhives farm (£1,034), Kilcalmkill farm (£310), and Portgower steading (£262).

13. The main expenditure under this head was on Brora Harbour

(£2,401), Golspie Inn (£896), Portgower Inn (£595), Brora Inn (£377) and Dunrobin Pier (£357).

14. Much of the expenditure under this head was on dyking, draining and enclosing in the neighbourhood of Golspie and in Dunrobin Glen; many of the items concerned cannot be precisely identified. Amongst identifiable subjects of expenditure were Dornoch Castle (£1,758), Morvich house (£1,570), Portgower seamen's cottages (£997), Golspie meal and flax mills (£876), Brora colliers' cottages (£775), Brora pilots' cottages (£676), and a willow plantation at Dunrobin (£238). It should be noted that these last figures are not comprehensive (see above p. 251, n. 9).

15. Under this head are included contributions towards the establishment and repair of the Burghead packet, the enterprise which first brought Young and Sellar to Sutherland (see above, p. xli), and also the cost of operating the sloop 'Dart'. This vessel, of Dutch design, was bought at Grangemouth for £133 in April 1814 and sailed to Brora with a cargo of 13,000 tiles. A Dutchman had to be brought from Caithness to teach the crew to navigate her. Thereafter she was used to carry coal and lime around the Moray Firth (and one cargo of freestone from Lossiemouth to the Mound), until she was wrecked off Hopeman harbour in March 1815. An attempt appears to have been made to repair her, but no further freights are recorded.

16. Meliorations to outgoing tenants were usually small, only twice exceeding £100. Advances at interest were made to Sellar (£1,500 on entering Culmaily in 1811, and £150 on entering Rhiloisk in 1816) and Gabriel Reid (£833 on entering Kilcalmkill in 1816). Several tenants received annuities in return for surrendering their leases: Mrs Boog of Skelbo, £115 per annum from 1812 onwards; Mrs Macleod of Morvich, £30 in 1814-15; and Rev. William Mackenzie of Assynt, £130 in 1814-15. In addition, lump sums were paid to the following for surrendering their leases: Lieut. William Gunn of Achnahow, £144 in 1814; Benjamin Ross of Achley, £410 in 1816; Robert McKay of Wester Helmsdale, £250 in 1816; and Robert Mackid of Kirkton, £1,352 in 1817.

17. After two experiments in 1804 and 1806, regular droves of Sutherland cattle were sent in August from 1808 onwards to Staffordshire for sale or fattening on the Leveson-Gower estate there.

The normal size of drove was between 50 and 80 beasts, but in 1811 two droves, totalling 121 beasts, were sent. Buying prices in Sutherland, after averaging between £4 10s. and £8 10s., rose steeply in 1812-14, in which last year £15 15s. was paid for prime cattle and £11 15s. for common beasts. In 1815 there was a sharp fall, prices coming back to between £6 and £10. No drove was sent in 1816; this may be related to the bad harvest, as a result of which cattle were later accepted in place of rents (see below, p. 262). In August 1817 Francis Suther sent 450 cattle received in this way to Trentham.

18. A small amount of expenditure incurred annually at Dornoch is included under this head. The higher figures recorded in some years are explained by parliamentary elections for the Sutherland county seat, or for the Northern Burghs, of which Dornoch was a part. In 1805 James McDonald (for whom see below, ii, 172) was elected member for the Northern Burghs. At the general election of 1806 William Dundas was elected for the county and Gen. John Randal Mackenzie of Suddie for the Northern Burghs. In the general election of 1807 both were re-elected, but in 1808 Dundas resigned and was succeeded by Suddie, who was in turn succeeded by W. H. Freemantle as member for the Burghs. On Suddie's death in action in 1809 George Macpherson Grant of Ballindalloch was elected member for the county. At the general election of 1812 James McDonald became member for the county and Hugh Innes of Lochalsh for the Burghs. On Macdonald's resignation in 1816, after a quarrel with the Marquis over a proposed allowance to the Duke of Cumberland, Macpherson Grant was elected in his place. William Mackenzie acted as the Sutherland family agent in political affairs, and came north to manage the elections; he acted in a similar capacity for the Seaforth family at Dingwall.

19. Paid on borrowed money, small sums deposited at interest with the factors, and (particularly in Young's term of office) bank overdrafts.

20. These were: 1808   celebration of Earl Gower's 21st birthday (8 August 1807).

1813   cattle sent to Armadale to graze, £753 (these do not reappear in the accounts, but may have been taken into Dunrobin and Skelbo farm stock).

1813   expenses of Kildonan Riots, £183.
         contribution to cost of the Mound, £1,202
         (see above, p. lxxv).
1814   subscription to Portmahomack pier.
1817   Sellar's legal expenses (see above, p. *c*).
21. These were: 1807   balance owed to Campbell on final settle-
         ment.
1811   balance owed to Falconer on final settle-
         ment.
1817   money advanced to new managers of Dun-
         robin Farm (£957) and Brora coal
         (£3,076), and to new factor (£100).

TABLE VII

ABSTRACT OF SUTHERLAND ESTATE CAPITAL TRANSACTIONS: 1803–1817

	1803	1804	1805	1806	1807	1808	1809	1810	1811[6]	1812	1813	1814	1815	1816	1817
Receipts															
Wadsets granted	2,543				1,107	1,610			1,330	1,647					
Sums borrowed		1,000	2,660												
Consigned sum recovered					1,094[2]										
Small transactions				40				200	163	230	107	252	10	40	20
Total	2,543	1,000	2,660	40	2,201	1,610	1,818	200	1,493	1,877	107	252	10	40	20
Expenditure															
Purchases of lands and titles	2,011[1]		2,304[1]	1,046[2]	791[3]	5,722[4]	1,818[5]			26,881[7]	25,690[8]	331[9]			
Redemption of wadsets					2,056			6,973		1,545	1,791		3,214	2,204	
Borrowings repaid						1,045								928	
Loans made						3,000									
Small transactions					40				100	153	257	22	90	373	
Total	2,011		2,304	1,046	2,887	9,767	1,818	6,973	100	28,579	27,738	353	3,304	3,505	

NOTES TO TABLE VII

This table has been mainly extracted from the Law Agent's Accounts, with the addition of a number of small loans and repayments recorded in Young's accounts. Loch recommended in 1816 (see above, p. 170) that the practice of accepting money at interest as an obligement to tenants and others should cease. The law agents did not maintain a separate capital account.

1. Heritable debts affecting the title to the Estate of Skelbo.
2. Sum consigned for redemption of Pronsie, a wadset on the Estate of Skelbo; recovered with interest.
3. Heritable debts affecting Pronsie.
4. Heritable debts affecting the title to the Estate of Skelbo, £4,022; purchase price of Strathskinsdale, first instalment, £1,700.
5. Purchase price of Strathskinsdale, second instalment, £1,818.
6. Figures for 1811 estimated.
7. Purchase price of Uppat, £8,104; purchase price of Carrol, £18,777.
8. Purchase price of Armadale.
9. Purchase price of Ardbeg.

R

Appendix B

THE FINANCE OF FAMINE RELIEF

FAILURE OF THE SUTHERLAND GRAIN CROP, evident by the early winter, had as its inevitable consequence shortage and famine in the following late spring and summer. When the seed corn was used to maintain men and beasts, the repercussions could stretch beyond a single year. In such situations, the urgent need, as seen by the estate management, was to find supplies in less affected areas and to transport them to Sutherland.[1] Once there, a distribution and accounting system existed which could handle the emergency, for the estate management was accustomed to receiving victual rents and issuing them on credit.[2]

It was, however, necessary to finance the purchases and the cost of their transport. While the management never envisaged free distribution on a large scale, although some charitable gifts were made, there still remained a time-lag between laying-out money and recovering it. Supplies were bought for ready cash, but most sales were on credit for settlement at the following Martinmas. Unfortunately, the surviving accounts throw only an intermittent light on these operations; even more unfortunately, they indicate that separate accounting methods were used at different times during the period. As a result, it has proved impossible to incorporate famine finance consistently into the tables given in Appendix A. An attempt will therefore be made to elucidate the different treatment of the various famine crises in the accounts, and to estimate their relevance to general estate finance.

1808

Falconer reported in January 1808 on the effects of the failure of

[1] For an earlier crisis and the steps taken to meet it, see *John Home's Survey of Assynt*, ed. R. J. Adam (Scottish History Society, 1960), xxvii–xxx.
[2] See above, pp. 245–6, n. 2.

the 1807 crop.[1] On 8 March William Mackenzie wrote to the Marchioness reporting his purchases of victual, and asking for funds to meet the payments.[2] He proposed to open a separate account for this purpose. Further purchases had to be made,[3] and vouchers preserved with Falconer's accounts show that the total cost was £4,050. Mackenzie must presumably have drawn on the Marquis for further funds, but his separate account does not survive to show this.

Once the total cost was known, Falconer charged himself with it, and discharged it in his Martinmas accounts for 1808, 1809 and 1810 (i.e., years 1809, 1810 and 1811). He received in all £4,703, leaving persistent debts of £56 which were then transferred to general arrears in Sellar's accounts. Only £1,500 was in fact remitted to Edinburgh (£600 in 1809 and £900 in 1810), the remainder being absorbed into management revenue. Mackenzie sent the first £600 to Drummonds in March 1809; there is no record of any further payment, but this may be an accident of the evidence.

The transactions show a profit of £653 (or almost 14%), indicating that Falconer's selling prices were well above the prime cost of the victual (26s. 9d.–29s. for oatmeal). Incidental charges were substantial. Mackenzie's original estimate was based on prime costs of £2,064, but his broker's final account showed prime costs of £2,124 and total costs of £2,386, expenses thus increasing the prime costs by over 12%. Also, the money expended was not recovered until 1810, for only £3,404 was repaid by buyers in 1809.

The overall effect of these transactions was that the Marquis injected £4,050 into the estate revenue in 1808, and was probably repaid £1,500 (actually £1,583, for Mackenzie added a balance of £83 to his remittance for £600) in 1809 and 1810. Falconer retained for estate purposes £3,203 between 1809 and 1811. In very broad terms, the result of the crisis was to inject £3,200 into the estate revenue over a period of four years.

1812–1815

Between 1812 and 1815 famine victual was required in every year (1812–1,754 bolls; 1813–3,370; 1814–2,051; 1815–802). The

[1] See above, pp. 11-13.
[2] See below, ii, p. 76.
[3] For total quantities, see above, p. 13; see also below, ii, p. 80.

accounting of these operations is difficult to trace, as Mackenzie does not appear to have been involved, and as Young did not incorporate them in his general accounts. Instead, he bought on his own responsibility, and operated a special meal ledger and account, which have not survived (although a large number of individual orders for issue of victual have done so). The only evidence surviving is:

(a) an abstract, dated May 1814, of the victual bought and sold in 1813, with a note on the proceeds of the 1812 operations.
(b) an undated sketch of meal imported in 1812-15, showing quantities, prime costs, and selling prices.
(c) an abstract, dated 2 July 1817, of arrears outstanding on meal sold in 1813, 1814 and 1815, with a note in James Loch's handwriting showing a final profit of £568, offset by arrears of £663 still outstanding.

Interpretation of these figures is not easy, particularly as (a) and (b) are not consistent with each other. But, if (b) is taken as a basis, prime costs were £2,328 in 1812, £5,563 in 1813, £2,191 in 1814, and £751 in 1815. There is some evidence to support these figures. On 13 May 1812 Young asked the Marchioness for permission to draw on the Marquis for £2,000–£3,000 for meal. On 16 May 1813 he reported that he was £3,000 in advance for meal. Assuming that he received a further draft at this time, and that he had received payment for the meal issued in 1812, a working hypothesis can be that the Marquis provided some £5,500 for famine relief in these two years. Repayments by those receiving the victual so bought would then provide the necessary funds for the purchases of 1814 and 1815.

It is possible to reach more detailed figures for the 1812 operations from (a) and (b). The selling prices in (b) vary (usually 1s. more for credit than for cash), but taking middle prices and bringing in the profit of £288 transferred to Young's general account in June 1814 (when only a negligible arrear of 9-10 bolls remained), the following figures are reached:

Prime cost	£2,328	(average cost 26s. 6d. per boll)
Charges	£234	
Receipts	£2,850	(cash price 32s.)
Profit	£288	

The following years present greater problems, but taking the figures in (*b*), together with the arrears and profit shown in (*c*), a conjectural table can be constructed as at 2 July 1817:

	1813	1814	1815	Total
Prime cost	£5,563 (35s.)	2,191 (21s. 4d.)	751 (18s. 9d.)	£8,505
Charges				647
Receipts	6,306 (39s.)	2,512 (24s.)	902 (22s.)	9,720
Profit				568
Deduct arrears				663

These figures are necessarily approximate, in view of the method used to calculate receipts. The total for charges appears on the low side, if compared with those for 1808 and 1812. No profit apparently was made on the operations, for there is no transfer to Young's general account of the type recorded for 1812. Young's estimate (in a letter to the Marchioness on 2 June 1812) of a return of 20% on money laid out for meal, twice as high as that secured on the 1812 operations, was certainly never reached.

Abstract (*a*), sent by Young to the Marchioness on 1 May 1814, suggests a different and more optimistic situation. He saw a large profit as likely to arise from the 1813 sales, if all debts were collected ('altho I never prosecuted a single creature nor brot a penny of expense on them I do not apprehend much loss'). He estimated prime costs of £5,563, receipts of £8,000, and profits of £671. This would indicate charges of £1,766, an impossibly high figure (30%) in relation to other years. The estimate of receipts in (*a*) must be assumed to be inflated, and the figures arising from it are not to be preferred to those extracted from (*b*) and (*c*).

As the meal accounts and ledger do not survive, there is no means of discovering what happened to the money advanced by the Marquis for famine relief in these years. At its height, in 1813, some £5,500 was involved. Since neither drafts from the Marquis nor repayments to him appear in Young's general accounts, it is to be assumed that the operation remained distinct and had no overall effect on the management accounts, beyond the small deficit remaining in 1817 on the 1813-15 transactions (the profit of £288 on the 1812 transactions is entered as management revenue in Table v).

1816-1817

The serious crisis of the winter of 1816–17 lies outside the period of Young's management. William Mackenzie received £3,600 from the Marquis on 10 December 1816, and a further £2,267 on 5 February 1817 (these sums are not included in the receipts columns of Table IV). They indicate, it may be noted in passing, that Young had not retained the £5,500 which had financed the purchases of 1812–15. Mackenzie, reverting to the methods used in 1808, spent this money immediately on famine supplies. In addition, between March 1817 and January 1818 Sellar paid a further £537 towards the cost of this victual (this item is not included in Table VI), and accepted some 450 cattle to the value of £1,064 in place of rents payable at Martinmas 1816 (this item has been taken at its cash value in Table V). Recovery of the cost of the victual issued in 1816–17 falls in Suther's factory, and so outside the scope of the present study.

To conclude, an estimate of the overall effect of famine victual operations in the period 1803–17 may be attempted:

1. Between 1808 and 1811, £4,050 was injected, £1,583 was repaid, and £3,203 management revenue was created.
2. Between 1812 and 1816, £5,500 was injected and repaid, and £288 management revenue was created.
3. In 1816–17, £5,867 was injected (repayment being carried forward to the new management) and £537 management revenue was expended.

Taking 1 and 3 together (2 being already allowed for in the general accounts) a total of £2,666 additional revenue resulted from these operations.

DATE DUE

HIGHSMITH # 45220